Lecture Notes in Computer Science   10146

Commenced Publication in 1973
Founding and Former Series Editors:
Gerhard Goos, Juris Hartmanis, and Jan van Leeuwen

More information about this series at http://www.springer.com/series/7410

Kerstin Lemke-Rust · Michael Tunstall (Eds.)

Smart Card Research
and Advanced Applications

15th International Conference, CARDIS 2016
Cannes, France, November 7–9, 2016
Revised Selected Papers

 Springer

Editors
Kerstin Lemke-Rust
Bonn-Rhein-Sieg University
  of Applied Sciences
St. Augustin
Germany

Michael Tunstall
Cryptography Research
San Francisco, CA
USA

ISSN 0302-9743   ISSN 1611-3349 (electronic)
Lecture Notes in Computer Science
ISBN 978-3-319-54668-1   ISBN 978-3-319-54669-8 (eBook)
DOI 10.1007/978-3-319-54669-8

Library of Congress Control Number: 2017932792

LNCS Sublibrary: SL4 – Security and Cryptology

Printed on acid-free paper

This Springer imprint is published by Springer Nature
The registered company is Springer International Publishing AG
The registered company address is: Gewerbestrasse 11, 6330 Cham, Switzerland

Preface

These proceedings contain the papers selected for presentation at the 15th International Conference on Smart Card Research and Advanced Applications (CARDIS 2016), held during November 7–9 and application of smart. The conference was organized by EURECOM and held at the Hôtel Barrière Le Gray d'Albion.

CARDIS has provided a forum for presenting exceptional research on smart cards and related technologies since 1994. Smart cards play an important role in our day-to-day lives, from bank cards to GSM SIMs, and security is vital to keep these systems functioning correctly. The CARDIS conference gathers researchers and technologists who focus on all aspects of the design, development, deployment, evaluation, and application of smart cards and secure elements in secure platforms or systems. The technology used in smart cards, and hence the attack vectors, are expanding to other areas, such as TPMs, HSMs, mobile phones, and the Internet of Things. It is, therefore, more important than ever that we understand how smart cards, and related systems, can be secured.

This year, CARDIS received 29 papers from 17 countries. Each paper was reviewed by at least three independent reviewers. The selection of 15 papers to fill the technical program was accomplished based on 114 written reviews. This task was performed by the 30 members of the Program Committee with the help of 38 external reviewers. The technical program also featured three invited talks. The first invited speaker, Eric Vétillard, from Prove & Run, France, presented "Three Views on IoT Security"; the second speaker, Ventzislav Nikov, from NXP Semiconductors, Belgium, presented "Security Outside the Black-Box Model: Challenges and Countermeasures"; and the third speaker, David Oswald, from the University of Birmingham, UK, presented "Breaking Automotive Remote Keyless Entry Systems, or: Why Your Car Is not a Safe Box."

We would like to thank the general chair, Aurélien Francillon, and the local Organizing Committee chairs, Ludovic Apvrille and Florian Lugou. We would also like to thank the Program Committee and the external reviewers for their thorough work, which enabled the technical program to achieve such a high quality, and the Steering Committee for giving us the opportunity to serve as program chairs at such a prestigious conference. The financial support of all the sponsors was highly appreciated and greatly facilitated the organization of the conference. In particular, we would like to thank the gold sponsors: NXP Semiconductors, Labex UCN and the Agence Nationale de la Sécurité des Systèmes d'Information (ANSSI). Furthermore, we would like to thank the authors who submitted their work to CARDIS 2016, without whom the conference would not have been possible.

January 2017

Keratin Lemke-Rust
Michael Tunstall

CARDIS 2016

15th International Conference on Smart Card Research and Advanced Applications

Cannes, France
November 7–9, 2016

General Chair

Aurélien Francillon   EURECOM, France

Local Arrangements Chair

Ludovic Apvrille   Telecom ParisTech, France

Web Chair

Florian Lugou   Telecom ParisTech, France

Program Chairs

Kerstin Lemke-Rust   Bonn-Rhein-Sieg University of Applied Sciences, Germany

Michael Tunstall   Cryptography Research, USA

Program Committee

Guillaume Barbu	Oberthur Technologies, France
Lejla Batina	Radboud University Nijmegen, The Netherlands
Guido Bertoni	ST Microelectronics, Italy
Elke De Mulder	Cryptography Research, USA
Hermann Drexler	Giesecke & Devrient, Germany
Thomas Eisenbarth	Worcester Polytechnic Institute, USA
Wieland Fischer	Infineon Technologies, Germany
Benedikt Gierlichs	Katholieke Universiteit Leuven, Belgium
Christophe Giraud	Oberthur Technologies, France
Cezary Glowacz	T-Systems, Germany
Sylvain Guilley	GET/ENST and CNRS/LTCI, France
Tim Güneysu	University of Bremen and DFKI, Germany
Johann Heyszl	Fraunhofer AISEC, Germany
Naofumi Homma	Tohoku University, Japan

Filippo Melzani
Shoei Nashimoto
Tobias Oder
Matheus Oliveira
Conor Patrick
Markus Peschina
Peter Pessl
Romain Poussier
Jürgen Pulkus
Joost Renes
Oscar Reparaz

Okan Seker
Victor Servant
Pascal Sasdrich
Ruggero Susella
Daisuke Suzuki
Rei Ueno
Felipe Valencia
Vincent Verneuil
Tobias Wagner
Erich Wenger
Ville Yli-Mäyry

Contents

Kernel Discriminant Analysis for Information Extraction in the Presence of Masking

Eleonora Cagli[1,2,4](✉), Cécile Dumas[1,2], and Emmanuel Prouff[3,4]

[1] Univ. Grenoble Alpes, 38000 Grenoble, France
{eleonora.cagli,cecile.dumas}@cea.fr
[2] CEA, LETI, MINATEC Campus, 38054 Grenoble, France
[3] Safran Identity and Security, Issy-les-Moulineaux, France
emmanuel.prouff@safrangroup.com
[4] Sorbonne Universités, UPMC Univ. Paris 06, CNRS, INRIA,
Laboratoire d'Informatique de Paris 6 (LIP6), Équipe PolSys,
4 place Jussieu, 75252 Paris Cedex 05, France

Abstract. To reduce the memory and timing complexity of the Side-Channel Attacks (SCA), dimensionality reduction techniques are usually applied to the measurements. They aim to detect the so-called *Points of Interest* (PoIs), which are time samples which (jointly) depend on some sensitive information (*e.g.* secret key sub-parts), and exploit them to extract information. The extraction is done through the use of functions which combine the measurement time samples. Examples of combining functions are the linear combinations provided by the Principal Component Analysis or the Linear Discriminant Analysis. When a masking countermeasure is properly implemented to thwart SCAs, the selection of PoIs is known to be a hard task: almost all existing methods have a combinatorial complexity explosion, since they require an exhaustive search among all possible d-tuples of points. In this paper we propose an efficient method for informative feature extraction in presence of masking countermeasure. This method, called Kernel Discriminant Analysis, consists in completing the Linear Discriminant Analysis with a so-called kernel trick, in order to efficiently perform it over the set of all possible d-tuples of points without growing in complexity with d. We identify and analyse the issues related to the application of such a method. Afterwards, its performances are compared to those of the Projection Pursuit (PP) tool for PoI selection up to a 4th-order context. Experiments show that the Kernel Discriminant Analysis remains effective and efficient for high-order attacks, leading to a valuable alternative to the PP in constrained contexts where the increase of the order d does not imply a growth of the profiling datasets.

Keywords: Higher-order side-channel attacks · Information extraction · Dimensionality reduction · Kernel Discriminant Analysis · Linear Discriminant Analysis

© Springer International Publishing AG 2017
K. Lemke-Rust and M. Tunstall (Eds.): CARDIS 2016, LNCS 10146, pp. 1–22, 2017.
DOI: 10.1007/978-3-319-54669-8_1

1 Introduction

1.1 Context

The dimensionality reduction of the acquired measurements is a fundamental pre-processing phase to get efficient and effective Side-Channel Attacks. The problem of performing an opportune dimensionality reduction goes hand in hand with the research of Points of Interests, which are the samples that (jointly) leak information about the sensitive cryptographic assets. Indeed, a convenient dimensionality reduction should enhance the contribution of such PoIs while reducing or nullify the one provided by non-interesting points.

A vast literature is dedicated to the problem of dimensionality reduction in the context of unprotected implementations. Some methods propose to select samples for which a given statistic exceeds a chosen threshold: this is *e.g.* the case of the T-test [2,15,25]. Other methods project the measurements into lower-dimensional spaces, through linear combinations of points: these are the Principal Components Analysis (PCA) [1,11,14], the Linear Discriminant Analysis (LDA) [4,28] and the recent approach based on Projection Pursuits (PP) [13]. These methods arouse a growing interest in last years due to their efficiency: indeed combining time samples in a convenient way raises the SNR of the contracted measurements, leading an attack to success with fewer side-channel traces.

The literature is more scattered in the context of implementations protected with masking (*aka* sharing) techniques, which are common countermeasures against SCAs. When applied, they ensure that every sensitive variable Z (*e.g.* the output of the non-linear sbox function for an AES implementation) is randomly split into multiple shares $M_1, M_2, \ldots, M_d$ in such a way that a relation $Z = M_1 \star \cdots \star M_d$ holds for a group operation $\star$ (*e.g.* the exclusive or for the Boolean masking). The value d plays the role of a security parameter and the method is usually referred to as $(d-1)$th-order masking (since it involves $d-1$ random values). In many cases, especially for software implementations, the shares are manipulated at different times, and no time sample therefore shows dependency on Z: in order to recover such information the attacker is obliged to join information held by each of the d shares, executing a so-called dth-order SCA. In the great majority of the published higher-order attacks, the PoI selection during the pre-attack characterization phase is either put aside or made under the hypothesis that the random shares are known. Actually, the latter knowledge brings the problem back to the unprotected case. In this paper we relax this hypothesis and we consider situations where the values of the random shares are unknown to the adversary. We however assume that the adversary can characterize the leakage before attacking the implementation, by controlling the value of the target variable Z. These two assumptions put our study in the classical context of *template attacks without knowledge of the masks*.

Before presenting our results, we motivate hereafter through a simplified but didactic example, the need for an efficient dimensionality reduction technique against masked implementations.

1.2   A Motivating Example

We consider here a side channel attack targeting an 8-bit sensitive variable Z which has been priorly split into d shares and we assume that a reverse engineering and signal processing have priorly been executed to isolate the manipulation of each share in a region of ℓ time samples. This implies that our SCA now amounts to extract a Z-dependent information from leakage measurements whose size has been reduced to $d \times \ell$ time samples. To extract such information the State-of-the-Art proposes three approaches to the best of our knowledge.

The first one consists in considering d time samples at a time, one per region, and in testing if they jointly contain information about Z (*e.g.* by estimating the mutual information [24] or by processing a Correlation Power Attack (CPA) using their centred product [9], etc.). Computationally speaking, this approach requires to evaluate ℓ^d d-tuples (*e.g.* 6.25 million d-tuples for $d = 4$ and $\ell = 50$), thus its complexity grows exponentially with d.

The second approach, that avoids the exhaustive enumeration of the d-tuples of time samples, consists in estimating the conditional pdf of the whole region: to this scope, a Gaussian mixture model is proposed in literature [18, 21] and the parameters of such a Gaussian mixture can be estimated through the expectation-maximization (EM) procedure. In [18] 4 variants of the procedure are proposed according to a trade-off between the efficiency and the accuracy of the estimations; the most rough leads to the estimation of $256^{(d-1)}(\ell d)$ parameters (*e.g.* $\approx$3.4 billion parameters for $d = 4$ and $\ell = 50$), while the finest one requires the estimation of $256^{(d-1)}(1 + \frac{3 \cdot \ell d}{2} + \frac{(\ell d)^2}{2} - 1)$ parameters (*e.g.* $\approx$87 trillion parameters). Once again, the complexity of the approach grows exponentially with the order d.

The third approach, whose complexity does not increase exponentially with d, is the application of the higher-order version of the PP tool for the PoI selection. As will be discussed later, its heuristic nature is the counterpart of the relatively restrained complexity of this tool.

The new approach proposed in this paper has similarities with the first one above as it also aims to exploit interesting d-tuples of time samples. It however improves it in several aspects. In particular, its complexity does not increase exponentially with d. Moreover, it may be remarked that the first approach allows the attacker to extract interesting d-tuples of points, but does not provide any hint to conveniently combine them. This is an important limitation since finding a convenient way to combine time samples would raise the SCA efficiency. This remark has already been made for the unprotected case and for the particular case of implementations protected by first-order masking [5]. Nevertheless in the SCA literature no specific method has been proposed for the general case $d > 2$. This paper aims to propose a new answer to this question, while showing that it compares favourably to the PP approach.

1.3   Our Contribution

The ideas developed in the paper are based on the so-called Kernel Discriminant Analysis (KDA) [16,26], which essentially consists in applying a so-called *kernel trick* to the LDA. The trick is a stratagem that allows performing the LDA over a higher-dimensional *feature space* (whose dimension can even raise exponentially with d) in which information about Z lies in single dimensions and can be enhanced through linear combinations, keeping the computational cost independent from the dimension of the feature space (thus independent from d).[1] This study is in line with other recent works aiming to apply machine learning techniques to the side-channel context, such as [17,19] which also exploit kernel functions to deal with non-linearly separable data.

We show that the application of the KDA comes with several issues that we identify and analyse. We afterwards apply it to attack masked operations implemented over an 8-bit AVR microprocessor Atmega328P. The experiments performed in 2nd-order, 3rd-order and 4th-order contexts confirm the effectiveness of the KDA: in all cases the dimensionality reductions provided by the KDA lead to efficient and successful key recovery template attacks.

The paper is organised as follows: in Sect. 2 the notations are established, together with the formalization of the treated problem. Moreover, some State-of-the-Art methods, efficient for the 1st-order context, are recalled. In Sect. 3, the KDA method is described. A discussion about issues related to the application of the KDA to the SCA is conducted in Sect. 4 on the basis of experimental results. Finally, a comparison with the PP approach is proposed in Sect. 5.

2   Dimensionality Reduction: Generalities and Linear Extractors

2.1   Notations and Goal

Throughout this paper we use calligraphic letters as $\mathcal{X}$ to denote sets, the corresponding upper-case letter X to denote random variables (random vectors if in bold $\mathbf{X}$) over $\mathcal{X}$, and the corresponding lower-case letter x (resp. $\mathbf{x}$ for vectors) to denote realizations of X (resp. $\mathbf{X}$). The i-th entry of a vector $\mathbf{x}$ is denoted by $\mathbf{x}[i]$. The symbol $\mathbb{E}$ denotes the theoretical expected value, and Var denotes the theoretical variance. A hat over these symbols (*e.g.* $\hat{\mathbb{E}}$) denotes an estimation. The empirical mean of some realizations $(\mathbf{x}_i)_{i=1,\dots,N}$ is denoted by $\overline{\mathbf{x}}$, while $\overline{\mathbf{x}}^z$ denotes the empirical mean of realizations belonging to a class z in presence of a labelled sample $(\mathbf{x}_i^{z_i})_{i=1,\dots,N}$ (the class z is the sub-sample composed of the $\mathbf{x}_i^{z_i}$ such that $z_i = z$). The statistic $\overline{\mathbf{x}}^z$ may also be viewed as the estimation of the mean $\mathbb{E}[\mathbf{X}|Z = z]$.

Side-channel traces will be viewed as realizations of a random column vector $\mathbf{X} \in \mathbb{R}^D$. The dimensionality reduction phase will hence be formalized as the

---

[1] Even if the complexity is independent of d, the amount of information extracted is still decreasing exponentially with d, as expected when $(d-1)$-th order masking is applied [9].

application of an *extractor* $\varepsilon \colon \mathbb{R}^D \to \mathbb{R}^C$, aiming to reduce the dimensionality of data, *i.e.* $C \le D$, in order to decrease the memory and time complexity of the attack phase while keeping the exploitable information held by data high enough to allow an SCA to succeed.

In order to construct an extractor, a training set $(\mathbf{x}_i)_{i=1,\dots N}$ of side-channel traces must be exploited. If the training phase is performed under the assumption that the values taken by the target Z are known, then a label z_i corresponding to the value manipulated by the device during the acquisition of $\mathbf{x}_i$ is assigned, leading to a labelled sample $(\mathbf{x}_i^{z_i})_{i=1,\dots N}$. In such a case, N_z denotes the number of traces in the class z.

In this paper the amount of information exploitable for an SCA by a given extractor ε will be measured by the *instantaneous* SNR, which is defined for every coordinate u by:

$$\mathrm{SNR}^\varepsilon(u) = \frac{\hat{\mathrm{Var}}_z(\hat{\mathbb{E}}_i[(\varepsilon(\mathbf{x}_i^z)[u])_{i:z_i=z}])}{\hat{\mathbb{E}}_z[\hat{\mathrm{Var}}_i((\varepsilon(\mathbf{x}_i^z)[u])_{i:z_i=z})]}. \tag{1}$$

The efficiency of a (univariate) SCA is related to the SNR of the acquisition: the higher the SNR, the fewer data are necessary to make the underlying attack succeed. Under given attack conditions (*e.g.* the noise), a target threshold for the SNR has to be achieved for the attack to succeed; in this context a sound extractor must reduce the measurements' dimensionality while ensuring that SNR is higher than such a threshold, at least in one point. It may be remarked that, while in the unprotected case the rough acquisitions (*i.e.* $\varepsilon = Id$) might already satisfy the condition over the SNR, in the masked case SNR^{Id} is asymptotically null and ε must therefore satisfy certain additional conditions to raise it, as it will be discussed in Sect. 2.3. In particular the extractors will be required to combine several time samples to reveal 1st-order leakages, as in the first approach of Sect. 1.2 (when a 1st-order CPA is subsequently applied).

2.2   State-of-the-Art Linear Extractors

In the literature different methods to combine time samples for non-masked implementations have been proposed, analysed and compared, especially those based on linear combinations of points, such as PCA [1,3,6], LDA [4,28] and PP [13]. These three methods provide extractors of the form:

$$\varepsilon(\mathbf{x}) = A\mathbf{x} \quad A \in M_{\mathbb{R}}(C, D). \tag{2}$$

Principal Components Analysis (PCA). The extractor $\varepsilon^{\mathrm{PCA}}$ is deduced from some eigenvectors $\boldsymbol{\alpha}_1, \dots, \boldsymbol{\alpha}_C$ that are stored as rows in the matrix A appearing in (2). Two versions of PCA exist, an *unsupervised* one and a *supervised* one:

- unsupervised version: the eigenvectors are those of the following matrix:

$$\mathbf{S} = \frac{1}{N} \sum_{i=1}^{N} (\mathbf{x}_i - \overline{\mathbf{x}})(\mathbf{x}_i - \overline{\mathbf{x}})^\mathsf{T}; \tag{3}$$

the interesting property of such an extractor is that it spreads the data as much as possible: the variance of the processed traces is maximal.
- supervised version: using the labelled set of traces the eigenvectors are those of the so-called *between-class scatter matrix*:

$$\mathbf{S_B} = \sum_{z \in \mathcal{Z}} N_z (\overline{\mathbf{x}}^z - \overline{\mathbf{x}})(\overline{\mathbf{x}}^z - \overline{\mathbf{x}})^\mathsf{T}; \tag{4}$$

in this case the extractor guarantees that the *inter-class variance* of the processed traces is maximal: the class-centroids $\overline{\varepsilon(\mathbf{x})}^z$ are spread as much as possible, maximizing the SNR numerator.

Linear Discriminant Analysis (LDA). The extractor $\varepsilon^{\mathrm{LDA}}$ is computed taking into account not only the inter-class variance of the data, but also their *intra-class variance*: minimizing the last one amounts to minimize the SNR denominator of the extracted traces (and thus to raise the class distinguishability). As widely discussed in the literature [6,14,28], the LDA method is more expensive than the PCA but more efficient.[2] As for the PCA, the construction of the matrix A is done through that of some eigenvectors, which correspond to those of the matrix $\mathbf{S_W^{-1} S_B}$, where $\mathbf{S_B}$ is defined as in (4) and $\mathbf{S_W}$ is known as the *within-class scatter matrix*:

$$\mathbf{S_W} = \sum_{z \in \mathcal{Z}} \sum_{i: z_i = z} (\mathbf{x}_i^{z_i} - \overline{\mathbf{x}}^z)(\mathbf{x}_i^{z_i} - \overline{\mathbf{x}}^z)^\mathsf{T}. \tag{5}$$

Projection Pursuits (PP). The extractor $\varepsilon^{\mathrm{PP}}$ also takes the form (2), with A reduced to a row vector $\boldsymbol{\alpha}$. The computation of this vector is iteratively performed: at each step of the procedure, an entry of $\boldsymbol{\alpha}$ is randomly picked up and its value is adapted in order to maximize an *objective function*. Two objective functions are primarily proposed in [13]; the first one is the SNR of the extracted traces set and the second one is based on the so-called *profiled CPA*: it involves two labelled training sets $(\mathbf{x}_i^{z_i})_i$ and $(\mathbf{y}_j^{z_j})_j$: the first-order estimations $\mathbf{m}_z = \hat{\mathbb{E}}(\boldsymbol{\alpha} \cdot \mathbf{x}_i^{z_i} \mid z_i = z)$ are deduced from the first set and the correlation coefficient is afterwards estimated between the (profiled) sample $(\mathbf{m}_{z_j})_j$ and the (test) sample $(\boldsymbol{\alpha} \cdot \mathbf{y}_j^{z_j})_j$.

Equipped with the SNR objective function the PP translates into an iterative procedure aiming to estimate the LDA extractor $\varepsilon^{\mathrm{LDA}} : \mathbb{R}^D \to \mathbb{R}^1$. Analogously, when using the profiled CPA objective function, the PP tool produces an estimation of $\varepsilon^{PCA} : \mathbb{R}^D \to \mathbb{R}^1$, up to a multiplicative factor. An advantage of the PP

---

[2] It has been shown to be optimal as preprocessing for a template attack under specific leakage models [4].

procedure is that the attacker can trade precision for complexity improvement. Moreover other objective functions can be chosen to *e.g.* detect higher-order leakages in first-order protected implementations (see [13] and Sect. 5). The disadvantage of the PP is its heuristic asset: the convergence of the method is not guaranteed, and this issue is especially difficult to deal with in higher-order contexts.

2.3   Getting Information from Masked Implementations

The SNR measures, point by point, the information held by the first-order moment of the acquisition, *i.e.* the mean, to which we can refer to as a *1st-order information*. In masked implementations, such information is null: in any time sample the mean is independent from Z due to the randomization provided by the shares, namely $f(z) = \mathbb{E}[\mathbf{X}|Z = z]$ is constant, which implies that the SNR is asymptotically null over the whole trace.

When a $(d-1)$th-order masking is applied, the information about the shared sensitive target Z lies in some dth-order statistical moments of the acquisition,[3] meaning that for some d-tuples of samples $(t_1, \ldots, t_d)$ the function $f(z) = \mathbb{E}[\mathbf{X}[t_1]\mathbf{X}[t_2] \cdots \mathbf{X}[t_d]|Z = z]$ (based on a dth-order raw moment) is not constant (equivalently, $f(z) = \mathbb{E}[(\mathbf{X}[t_1] - \mathbb{E}[\mathbf{X}[t_1]]) \cdots (\mathbf{X}[t_d] - \mathbb{E}[\mathbf{X}[t_d]])|Z = z]$ is not constant, using the central moment). We can refer to such information as dth-order information. In order to let the SNR reveal it, and consequently let such information be directly exploitable, the attacker must pre-process the traces through an extractor ε that renders the mean of the extracted data dependent on Z, *i.e.* such that $f(z) = \mathbb{E}[\varepsilon(\mathbf{X})|Z = z])$ is not constant. In this way, the dth-order information is brought back to a 1st-order one.

Property 1 (SCA efficiency necessary condition). Let us denote by Z the SCA target and let us assume that Z is represented by a tuple of shares M_i manipulated at d different times. Denoting $t_1, \ldots, t_d$ the time samples[4] where each share is handled, the output of an effective extractor needs to have at least one coordinate whose polynomial representation over the variables given by the coordinates of $\mathbf{X}$ contains at least one term divisible by the the dth-degree monomial $\prod_{i=1,\ldots,d} \mathbf{X}[t_i]$ (see *e.g.* [7] for more information).

Remark 1. The use of central moments has been experimentally shown to reveal more information than the use of the raw ones [9,23]. Thus we will from now on suppose that the acquisitions have previously been normalized, so that $\hat{\mathbb{E}}(\mathbf{x}_i) = \mathbf{0}$ and $\hat{\text{Var}}(\mathbf{x}_i) = \mathbf{1}$. In this way a centred product coincides with a non-centred one.

The necessary condition exhibited in Property 1 explains why the linear extractors presented in Sect. 2.2 are ineffective in masked contexts. The KDA technique that we present in the following section provides an efficient strategy to construct an effective extractor in higher-order contexts.

---

[3] Whence the name *dth-order attacks.*
[4] Not necessary distinct.

3   Kernel Discriminant Analysis for High-Order Dimensionality Reduction

As described in Sect. 2.3, the hard part of the construction of an effective extractor is the detection of d time samples $t_1, \ldots, t_d$ where the shares leak. A naive solution, depicted in Fig. 1, consists in applying to the traces the centred product preprocessing for each d-tuple of time samples. Formally it means immerse the observed data in a higher-dimensional space, via a non-linear function

$$\Phi \colon \mathbb{R}^D \to \mathcal{F} = \mathbb{R}^{\binom{D+d-1}{d}}. \tag{6}$$

Using the machine learning language the higher-dimensional space $\mathcal{F}$ will be called *feature space*, because in such a space the attacker finds the features that discriminate different classes. Procedures involving a feature space defined as in (6) imply the construction, the storage and the management of $\binom{D+d-1}{d}$-sized traces; such a combinatorially explosion of the size of $\mathcal{F}$ is undoubtedly an obstacle from a computational standpoint.

$$\mathbb{R}^D \xrightarrow{\ \Phi\ } \mathcal{F} \xrightarrow[\varepsilon^{\mathrm{LDA}}]{\varepsilon^{\mathrm{PCA}}} \mathbb{R}^C$$

Fig. 1. Performing LDA and PCA over a high-dimensional feature space.

3.1   Kernel Trick for Discriminant Analysis

In machine learning a stratagem known as *kernel trick* is available for some linear classifiers, such as Support Vector Machine (SVM), PCA and LDA, to turn them into non-linear classifiers, providing an efficient way to implicitly compute them into a high-dimensional feature space. This section gives an intuition about how the kernel trick acts. It explains how it can be combined with the LDA, leading to the so-called KDA algorithm, that enables an attacker to construct some non-linear extractors that concentrate in few points the d-th order information held by the side-channel traces, without requiring computations into a high-dimensional feature space, see Fig. 2.

The central tool of a kernel trick is the *kernel function* $K \colon \mathbb{R}^D \times \mathbb{R}^D \to \mathbb{R}$, that has to satisfy the following property, in relation with the function Φ:

$$K(\mathbf{x}_i, \mathbf{x}_j) = \Phi(\mathbf{x}_i) \cdot \Phi(\mathbf{x}_j), \tag{7}$$

for each $i, j = 1, \ldots, N$, where $\cdot$ denote the dot product.

Every map Φ has an associated kernel function given by (7), for a given set of data. The converse is not true: all and only the functions $K \colon \mathbb{R}^D \times \mathbb{R}^D \to \mathbb{R}$ that satisfy a convergence condition known as *Mercer's condition* are associated to some map $\Phi : \mathbb{R}^D \to \mathbb{R}^F$, for some F. Importantly, a kernel function is interesting only if it is computable directly from the rough data $\mathbf{x}_i$, without evaluating the function Φ.

The notion of kernel function is illustrated in the following example.

Example 1. Let $D = 2$. Consider the function

$$K \colon \mathbb{R}^2 \times \mathbb{R}^2 \to \mathbb{R}$$
$$K \colon (\mathbf{x}_i, \mathbf{x}_j) \mapsto (\mathbf{x}_i \cdot \mathbf{x}_j)^2, \tag{8}$$

After defining $\mathbf{x}_i = [a, b]$ and $\mathbf{x}_j = [c, d]$, we get the following development of K:

$$K(\mathbf{x}_i, \mathbf{x}_j) = (ac + bd)^2 = a^2 c^2 + 2abcd + b^2 d^2, \tag{9}$$

which is associated to the following map from $\mathbb{R}^2$ to $\mathbb{R}^3$:

$$\Phi(u, v) = [u^2, \sqrt{2}uv, v^2] \tag{10}$$

Indeed $\Phi(\mathbf{x}_i) \cdot \Phi(\mathbf{x}_j) = a^2 c^2 + 2abcd + b^2 d^2 = K(\mathbf{x}_i, \mathbf{x}_j)$. This means that to compute the dot product between some data mapped into the 3-dimensional space $\mathcal{F}$ there is no need to apply Φ: applying K over the 2-dimensional space is equivalent. This trick allows the short-cut depicted in Fig. 2.

In view of the necessary condition exhibited by Property 1, the function $K(\mathbf{x}_i, \mathbf{x}_j) = (\mathbf{x}_i \cdot \mathbf{x}_j)^d$, hereafter named *dth-degree polynomial kernel function,* is the convenient choice for an attack against implementations protected with $(d - 1)$th-order masking. It corresponds to a function Φ that brings the input coordinates into a feature space $\mathcal{F}$ containing all possible d-degree monomials in the coordinates of $\mathbf{x}$, up to constants. This is, up to constants, exactly the Φ function of (6).[5]

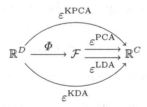

Fig. 2. Applying KDA and KPCA permits to by-pass computations in $\mathcal{F}$.

---

[5] Other polynomial kernel functions may be more adapted if the acquisitions are not free from d'th-order leakages, with $d' < d$. Among non-polynomial kernel functions, we effectuated some experimental trials with the most common Radial Basis Function (RBF), obtaining no interesting results. This might be caused by the infinite-dimensional size of the underlying feature space, that makes the discriminant components estimation less efficient.

As shown in 7, the kernel function K allows us to compute the dot product between elements mapped into the feature space $\mathcal{F}$ (7), and more generally any procedure that is only composed of such products. Starting from this remark, the authors of [27] have shown that the PCA and LDA procedures can be adapted to satisfy the latter condition, which led them to define the KPCA and KDA algorithms. The latter one is described in the following procedure.

Procedure 1 (KDA for dth-order masked side-channel traces). Given a set of labelled side-channel traces $(\mathbf{x}_i^{z_i})_{i=1,\ldots,N}$ and the kernel function $K(\mathbf{x}, \mathbf{y}) = (\mathbf{x} \cdot \mathbf{y})^d$:

(1) Construct a matrix $\mathbf{M}$ (acting as *between-class scatter matrix*):

$$\mathbf{M} = \sum_{z \in \mathcal{Z}} N_z (\mathbf{M}_z - \mathbf{M_T})(\mathbf{M}_z - \mathbf{M_T})^{\mathsf{T}}, \tag{11}$$

where $\mathbf{M}_z$ and $\mathbf{M_T}$ are two N-size column vectors whose entries are given by:

$$\mathbf{M}_z[j] = \frac{1}{N_z} \sum_{i:z_i=z}^{N_z} K(\mathbf{x}_j^{z_j}, \mathbf{x}_i^{z_i}) \tag{12}$$

$$\mathbf{M_T}[j] = \frac{1}{N} \sum_{i=1}^{N} K(\mathbf{x}_j^{z_j}, \mathbf{x}_i^{z_i}). \tag{13}$$

(2) Construct a matrix $\mathbf{N}$ (acting as *within-class scatter matrix*):

$$\mathbf{N} = \sum_{z \in \mathcal{Z}} \mathbf{K}_z (\mathbf{I} - \mathbf{I}_{N_z}) \mathbf{K}_z^{\mathsf{T}}, \tag{14}$$

where $\mathbf{I}$ is a $N_z \times N_z$ identity matrix, $\mathbf{I}_{N_z}$ is a $N_z \times N_z$ matrix with all entries equal to $\frac{1}{N_z}$ and $\mathbf{K}_z$ is the $N \times N_z$ sub-matrix of $\mathbf{K} = (K(\mathbf{x}_i^{z_i}, \mathbf{x}_j^{z_j}))_{\substack{i=1,\ldots,N \\ j=1,\ldots,N}}$ storing only columns indexed by the indices i such that $z_i = z$.

(2bis) Regularize the matrix $\mathbf{N}$ for computational stability:

$$\mathbf{N} = \mathbf{N} + \mu \mathbf{I} \quad \text{see Sect 4.2;} \tag{15}$$

(3) Find the non-zero eigenvalues $\lambda_1, \ldots, \lambda_Q$ and the corresponding eigenvectors $\boldsymbol{\nu}_1, \ldots, \boldsymbol{\nu}_Q$ of $\mathbf{N}^{-1}\mathbf{M}$;
(4) Finally, the projection of a new trace $\mathbf{x}$ over the ℓ-th non-linear d-th order discriminant component can be computed as:

$$\varepsilon_\ell^{\text{KDA}}(\boldsymbol{x}) = \sum_{i=1}^{N} \boldsymbol{\nu}_\ell[i] K(\mathbf{x}_i^{z_i}, \mathbf{x}). \tag{16}$$

For the reasons discussed in the introduction of this section, the right-hand side of (16) may be viewed as an efficient way to process the ℓ-coordinate of the vector $\varepsilon^{LDA}(\varPhi(\mathbf{x})) = \mathbf{w}_\ell \cdot \varPhi(\mathbf{x})$, without evaluating $\varPhi(\mathbf{x})$. The entries of $\mathbf{w}_\ell$ are never computed, and will thus be referred to as *implicit coefficients* (see Remark 2). It may be observed that each discriminant component $\varepsilon_\ell^{\mathrm{KDA}}(\cdot)$ depends on the training set $(\mathbf{x}_i^{z_i})_{i=1,\dots,N}$, on the kernel function K and on the regularization parameters μ.

Remark 2 (The implicit coefficients). As already said, the KDA, when the dth-degree polynomial kernel function is chosen as kernel function, operates implicitly in the feature space of all products of d-tuples of time samples. In order to investigate the effect of projecting a new trace $\mathbf{x}$ over a component $\varepsilon_\ell^{\mathrm{KDA}}(\mathbf{x})$, we can compute for a small d the implicit coefficients that are assigned to the d-tuples of time samples through (16). For $d = 2$ we obtain that in such a feature space the projection is given by the linear combination computed via the coefficients shown below:

$$\varepsilon_\ell^{\mathrm{KDA}}(\mathbf{x}) = \sum_{j=1}^{D}\sum_{k=1}^{D}[(\mathbf{x}[j]\mathbf{x}[k])\,\underbrace{(\sum_{i=1}^{N}\boldsymbol{\nu}_\ell[i]\mathbf{x}_i[j]\mathbf{x}_i[k])}_{\text{implicit coefficients}}] \tag{17}$$

3.2 Computational Complexity Analysis

The order d of the attack does not significantly influence the complexity of the KDA algorithm. Let N be the size of the training trace set and let D be the trace length, then the KDA requires:

- $\frac{N^2}{2}D$ multiplications, $\frac{N^2}{2}(D-1)$ additions and $\frac{N^2}{2}D$ raising to the d-th power, to process the kernel function over all pairs of training traces,
- $(D+C)$ multiplications, $(D+C-2)$ additions and 1 raising to the d-th power for the projection of each new trace over C KDA components,
- the cost of the eigenvalue problem, that is $O(N^3)$.

4 The KDA in Practice

In this section we discuss the practical problems an attacker has to deal with when applying the KDA. The argumentation is conducted on the basis of experimental results whose setup is described in the next section.

4.1 Experimental Setup

The target device is an 8-bit AVR microprocessor Atmega328P and we acquired power-consumption traces thanks to the ChipWhisperer platform [22].[6]

---

[6] This choice has been done to allow for reproducibility of the experiments.

From the acquisitions we extracted some traces composed of 200 time samples, corresponding to 4 clock cycles (see Fig. 7(a) or (b) upper parts). Depending on the attack implementation, we ensure that the acquisitions contain either 2, 3 or 4 shares respectively for $d = 2, 3$ or 4. The shares satisfy $M_1 \oplus \cdots \oplus M_d = Z$, where $Z = \mathrm{Sbox}(P \oplus K^\star)$. The goal of the attack is to recover the subkey $K^\star$. The plaintext P is assumed to be known and the M_i are assumed to be unknown random uniform values. For the characterization phase, the subkey $K^\star$ is also known. The training set has size $N = 8960$, and the plaintexts p_i have been chosen to balance the number of classes ($N_z = \frac{8960}{256} = 35$ for each $z \in \mathbb{F}_2^8$). We fixed the dimension C, *aka* the dimension of the extractor output, at the value 2 (except for the 2-class KDA for which we chose $C = 1$, see Remark 7): we therefore tried to build extractors $\varepsilon^{\mathrm{KDA}}(\cdot) = (\varepsilon_1^{\mathrm{KDA}}(\cdot), \varepsilon_2^{\mathrm{KDA}}(\cdot))$ mapping traces of size 200 samples into new traces composed of 2 coordinates.[7] Afterwards, a bivariate template attack [10] is then performed: some new profiling traces are used to estimate a Gaussian template for each class, and a maximum likelihood matching phase has then been performed to recover an unknown key $K^\star$ from some attack traces.

As discussed in Remark 1, the training traces are normalized. The average trace and the standard deviation trace used to perform the normalization are stored and reused to center the profiling and attack traces before projecting them onto the KDA components. In this way the new traces present a form as similar as possible to the training ones. Remark that, due to the over-fitting risk that will be discussed in Sect. 4.2, it is worth to not reusing the training traces as profiling traces in the attack phase: the extractor $\varepsilon^{\mathrm{KDA}}$ has a different behaviour when applied to the traces used to train it and to some new traces, and this might corrupt the profiling phase.

4.2   The Regularization Problem

By construction the matrix $\mathbf{N}$ in (14) is not positive-definite, which is one of the reasons why [26] proposes the regularization (15) recalled hereafter:

$$\mathbf{N} = \mathbf{N} + \mu \mathbf{I}. \tag{18}$$

When applying such a regularization, the choice of the constant μ is crucial. For sure it has to be large enough to ensure that $\mathbf{N}$ turns to a positive-definite matrix, but we experimentally observed that the minimal μ for which the positive-definitiveness of $\mathbf{N}$ is attained is often far from being the one that provides a good extractor. In Fig. 3 (left) we observe the efficiency of a template

---

[7] For PCA and LDA methods, it is known that a good component selection is fundamental to obtain an efficient subspace [6], and that the first components not always represent the best choice. This is likely to be the case for the KDA as well, but in our experiments the choice of the two first components $\varepsilon_1^{\mathrm{KDA}}, \varepsilon_2^{\mathrm{KDA}}$ turns out to be satisfying, and therefore to simplify our study we preferred to not investigate other choices.

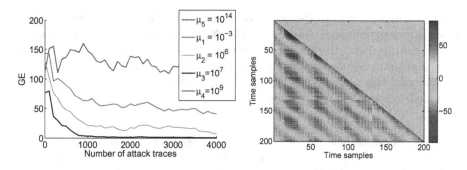

Fig. 3. On the left: template attack guessing entropy vs. the number of traces for the attack phase, varying for choices of the constant μ (15). On the right: the implicit coefficients assigned to pairs of time samples for μ_3 (upper triangular part) and μ_5 (lower triangular part).

attack run in combination with a KDA extractor. The matrix **N** is positive-definite for $\mu_1 = 10^{-3}$ but the value that provides the best extractor is much higher (namely $\mu_3 = 10^7$). Still raising the value of μ degrades the quality of the extractor. The right part of Fig. 3 shows the implicit coefficients of the extractor (see (17)) obtained under μ_3 (upper triangular part) and under μ_5 (lower triangular part). The extractor corresponding to the former one leads to a successful attack and has high values concentrated over the interesting windows; the extractor corresponding to the latter one leads to an unsuccessful attack and shows lack of localization around interesting parts of the trace, highlighting the fact that the KDA tool failed in detecting generalisable class-distinguishing features in this case.

As explained in [26], the regularization (15) is not only a way to make the problem computationally stable (which explains why the minimal μ making **N** positive-definite may not be a good choice). It is also an answer to the fact that kernel methods are generally prone to over-fitting, *i.e.* the aptitude to perfectly learn the training set without having the capacity to correctly classify new examples. This means, in the case of the KDA, that $\varepsilon^{\mathrm{KDA}}$ risks to perfectly separate the training traces in their classes, while failing in separating the attack traces. A regularization acts as an additional constraint of the problem, that makes the method less accurate in the learning phase, but in some cases more likely to correctly operate on new examples. The regularization (15) corresponds in particular to the additional requirement for ν to have a small norm $\|\nu\|^2$.

Remark 3. Another regularization strategy may be to search for sparse vectors of implicit coefficients (see (17)). This alternative might be more suitable for the side-channel context, since it would promote localized solutions, *i.e.* projections for which only a few d-tuples of time samples contribute to the construction of the extractor (see [6] for an analogy in 1*st*-order context). This approach is left for future developments.

Some heuristics exist to choose the constant μ; *e.g.* the average of the diagonal entries [20] or the minimal constant that let $\mathbf{N}$ be diagonally dominant (implying positive-definite), etc. In [8] Centeno *et al.* propose a maximization strategy to find the optimal regularization parameter, based on a probabilistic approach. The study of this approach is left for future works. For our study we simply performed experiments for various values of μ and we kept the best obtained results.

Remark 4. A criterion to decide whether the chosen regularization is convenient consists in comparing the SNR computed over the extracted training traces $(\varepsilon^{\mathrm{KDA}}(\mathbf{x}_i^{z_i}))_{i=1,\ldots,N}$ with the one computed over some extracted new traces $\mathbf{y}_i^{z_i}$ (*e.g.* the profiling traces $(\varepsilon^{\mathrm{KDA}}(\mathbf{y}_i^{z_i}))_{i=1,\ldots,N_p}$, being N_p the number of available profiling traces). If the latter is significantly lower than the former, the regularization failed and it is worth to try with another constant μ.

4.3   The Multi-class Trade-Off

As discussed in Sect. 2.2, the LDA, and by consequence the KDA, looks for a subspace of the feature space to optimally separate some given classes (for a well-chosen distance). Intuitively the more examples (*i.e.* training traces) available the more accurate the resulting KDA. Nevertheless, the number of examples might be bounded by the acquisition context. Actually even when the number N can be very high, it may be interesting to minimize it since the KDA complexity is $O(N^3)$. A trade-off must therefore be found between accuracy and efficiency. Assuming that the size of the training set is fixed to N, which controls the efficiency, a way to gain in accuracy may be found by appropriately adjusting

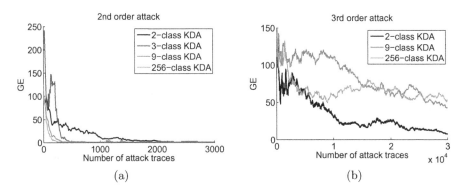

Fig. 4. Comparison between 2-class, 3-class, 9-class and 256-class KDA in 2nd-order context (a) and in 3rd-order context (b). For 2nd-order the KDA is efficient in providing separability between 256 classes, allowing an optimal attack. In 3rd-order context the training data are not enough to succeed the 256-class learning phase. Decreasing the number of classes to be distinguished raises the efficiency of the learning problem and thus of the attack.

the number of classes to distinguish: again intuitively, the more examples per class, the more accurate the detection of a separating subspace. Then, if the total number of training traces is fixed, in order to raise the number of traces per class, a smaller number of classes must be considered. To do so, a non-injective model $m(\cdot)$ can be introduced, to create a smaller set of labels $m(\mathcal{Z})$ from the initial set $\mathcal{Z}$. In the rest of the paper, the reduced number of classes, *i.e.* the number of labels assigned to the training set after applying the model m, will be denoted by W (it is the cardinality of $m(\mathcal{Z})$). In order to not corrupt the soundness of the KDA method in the SCA context, it is worth choosing a meaningful model. Since a widely-accepted power-consumption model for side-channel traces is provided by the Hamming Weight (HW) function, it makes sense to group the different values of Z according to their Hamming weights. In Fig. 4 we compared a 2-class model $(m(z) = 0$ if $\mathrm{HW}(z) < 4$, $m(z) = 1$ if $\mathrm{HW}(z) \geq 4)$, a 3-class model $(m(z) = 0$ if $\mathrm{HW}(z) < 4$, $m(z) = 1$ if $\mathrm{HW}(z) = 4$, $m(z) = 2$ if $\mathrm{HW}(z) > 4)$ and a 9-class one $(m(z) = \mathrm{HW}(z))$.

Remark 5. A balanced training set of size $N = 9000$ (instead of 8960) has been used to run the experiments for 2-class, 3-class and 9-class KDA.

Remark 6. For the sake of consistency[8] between the pre-processing phase and the attack phase, when a non-injective model is applied to the labels of the training set to reduce the number of classes, the same model is exploited to run the template attack: W templates (one per each class) are computed and compared to the matching traces. Thus, in Fig. 4 the different multi-class extractors are compared using different template attacks. It may be remarked that as W decreases the efficiency of the attack is supposed to decrease as well, because each attack trace contributes in distinguishing the right key $K^\star$ only from a growing-size set of indistinguishable hypotheses.

In 2nd-order context, it can be observed in Fig. 4 that the KDA is provided with sufficient training traces to succeed a 256-class separation, which allows the finest characterization of the leakage, and leads as expected (see Remark 6), to the most efficient template attack. Moving to the 3-rd order context, the available training set is insufficient to make the multi-class approach succeed; nevertheless, turning the problem into a 2-class problem turns out to be a good strategy to trade extraction accuracy for attack efficiency.

Remark 7. The separating subspace given by the KDA has maximal dimension $(W - 1)$, *i.e.* $Q \leq (W - 1)$ in point 4 of Procedure 1. When $W = 2$ a single discriminant component $\varepsilon_1^{\mathrm{KDA}}$ is available, then we run a univariate template attack, instead of a bivariate one.

4.4 Multi-class vs. 2-class Approach

An idea to avoid an excessive reduction of the number of separable classes W can be found in the machine learning literature dealing with the so-called *multi-class*

---

[8] A different approach is analysed in Sect. 4.5.

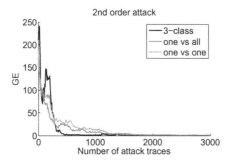

Fig. 5. Performance of template attacks run over 3-class KDA subspaces: multi-class, one vs. one and one vs. all approaches compared.

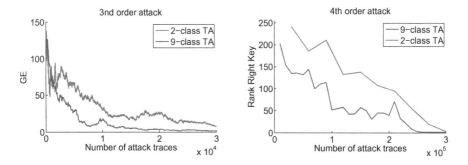

Fig. 6. Left: guessing entropy (over 10 independent tests) for a 2-class and a 9-class 3rd-order template attack. Right: right key rank of a 2-class and a 9-class 4th-order template attack.

classification problems. It consists in treating the W-class problem as multiple 2-class problems. Two different *modus operandi* exist: the *one-vs-one* and the *one-vs-all*. When applied to our context, the one-vs-one approach determines for each pair of classes the 1-dimensional subspace that best separates them and exploits all the obtained subspaces to run an attack (for W classes we obtain $\binom{W}{2}$ dimensions and we run a $\binom{W}{2}$-variate template attack). The one-vs-all approach looks for dimensions that best separate each class from all the others (obtaining W projections in total).

We tested this approach in the 3-class case: in this way the one-vs-one and the one-vs-all approaches provide both 3 dimensions that we use to run a 3-variate template attack, and that we compare to the 3-class multi-class approach with bivariate template attack. Our experimental results, summed up in Fig. 5, show that no gain is obtained by the 2-classes strategies.[9] We therefore chose to not consider them for our higher-order experiments.

---

[9] We think that is result is quite data-dependant, so the use of such an approach is not discouraged in general.

4.5 Asymmetric Preprocessing/Attack Approach

In Remark 6 we appealed a consistency principle to justify the choice of running a W-class template attack after a W-class KDA extraction. Here we propose a different reasoning: the consistency principle does not grant that an extractor ε^{KDA} trained with W classes is not able to separate W' classes with $W' > W$. As seen in Remark 2, an extractor ε^{KDA} always implicitly performs a weighed sum, via the implicit coefficients, of centred products of time samples. If ε^{KDA} is effective, the implicit coefficients which have the highest magnitude must correspond to time samples corresponding to the manipulation of sensitive data (*e.g.* the variable shares when masking is applied). This property is not necessarily related to the number of classes used to train the extractor.

Based on the reasoning above and on the observations reported in Remark 6, we performed in 3rd-order and 4th-order contexts a 9-class template attack after the 2-class KDA preprocessing. The results are depicted in Fig. 6 and confirm that, for our experimental data, this approach is sound: in both cases, using the same extractor trained with 2 classes and the same attack traces, the 9-class approach outperforms the 2-class one.

Remark 8. We choose to run the 9-class instead of the 256-class template attack in order to raise the accuracy of the profiling phase, being limited in terms of profiling traces.

5 A Comparison with the Projection Pursuits Technique

As discussed in the introduction, the PP approach [13] is nowadays in the side-channel literature the sole PoI detection technique that shares with the KDA the following characteristics: (1) it is applicable at any order d, (2) it does not assume the knowledge of the target random shares and (3) its computational complexity does not grow exponentially with d.[10] In this section the differences between the two approaches are discussed and an experimental comparison is performed.

5.1 An Outline of the PP Algorithm

The dth-order version of PP makes use of the so-called *Moment against Moment Profiled Correlation* (MMPC) as objective function. The extractor ε^{PP} has the following form:

$$\varepsilon^{PP}(\mathbf{x}) = (\boldsymbol{\alpha} \cdot \mathbf{x})^d, \tag{19}$$

where $\boldsymbol{\alpha}$ is a sparse projecting vector with d non-overlapping windows of coordinates set to 1, where the method has identified points of interest. Actually, as will be discussed in Sect. 5.2, authors of [13] propose to exploit $\boldsymbol{\alpha}$ as a pointer of PoIs, but do not encourage the use of ε^{PP} as an attack preprocessing. The

---

[10] At the cost of adjust some parameters in a way that might affect the accuracy of the method, see [13] for a discussion.

procedure is divided into two parts: a global research called *Find Solution* and a local optimization called *Improve Solution*. At each step of *Find Solution*, d windows are randomly selected to form a primordial $\boldsymbol{\alpha}$, thus a primordial ε^{PP}. A part of the training traces are then processed via ε^{PP} and used to estimate the dth-order statistical moments $\mathbf{m}_z^d = \hat{\mathbb{E}}_i[(\varepsilon^{PP}(\mathbf{x}_i^z))_{i:z_i=z}])$, for each value of z. Then the Pearson correlation coefficient $\hat{\rho}$ between such estimates and the same estimates issued from a second part of the training set is computed. If $\hat{\rho}$ is higher than some threshold T_{det}, the windows forming $\boldsymbol{\alpha}$ are considered interesting[11] and *Improve Solution* optimises their positions and lengths, via small local movements. Otherwise, the $\boldsymbol{\alpha}$ is discarded and another d-tuple of random windows is selected.

The threshold T_{det} plays a fundamental role in this crucial part of the algorithm: it has to be small enough to promote interesting windows (avoiding false negatives) and high enough to reject uninteresting ones (avoiding false positives). A hypothesis test is used to choose a value for T_{det} in such a way that the probability of $\hat{\rho}$ being higher than T_{det} given that no interesting windows are selected is lower than a chosen significance level β.[12]

5.2 Comparison with the KDA Approach

A first difference between the PP algorithm and the KDA approach is that they do not have exactly the same purposes. The PP, whose output $\boldsymbol{\alpha}$ consists in a projecting vector showing only d windows of coordinates set to 1, is a tool for the research of PoIs, but does not aim to provide an efficient way to combine the found points: the extractor ε^{PP} provides a non-null SNR but it does not aim to somehow raise it. On the contrary, the KDA looks for a way to efficiently combine the time samples of the traces, but does not give to the attacker the intuition about where the interesting points are (the explicit computation of the implicit coefficients is necessary to have such an intuition, see Remark 2).

A second remarkable difference is that the KDA is deterministic. On the contrary, the PP is an heuristic algorithm, whose convergence is not guaranteed as agreed by the authors of [13].

A third difference is that, once the Kernel function is chosen in a meaningful way, the KDA algorithm demands to set a single parameter: the regularization constant μ discussed in Sect. 4.2. By contrast several parameters have to be set when running the PP algorithm, and the choice of each one can be crucial: the ones related to the windows size (W_len, $minWS$ and $maxWS$), the number of

---

[11] A further validation is performed over such windows, using other two training sets to estimate $\hat{\rho}$, in order to reduce the risk of false positives.

[12] Interestingly, the threshold T_{det} depends on size of $\mathcal{Z}$ and not on the size of the training sets of traces. This fact disables the classic strategy that consists in enlarging the sample, making T_{det} lower, in order to raise the statistical power of the test (*i.e.* Prob$[\hat{\rho} > T_{det}|\rho = 1]$). Some developments of this algorithm have been proposed [12], also including the substitution of the MMPC objective function with a *Moments against Samples* one, that would let T_{det} decrease when increasing the size of the training set.

iterations and the number of maximal stationary steps (N_r^f, N_r^i and max_stagn), the initialization vector $\boldsymbol{\alpha}$, the hypothesis test threshold T_det, the number of best neighbours considered in the improve solution phase (N_n), the lengths of windows movements for global search (num_hops), the windows moves for local optimization ($move\_steps$), the allowed resize steps ($resize\_steps$).

Finally, while the computational complexity $O(N^3)$ of the KDA is strongly impacted by the training set size, the relation between the training set size and the complexity of the PP is not so easily determinable. Indeed, raising N implies an increasing cost in evaluating the objective function, but at the same time allows (thanks to the better averaging of noise) to enlarge the windows length W_{len}. The exploitation of larger windows implies a faster convergence of the *Find Solution* part of the algorithm, thus a decrement of the number of evaluations of the objective function.

5.3   Experimental Results

To get a fair comparison, we run the PP algorithm over the same training set used to evaluate the KDA in Sect. 4. The best results in the 2nd-order context were obtained with the HW model (*i.e.* $|\mathcal{Z}| = 9$). In this case T_{det} is fixed to 0.7. Since 4 training sets are required, the 9000 training traces are split in 4 equally-sized groups. Experimental observations allowed to fix $W_{len} = 5$, consequently suggesting $minWS = 1$, $maxWS = 15$ and consistent global and local movements and resizes. Given the heuristic asset of the algorithm, we run it 1000 times for $d = 2$ and for $d = 3$. An overview of the global behaviour of the obtained results is depicted in Figs. 7(a) and (b): the lower parts of the figures show the sum of the 1000 outputs of the algorithm. We recall that each coordinate of $\boldsymbol{\alpha}$ is set to 1 for the windows identified to be of interest, and to 0 elsewhere, so for each time sample the sum of the values (0 or 1) assigned by the 1000 attempts give an intuition about its likelihood to be considered as interesting by the PP method. It can be observed that in the 2-nd order case (Fig. 7(a)) the results are excellent: 100% of the tests highlight an informative part of the two clock-cycles where the sensitive shares are manipulated.[13] It means that $\varepsilon^{PP}(\mathbf{X})$ always contains information about Z and a successful attack can be mounted over such extracted traces. The efficiency of such an attack depending on many factors, there is no interest in comparing it to the performances of the template attacks run in 2nd-order context using ε^{KDA} and depicted in Fig. 4(a). As it may be observed in Fig. 7(b), in the 3-rd order case the experimental results are completely different: almost no $\boldsymbol{\alpha}$ selects the clock-cycle where the second share is manipulated. Thus in this case the PP approach fails: $\varepsilon^{PP}(\mathbf{X})$ does not contain information about Z, so any attack launched over the extracted traces would fail, while ε^{KDA} still allows successful attacks in 3rd-order and 4th-order case, as depicted in Fig. 6.

---

[13] It can be observed that the regions selected by ε^{PP} correspond to those for which the ε^{KDA} exhibits the highest magnitude implicit coefficients (Fig. 3, upper-triangular part on the right).

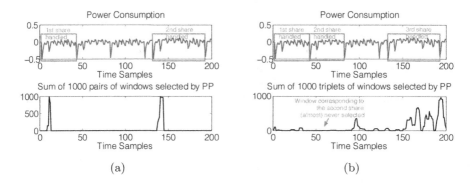

Fig. 7. (a) Overview of PP outputs in 2nd-order context. (b) Overview of PP outputs in 3rd-order context.

We conclude that the KDA approach is a valuable alternative to the PP one, especially in contexts where the training set size is bounded and independent from the order d of the attack.

6   Conclusions

In this work we proposed the use of the KDA method to extract small-sized informative features from side-channel acquisitions protected by a $(d-1)$th-order masking countermeasure. The KDA naturally extends the LDA technique to the generic dth-order context. It requires the choice of a so-called kernel function. We proposed to choose a polynomial kernel function, because it seems to perfectly fit the higher-order side-channel context. Indeed, in this way the obtained extractor provides the linear combination of all possible d-tuples of time samples which maximises the instantaneous SNR. In the State-of-the-Art the main obstacle to the problems of PoI selection and dimensionality reduction in higher-order side-channel context is given by the fact the size of the space containing all possible d-tuples of time samples explodes combinatorially while d grows. Nevertheless, the KDA only implicitly operates in such a space, by means of a so-called kernel trick, implying that its complexity is independent from the order d. This property represents the main advantage of the KDA, making it the only non-heuristic method for dimensionality reduction, computationally efficient in higher-order context. The main issue an attacker has to deal with to apply the KDA is related to the choice of a regularization parameter. Moreover the computational cost of the method is affected by the number of side-channel traces it uses for the training. For this reason, in order to achieve good results, the attacker has to find a good trade-off between the efficiency of the information extraction, its accuracy and the efficiency of the underlying attack, through a careful choice of the target classification model. A discussion about such a calibration has been presented in this paper and experimental results confirmed the effectiveness of the proposed technique in a 2nd-order, 3rd-order and 4th-order cases.

References

1. Archambeau, C., Peeters, E., Standaert, F.-X., Quisquater, J.-J.: Template attacks in principal subspaces. In: Goubin, L., Matsui, M. (eds.) CHES 2006. LNCS, vol. 4249, pp. 1–14. Springer, Heidelberg (2006). doi:10.1007/11894063_1
2. Bär, M., Drexler, H., Pulkus, J.: Improved template attacks. In: COSADE 2010 (2010)
3. Batina, L., Hogenboom, J., van Woudenberg, J.G.J.: Getting more from PCA: first results of using principal component analysis for extensive power analysis. In: Dunkelman, O. (ed.) CT-RSA 2012. LNCS, vol. 7178, pp. 383–397. Springer, Heidelberg (2012). doi:10.1007/978-3-642-27954-6_24
4. Bruneau, N., Guilley, S., Heuser, A., Marion, D., Rioul, O.: Less is more: dimensionality reduction from a theoretical perspective. In: Güneysu, T., Handschuh, H. (eds.) CHES 2015. LNCS, vol. 9293, pp. 22–41. Springer, Heidelberg (2015). doi:10.1007/978-3-662-48324-4_2
5. Bruneau, N., Danger, J.-L., Guilley, S., Heuser, A., Teglia, Y.: Boosting higher-order correlation attacks by dimensionality reduction. In: Chakraborty, R.S., Matyas, V., Schaumont, P. (eds.) SPACE 2014. LNCS, vol. 8804, pp. 183–200. Springer, Heidelberg (2014). doi:10.1007/978-3-319-12060-7_13
6. Cagli, E., Dumas, C., Prouff, E.: Enhancing dimensionality reduction methods for side-channel attacks. In: Homma, N., Medwed, M. (eds.) CARDIS 2015. LNCS, vol. 9514, pp. 15–33. Springer, Heidelberg (2016). doi:10.1007/978-3-319-31271-2_2
7. Carlet, C., Danger, J.-L., Guilley, S., Maghrebi, H., Prouff, E.: Achieving side-channel high-order correlation immunity with leakage squeezing. J. Cryptographic Eng. 4(2), 107–121 (2014)
8. Centeno, T.P., Lawrence, N.D.: Optimising kernel parameters and regularisation coefficients for non-linear discriminant analysis. J. Mach. Learn. Res. 7, 455–491 (2006)
9. Chari, S., Jutla, C.S., Rao, J.R., Rohatgi, P.: Towards sound approaches to counteract power-analysis attacks. In: Wiener, M. (ed.) CRYPTO 1999. LNCS, vol. 1666, pp. 398–412. Springer, Heidelberg (1999). doi:10.1007/3-540-48405-1_26
10. Chari, S., Rao, J.R., Rohatgi, P.: Template attacks. In: Kaliski, B.S., Koç, K., Paar, C. (eds.) CHES 2002. LNCS, vol. 2523, pp. 13–28. Springer, Heidelberg (2003). doi:10.1007/3-540-36400-5_3
11. Choudary, O., Kuhn, M.G.: Efficient template attacks. In: Francillon, A., Rohatgi, P. (eds.) CARDIS 2013. LNCS, vol. 8419, pp. 253–270. Springer, Cham (2014). doi:10.1007/978-3-319-08302-5_17
12. Durvaux, F., Standaert, F.-X.: From improved leakage detection to the detection of points of interests in leakage traces. IACR Cryptology ePrint Archive, p. 536 (2015)
13. Durvaux, F., Standaert, F.-X., Veyrat-Charvillon, N., Mairy, J.-B., Deville, Y.: Efficient selection of time samples for higher-order DPA with projection pursuits. In: Mangard, S., Poschmann, A.Y. (eds.) COSADE 2014. LNCS, vol. 9064, pp. 34–50. Springer, Cham (2015). doi:10.1007/978-3-319-21476-4_3
14. Eisenbarth, T., Paar, C., Weghenkel, B.: Building a side channel based disassembler. In: Gavrilova, M.L., Tan, C.J.K., Moreno, E.D. (eds.) Trans. on Comput. Sci. X. LNCS, vol. 6340, pp. 78–99. Springer, Heidelberg (2010). doi:10.1007/978-3-642-17499-5_4
15. Gierlichs, B., Lemke-Rust, K., Paar, C.: Templates vs. stochastic methods. In: Goubin, L., Matsui, M. (eds.) CHES 2006. LNCS, vol. 4249, pp. 15–29. Springer, Heidelberg (2006). doi:10.1007/11894063_2

16. Hofmann, T., Schölkopf, B., Smola, A.J.: Kernel methods in machine learning. Ann. Stat. **36**, 1171–1220 (2008)
17. Hospodar, G., Gierlichs, B., De Mulder, E., Verbauwhede, I., Vandewalle, J.: Machine learning in side-channel analysis: a first study. J. Cryptographic Eng. **1**(4), 293–302 (2011)
18. Lemke-Rust, K., Paar, C.: Gaussian mixture models for higher-order side channel analysis. In: Paillier, P., Verbauwhede, I. (eds.) CHES 2007. LNCS, vol. 4727, pp. 14–27. Springer, Heidelberg (2007). doi:10.1007/978-3-540-74735-2_2
19. Lerman, L., Poussier, R., Bontempi, G., Markowitch, O., Standaert, F.-X.: Template attacks vs. machine learning revisited (and the curse of dimensionality in side-channel analysis). In: Mangard, S., Poschmann, A.Y. (eds.) COSADE 2014. LNCS, vol. 9064, pp. 20–33. Springer, Cham (2015). doi:10.1007/978-3-319-21476-4_2
20. Li, T., Zhu, S., Ogihara, M.: Using discriminant analysis for multi-class classification: an experimental investigation. Knowl. Inf. Syst. **10**(4), 453–472 (2006)
21. Lomné, V., Prouff, E., Rivain, M., Roche, T., Thillard, A.: How to estimate the success rate of higher-order side-channel attacks. In: Batina, L., Robshaw, M. (eds.) CHES 2014. LNCS, vol. 8731, pp. 35–54. Springer, Heidelberg (2014). doi:10.1007/978-3-662-44709-3_3
22. O'Flynn, C., Chen, Z.D.: ChipWhisperer: an open-source platform for hardware embedded security research. In: Prouff, E. (ed.) COSADE 2014. LNCS, vol. 8622, pp. 243–260. Springer, Cham (2014). doi:10.1007/978-3-319-10175-0_17
23. Prouff, E., Rivain, M., Bevan, R.: Statistical analysis of second order differential power analysis. IEEE Trans. Comput. **58**(6), 799–811 (2009)
24. Reparaz, O., Gierlichs, B., Verbauwhede, I.: Selecting time samples for multivariate DPA attacks. In: Prouff, E., Schaumont, P. (eds.) CHES 2012. LNCS, vol. 7428, pp. 155–174. Springer, Heidelberg (2012). doi:10.1007/978-3-642-33027-8_10
25. Schneider, T., Moradi, A.: Leakage assessment methodology. In: Güneysu, T., Handschuh, H. (eds.) CHES 2015. LNCS, vol. 9293, pp. 495–513. Springer, Heidelberg (2015). doi:10.1007/978-3-662-48324-4_25
26. Schölkopf, B., Müller, K.-R.: Fisher discriminant analysis with kernels. In: Neural Networks for Signal Processing IX, vol. 1, p. 1 (1999)
27. Schölkopf, B., Smola, A., Müller, K.-R.: Nonlinear component analysis as a kernel eigenvalue problem. Neural Comput. **10**(5), 1299–1319 (1998)
28. Standaert, F.-X., Archambeau, C.: Using subspace-based template attacks to compare and combine power and electromagnetic information leakages. In: Oswald, E., Rohatgi, P. (eds.) CHES 2008. LNCS, vol. 5154, pp. 411–425. Springer, Heidelberg (2008). doi:10.1007/978-3-540-85053-3_26

Defeating Embedded Cryptographic Protocols by Combining Second-Order with Brute Force

Benoit Feix[✉], Andjy Ricart, Benjamin Timon, and Lucille Tordella

UL Transaction Security Lab, Basingstoke, England
{benoit.feix,andjy.ricart,benjamin.timon,lucille.tordella}@ul.com

Abstract. Side-channel analysis is a well-known and efficient hardware technique to recover embedded secrets in microprocessors. Counter-measures relying on random masking have been proven to be sound protections against such threats and are usually added to protect sensitive intermediate data during the algorithm process. However, Second-Order Side-Channel Analysis have proven to allow secret key recovery in the presence of random masking. In [4] an attack was introduced which exploits the information exchange at the cryptographic protocol level in order to disclose the secret key of the ISO/IEC 9797-1 MAC algorithm 3 using DES operations. A countermeasure suggestion was for a mask to be applied at the protocol level in order to protect all secret data. This paper extends the attack idea previously published to second order attacks on masked implementations of the ISO/IEC 9797-1 MAC algorithm 3 and shows that securing against such attacks must be done with care.

Keywords: Side-channel analysis · DES · MAC ISO/IEC 9797-1 · HODPA · Masking · Exhaustive search

1 Introduction

Since its first introduction in 1996 by Kocher [10] side-channel analysis has proved to be a powerful threat for embedded cryptosystems. The fast paced growth of published attacks using side-channel techniques challenge cryptographic algorithms designers to constantly counteract these attacks.

While many countermeasures already exists to protect cryptographic algorithms against those attacks, [4] showed that these protections shall not be confined to the cryptographic layer only but shall be extended to the cryptographic protocol level. Indeed the authors presented an attack targeting the ISO9797-1 MAC Algorithm 3 [8] protocol mostly used on secure elements. The attack uses the fact that for this protocol, a data usually considered as a public value (the resulting ciphertext of a DES operation) could lead to the recovery of the 112-bits secret key of the algorithm combining statistical side-channel and brute-force attacks.

In [4], the authors suggested to prevent the intermediate information between the DES operation to appear in plain in order to withstand the presented attack.

© Springer International Publishing AG 2017
K. Lemke-Rust and M. Tunstall (Eds.): CARDIS 2016, LNCS 10146, pp. 23–38, 2017.
DOI: 10.1007/978-3-319-54669-8_2

This paper presents how, in some attack scenarios, an implementation of the ISO9797-1 MAC Algorithm 3 [8] protocol secured with boolean masking could still be vulnerable to higher order side-channel analysis.

The paper is organized as follows. Section 2 reminds the structure of the ISO9797-1 MAC algorithm 3. The necessary knowledge and background on side-channel analysis to understand our second order attacks are also presented. In Sect. 3 describes our work to recover the secret keys of masked MAC computations. The practical results obtained are then presented in Sect. 4. In Sect. 5 we provide recent status on DES crackers capabilities and Sect. 6 is a discussion of the classical countermeasures and their efficiency to prevent our attack. Finally we conclude in Sect. 7.

2   Preliminaries

2.1   Side-Channel Analysis Background

Side-channel analysis has been studied for years since it has been introduced by Kocher [10]. Many attack paths have been published on the different cryptosystems like DES [5] and RSA [15] which are widely used in the majority of the hardware embedded devices like Banking or Identity products. In the same time many statistical attack techniques have improved the original Differential Side-Channel Analysis (DSCA) (i.e. Difference of Mean - DoM) from Kocher et al. [11]. We can for instance mention the Correlation Side-Channel Analysis (CSCA) introduced by Brier et al. [2], the Mutual Information Side-Channel Analysis (MISCA) from Gierlichs et al. [7] or the Linear Regression Side-Channel Analysis [3,16].

Second Order Side-Channel Attacks. Second order Side-channel analysis is an attack category allowing to recover a secret data in the presence of a first order countermeasure (i.e. where classical first-order side-channel attacks are failing). It has been originally introduced by Messerges [13]. For years now second-order attacks are mainly focused on attacks relying on the Hamming Weight.

When a boolean masking is implemented as a countermeasure, the intermediate data is replaced by $v_K^* = v_K \oplus M$ with $M \in \mathbb{F}_2^n$ and n being the bit length of v_K. By doing so, the sensitive data is no longer linked to the side-channel leakage. But it is still possible to succeed the attack on such an implementation with the knowledge of the mask side-channel emanations as explained in [9,14,17].

The core idea of SODPA is that if the attacker knows (or guesses) the time frames T_M and T_v where the mask and the masked sensitive data are respectively manipulated, he can combined them in order to decrease the mask efficiency. Both the guess on the intermediate values and the traces during T_M and T_v have to be combined.

The intermediate values v_K^* and M can be combined using $S = HW(v_K^* \oplus M)$.

A study of combination methods for the traces has been conducted in [14] by comparing mainly the *Absolute Difference* processing traces such as $T = |T_M - T_v|$ and the *Multiplicative Combining* processing traces such as $T = (T_M - \mu_M) * (T_v - \mu_v)$ with μ_M and μ_v the mean values of the sets of traces T_M and T_v. It concluded the latest is the most efficient.

A correlation between S and the combined signal would then allow to recover K.

2.2 Background on ISO 9797-1 MAC Algo 3

The ISO/IEC-9797-1 MAC Algorithm 3 with DES (also known as retail MAC) computes the MAC of data using a 112-bit secret key. For a k 8-byte blocks data, the $k - 1$ first blocks are processed through Single DES operations in CBC mode using 56 bits of the key and a triple DES is performed on the final block using a 112 bits secret key and the result of the processing of the $k - 1$ first blocks as IV. The security of this protocol relies on the Triple DES but the use of a CBC-DES chain allow a reasonable computation time. Figure 1 describes the MAC algorithm 3 when the encryption algorithm selected is the standard DES.

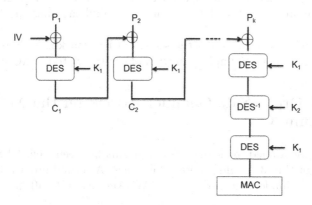

Fig. 1. ISO 9797-1 MAC Algo 3 Description with DES cipher

In the following we define K as the 112 bits key used for the calculation, divided into two subkeys K_1 and K_2 of equal length such as $K = (K_1, K_2)$. The ith occurrence of the algorithm $MAC^{(i)}$ is the result value CBC-MAC-Algo3$(P_1^{(i)} P_2^{(i)} \ldots P_k^{(i)})$ with $IV = 0$ and the nth ciphertext is defined as $C_n^{(i)} = DES_{K_1}(P_{n-1}^{(i)} \oplus C_{n-2}^{(i)})^1$.

Side-Channel Attack on MAC Algo 3. The attack introduced in [4] targets the 112 bit-length master key used by the ISO 9797-1 MAC algorithm. The result of such an attack could be the disclosure of the whole master key. In the following, the different steps for implementing this attack are reminded.

---

[1] $\oplus$ represents the bitwise exclusive OR operation.

The first step of the attack is to recover one couple of value (plaintext P, ciphertext C) from a single DES computation from a set of ℓ executions of the ISO9797-1 MAC algorithm 3 using side channel traces collected from the targeted device during the MAC Algorithm 3 computation.

In order to recover the nth block intermediate result, C_n has to be a fixed value. Hence, the n first 8-byte long blocks value $P_1^{(i)}, \ldots, P_n^{(i)}$ must be set to a constant value $P = P_1, \ldots, P_n$, identical for all of the ℓ MAC computation $MAC^{(1)}, \ldots, MAC^{(\ell)}$. The $n+1^{th}$ block $P_{n+1}^{(i)}$ must then be chosen randomly or at least with a high entropy across the transaction set.

As the input $P_{n+1}^{(i)}$ is a known random value, it is possible to guess the value $D^{(i)} = C_n \oplus P_{n+1}^{(i)}$ from side channel traces using statistical attacks and to recover C_n.

Once recovered, a brute force attack can then be conducted to deduce the value of the 56-bit key K_1 from the couple (P_n, C_n), which in turn allows the recovery of K_2 with some more effort.

In [4] masking the operations between each DES operations of the MAC Algorithm 3 is proposed as a countermeasure against such an attack. This paper will however show that high order attacks could still be possible in some cases and that therefore care should be taken when implementing such a masking scheme.

In the following section we use the second order attack as well as the results from [4] to target a masked implementation of the ISO9797-1 MAC Algorithm 3.

3   Second Order Side-Channel Attack on the MAC Algorithm 3

As previously mentioned, masking the operations between each DES operation of a MAC Algorithm 3 should be done with care. A second order attack on two different masked implementations of a MAC Algorithm 3 will be presented in this section.

3.1   All DES Inputs Masked with the Same Mask

The first masking scheme is presented on Fig. 2. While this implementation is secure against the first order attack presented in [4], should the same mask M be used for all the DES of the same transaction it would then be possible to mount a second order attack against this implementation by combining two DES inputs as explained in Sect. 2.1.

Indeed, considering $P_n \oplus M$ the nth DES input and $C_n \oplus P_{n+1} \oplus M$ the $(n+1)^{th}$ DES input, it is possible to perform a second order CPA in order to retrieve C_n.

As for the first order attack, a set of side channel traces focusing on the execution of both the first and second DES operations is collected with $P_0 \ldots P_n$ fixed and P_{n+1} randomized.

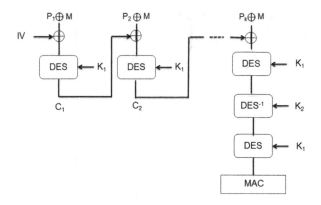

Fig. 2. ISO 9797-1 MAC Algo 3 Description with DES cipher

To cancel the unknown mask value, the first and second DES inputs can be combined as follows: $(P_n \oplus M) \oplus (C_n \oplus P_{n+1} \oplus M) = C_n \oplus P_n \oplus P_{n+1}$.

Therefore the two areas of the side channel traces corresponding to the two DES inputs processing, from the same transaction i, have to be combined. For $T_1^{(i)}$ and $T_2^{(i)}$ corresponding to these two parts of the signal $D_1 = (P_n \oplus M)$ and $D_2 = C_n \oplus P_{n+1} \oplus M$, any combination function $F(T_1, T_2)$ can be used as explained in [14].

A correlation between $D_1 \oplus D_2$ and the combined signal $F(T_1, T_2)$ would then enable the recovery of C_n which would then lead to the retrieval of keys K_1 and K_2 using brute force technique. It can be highlighted that if the value of P_n is fixed to 0, then the targeted intermediate state is the same as for the first order attack: $C_n \oplus P_{n+1}$. In this case, the mask is directly manipulated by the device during the data loading. A legitimate question is to know if fixing P_{n+1} to 0 improves the attack. This question will be studied in Sect. 4.

3.2 All DES Inputs Masked with Different Masks, Mask Is only 1 Byte

In the case of each block being masked with a different value, as presented in Fig. 3, the previous attack cannot be applied. In the specific case of these masks being only 8-bit masks (i.e. for the nth block, $M_n = (R_n|R_n|\dots|R_n)$ with R_n an 8-bit random) then a more complex attack can still reveal the secret key.

Indeed in this case the input of one DES operation can be combined with itself to cancel the mask as such: $(C_{n,j} \oplus P_{n,j} \oplus R_n) \oplus (C_{n,j+1} \oplus P_{n,j+1} \oplus R_n) = C_{n,j} \oplus P_{n,j} \oplus C_{n,j+1} \oplus P_{n,j+1}$ (for each byte j of the ciphertext). As for the previous attack, the two parts of the signal T_1 and T_2 corresponding to the processing of respectively $D_1 = (C_{n,j} \oplus P_{n,j} \oplus R_n)$ and $D_2 = (C_{n,j+1} \oplus P_{n,j+1} \oplus R_n)$ are combined using the function $F(T_1, T_2)$.

In order to compute the value $D_1 \oplus D_2$ the attacker has to guess the value of $C_{n,1}$ and $C_{n,2}$, therefore the complexity of the correlation attack will be higher

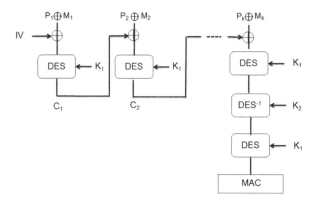

Fig. 3. ISO 9797-1 MAC Algo 3 Description with DES cipher

than the attack presented earlier. If successful, this attack would then enable the recovery of $C_{n,j} \oplus C_{n,j+1}$. In order to recover the ciphertext C_n, the attacker would still have a 1-byte uncertainty due to the XOR operation between the bytes. Although the complexity of the brute force key recovery on the MAC Algorithm 3 would be higher, the effort would remain affordable as explained in Sect. 5.

4   Practical Results

Several practical experimentations were conducted to assert the feasibility of the attacks we proposed in Sect. 3. Tests were first conducted on simulated power traces relying on a standard Hamming weight leakage model with a white Gaussian noise. An ISO9797-1 MAC algorithm 3 implemented on a 32-bit AT-Mega microprocessor was then targeted, the tests focusing on the electromagnetic emanations of the device collected during several MAC computations. All of the results are presented in this section.

4.1   Simulated Traces

Tests on Fixed Mask. Simulations were performed in order to validate the proposed attack path. Another goal of the simulations was to determine whether or not, the choice of the fixed value P_n (fixed to 0 or not) can influence the result of the attack. We chose to attack the 1st DES output C_1. To do so, we use the classic power model $L(x) = HW(x) + N(\alpha, \sigma)$, where $HW(x)$ refers to the Hamming weight of the value x, and N is a Gaussian noise of mean α and standard deviation[2] σ. We simulated the attack on an 8-bit architecture.

---

[2] Regarding the standard deviation of the noise, a unit corresponds to the side-channel difference related to a one bit difference in the Hamming weight.

Simulation Protocol. Draw an 8-byte random P_1 to simulate the first fixed data block and an 8-byte random K_1 the DES key used in Fig. 1. For each simulated trace proceed as follows:

- Draw an 8-byte random M as mask value,
- Compute $D_1^{(i)} = P_1^{(i)} \oplus M^{(i)}$ and $C_1 = \text{DES}_{K_1}(P_1)$,
- Draw an 8-byte random $P_2^{(i)}$ to as random second data block,
- Compute the next masked value $P_2^{(i)} \oplus M^{(i)}$,
- Compute the next DES operation input $D_2^{(i)} = C_1 \oplus P_2^{(i)} \oplus M^{(i)}$,
- Compute the combination for the second order attack $D_1^{(i)} \oplus D_2^{(i)}$.

The power consumption of the described sequence was simulated using the power model previously defined. The DES operation was not included in the simulation to avoid any risk of leakage from this process. The second order attack as previously proposed was implemented and tested. Figures 4 and 5 show the attack success on the bytes 3 and 6 of C_1 to illustrate the results (all bytes showed similar results).

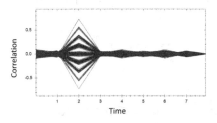

Fig. 4. 2^8 correlation traces attack result on byte 3 of C_1 for $\ell = 100$ traces and $\sigma = 1$

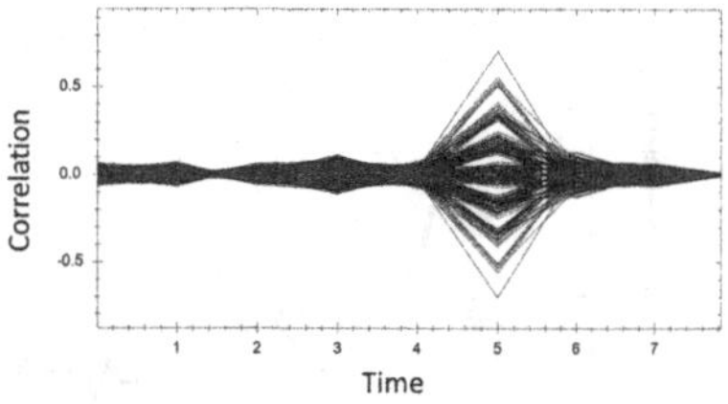

Fig. 5. 2^8 correlation traces attack result on byte 6 of C_1 for $\ell = 100$ traces and $\sigma = 1$

The success rate of our attack technique was assessed by performing 100 experiments as described earlier. The tests have been performed for different noise standard deviation values, from $\sigma = 0.1$ to $\sigma = 7$. The results are presented in Fig. 6. These tests confirmed in practice the relevance of the theoretical attack presented in Sects. 4.2 and 4.3.

Next, experiments were performed in order to conclude about the influence of P_1 on the results. First, the attack was performed with P_1 fixed to 0 and then with P_1 fixed to a random non-null value. The result of these attacks are presented in Fig. 7.

As it can be observed, the correlation levels are similar in both cases, which means that the chosen value of the fixed data P_1 does not influence the result of the attack.

Tests on 1-Byte Random Masks. The same power model was kept for the simulation $L(x) = HW(x) + N(\alpha, \sigma)$. Here, the attack was simulated on an 8-bit architecture.

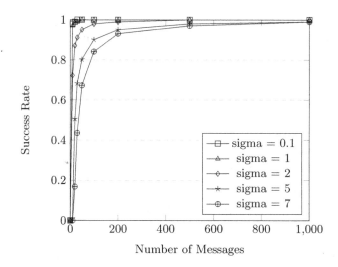

Fig. 6. Attack success rate for different noise value - Recover the full ciphertext

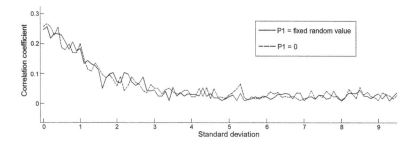

Fig. 7. Comparison of the attack efficiency depending on the value of P1.

Simulation Protocol. Draw an 8-byte random P_1 to simulate the first fixed data block and an 8-byte random K_1 the DES key used for the CBC DES chain of the protocol. For each trace simulation proceed as follows:

- Draw a 1-byte random $M_1^{(i)}$ as mask value,
- Compute $D_1^{(i)} = P_1^{(i)} \oplus M_1^{(i)}$ and $C_1 = \text{DES}_{K_1}(P_1)$,
- Draw an 8-byte random $P_2^{(i)}$ as random second data block,
- Draw a new 1-byte random $M_2^{(i)}$ to simulate the new mask value,
- Compute the next masked value $P_2^{(i)} \oplus M_2^{(i)}$,
- Compute the next DES operation input $D_2^{(i)} = C_1 \oplus P_2^{(i)} \oplus M_2^{(i)}$,
- Compute the combination for the second order attack $D_{2,j}^{(i)} \oplus D_{2,j+1}^{(i)}$ (for each byte j of the ciphertext).

The power consumption of the described sequence was simulated using the power model previously defined. The DES operation was not included in the simulation to avoid any risk of leakage from this process. The second order attack as previously proposed was implemented and tested. Figures 8 and 9 show the attack success on some of the bytes of C_1 to illustrate the results (all the bytes showed similar results).

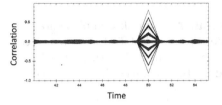

Fig. 8. 2^8 correlation traces attack result on $C_{1,3} \oplus C_{1,4}$ for $\ell = 100$ traces and $\sigma = 1$

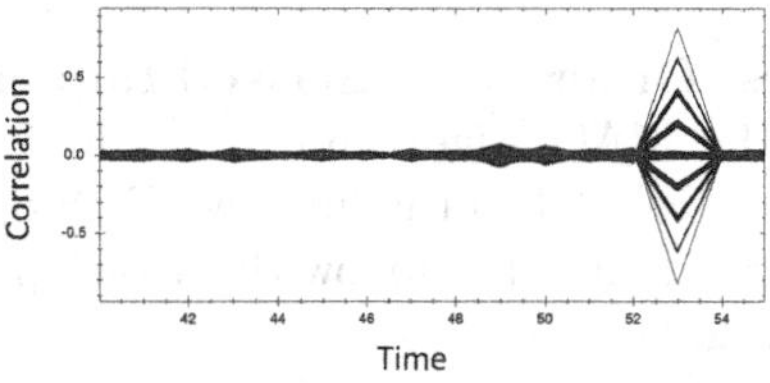

Fig. 9. 2^8 correlation traces attack result on $C_{1,6} \oplus C_{1,7}$ for $\ell = 100$ traces and $\sigma = 1$

The success rate of our attack technique was assessed by performing 100 experiments as described earlier. The tests have been performed for different noise standard deviation values, from $\sigma = 0.1$ to $\sigma = 7$. The results are presented in Fig. 10.

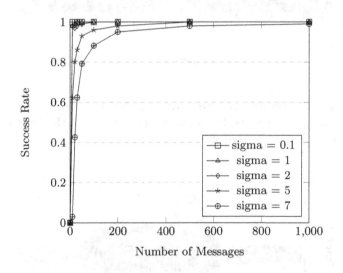

Fig. 10. Attack success rate for different noise value

4.2   Tests on an 32-Bit AT-Mega Microprocessor

The single DES operations of an ISO9797-1 MAC algorithm 3 were implemented on a 32-bit Arduino board. Different tests were conducted to validate the previous attacks presented on a real device as well as to corroborate the results computed from the simulation traces. First, an unmasked implementation of the MAC Algorithm 3 was targeted to reproduce the results of [4]. Tests on a masked implementation of the MAC Algorithm 3 were then conducted. The results of the different test are presented in the following.

First Order on Unmasked Implementation. An unmasked implementation of the MAC Algorithm 3 was first targeted. Around 10,000 Electromagnetic traces related to the first two DES operations were collected, with P1 fixed and P2 randomised to follow the attack presented in [4]. The area of interest is shown in Fig. 11.

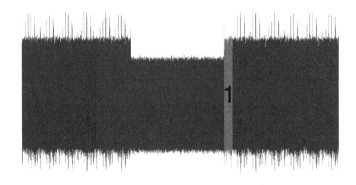

Fig. 11. Area or interest - $P_2 \oplus C_1$ (area 1)

Less than 130 traces were needed to recover all 8 bytes of the targeted ciphertext. As an example of results, Fig. 12 shows the results for the fourth byte. The results for the other bytes were similar.

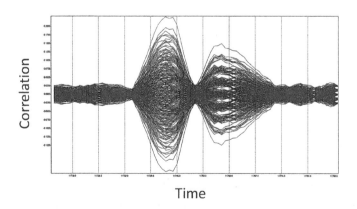

Fig. 12. Correlation peak on byte 4 of C_1 for the First Order attack

The detailed summary of the number of traces needed to recover each of the bytes of the targeted ciphertext is presented in Table 1.

Table 1. Number of traces needed to recover the targeted bytes, first order attack on an unmasked implementation

Targeted byte	Byte 1	Byte 2	Byte 3	Byte 4	Byte 5	Byte 6	Byte 7	Byte 8
Traces needed	30	70	50	90	70	90	130	90

Tests on a Masked Implementation. Tests were then conducted on a masked implementation of the MAC Algorithm 3. For these tests, a 8-byte mask $M^{(i)}$ was randomly generated for each $MAC^{(i)}$ computation and applied to each DES operation in order to conceal the XOR operations $D_{k+1}^{(i)} = C_k \oplus P_{k+1}^{(i)}$ and prevent the recovery of C_k with first order statistical attacks. It is to be noted that the DES operations themselves were modified following the scheme proposed in [1] to ensure that the input of each DES would remain masked during the entire computation and prevent any leakage from the DES internal computations.

100,000 traces were collected, with the input block P_1 fixed to zero. A first order attack was conducted focusing on the area of leakage previously identified in order to ensure that the masking scheme is efficient enough to prevent any first order leakage. The correlation traces corresponding to the bytes of the targeted ciphertext showed that no peak could be obtained of the previously leaking area thus proving that the implemented masking scheme is sufficient to prevent such an attack.

The leakage areas T_1 and T_2 corresponding respectively to $D_1 = (P_1 \oplus M)$ and $D_2 = (P_2 \oplus M \oplus C_1)$ were identified on the traces as shown on Fig. 13.

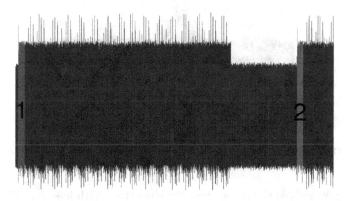

Fig. 13. Areas of interest - $D_1 = P_1 \oplus M$ (area 1) and $D_2 = P_2 \oplus M \oplus C_1$ (area 2)

The previously explained second order attack was firstly performed by combining T_1 and T_2 such as $T_{sec} = \|T_2 - T_1\|$ with T_{sec} the traces targeted by the attack. Correlation peaks allowed the recovery of each bytes of the targeted value, Fig. 14 shows the example of the fourth byte.

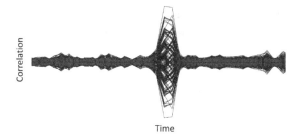

Fig. 14. Correlation peak on byte 4 of C_1 on traces using *Absolute Difference*

Table 2. Number of traces needed to recover the targeted bytes, second order attack with $P_1 = 0$ using *Absolute Difference*

Targeted byte	Byte 1	Byte 2	Byte 3	Byte 4	Byte 5	Byte 6	Byte 7	Byte 8
Traces needed	3,500	34,000	7,100	4,000	6,800	8,000	4,200	5,300

This attack enabled the recovery of the ciphertext with less than 34000 traces. Table 2 shows the number of traces needed to recover each bytes of the ciphertext.

The exact same attack was performed but combining T_1 and T_2 such as $T_{sec} = (T_2 - \mu_{T_2}) * (T_1 - \mu_{T_1})$ with T_{sec} the traces targeted by the attack. Again, correlation peaks allowed the recovery of each bytes of the targeted value, Fig. 15 shows the example of the fourth byte.

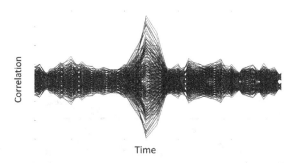

Fig. 15. Correlation peak on byte 4 of C_1 on traces using *Multiplicative Combining*

This attack enabled the recovery of the ciphertext with less than 8500 traces. Table 3 shows the number of traces needed to recover each bytes of the ciphertext.

These results prove that the attacks we presented in Sect. 3 can be a threat to some masked MAC Algorithm 3 computations. The following section will present possible countermeasures against those second order attacks.

Table 3. Number of traces needed to recover the targeted bytes, second order attack with $P_1 = 0$ using *Multiplicative Combining*

Targeted byte	Byte 1	Byte 2	Byte 3	Byte 4	Byte 5	Byte 6	Byte 7	Byte 8
Traces needed	1,400	1,000	8,500	4,200	3,000	4,900	4,000	4,800

4.3   Tests on a Secure Integrated Circuit from the Industry

This attack was also performed this attack on a more secure integrated circuit than a commercial Arduino. Indeed it embeds several hardware security mechanisms. The objective was to measure the effectiveness of this attack path on a state-of-the-art security product. The same second order attack has been conducted with success on this device, with P_1 fixed to zero. In this case it was also possible to recover all bytes of C_1 with less than $65,535$ traces which is the maximum number of traces available for such a protocol for some banking products.

5   Follow-Up: How to Complete the Attack - The Efficiency of DES Crackers

Once we have recovered with side-channel analysis the couple of values (P_n, C_n), it is required to perform a brute force attack to recover the first single DES 56-bit key K_1 of the MAC algorithm 3. Today performing such a single DES brute force can be achieved for a low cost in a short time period: from few hours to 1 week depending on the solution chosen.

It can be performed using a dedicated hardware such as the Rivyera engine sold by the SciEngines company based on the COPACABANA DES cracker [12] presented initially at the CHES 2009 conference. Using such an engine enable the recovery of a single DES key in 1–2 days. Once this secret key K_1 is recovered a second brute force is performed to recover K_2.

The attack presented here requires the value P to be fixed to a unique constant value (e.g. plaintext $P = 0$) that can be chosen or at least is known by the attacker. Therefore it is also possible to use DES rainbow table - constructed on this given plaintext value - to perform the DES brute force operation.

In 2015 two students and their professor from Limoges University succeeded to build a DES rainbow table in less than 1 month using GPU from the university [6]. Once the DES rainbow table is available (128 Gigabyte in this case) only few days on a computer are necessary to recover with high probability the secret key. This example shows that no expensive or complicated hardware is necessary. Indeed a student can use a classroom and rainbow tables found on the internet and brute force a single DES key in only a few days.

More recently it has been published on twitter it is possible to brute force a DES in less than 60 hours for $\sim$5000\$ using hashcat.

6   Countermeasures

Session keys: a first protection to consider relies on the protocol level design. Using session keys instead of a master key when computing ISO9797-1 MAC Algorithm 3 cryptograms, the session keys being regenerated for each transaction, is still considered as the strongest countermeasure against the first and second (and higher) order attacks presented here.

Enhanced random masking: the classical technique consisting in using several random mask is still efficient if properly designed. Indeed if a masking scheme similar to the one presented in Sect. 3 is used to protect the MAC Algorithm 3 against first order attacks, the developer should make sure that each DES block are masked using a different mask, even if this requires more resources. If the RNG used to generate the different masks is not biased, it would then insure protection against first and second order attacks.

Execution counter: as a second order attack on the MAC Algorithm 3 might require more traces than a first order attack to be successful, limiting the number of MAC computations can still be considered as a temporary solution against this attack. However, our experiments showed that this cannot be always considered enough to protect an implementation against this attack. Tests should therefore still be done to ensure that the limit counter chosen would be sufficient. However improving the attack efficiency in the future could still defeat this light protection.

Signal desynchronization: adding noise to the signal in order to lower the signal to noise ratio should also reduce the efficiency of any attack, as for the first order but that should not be considered enough and needs to be combined with another security measure.

7   Conclusion

In this paper we have explained how much it can be difficult to prevent some cryptographic protocols (i.e. MAC algorithm 3) implementation from state-of-the-art side-channel attacks. Indeed we have presented successful practical second order attacks that can defeat masked implementations of the MAC algorithm 3 designed to be resistant to the original side-channel attack presented in 2014 by Feix et al. These new results highlight the serious need for strong high-order side-channel resistant countermeasures at the protocol level and not only during the DES cryptographic operations. Hence random masks applied on DES inputs and outputs - as well as during the XOR operations - must be updated very regularly. It requires developers to apply random mask values from the beginning of the CBC chain to the end of the MAC computation by refreshing the random masks for each plaintext and ciphertext block manipulated. Nowadays the efficiency of high-order side-channel attacks combined with the fact it has become quite simple to access DES cracker computations make such attacks very realistic and practical on secure products. It is then very important to embed strong countermeasures when performing MAC algorithm 3 computations with master keys.

Acknowledgements. The authors would like to thank Loic Thierry for the fruitful discussions we had on this subject in the past.

References

1. Akkar, M.-L., Giraud, C.: An implementation of DES and AES, secure against some attacks. In: Koç, Ç.K., Naccache, D., Paar, C. (eds.) CHES 2001. LNCS, vol. 2162, pp. 309–318. Springer, Heidelberg (2001). doi:10.1007/3-540-44709-1_26
2. Brier, E., Clavier, C., Olivier, F.: Correlation power analysis with a leakage model. In: Joye, M., Quisquater, J.-J. (eds.) CHES 2004. LNCS, vol. 3156, pp. 16–29. Springer, Heidelberg (2004). doi:10.1007/978-3-540-28632-5_2
3. Doget, J., Prouff, E., Rivain, M., Standaert, F.-X.: Univariate side channel attacks and leakage modeling. IACR Cryptology ePrint Archive, 2011:302 (2011)
4. Feix, B., Thiebeauld, H.: Defeating ISO9797-1 MAC Algo 3 by Combining Side-Channel and Brute Force Techniques. Cryptology ePrint Archive, Report 2014/702 (2014)
5. Federal Information Processing Standards Publication (FIPS). Data Encryption Standard - DES, FIPS PUB 46-3 (1999)
6. Fournier, R.: Implementation et Evaluation des Attaques par Brute-Force et par Analyse de Canaux Auxiliaires sur des Algorithmes Cryptographiques l'Aide de Processeurs Graphiques. Intership Limoges University (2015)
7. Gierlichs, B., Batina, L., Tuyls, P., Preneel, B.: Mutual information analysis. In: Oswald, E., Rohatgi, P. (eds.) CHES 2008. LNCS, vol. 5154, pp. 426–442. Springer, Heidelberg (2008). doi:10.1007/978-3-540-85053-3_27
8. ISO/IEC. Information technology - Security techniques - Message Authentication Codes (MACs). ISO/IEC Standards (1999)
9. Joye, M., Paillier, P., Schoenmakers, B.: On second-order differential power analysis. In: Rao, J.R., Sunar, B. (eds.) CHES 2005. LNCS, vol. 3659, pp. 293–308. Springer, Heidelberg (2005). doi:10.1007/11545262_22
10. Kocher, P.C.: Timing attacks on implementations of Diffie-Hellman, RSA, DSS, and other systems. In: Koblitz, N. (ed.) CRYPTO 1996. LNCS, vol. 1109, pp. 104–113. Springer, Heidelberg (1996). doi:10.1007/3-540-68697-5_9
11. Kocher, P., Jaffe, J., Jun, B.: Differential power analysis. In: Wiener, M. (ed.) CRYPTO 1999. LNCS, vol. 1666, pp. 388–397. Springer, Heidelberg (1999). doi:10.1007/3-540-48405-1_25
12. Kumar, S., Paar, C., Pelzl, J., Pfeiffer, G., Schimmler, M.: Breaking ciphers with COPACOBANA –a cost-optimized parallel code breaker. In: Goubin, L., Matsui, M. (eds.) CHES 2006. LNCS, vol. 4249, pp. 101–118. Springer, Heidelberg (2006). doi:10.1007/11894063_9
13. Messerges, T.S.: Using second-order power analysis to attack DPA resistant software. In: Koç, Ç.K., Paar, C. (eds.) CHES 2000. LNCS, vol. 1965, pp. 238–251. Springer, Heidelberg (2000). doi:10.1007/3-540-44499-8_19
14. Prouff, E., Rivain, M., Bevan, R.: Statistical analysis of second order differential power analysis. IEEE Trans. Comput. **58**(6), 799–811 (2009)

15. Rivest, R.L., Shamir, A., Adleman, L.: A method for obtaining digital signatures and public-key cryptosystems. Commun. ACM **21**, 120–126 (1978)
16. Schindler, W., Lemke, K., Paar, C.: A stochastic model for differential side channel cryptanalysis. In: Rao, J.R., Sunar, B. (eds.) CHES 2005. LNCS, vol. 3659, pp. 30–46. Springer, Heidelberg (2005). doi:10.1007/11545262_3
17. Waddle, J., Wagner, D.: Towards efficient second-order power analysis. In: Joye, M., Quisquater, J.-J. (eds.) CHES 2004. LNCS, vol. 3156, pp. 1–15. Springer, Heidelberg (2004). doi:10.1007/978-3-540-28632-5_1

Side-Channel Analysis of the TUAK Algorithm Used for Authentication and Key Agreement in 3G/4G Networks

Houssem Maghrebi$^{(\boxtimes)}$ and Julien Bringer

Safran Identity and Security, Paris, France
{houssem.maghrebi,julien.bringer}@morpho.com

Abstract. Side-channel attacks are nowadays well known and most designers of security embedded systems are aware of them. Yet, these attacks are still major concerns and several implementations of cryptographic algorithms are still being broken. In fact, a recent work has exhibited a successful Differential Power Attack (DPA) on the MILENAGE algorithm used for authentication and key agreement in UMTS/LTE networks. Surprisingly, the targeted MILENAGE implementations in different USIM cards, coming from several mobile network operators, didn't systematically take advantage of the large panel of the well-known side-channel countermeasures. Recently, a new algorithm called TUAK, based on the KECCAK permutation function, has been proposed as alternative to MILENAGE. Although KECCAK was deeply analyzed in several works, the TUAK algorithm needs to be well investigated to assess its security level and to avoid inappropriate apply of KECCAK. In this paper, we present a side-channel analysis of an unprotected TUAK implementation and we demonstrate that a successful side-channel attack is possible if the state-of-the-art countermeasures are not considered. Our results show that a few hundred of traces would roughly be needed to recover the subscriber key and other authentication secrets fixed by mobile operators. Actually, this work raises a warning flag to embedded systems developers alerting them to rely on adequate countermeasures, which effect shall be confirmed with thorough security analysis, when implementing cryptographic primitives in USIM cards.

Keywords: TUAK · KECCAK · Side-channel analysis · Authentication and key agreement · UMTS · LTE · USIM cards

1 Introduction

Side-Channel Attacks. Side-channel attacks (SCA) are a serious threat against modern cryptographic implementations. They exploit information leaked from the physical implementations of cryptographic algorithms. Since this leakage (*e.g.* the power consumption or the electromagnetic radiation) depends

This work has been partially funded by the ANR project SERTIF.

© Springer International Publishing AG 2017
K. Lemke-Rust and M. Tunstall (Eds.): CARDIS 2016, LNCS 10146, pp. 39–56, 2017.
DOI: 10.1007/978-3-319-54669-8_3

on the internally used secret key, the adversary may perform an efficient key-recovery attack to reveal this sensitive data. During the two last decades, the development of the smart card industry has urged the cryptographic research community to carry on with this new concept of attacks and many papers describing either countermeasures or attacks improvement have been published. Amongst the side-channel attacks, two classes may be distinguished. The set of so-called *profiling SCA*: is the most powerful kind of side-channel attacks and consists of two steps. First, the adversary procures a copy of the *target device* and uses it to characterize the physical leakage. Second, she performs a key-recovery attack on the target device. This set of profiled attacks includes Template attacks [15] and Stochastic models (*aka* Linear Regression Analysis) [17,30,31]. The set of so-called *non-profiling SCA*: corresponds to a much weaker adversary who has only access to the physical leakage captured on the target device. To recover the internally used secret key, she performs some statistical analyses to detect the dependency between the leakage measurements and this sensitive variable. This set of non-profiled attacks includes Differential Power Analysis (DPA) [22], Correlation Power Analysis (CPA) [13] and Mutual Information Analysis (MIA) [18].

On the Vulnerability of Cryptographic Algorithms Used in Cellular Networks. Till recent times, research towards the security of cryptographic algorithms used in *mobile cellular networks* has been essentially concerned with classical cryptanalytic attacks [8,34]. Even if the cryptographic algorithm is mathematically sound [7], an adversary can mount a side-channel attack on a Universal Subscriber Identity Module (USIM) card implementing it to recover the internally used secret key. Indeed, authors in [28] have described a successful side-channel attack on the popular GSM authentication algorithm COMP128. Mainly, the entire 128-bit key of COMP128 can be recovered with only 8 adaptively chosen inputs.

Recently, Liu *et al.* have assessed in [24] a physical security analysis of the MILENAGE algorithm [4]. This primitive is used for authentication and key agreement in UMTS (Universal Mobile Telecommunications System)/LTE (Long-Term Evolution) networks and it is based on the AES algorithm [16]. The authors have concluded that the targeted MILENAGE implementations in several USIM cards didn't systematically take advantage of state-of-the-art countermeasures against side-channel attacks. In fact, when performing a DPA attack, an adversary is able to recover the subscriber key and other secrets fixed by the mobile network operator within a few hundred of traces for the unprotected USIM cards which have been analyzed. The results of this security analysis have been also presented at BlackHat 2015 [23].

Our Contribution. The 3rd Generation Partnership Project (3GPP) has proposed the TUAK algorithm as an alternative to MILENAGE to enhance security and privacy of UMTS/LTE mobile cellular networks [5]. The design of TUAK is based upon the winner of the SHA-3 competition, KECCAK [11]. When looking carefully at the technical specification of the TUAK algorithm [5, Sect. 7.3], one can clearly notice that it is highly recommended to protect its implementation against side-channel attacks, as it was the case for MILENAGE [4, Sect. 5.4]. In this paper, we try to answer the following question:

Is the straightforward TUAK implementation, in a USIM card, protected against side-channel attacks?

Actually, we answer this question negatively. In fact, our conducted security analysis has led to the same conclusions as those obtained in [24]. Mainly, we show first that it is possible to recover the involved secret parameters with roughly a few hundred of TUAK invocations. Then, we try to bridge the gap between the physical implementation of this new cryptographic primitive in USIM cards and the existing investigations on dedicated countermeasures to thwart side-channel attacks by proposing some defensive strategies.

Our paper provides, to the best of our knowledge, the first complete side-channel analysis of the TUAK algorithm. The only publicly available security analysis was performed in [26], where authors have theoretically evaluated the robustness of the TUAK implementation against timing attacks [21].

Paper Outline. The paper is organized as follows. In Sect. 2, we first overview the AKA protocol used for mutual authentication and key agreement in 3G/4G mobile cellular networks. Then, we describe the main characteristics of the TUAK algorithm and the KECCAK permutation function. In Sect. 3, we detail our SCA strategy and provide the practical results of our proposal. This is followed in Sect. 4 by a discussion of some well-known side-channel countermeasures and other defensive strategies that could be applied to protect the TUAK algorithm when implemented in USIM cards. Finally, Sect. 5 draws general conclusions.

2 Background

2.1 Overview of the AKA Protocol

The 3GPP is a collaboration agreement that was established in 1998 between international telecommunications standards bodies. It aims, inter alia, at the development of technical specifications for the third and the fourth generation (3G/4G) mobile cellular networks. To enhance the security of the authentication procedure through these new generation networks, the 3GPP has proposed a mutual Authentication and Key Agreement (AKA) protocol [1]. In Fig. 1, we describe the sequence diagram of this protocol in a unified way for 3G and 4G networks[1]. Without loss of generality, the 3G/4G networks are composed of:

- The user equipment: comprises the mobile equipment (*e.g.* a cellular phone) and the USIM card issued by a mobile operator to a subscriber and that contains mainly: the International Mobile Subscriber Identity (IMSI), which

---

[1] The AKA 4G protocol slightly differs from the 3G one, in particular on the way that the session keys are computed.

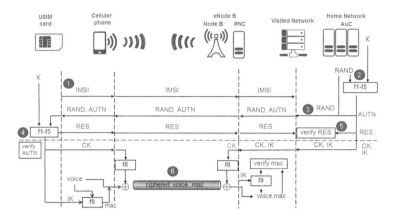

Fig. 1. Unified AKA protocol between the USIM card and the authentication center in 3G/4G networks.

is the permanent key of the subscription, and the cryptographic keys and algorithms required for the authentication protocol.

- The radio access network: which contains the Node B's and the Radio Network Controllers (RNC) for the 3G network and is composed only by the Evolved Node B's for the 4G network. It provides and manages wireless connection between mobile equipment and the core network.
- The visited network: it acts as the manager of network connectivity and is responsible for the subscriber authentication.
- The home network: which contains and maintains the Authentication Center (AuC) server. The latter contains the keys of all operator's subscribers and generates temporary tokens used to establish authentication, to set up session keys and to enable the communication.

The AKA protocol is executed between the user, the visited network and the home network as follows: when the mobile equipment is powered on, it sends through wireless communication the IMSI to the visited network. The latter forwards the request to the AuC. Upon receipt of this request, the AuC generates a fresh nonce (RAND) and fetches the subscriber key K to generate a batch of authentication vectors by computing the cryptographic functions (f_1, f_2, f_3, f_4, f_5). Each authentication vector is composed of:

- RES: the expected response value,
- CK, IK: respectively the cipher and the integrity session keys, and
- AUTN: the authentication token which contains several concatenated fields such that:

$$AUTN = (SQN \oplus AK)\|AMF\|MAC, \qquad (1)$$

where SQN is the sequence number, AK is the anonymity key, AMF is the authentication management field and MAC is the message authentication code. The ($\|$) and ($\oplus$) symbols denote respectively the concatenation and the exclusive-or (XOR) operations. Then, the AuC sends the AUTN and the challenge (RAND) to the user equipment and keeps the other related security parameters (RES, CK and IK). Once receipt of (AUTN, RAND), the USIM card executes symmetrically the same security functions (f_1, f_2, f_3, f_4, f_5) to check the parameters of the authentication token AUTN. First, it computes the anonymity key AK (by performing f_5 function) and retrieves the SQN = (SQN$\oplus$AK)$\oplus$AK. Second, it computes the MAC (by executing f_1 function) and then compares it to that contained in AUTN. If they are equal, then the USIM card performs a check on the SQN sent by the AuC and that maintained inside the USIM card. If either of these two checks fails, then the USIM card sends some error messages. Otherwise, it generates the session keys (CK, IK), computes the response RES and sends it to the visited network. Next, the visited network compares the response received from the AuC and the one received from the USIM card. If the check succeeds, then the AKA protocol is completed. Finally, the subscriber could start his communication. His voice is encrypted and integrity protected (with a MAC) by the mobile (and the network) using the security functions (f_8, f_9) and the generated session keys (CK, IK). For further details on how these ciphering and integrity functions are used, we refer the reader to [2,3].

The AKA protocol is compatible with either MILENAGE or TUAK algorithms. The main difference is the security functions used (f_1, f_2, f_3, f_4, f_5). In fact, while MILENAGE security functions are based on the AES-128, the TUAK ones are based on the KECCAK permutation.

2.2   The TUAK Algorithm

The TUAK algorithm is composed of several encryption functions that are based on the KECCAK permutation. Mainly, it contains 8 different functions:

- the derivation function: used to compute a 256-bit value, called TOP$_c$, from the TOP, a secret constant value chosen by the mobile operator, and the subscriber key K. As stated in [5, Sect. 7.1], this function is preferably performed off-card and only the output (*aka* TOP$_c$) is stored in the USIM card. For the rest of this paper, we will consider this recommendation as part of our assumptions.
- f_1: used to generate the message authentication code (MAC).
- f_2: used to generate the response (RES).
- f_3: used to generate the cipher session key (CK).
- f_4: used to generate the integrity session key (IK).
- f_5: used to generate the anonymity key (AK).
- f_1^* and f_5^*: used to recompute MAC and AK in case of authentication failure (*aka* re-synchronization phase) to determine the error messages to send.

All the previously described functions take 1600-bit as input. However, the output length varies according to each function.

Without loss of generality, we will focus in this work on the implementation of the f_1 function on the USIM card side. We stress the fact that our attack strategy could be applied to any other TUAK functions. However, in realistic scenarios if the MAC comparison fails, the authentication is aborted and the rest of TUAK functions (*i.e.* f_2, f_3 and f_4) will not be processed. Moreover, we argue that our choice differs from that in [24], where the authors have focused on f_5 and justified their choice by the fact that this function is the first one to be executed. But, when looking at the technical specification, we noticed that during the establishment of the AKA protocol the use of f_5 function is optional [1, Sect. 5.1.6.7] which further supports our choice towards targeting the f_1 function. In fact, most of mobile network designers omit this calculation aiming at enhancing the performance of the authentication process. Indeed, in such a case, the SQN field is sent in clear (*i.e.* not XORed with the anonymity key AK as detailed in Eq. (1) and hence, AUTN = SQN∥AMF∥MAC). We will use this technical detail when exhibiting our attack strategy.

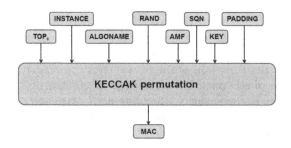

Fig. 2. The f_1 function of TUAK.

As depicted in Fig. 2, f_1 function takes as input:

- TOP$_c$: a 256-bit secret value.
- INSTANCE: an 8-bit constant value that depends on the subscriber key length (128-bit or 256-bit) and the outputted MAC length (64-bit, 128-bit or 256-bit). In the sequel, we fix the INSTANCE field at the hexadecimal value 0x10. Said differently, we assume a subscriber key of 128-bit length and an outputted MAC of 64-bit length[2].
- ALGONAME: a 56-bit constant value equals to the ASCII representation of the string "TUAK1.0"[3].
- RAND: a 128-bit value standing for the nonce generated by the AuC.
- AMF: a 16-bit value standing for the authentication management field.
- SQN: a 48-bit value standing for the sequence number.
- KEY: the subscriber key of 128 or 256 bits length. As explained above, we will fix the key length at 128-bit.
- PADDING: an 832-bit value to reach the 1600-bit required size for the input.

---

[2] We refer the reader to [5, Sect. 6.2] for further information about the specifications of the INSTANCE field.

[3] Explicitly, the successive ALGONAME field bytes are: 0x30, 0x2E, 0x31, 0x4B, 0x41, 0x55 and 0x54.

Yet, we notice that for the other TUAK functions, the same inputs are used except for the INSTANCE field which changes according to the required output to be calculated (*e.g.* CK, IK, RES).

To compute the MAC, f_1 function performs the KECCAK permutation on the 1600-bit input described above. In the following subsection, we will detail the KECCAK permutation.

2.3   The KECCAK Permutation

In 2012, the NIST selected KECCAK as the winner of the SHA-3 contest due to its novel design and excellent performance both in resistance to various attacks and implementation in software and hardware. The structure of KECCAK [11] is based on the so-called *sponge function* which is a generalized hash function that accepts an arbitrary length inputs (of the message and key) and generates digests of any desired bit size. Thus, KECCAK could be used in several ways: to perform a regular hashing, to compute a MAC, to derive keys, *etc.*

Concerning the internal KECCAK permutation function, there are 7 instances with an input width ranging from 25 to 1600 bits increasing in powers of two (*i.e.* the permutation width is equal to 25×2^l, *s.t.* $l \in [0, 6]$). The default input width value is 1600 bits [11], as it is the case for the TUAK security functions [5].

Besides, several bit-width implementations of the KECCAK permutation could be considered. For instance, in [5, Annex. E], the 3GPP technical specification provides examples of source code for an 8, 32 and 64 bits implementation of the KECCAK permutation. In the sequel, we will focus on the 32-bit version since it especially suitable for the USIM card we targeted for our side-channel analysis. Doing so, the 1600-bit state of the KECCAK permutation (*i.e.* the input of the TUAK f_1 function) are represented as 50 blocks of 32 bits each. We recall the source code of the 32-bit implementation, that we will use, in Listing 1.

From Listing 1, one can notice that the KECCAK permutation consists of 24 rounds, each round is composed of 5 functions:

- θ function: consists of bitwise XOR operations of the input.
- ρ function: consists of bitwise rotation of the input.
- π function: is a simple permutation over the bits of the state.
- χ function: is the unique non-linear function of the KECCAK permutation. It consists of a mix between XOR, AND and NOT binary operations.
- ι function: is a bitwise XOR with a round constant.

We recall that these functions operate on states of 32-bit each, *i.e.* $s[i]$ in Listing 1. According to this implementation version, we describe in Fig. 3 how the 1600-bit inputs of the TUAK f_1 function are represented. So, each line corresponds to a state of 32-bit.

```
1   void KECCAK_f_32(uint32 s[50])
2   {
3       uint32 t[10];
4       uint8 i, j, round, k;
5
6       for(round=0; round<24; ++round)
7       {
8           /* Theta function */
9           for(i=0; i<10; i=i+2)
10          {
11              t[i] = s[i] ^ s[10+i] ^ s[20+i] ^ s[30+i] ^ s[40+i];
12              t[i+1]=s[i+1]^s[10+i+1]^s[20+i+1]^s[30+i+1]^s[40+i
    +1];
13          }
14
15          for(i = 0; i < 5; ++i, s+=10)
16          {
17              s[0] ^= t[8] ^ ((t[2]<<1)|(t[3]>>31));
18              s[1] ^= t[9] ^ ((t[3]<<1)|(t[2]>>31));
19              s[2] ^= t[0] ^ ((t[4]<<1)|(t[5]>>31));
20              s[3] ^= t[1] ^ ((t[5]<<1)|(t[4]>>31));
21              s[4] ^= t[2] ^ ((t[6]<<1)|(t[7]>>31));
22              s[5] ^= t[3] ^ ((t[7]<<1)|(t[6]>>31));
23              s[6] ^= t[4] ^ ((t[8]<<1)|(t[9]>>31));
24              s[7] ^= t[5] ^ ((t[9]<<1)|(t[8]>>31));
25              s[8] ^= t[6] ^ ((t[0]<<1)|(t[1]>>31));
26              s[9] ^= t[7] ^ ((t[1]<<1)|(t[0]>>31));
27          }
28          s -= 50;
29
30          /* Rho function */
31          for(i=2; i<50; i+=2)
32          {   k = Rho[i>>1] & 0x1f;
33              t[0] = (s[i+1] << k) | (s[i] >> (32-k));
34              t[1] = (s[i] << k) | (s[i+1] >> (32-k));
35              k = Rho[i>>1] >> 5;
36              s[i] = t[1-k], s[i+1] = t[k];
37          }
38
39          /* Pi function */
40          for(i=2, t[0]=s[2], t[1]=s[3]; (j=(Pi[i>>1]<<1))>2; i=j)
41          {
42              s[i]=s[j], s[i+1]=s[j+1];
43              s[i]=t[0], s[i+1]=t[1];
44          }
45
46          /* Chi function */
47          for(i=0; i<5; ++i, s+=10)
48          {
49              for(j=0; j<10; ++j)
50                  t[j] = (~s[(j+2)
51              for(j=0; j<10; ++j)
52                  s[j] ^= t[j];
53          }
54          s -= 50;
55
56          /* Iota function */
57          t[0] = Iota[round];
58          s[0] ^= (t[0] | (t[0]<<11) | (t[0]<<26)) & 0x8000808B;
59          s[1] ^= (t[0]<<25) & 0x80000000;
60      }
61  }
```

Listing 1. Source code of the 32-bit version of the KECCAK permutation function, inspired from [5, 12].

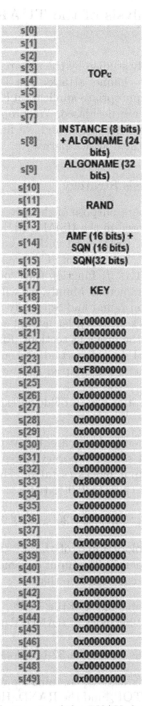

s[0]	
s[1]	
s[2]	
s[3]	TOPc
s[4]	
s[5]	
s[6]	
s[7]	
s[8]	INSTANCE (8 bits) + ALGONAME (24 bits)
s[9]	ALGONAME (32 bits)
s[10]	
s[11]	RAND
s[12]	
s[13]	
s[14]	AMF (16 bits) + SQN (16 bits)
s[15]	SQN(32 bits)
s[16]	
s[17]	KEY
s[18]	
s[19]	
s[20]	0x00000000
s[21]	0x00000000
s[22]	0x00000000
s[23]	0x00000000
s[24]	0xF8000000
s[25]	0x00000000
s[26]	0x00000000
s[27]	0x00000000
s[28]	0x00000000
s[29]	0x00000000
s[30]	0x00000000
s[31]	0x00000000
s[32]	0x00000000
s[33]	0x80000000
s[34]	0x00000000
s[35]	0x00000000
s[36]	0x00000000
s[37]	0x00000000
s[38]	0x00000000
s[39]	0x00000000
s[40]	0x00000000
s[41]	0x00000000
s[42]	0x00000000
s[43]	0x00000000
s[44]	0x00000000
s[45]	0x00000000
s[46]	0x00000000
s[47]	0x00000000
s[48]	0x00000000
s[49]	0x00000000

Fig. 3. The inputs of the TUAK f_1 function.

3 Side-Channel Analysis of the TUAK Implementation in USIM Cards

Despite KECCAK was carefully studied by the researchers [10,25,32,35] to assess its security level against side-channel attacks, the TUAK algorithm need to be well investigated to avoid inappropriate application KECCAK such that the security properties of the latter are decreased. We propose in this section a side-channel analysis of the TUAK algorithm and we first start by describing our attack strategy and the identified attack paths.

3.1 Side-Channel Analysis Strategy

As detailed in [24], the ultimate purpose of the adversary is to recover the subscriber key and the TOP_c stored in the USIM card, and then to create a cloned one by personalizing a blank USIM card with these secret values. In order to recover the key and the TOP_c by means of SCA, we identify in what follows the sensitive operations of the TUAK f_1 function that could leak information about the internally used secret parameters. Mainly, we will focus on the execution of the first KECCAK permutation round and especially on the θ function.

Before detailing our attack strategy, let us first recall the different assumptions considered throughout the previous sections. First, the TOP_c is computed off-card and stored in the USIM card. Second, the subscriber key length is 128-bit. Third, the TUAK f_5 function is omitted since optional. Thus, the SQN is known to the adversary.

Under the previous assumptions, we provide hereafter an in-depth description of our attack proposal.

Recovering the TOP_c. When looking carefully at the loop in Lines (9–13) of Listing 1, one can notice that some temporary states are computed by XORing the KECCAK permutation input blocks (s table). For instance, when the loop index i equals 0, the temporary state $T[0]$ satisfies:

$$T[0] = s[0] \oplus s[10] \oplus s[20] \oplus s[30] \oplus s[40] \ , \tag{2}$$

where $s[i]$ is the ith 32-bit block input of the TUAK f_1 function. Now, when focusing on Fig. 3, one can identify the input parameters standing for each $s[i]$ block of Eq. (2). In fact, one can conclude that:

– $s[0]$: stands for the first 32-bit block of the TOP_c.
– $s[10]$: stands for the first 32-bit block of RAND. We recall that the latter value is known to the adversary.
– $s[20]$, $s[30]$ and $s[40]$: stands each for a 32-bit block of zero-padding.

Consequently, the temporary state $T[0]$ contains the result of the bitwise XOR of the first 32-bit blocks of the TOP_c and the RAND. Hence, a *divide-and-conquer* side-channel attack could be performed to recover separately the first 4 bytes of the TOP_c ($s[0]$).

The same strategy is adapted to retrieve the second, third and fourth blocks of the secret variable TOP_c ($s[1]$, $s[2]$ and $s[3]$). For instance, the adversary can perform a side-channel when targeting the computation of the temporary states $T[1]$, $T[2]$ and $T[3]$ respectively. Besides, all the latter computation involves a XOR of 32-blocks of both TOP_c and RAND.

Now, we will describe how to recover the fifth and the sixth 32-bit blocks of the TOP_c. To do so, we have to look at the loop in Lines (15–27) of Listing 1 when the loop index i equals 0. At Lines 21 and 22, the fifth ($s[4]$) and the sixth ($s[5]$) blocks of the TOP_c are XORed with the temporary states $T[2]$ and $T[3]$ respectively. The latter values are known to the adversary if she has succeeded his side-channel attack as described above ($s[2]$ and [3] have been recovered). In fact, $T[2]$, respectively $T[3]$, contains the XOR results of the third, receptively the fourth, blocks of TOP_c and the RAND. All in all, the adversary could perform a side-channel attack when targeting the XOR operations in Lines 21 and 22 to carry out the fifth and the sixth blocks of the TOP_c.

Given that $T[4]$ and $T[5]$ are already known[4], the attacker could perform as well a successful side-channel attack when targeting the XOR operations at Lines 23 and 24 when the loop index i equals 0 to guess the last two 32-blocks of TOP_c ($s[6]$ and $s[7]$).

Hence, the attacker recovers the 256-bit value of the secret variable TOP_c. We stress the fact that other XOR operations could be targeted to carry out some blocks of the TOP_c. For instance, to find the fifth and the sixth 32-bit blocks of the TOP_c, one could directly target the computation of temporary states $T[4]$ and $T[5]$. There are, in fact, several possibilities to mount the attack on the TOP_c, depending on the targeted operations the adversary chooses.

Recovering the Subscriber Key. To recover the 16-byte values of the key, the attacker should target the XOR operations performed at Lines 17, 18, 23 and 24 when the loop index i equals 1.

In fact, at Line 17 when computing $s[10] \oplus T[8]$, we are actually performing a 32-bit XOR operation of: the first 32-bit block of RAND ($s[10]$), the third block of the key ($s[18]$) and the INSTANCE byte concatenated to the first three bytes of the ALGONAME. The latter 4-byte value ($s[8]$) is constant and known to the attacker (*i.e.* the successive bytes values are 0x10, 0x30 0x2E 0x31).

Alike, at Line 18 when computing $s[11] \oplus T[9]$, we are executing a 32-bit XOR operation of: the second 32-bit block of RAND ($s[11]$), the last 4 bytes of the ALGONAME ($s[9]$, *i.e.* the successive bytes values are 0x4B, 0x41 0x55 0x54) and the fourth block of the key ($s[19]$).

Hence, a side-channel attack when targeting the above detailed XOR operations should recover the last 8 bytes of the subscriber key ($s[18]$ and $s[19]$).

---

[4] In fact, both $T[4]$ and $T[5]$ depend on the SQN and AMF fields which are sent in clear, so known to the adversary, since we have assumed that f_5 function is not executed. Indeed, these fields vary from an authentication session to another one (*e.g.* the SQN is incremented by one for each authentication request) which enables performing a side-channel attack.

Finally, since $T[4]$ and $T[5]$ are known, the first 8 bytes of the subscriber key ($s[16]$ and $s[17]$) can also be recovered with a divide-and-conquer side-channel attack when targeting the XOR operations at Lines 23 and 24.

Doing so, the adversary succeeds to recover all the needed secret data enabling him to clone the USIM card and use it illegally.

3.2 Evaluation Methodology and Setup

To perform our practical analysis, we have first implemented the 32-bit version of the TUAK f_1 function, described in Listing 1, in a 32-bit processor core running at up to 25 MHz. Then, the USIM card is inserted into a self-made card reader (with a resistor integrated to measure the voltage drop and enable the power acquisition) that has been connected to a monitoring PC via an USB link. In our setup, the PC is playing the role of the AuC. So, it sends the authentication token AUTN and the RAND to the USIM card to initiate the execution of the implemented TUAK f_1 function. While processing the messages, the power consumption traces of the USIM card were collected on a Lecroy WavePro 725Zi oscilloscope with 1.5 GHz bandwidth and a maximal sampling rate of 40 GSa/s. We provide in Fig. 4 a high-level description of our measurement setup.

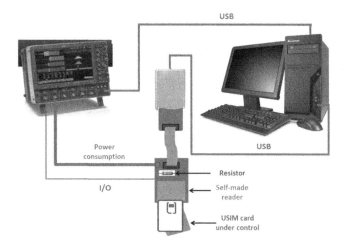

Fig. 4. The measurement setup used for our analysis.

Actually, our side-channel evaluation consists of two steps. First, we will perform a Simple Power Analysis (SPA) to identify the executed operations during the TUAK f_1 function and especially the target area for the attack (*i.e.* the θ function of KECCAK). Second, we will perform a statistical analysis via a Correlation Power attack (CPA) [13], to evaluate whether it is possible to recover the secret data used.

For illustration, the yellow curve at the top of Fig. 5 gives a big view of a captured power trace[5] where we clearly identify the 24 regular rounds of the KECCAK permutation. A zoom on the beginning of the first round is provided at the bottom of Fig. 5.

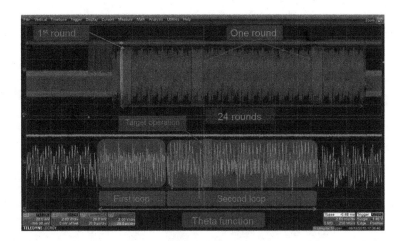

Fig. 5. Simple power analysis of the TUAK f_1 function.

When looking inside the first round, one can easily identify the θ function of the KECCAK permutation. Mainly, it is composed of two loops of 5 iterations each: the first loop consists in computing the temporary states and the second one stands for updating the state values with the XOR results. These observations are in-line with the source code of the KECCAK permutation detailed in Listing 1 (*i.e.* the loops in Lines (9–13) and (15–27)).

For the sake of conciseness and simplicity, we restrict our practical side-channel analysis to target the third and the fourth 32-bit blocks of the subscriber key. We stress the fact that the same results were essentially obtained for the other key bytes and the TOP_c. As detailed in Sect. 3.1, the third and the fourth 32-bit blocks of the key are processed during the beginning of the second iteration of the second loop. This target area is highlighted in red at the bottom of Fig. 5.

3.3 Experimental Results

Once the target operation has been identified, we have first acquired 100.000 power consumption traces of 70.000 samples each. Then, the traces were synchronized by applying a cross-correlation technique [20] to remove the misalignment caused by inaccuracies in triggering the power measurements. In fact, we choose a unique signal pattern representing the beginning of the second loop of the θ function (*e.g.* that detected on the first acquired trace). Then, for each

---

[5] The pink curves describe the input/output signal.

trace, we search this pattern by computing the cross-correlation and then by taking the sample index that maximizes it. No further pre-processing techniques were applied since the noise level has been relatively low as one can see in Fig. 5 and the executed operations are easily identified. For illustration, we provide in Fig. 6 a superimposition of five synchronized traces.

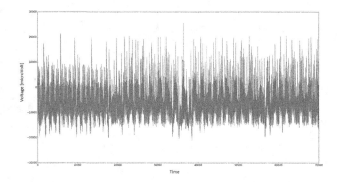

Fig. 6. Superimposition of five synchronized traces.

From Fig. 6, one can identify the last four iterations of the first loop of θ function followed by three iterations of the second loop. As described in Sect. 3.1, we will target the second iteration of the second loop which starts around the time sample 39.000 in Fig. 6.

Once the traces are aligned, we performed a first-order CPA attack using the 100.000 acquired traces. The attack results on the first key byte are shown in Fig. 7. The correlation peak was clearly sufficient to recover the good key byte value without ambiguity. Moreover, the correlation peak appears around the time sample 40.000 and this is in-line with our previous observations concerning the targeted attack area. The same results were obtained for the other targeted key bytes. For the sake of clarity, these results are not shown.

Finally, to estimate the minimum number of traces needed to disclose the key byte values through a side-channel analysis, we conducted 50 independent CPA attacks by using 50 independent sets of 2.000 power traces each. The evolution of the averaged ranks of the correct target key bytes is plotted in Fig. 8.

From Fig. 8, one can conclude that 700 traces are roughly needed to disclose the eight correct key byte values. The same results were obtained when target-ing the XOR operations involving the TOP_c bytes. In addition and similarly to [24], we have estimated the complexity and the time needed to perform our attack including: the power traces acquisition, the traces alignment and the CPA attack processing. In fact, about 2 h are roughly sufficient to recover the secret values used during the authentication protocol and hence to procure a cloned USIM card. Relatively cheap to perform, our attack strategy raises a warning flag to alert embedded systems developers to give further considerations when implementing cryptographic functions inside a USIM card.

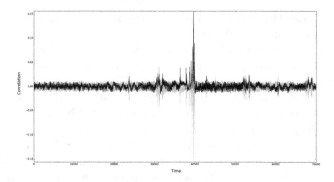

Fig. 7. CPA attack results when targeting the first key byte.

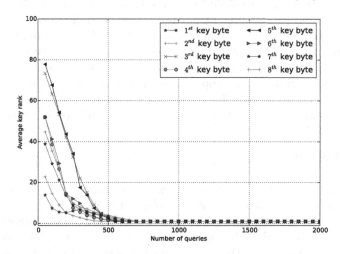

Fig. 8. Evolution of the correct key rank according to the number of observations.

4 Countermeasures and Discussions

Our side-channel analysis have pinpointed the requirement of protecting the TUAK algorithm against classical side-channel attacks. In fact, embedded systems developers have access to a large panel of countermeasures and they should take advantage of the broad literature on secure cryptographic implementations. Amongst side-channel countermeasures one should consider to ensure protection is masking [6,14,19,27]. Indeed, a solution could consist in masking the TUAK f_1 function input states. Doing so, a first-order side-channel attack could be thwarted. Another way to counter SCA, is to use shuffling techniques [33] which consist in randomizing the execution order of independent operations. Even better, shuffling could be combined with masking to reinforce the protection [29]. Recently, authors in [9] have emphasized the use of secret sharing techniques to protect the KECCAK permutation function. To summarize, it is up to the designers to choose the suitable type of countermeasure that guarantees the best performance-security trade-off.

Another protection approach will consist, first, in setting the subscriber key at 256-bit, which leads to hardening our attack process. For instance, when the adversary tries to recover the first 32-bit block of TOP_c (*i.e.* $s[0]$) as described in Sect. 3.1, actually she will recover $s[0] \oplus s[20]$ where $s[20]$ is the sixth 32-bit block of key. Said differently, the attacker will recover a XOR of both secrets and hence he needs to perform a brute force attack to carry-out one secret and then to get the other one. Second, the f_5 function could systematically be executed despite the associated extra overhead. Doing so, attacking the first and the second 32-bit blocks of the subscriber key become more challenging since the SQN is protected by the anonymity key (AK) as described in Sect. 2.

We believe that the latter defensive strategy is insufficient to completely counter our attack; it only aims at making it more complicated. In fact, albeit increasing the key size and executing the f_5 function, the TUAK implementation still leaks information about its secret values. For instance, recovering the third and the fourth 32-bit blocks of the key ($s[18]$ and $s[19]$) is still possible with our proposal: the adversary can apply the same procedure described in Sect. 3.1. Therefore, we emphasize combining the latter protection approach and some side-channel countermeasures to guarantee an acceptable security level.

5 Conclusion

In this work, we have demonstrated that with a classical CPA attack it is possible to break an unprotected software implementation of the TUAK algorithm being part of the authentication protocol of the 3G/4G mobile cellular networks. In fact, we have shown that the attack complexity is quite conservative and few hours are needed to recover the secret data if the state-of-the-art countermeasures are not considered. Through this side-channel analysis, we want to put more emphasis on taking advantage of the existing research investigations on dedicated protections against side-channel attacks. Indeed, the security designers are free to choose the most adequate countermeasure with respect to the expected performance requirements for the authentication protocol. What matters is to follow the 3GPP recommendations and to take into account the physical security issues when implementing cryptographic algorithms in USIM cards.

References

1. ETSI TS 133 105; universal mobile telelecommunications system (UMTS); LTE; 3G security; cryptographic algorithm requirements (2016). 3GPP TS 33.105 version 13.0.0 release 13, 01/2016
2. ETSI, TS 133 202; universal mobile telelecommunications system (UMTS); LTE; 3G security; specification of the 3GPP. Confidentiality, integrety algorithms; document 2: Kasumi specification (2016). 3GPP TS 35.202 version 13.0.0 release 13, 01/2016

3. ETSI, TS 135 201; universal mobile telelecommunications system (UMTS); LTE; 3G security; specification of the 3GPP. Confidentiality, integrety algorithms; document 1: f_8 and f_9 specification (2016). 3GPP TS 35.201 version 13.0.0 release 13, 01/2016

4. 3GPP specification: 135.206 (2016). Specification of the Milenage algorithm set, V13.0.0, 01/2016

5. 3GPP specification: 135.231 (2016). Specification of the Tuak algorithm set, V13.0.0, 01/2016

6. Akkar, M.-L., Giraud, C.: An implementation of DES and AES, secure against some attacks. In: Koç, Ç.K., Naccache, D., Paar, C. (eds.) CHES 2001. LNCS, vol. 2162, pp. 309–318. Springer, Heidelberg (2001). doi:10.1007/3-540-44709-1_26

7. Alt, S., Fouque, P.-A., Macario-rat, G., Onete, C., Richard, B.: A cryptographic analysis of UMTS/LTE AKA. In: Manulis, M., Sadeghi, A.-R., Schneider, S. (eds.) ACNS 2016. LNCS, vol. 9696, pp. 18–35. Springer, Heidelberg (2016). doi:10.1007/978-3-319-39555-5_2

8. Barkan, E., Biham, E., Keller, N.: Instant ciphertext-only cryptanalysis of GSM encrypted communication. In: Boneh, D. (ed.) CRYPTO 2003. LNCS, vol. 2729, pp. 600–616. Springer, Heidelberg (2003). doi:10.1007/978-3-540-45146-4_35

9. Bertoni, G., Daemen, J., Debande, N., Le, T., Peeters, M., Assche, G.V.: Power analysis of hardware implementations protected with secret sharing. In: 45th Annual IEEE/ACM, MICRO 2012, Workshops Proceedings, Vancouver, BC, Canada, 1–5 December 2012, pp. 9–16 (2012)

10. Bertoni, G., Daemen, J., Peeters, M., Assche, G.V.: Note on side-channel attacks and their countermeasures. In: Comment on the NIST Hash Competition Forum, May 2009

11. Bertoni, G., Daemen, J., Peeters, M., Assche, G.V.: The Keccak reference, January 2011

12. Bertoni, G., Daemen, J., Peeters, M., Assche, G.V.: Keccak implementation overview, Version 3.2, 29 May 2012

13. Brier, E., Clavier, C., Olivier, F.: Correlation power analysis with a leakage model. In: Joye, M., Quisquater, J.-J. (eds.) CHES 2004. LNCS, vol. 3156, pp. 16–29. Springer, Heidelberg (2004). doi:10.1007/978-3-540-28632-5_2

14. Chari, S., Jutla, C.S., Rao, J.R., Rohatgi, P.: Towards sound approaches to counteract power-analysis attacks. In: Wiener, M. (ed.) CRYPTO 1999. LNCS, vol. 1666, pp. 398–412. Springer, Heidelberg (1999). doi:10.1007/3-540-48405-1_26. ISBN: 3-540-66347-9

15. Chari, S., Rao, J.R., Rohatgi, P.: Template attacks. In: Kaliski, B.S., Koç, K., Paar, C. (eds.) CHES 2002. LNCS, vol. 2523, pp. 13–28. Springer, Heidelberg (2003). doi:10.1007/3-540-36400-5_3

16. Daemen, J., Rijmen, V.: The Design of Rijndael: AES - The Advanced Encryption Standard. Springer, Heidelberg (2002)

17. Doget, J., Prouff, E., Rivain, M., Standaert, F.-X.: Univariate side channel attacks and leakage modeling. J. Cryptogr. Eng. 1(2), 123–144 (2011)

18. Gierlichs, B., Batina, L., Tuyls, P., Preneel, B.: Mutual information analysis. In: Oswald, E., Rohatgi, P. (eds.) CHES 2008. LNCS, vol. 5154, pp. 426–442. Springer, Heidelberg (2008). doi:10.1007/978-3-540-85053-3_27

19. Goubin, L., Patarin, J.: DES and differential power analysis the "Duplication" method. In: Koç, Ç.K., Paar, C. (eds.) CHES 1999. LNCS, vol. 1717, pp. 158–172. Springer, Heidelberg (1999). doi:10.1007/3-540-48059-5_15

20. Homma, N., Nagashima, S., Sugawara, T., Aoki, T., Satoh, A.: A high-resolution phase-based waveform matching and its application to side-channel attacks. IEICE Trans. **91**-A(1): 193–202. New Orleans. Louisiana, USA (2008). doi:10.1109/ISCAS.2007.378024

21. Kocher, P.C.: Timing attacks on implementations of diffie-hellman, RSA, DSS, and other systems. In: Koblitz, N. (ed.) CRYPTO 1996. LNCS, vol. 1109, pp. 104–113. Springer, Heidelberg (1996). doi:10.1007/3-540-68697-5_9

22. Kocher, P., Jaffe, J., Jun, B.: Differential power analysis. In: Wiener, M. (ed.) CRYPTO 1999. LNCS, vol. 1666, pp. 388–397. Springer, Heidelberg (1999). doi:10.1007/3-540-48405-1_25

23. Liu, J., Yu, Y., Standaert, F.-X., Guo, Z., Gu, D., Sun, W., Ge, Y., Xie, X.: Cloning 3G/4G sim cards with a pc and an oscilloscope: lessons learned in physical security. In: BlackHat (2015)

24. Liu, J., Yu, Y., Standaert, F.-X., Guo, Z., Gu, D., Sun, W., Ge, Y., Xie, X.: Small tweaks do not help: differential power analysis of MILENAGE implementations in 3G/4G USIM cards. In: Pernul, G., Ryan, P.Y.A., Weippl, E. (eds.) ESORICS 2015. LNCS, vol. 9326, pp. 468–480. Springer, Heidelberg (2015). doi:10.1007/978-3-319-24174-6_24

25. Luo, P., Fei, Y., Fang, X., Ding, A.A., Kaeli, D.R., Leeser, M.: Side-channel analysis of MAC-Keccak hardware implementations. In: Proceedings of the Fourth HASP, pp. 1:1–1:8. ACM, New York, NY, USA (2015)

26. Mayes, K., Babbage, S., Maximov, A.: Performance evaluation of the new Tuak mobile authentication algorithm. In: The Eleventh International Conference on Systems ICONS 2016, pp. 38–44 (2016). Related to work done in support of the ETSI SAGE group for mobile authentication standards

27. Messerges, T.S.: Securing the AES finalists against power analysis attacks. In: FSE 2000, pp. 150–164. Springer, New York (2000)

28. Rao, J.R., Rohatgi, P., Scherzer, H., Tinguely, S.: Partitioning attacks: or how to rapidly clone some GSM cards. In: Proceedings of the 2002 IEEE Symposium on Security and Privacy, SP 2002, p. 31, Washington, DC, USA (2002)

29. Rivain, M., Prouff, E., Doget, J.: Higher-order masking and shuffling for software implementations of block ciphers. In: Clavier, C., Gaj, K. (eds.) CHES 2009. LNCS, vol. 5747, pp. 171–188. Springer, Heidelberg (2009). doi:10.1007/978-3-642-04138-9_13

30. Schindler, W.: Advanced stochastic methods in side channel analysis on block ciphers in the presence of masking. J. Math. Crypt. **2**(3), 291–310 (2008)

31. Schindler, W., Lemke, K., Paar, C.: A stochastic model for differential side channel cryptanalysis. In: Rao, J.R., Sunar, B. (eds.) CHES 2005. LNCS, vol. 3659, pp. 30–46. Springer, Heidelberg (2005). doi:10.1007/11545262_3

32. Taha, M.M.I., Schaumont, P.: Side-channel analysis of MAC-Keccak. In: 2013 IEEE International Symposium on Hardware-Oriented Security and Trust, HOST 2013, Austin, TX, USA, 2–3 June 2013, pp. 125–130 (2013)

33. Veyrat-Charvillon, N., Medwed, M., Kerckhof, S., Standaert, F.-X.: Shuffling against side-channel attacks: a comprehensive study with cautionary note. In: Wang, X., Sako, K. (eds.) ASIACRYPT 2012. LNCS, vol. 7658, pp. 740–757. Springer, Heidelberg (2012). doi:10.1007/978-3-642-34961-4_44

34. Wagner, D., Schneier, B., Kelsey, J.: Cryptanalysis of the cellular message encryption algorithm. In: Kaliski, B.S. (ed.) CRYPTO 1997. LNCS, vol. 1294, pp. 526–537. Springer, Heidelberg (1997). doi:10.1007/BFb0052260

35. Zohner, M., Kasper, M., Stottinger, M., Huss, S.: Side channel analysis of the SHA-3 finalists. DATE **2012**, 1012–1017 (2012)

Reverse Engineering Flash EEPROM Memories Using Scanning Electron Microscopy

Franck Courbon[1($\boxtimes$)], Sergei Skorobogatov[1], and Christopher Woods[2]

[1] Computer Laboratory, University of Cambridge, Cambridge, UK
{frc26,sps32}@cam.ac.uk
[2] Quo Vadis Labs, London, UK
chris@quovadislabs.com

Abstract. In this article, a methodology to extract Flash EEPROM memory contents is presented. Samples are first backside prepared to expose the tunnel oxide of floating gate transistors. Then, a Scanning Electron Microscope (SEM) in the so called Passive Voltage Contrast (PVC) mode allows distinguishing '0' and '1' bit values stored in individual memory cell. Using SEM operator-free acquisition and standard image processing technique we demonstrate the possible automating of such technique over a full memory. The presented fast, efficient and low cost technique is successfully implemented on $0.35\,\mu m$ technology node microcontrollers and on a $0.21\,\mu m$ smart card type integrated circuit. The technique is at least two orders of magnitude faster than state-of-the-art Scanning Probe Microscopy (SPM) methods. Without adequate protection an adversary could obtain the full memory array content within minutes. The technique is a first step for reverse engineering secure embedded systems.

Keywords: Reverse engineering · Flash EEPROM · Scanning Electron Microscope (SEM) · Passive Voltage Contrast (PVC)

1 Introduction

Reverse engineering techniques have historically been developed to perform the opposite of a typical process flow used to build Integrated Circuits (IC). IC reverse engineering can be used for validation, debugging, patent infringment/malicious circuit modification/backdoors detection and failure analysis. Typical reverse engineering flow [22] is expensive in terms of equipements, time and skills and is composed of:

- circuit depackaging
- layer by layer deprocessing
- hundreds of SEM acquisitions for each layer
- cross-layer alignment
- individual element annotation
- netlist reconstruction and analysis

© Springer International Publishing AG 2017
K. Lemke-Rust and M. Tunstall (Eds.): CARDIS 2016, LNCS 10146, pp. 57–72, 2017.
DOI: 10.1007/978-3-319-54669-8_4

Today, embedded systems rely heavily on non-volatile memory (ROM, EEP-ROM, Flash) to store code and data. There is a constantly growing demand for the confidentiality of the information stored in embedded devices for Intellectual Property (IP) protection and sensitive data such as passwords and cryptographic keys. Hence the interest of using reverse engineering to extract memory contents such as performed by Kommerling and Kuhn in 1999 [14]. They show that Mask ROM contents (most secure type of ROM) can be revealed using a microscope after sample preparation (selective dash etching). Since then Mask ROMs have not been considered to be secure unless encrypted or at least obfuscated. This paper targets EEPROM/FLASH non volatile memories.

Originally EEPROM was referred to as a two-transistor electrically re-programmable cell, while Flash was introduced later and had a single transistor [2]. These days both structures are usually referred to as a Flash memory. Each semiconductor manufacturer has many different designs with a unique layout for Flash memory cells. But they all have something in common - the information is stored in a form of electric charge inside the memory transistor. The actual number of electrons varies from 10^5 in old technologies to less than 10^3 in modern chips. These electrons shift the threshold voltage of the memory transistor and this is then detected by a readout circuit. The electrons are placed into a memory transistor by applying high voltages to the memory transistor employing either one of two mechanisms: Fowler-Nordheim tunneling or Channel Hot Electron (CHE) injection. In order to erase the cell another combination of high voltages is applied which force the electrons to tunnel through a very thin oxide barrier. Flash EEPROM is widely used as a protection against reverse engineering because conventional de-processing methods only reveal the transistor structure and not its state.

Several publications exist which refer to Scanning Probe Microscopy (SPM) techniques being used to highlight differences between '0' and '1' in Flash EEP-ROM. For instance, the use of a current applied on a conductive tip allows us to see some interaction whenever electron charges are present within memory cells. Following Skorobogatov's conclusions [18], the first investigations using SPM-based techniques have been performed by De Nardi et al. [6,7] and, recently, similarly performed again by different teams; Konopinski et al. [15], Hanzii et al. [11] and Dhar et al. [9,10].

Nevertheless, some key micro-electronics companies, such as Sharp in 2005 [19], Cypress in 2008 [17], Virage Logic in 2009 [12] and Synopsys in 2011 [25] noted the security threat relating to the possibility of memory extraction using SEM. Actually, without waves, at CHES 2000, Weingart [24] first introduced that a Scanning Electron Microscope can be used to read individual bits in a EEPROM. Later, De Nardi's inconspicuous PhD. manuscript details the technique applied with success [8]. Today, we open the technique to the community with our own application. We thus disclose a low cost sample preparation, validate the methodology on smaller technology node EEPROM and show that some '0'/'1' contrast can be seen in single transistor technology. We also anticipate on the capability to have a non destructive readout and give different image processing approaches to effectively extract memory contents.

However, due to SPM limitations, only slow and reduced area Flash EEP-ROM cell measurements are documented to date. The main drawbacks of SPM techniques are the low scanning speed, the small area covered, replacement of the tip, and an operator intervention to read a full memory array. This results in an impractical technique of reading out the complete memory of several mm². Whereas in the security community, Scanning Electron Microscopy has been recently used for hardware trojan detection [5, 21] and for spatially resolved laser fault injection [4]. Following those investigations, we show in this paper how Flash EEPROM contents commonly thought unreachable are retrieved using artefact free backside sample preparation, fined tuned SEM acquisitions (Voltage Contrast mode) and efficient image processing.

Voltage Contrast imaging is one of the first use of Scanning Electron Microscope [20]. The depicted technique is actually based on a mode which corresponds to the setup where no external bias is applied to the sample while setup parameters permit to obtain various information on the sample. In the literature, one can also find PVC variants as Capacitive Coupling Voltage Contrast (CCVC) [23] and Low Energy Electron Microscopy (LEEM) [1].

After a primary electron beam hits a specimen surface, a secondary electron signal results from the sample interaction. This collected signal depends on the primary beam features, the sample's atomic number, the nature of the area scanned, the doping level, short/open circuit [13] and as depicted in this communication the presence of local charges trapped in an oxide.

We thus open to the academic community the technique where floating gate accumulated electrons (image of '0' and '1' memory cell content) can be probed by SEM as illustrated in Fig. 1. It can be seen as a first step for secure IC reverse engineering investigations.

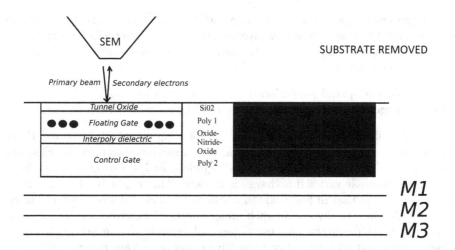

Fig. 1. Technique global flow, use of SEM after backside removal

2 Passive Voltage Contrast (PVC) for Flash/EEPROM Memory Content Extraction

We acknowledge that neither the sample preparation nor the passive voltage contrast nor the image processing are new techniques but their combination results in a fast and effective approach for characterizing Flash EEPROM. On one hand, the sample preparation consisting in removing the substrate until tunnel oxides follows Korchnoy's approach [16]. On the other hand, the image acquisition using SEM is based on previous work of Cole [3]. The complete methodology is illustrated in Table 1.

Table 1. Methodology recipe

Step	Task	Goal	Overview
Sample preparation	Lapping, polishing, wet etching	Successively remove Si down to $20\mu m$, get a mirror aspect and then remove remaining substrate by wet etching	
Image acquisition	Move to & define area of interest, apply SEM parameters, load acquisition macro	Set best SEM parameters for charge differentiation and perform automated large scan	
Image processing	Image registration, contrast enhancement, image segmentation	Gather individual images to cover all memory, '0s' and '1s' bit value extraction	

Sample preparation goal is to remove all Silicon down to the tunnel oxide while leaving the charge blocking layer intact and such over a large area. Once the sample preparation performed, the acquisition is based on two principles for the dedicated application:

– Have sufficient spatial resolution to distinguish memory states
– Limit charge-up inherent to the use of an electron beam over a dielectric

The bit cell information is present at the Floating Gate/SiO$_2$ interface. However we do not directly probe the memory information stored in the Floating Gate. Indeed, a mirrored charge is SEM acquired at the tunnel oxide surface. The image contrast varies if a charge is present. This might be due to a local field modification that in fine leads to a different number of secondary electrons collected. To successfully obtain such image contrast, we give some information about the SEM parameters to use. They follow state of the art publications about passive voltage contrast or capacitive coupling voltage contrast [23].

No success was achieved with standard secondary electrons detectors. We select the through the lens (or InLens) detector combined with a small working distance to maximise the number of secondary electrons collected. To limit the charge-up phenomenon, we use an accelerating voltage around 2.5 keV, the characteristic energy of SiO_2. At such low accelerating voltage, the beam does not create a conductive path between floating and control gates (so the memory information remains). Regarding the probe current, a small diaphragm aperture is chosen for this. We also limit the number of incident electrons using a low magnification. The chosen magnification still requires enough pixels to characterize each memory cell individually. The magnification directly affects the time spent on a memory point. It also affects the global scanning time for large scans. To still limit the incidence of the primary beam, the fastest scanning speed possible is used. At such a fast scanning speed (25/50 ns per pixel) the noise becomes an issue, thus, multiple acquisitions are taken and integrated to achieve a final, high quality image.

Under a SEM, an automated acquisition routine can be launched. Scanning area and magnification need to be first defined. It permits to collect a large set of images over a full memory without the presence of an operator. At last, image processing enables us to align all acquisitions together, to enhance the image contrast and to extract '0s' and '1s' in an automate way. It also allows us correlating the extracted data with the one load into the samples.

The technique combines steps coming from different field. To clarify the technique and for a better understanding, orders of magnitude of setup/tuning and operating time are given in Table 2 along the main considerations for each step.

Table 2. List of parameters and considerations to have all along the methodology

Step	Parameters/Considerations	Operating time	Setup/tuning time
Sample preparation	Rotation speed, disks roughness & grit, time, acid concentration, temperature/etch time, final etch control	Half a day	Days
Image acquisition	Detector type, accelerating voltage, probe current, working distance, scanning speed, contrast/luminosity, tilt, scan orientation and type	A couple of hours	A couple of days
Image processing	Method, algorithm, threshold value, array size, data convention, bit number, MSB/LSB direction	Minutes	Days

3 Flash/EEPROM Reverse Engineering: Sample Preparation

Device Under Test. We demonstrate the technique on three different samples:

- ATMEL ATmega32U4 0.35 μm 2T memory cell (microcontroller)
- ATMEL AT90SCxx 0.21 μm 2T memory cell (smart card type IC)
- Texas Instruments MSP430 0.35 μm 1T memory cell (microcontroller)

Using an universal programmer it was possible to load a specific pattern into the microcontrollers samples to ensure that charge differences would be noticeable no matter what the physical layout of the memory. However, due to the higher security of the smartcard we were unable to program arbitrary data; still, some regions were readable, so that at least we knew the data structure.

Accessing the Area of Interest. Two approaches are currently documented regarding accessing floating gate transistors: either frontside with delayering down to the inter-poly dielectric layer or backside down to the tunnel oxide layer. Due to the charge nature, high energetic solutions cannot be used (plasma etching or a high temperature approach). Moreover, the surface roughness needs to be even over a large surface. Frontside approach has shown that tunnel oxides are affected by the preparation. Thus, as in previous successful experiments, we use a backside approach where most of the silicon substrate is removed using mechanical polishing before a selective wet etching allows removing the remaining Silicon thickness. Floating gates tunnel oxides remain unspoiled.

Parallel Polishing. The samples are prepared using a simple polishing/lapping machine with devices mounted on a sample holding jig to assist precise thickness control and parallel lapping surface. As a backside approach is used, the mechanical grinding tool first encounters and removes a copper heatsink. Once removed, we successively use hard diamond discs to remove silicon down to a $100\,\mu m$ thickness. Then we use high grit abrasive discs to slowly reduce the thickness down to $20(+/-5)\,\mu m$. Scratches are removed using polishing paste, a mirror polish aspect with a fairly constant roughness is obtained. We show, in Fig. 2, intermediate backside Silicon removal images at the copper heatsink level, at $100\,\mu m$ Si, at $20\,\mu m$ Si and once polished at $20\,\mu m$ Si for the ATmega32U4 sample.

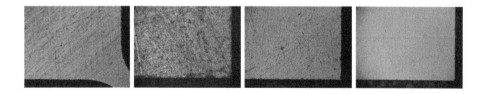

Fig. 2. Si. removal down to copper heatsink, $100\,\mu m$ Si., $20\mu m$ Si. and once polished

Wet Etching. Once the $20(+/-5)\,\mu m$ thickness is obtained, we use wet chemical etching to access the floating gate transistor's tunnel oxide for all samples, Fig. 3. We use the same approach as the one developed by Korchnoy [16]

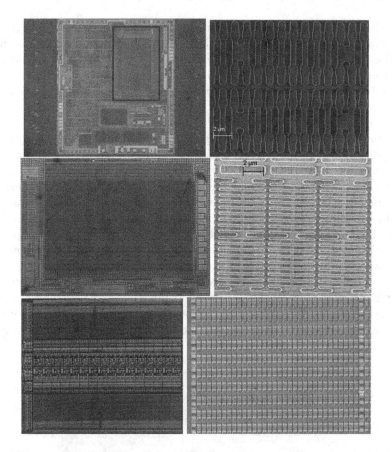

Fig. 3. IC/memory field of view (left col.) and memory structures zoom in (right col.)

and re-used in various AFM works [10]. We use Choline Hydroxide to remove the remaining substrate ($20\,\mu m$) without damaging the thin tunnel oxide (10 nm). The solution was heated to 90°C to speed the etching process up while keeping a sufficient Si/SiO_2 selectivity ratio (about 5000).

4   Flash/EEPROM Reverse Engineering: Image Acquisition

4.1   0.35 μm 2T Memory Cell

We move to the next step of the methodology, the SEM imaging. Parameters were chosen in accordance with PVC state-of-the-art approaches. These involved using an InLens detector, a short working distance of 2 mm to 5 mm, 1 kV to 3 kV accelerating voltage and a minimal probe current. The magnification was chosen to fit the 1024×768 resolution of the image in a way that each memory cell was distinguishable from its neighbouring one. Depending on individual settings this resulted in magnifications between 1 kX and 5 kX - leading to about 8 to 16 pixels characterizing each memory cell. The scan speed was set to tens of milliseconds with integration over tens of frames.

Non exhaustively, the best image quality and contrast was achieved for the working distance of 5.3 mm and for the accelerating voltage of 2.5 kV - a compromise between the best contrast and a reasonable number of frames we can acquire before the charge disappears from the floating gate of the memory transistors. The probe current was about 20 pA with these settings. All those parameters allowed us to obtain clear differences between '0' and '1' states as seen in Fig. 4. It has to be noted that this image is obtained without additional image processing to highlight differences between '0' and '1' states. From the programmed test data we worked out that '0' state of a programmed cell corresponds to the darker memory cell, while '1' state of an erased cell corresponds to the brighter cell. Plus, it is possible to control the process of injecting and removing charge by adjusting the accelerating voltage and probe current. For instance, concentrating a high energetic electron beam over a structure will brighten the structure.

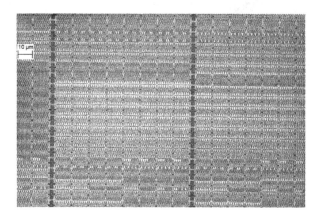

Fig. 4. $0.35\,\mu m$ 2T memory cell content extraction

Using Fig. 4, it is quite interesting to analyze the reading out speed of the technique. This image has been obtained in 9.5 s (number of frames integration and scanning speed dependant). There are 40 lines containing each 128 bits (magnification dependant), 640 bytes in total. The SEM reading throughput is thus about 67 bytes/s, or approximately 241 kbytes per hour.

Transistors states can be clearly distinguished as the dark (holes, positive charge) and the bright (electrons, negative charge) areas respectively. It is convention dependant for each integrated circuit (convention dark = '0' and bright = '1' for this ATMEL sample). The intermediary contrast at the word line is confirmed by the theory. Unlike 1T cell, the theoretical 2T cell contrast difference between programmed and erased are equal to twice the charge (as a 1T depleted cell has a null charge).

We also figured out the physical layout of the memory from the test pattern was programmed into this sample. The array was split into 16 blocks each representing one bit of data from the bit0 being the most right one to the bit15 located on the left. The addresses were going sequentially from right to left and each upper line had its corresponding address 128 bytes higher. For this sample, the complete memory content extraction (32 kbytes) would approximately take 8 min of SEM acquisitions (less than 10 min including a 10% image overlap). The practical implementation of the depicted technique is about 250 times faster than published state of the art EEPROM reverse engineering techniques (AFM based).

4.2   0.21 μm 2T Memory Cell

We then apply the technique over the AT90SCxx sample, which uses a more recent technology node (0.21 μm vs 0.35 μm). The idea is to see how far the technique could work, despite the smaller number of electrons to be probed. As a result, Fig. 5, the charges are still differentiated for each of the individual memory point.

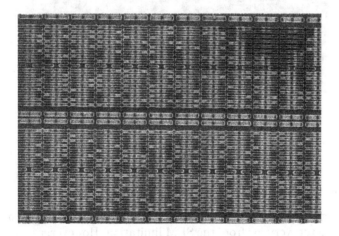

Fig. 5. 0.21 μm 2T memory cell content extraction

The sample prepration is not sample depedant, only the SEM parameters were modified for this second sample. Indeed, after initially using the same stetings, we first had to increase the magnification to have enough pixels covering each memory point. The working distance was also decreased to maximize the number of secondary electrons collected.

Moreover, due to the higher magnification and smaller technology node, it was only possible to integrate over less frames. Indeed, beyond a certain number of frames all memory cells look alike. One of the reasons for that is because incident electron beam density is too important for such probing. Observing charge fluctuations with the help of a Scanning Electron Microscope is thus also successful over this $0.21\,\mu m$ technology node integrated circuit.

4.3 $0.35\,\mu m$ 1T Memory Cell

To finish with, we target the memory of the third sample. Each individual cell structure is made of a single transistor. The raw SEM image, Fig. 6, does not permit to easily dinstinguish '0' and '1' cells. However, some charge fluctuations can be seen over this 1T memory cell structure. More research on each of the methodology step has to be undertaken to clarify this possibility.

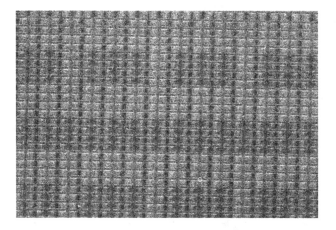

Fig. 6. $0.35\,\mu m$ 1T memory cell content extraction

4.4   Optimal Setup: A Look over $0.35\,\mu m$ 2T

In our investigations, we only use about a 3kX magnification and we are, regarding this parameter, very far from the SEM limitation. However, as seen in Fig. 7 - covering about a sixth of the full memory, contrast can still be obtained at very low magnification. Moreover, using such magnification show about no information decay compare to the setup previously defined. The reading step can thus be non destructive. Figure 7 is a first answer towards the technique improvement where a 218 times magnification also allows charge differentiation.

Fig. 7. 0.35 μm 2T '0s' and '1s' differentiating at 218 times magnification

5 Flash/EEPROM Reverse Engineering: Image Processing

5.1 Area of Acquisition Definition and Acquisition Routine Creation

We then want to show that the technique is industry compliant and interesting in the security field - as cell extraction contents can both be operator-free and cover a full memory.

The methodology being demonstrated, we then use the intrinsic features of a SEM - the ease to make automated and large scans. The goal is to extract the complete memory. We set the region of interest as the full memory of the integrated circuit by simply drawing a rectangle over it. Then we set the SEM acquisition parameters previously used. Given the magnification and the size of the memory, a certain amount of images to acquire are indicated. This number increases with the percentage of overlap desired. Ideally, we want to have successive images overlapping area where no data are present (between current and next 8 bits and between current and next address).

The area to scan being defined, the process is then to create and launch an acquisition macro saving each image in a repository. No operator is thus needeed to acquire large set of tens or hundreds images. It has to be noted that the capability to create macros is not included for all SEMs.

5.2 Offline Image Registration

The usage of the SEM over, the multiple image registration is done offline by the use of open source softwares or matlab commands based on phase transform.

Such exemple is given for two successive acquisitions (1024 × 768 each) with X (33pix.) and Y (139pix.) shifts. Despite the repetitive cell structure, no artefacts over the final reconstructed image (1057 × 907) are present, Fig. 8.

Fig. 8. Image alignment over 2 acquisitions without charges

However, this can be a bit trickier to acquire successive images with charges and to align them. We tackle the typical use case for large memory reverse engineering and give, Fig. 9, the registration of two successive images. It is thus possible to obtain an image of the complete memory array without operator. Having such data, the next step is to extract '0s' and '1s' information in an automated way.

Fig. 9. Image alignment over 2 acquisitions with charge

5.3   0s and 1s Extraction Using Intensity Values Variation

A straightforward way to extract data is to process gray scale intensities to differentiate cells with a charge to the ones without. High intensity values correspond to the presence of a negative charge and subsequently a '1' for this device. We first use standard image processing technique to enhance the signal contrast of '1s' over '0s'. Then, we set a threshold to distinguish '0s' and '1s' cells. We illustrate such on Fig. 10. In fine, a grid can be created as data follows a repetitive pattern (rows and columns).

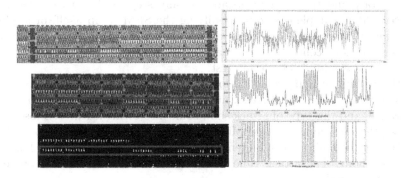

Fig. 10. Top: Raw profile line, middle: after processing bottom: after thresholding

5.4   0s and 1s Extraction Subtracting Successive Acquisitions

An other approach for charge differentiation is to acquire a first SEM acquisition followed by a second acquisition where charges are not noticeable anymore. The idea is to get advantage of the incident electron beam effect. In Fig. 11 are the two SEM acquisitions (left and middle) and the final subtraction (right) giving the data pattern.

Fig. 11. Left: SEM acq. w/ charge, middle: SEM acq. w/o charges, right: subtraction

Depending on the convention used by the manufacturer, the bit number layout, the MSB/LSB layout, one can correlate an input data pattern loaded into the sample and then read it back using the depicted methodology. The practical methodology is thus theoretically applicable over a large area and automatable.

6 Discussion: Recent Integrated Circuits and Methodology Pros & Cons

6.1 Towards Recent Integrated Circuits Application

Within this paper, a reverse engineering attack is discussed and is practically implemented over different integrated circuits. Nevertheless, those integrated circuits are about 15 years old. It would be interesting to challenge the technique where fewer electrons are stored in Flash EEPROM floating-gate transistors (smaller technology node). Multiple approaches seem possible to improve the SEM contrast and they can be located at any step of the methodology. For instance, adding sample coatings, modifying the SEM setup itself, or applying further image processing could be some options. Moreover, reverse engineering the whole memory contents to estimate the error rate and application ease of this technique would also be of interest.

If the technique is proven functional over smaller technology node, attack ratings could be impacted. Indeed, attacks are being ranked (common criteria for instance) and this type of attack show some interesting features, Subsect. 6.2. We recall that Scanning Electron Microscope are still classified as bespoke (such as FIB) even though they can be rented in many facilities for less than hundreds dollars per hour. The attack time is relatively weak and a small number of samples is required.

6.2 Methodology Pros and Cons

The technique gets advantages of the inherent SEM features to extract memory cells content, Table 3. However, using this sole depicted technique won't enable the attacker to get over scrambling and encryption. To sum up, the depicted methodology is fast - only a day of work is necessary, low-cost - about 100$ of consumables are necessary and Scanning Electron Microscopes can be rented for an additional 100$ per hour, repeatable - technique is efficient, large scale compliant - SEMs permit to image a full memory area and is non software dependent - as it directly addresses the hardware of the device. The hardware dependancy is also seen as a drawback as SEM parameters needs to be adjusted depending on the hardware structure.

Table 3. SEM-based content extraction main features

Advantages	Drawbacks
Low cost	Data decay
Fast	Invasive approach with destructive reading
Efficient	Do not tackle encryption nor scrambling
Large area compliant	Only validated down to 0.21 μm technology
Hardware dependant	Hardware dependant

7   Conclusion

We successfully reverse engineer Flash EEPROM using backside sample preparation and Scanning Electron Microscopy (SEM). The technique only requires a polishing tool, wet etching acid and few hours' access to a SEM. The methodology is proven fast, low-cost and repeatable and above all is shown automatable. Beside explaining methodology steps, we also validate it over different integrated circuits. For a $0.35\,\mu m$ technology node 2T EEPROM cell microcontroller, we get an imaging throughput of 241k bytes per hour without optimization. It beats published current state of the art memory content extraction (AFM based) by a factor of approximately 250 and it opens a novel research area for hardware security, reverse engineering but also image processing for hardware security purposes. As previous investigations showing weaknesses of ROM (also non volatile memory), this paper highlights the security vulnerabilities of Flash EEPROM. The methodology can definitely be seen as a first step for reverse engineering secure integrated circuit memory contents. Additional research grant would permit to judge the application of such technique over current integrated circuits and to characterize possible encryption/scrambling vulnerabilities.

References

1. Bauer, E.: Low energy electron microscopy. Rep. Prog. Phys. **57**(9), 895 (1994). http://stacks.iop.org/0034-4885/57/i=9/a=002
2. Brown, W., Brewer, J.: Nonvolatile Semiconductor Memory Technology: A Comprehensive Guide to Understanding and Using NVSM Devices. IEEE Press Series on Microelectronic Systems. Wiley, New York (1997)
3. Cole Jr., E.I.: Beam-based defect localization techniques. In: Ross, R.J. (ed.) Microelectronics Failure Analysis: Desk Reference, 6th edn., pp. 246–262. ASM International (2011)
4. Courbon, F., Loubet-Moundi, P., Fournier, J.J.A., Tria, A.: Increasing the efficiency of laser fault injections using fast gate level reverse engineering. In: IEEE International Symposium on Hardware-Oriented Security and Trust, HOST (2014)
5. Courbon, F., Loubet-Moundi, P., Fournier, J.J.A., Tria, A.: A high efficiency hardware trojan detection technique based on fast SEM imaging. In: Proceedings of the 2015 Design, Automation & Test in Europe Conference & Exhibition, DATE 2015, Grenoble, France, 9–13 March 2015, pp. 788–793 (2015)
6. De Nardi, C., Desplats, R., Perdu, P., Beaudoin, F., Gauffier, J.-L.: Oxide charge measurements in EEPROM devices. Microelectron. Reliab. **45**(9–11), 1514–1519 (2005). http://dx.doi.org/10.1016/j.microrel.2005.07.055. ISSN: 0026-2714
7. De Nardi, C., Desplats, R., Perdu, P., Gurin, C., J.-L., G., Amundse, T.: Direct measurements of charge in floating gate transistor channels of flash memories using scanning capacitance microscopy. In: ISTFA 2006 (2006)
8. De Nardi, C.: Techniques d'analyse de défaillance de circuits intégrés appliquées au descrambling et à la lecture de données sur des composants mémoires non volatiles. Ph.D. thesis, Toulouse, INSA (2009)
9. Dhar, R., Dixon-Warren, S., Campbell, J., Green, M., Ban, D.: Direct charge measurements to read back stored data in nonvolatile memory devices using scanning capacitance microscopy (2013)

10. Dhar, R., Dixon-Warren, S., Kawaliye, Campbell, J., Green, M., Ban, D.: Read back of stored data in non volatile memory devices by scanning capacitance microscopy (2013)
11. Hanzii, D., Kelm, E., Luapunov, N., Milovanov, R., Molodcova, G., Yanul, M., Zubov, D.: Determining the state of non-volatile memory cells with floating gate using scanning probe microscopy. vol. 8700, p. 87000V–87000V-11 (2013)
12. Humes, T.: Ensuring data security in logic non-volatile memory applications: Floating-gate versus oxide rupture. In: Virage logic (2009)
13. Jenkins, M., Tangyunyong, P., Cole Jr., E., Soden, J., Walraven, J., Pimentel, A.: Floating substrate passive voltage contrast. In: ISTFA 2006 (2006)
14. Kömmerling, O., Kuhn, M.G.: Design principles for tamper-resistant smartcard processors. In: Proceedings of the USENIX Workshop on Smartcard Technology, WOST 1999, p. 2 (1999)
15. Konopinski, D.: Forensic applications of atomic force microscopy (2013)
16. Korchnoy, V.: Investigation of choline hydroxide for selective silicon etch from a gate oxide failure analysis standpoint (2002)
17. Ramkumar, K.: Cypress SONOS technology, Cypress (2008)
18. Skorobogatov, S.P.: Semi-invasive attacks - a new approach to hardware security analysis (2005)
19. Smith, G.: Addressing security concerns of flash memory in smart cards, Sharp (2005)
20. Smith, K.C., Wells, O.C., McMullan, D.: The fiftieth anniversary of the first applications of the scanning electron microscope in materials research. Phys. Procedia **1**(1), 3–12 (2008)
21. Sugawara, T., Suzuki, D., Fujii, R., Tawa, S., Hori, R., Shiozaki, M., Fujino, T.: Reversing stealthy dopant-level circuits. In: Batina, L., Robshaw, M. (eds.) CHES 2014. LNCS, vol. 8731, pp. 112–126. Springer, Heidelberg (2014). doi:10.1007/978-3-662-44709-3_7
22. Torrance, R., James, D.: The state-of-the-art in IC reverse engineering. In: Clavier, C., Gaj, K. (eds.) CHES 2009. LNCS, vol. 5747, pp. 363–381. Springer, Heidelberg (2009). doi:10.1007/978-3-642-04138-9_26
23. Watanabe, Y., Fukuda, Y., Jinno, T.: Analysis of capacitive coupling voltage contrast in scanning electron microscopy. Jpn. J. Appl. Phys. **24**(10R), 1294 (1985)
24. Weingart, S.H.: Physical security devices for computer subsystems: A survey of attacks and defences. In: Proceedings of the Cryptographic Hardware and Embedded Systems - CHES 2000, Worcester, MA, USA, August 17–18, 2000, pp. 302–317 (2000)
25. Zajac, C.: Protect your electronic wallet against hackers, Synopsys (2011)

SpecTre: A Tiny Side-Channel Resistant Speck Core for FPGAs

Cong Chen[1(✉)], Mehmet Sinan İnci[1], Mostafa Taha[2], and Thomas Eisenbarth[1]

[1] Worcester Polytechnic Institute, Worcester, MA, USA
{ccong3,msinci,teisenbarth}@wpi.edu
[2] University of Western Ontario, London, ON, Canada
mtaha9@uwo.ca

Abstract. Emerging applications such as the Internet of Things require security solutions that are small, low power and low cost, yet provide solid protection against a wide range of sophisticated attacks. Lightweight cryptographic schemes such as the Speck cipher that was recently proposed by the NSA aim to solve some of these challenges. However, before using Speck in any practical application, sound protection against side-channel attacks must be in place. In this work, we propose a bit-serialized implementation of Speck, to achieve minimal area footprint. We further propose a Speck core that is provably secure against first-order side-channel attacks using a Threshold Implementation technique which depends on secure multi-party computation. The resulting design is a tiny crypto core that provides AES-like security in under 40 slices on a low-cost Xilinx Spartan 3 FPGA. The first-order side-channel resistant version of the same core needs less than 100 slices. Further, we validate the security of the protected core by state-of-the-art side-channel leakage detection tests.

1 Introduction

Lightweight cryptography aims to answer the need for smaller, less energy consuming security tokens as commonly used for authentication and micro-payments. Lightweight cryptographic implementations are commonly used in hardware modules in RFID tokens, remotes, and all types of devices for the Internet of Things (IoT). In these application scenarios the available area footprint as well as the computation power and the battery life are heavily constrained, where the commonly used and trusted standard ciphers like the AES [9] are too costly. Here comes the arena of Speck [4] as a lightweight block cipher. For more information on lightweight cryptography, please refer to [11].

Another major concern for embedded security solutions—besides cost—is side-channel attacks. Given potential physical access to the device, an attacker can collect and exploit various emanations from the electrical circuits, like electromagnetic waves, power consumption, sound or execution timings to recover secret information [15]. Over the last decade, a vast body of work has been performed to find effective methods to prevent these powerful attacks, especially

© Springer International Publishing AG 2017
K. Lemke-Rust and M. Tunstall (Eds.): CARDIS 2016, LNCS 10146, pp. 73–88, 2017.
DOI: 10.1007/978-3-319-54669-8_5

the *differential power analysis* (DPA) attack. Usually, the implementation is hardened by adding *masking* or *hiding* countermeasures [17]. One of the promising and fairly generic masking techniques is Threshold Implementation [20]. While fairly expensive to apply on standard ciphers like AES [6,19], its application to lightweight ciphers (e.g. Simon and KATAN) comes at reasonable overheads [7,24]. More importantly, prior work verified its postulated resistance to first-order side-channel attacks [6,7,19,24], making the introduced area overhead worthwhile.

Speck and its sister Simon are two lightweight block ciphers proposed by NSA as versatile alternatives to the AES [2]. Speck was optimized for software applications, while Simon was optimized for hardware applications. Speck supports various key sizes (64, 72, 96, 128, 144, 192 and 256 bits) and block sizes (32, 48, 64, 96 and 128 bits), making it suitable candidate for a broad range of applications. The design of Speck depends entirely on modular addition, rotation and XOR in a number of rounds ranging from 22, to 34 (depending on key and block sizes). Although Simon showed a small footprint on FPGAs (only 36 slices) [1], its throughout was not promising (3.6 Mbps). Moreover, in most IoT applications, the infrastructure is mixed where some nodes are equipped with low-power micro-controllers, others with dedicated hardware or even FPGAs. If one block cipher is to be adopted in both platforms, Simon will cause a huge hit in performance. On the other hand, Speck was optimized for software and shows good throughput that is comparable to AES (while being more than double the throughput of Simon) on both low-end and high-end processors [2,3]. Also note that area and throughput optimized Simon and Speck designs were proposed and implemented (in ASIC) in [2] and later on FPGAs in [4]. Authors used bit-serialized implementation to reduce the area and iterated implementation to increase the performance. However, these designs were unprotected against first order side-channel attacks.

In this paper, we propose a bit-serialized threshold implementation of Speck with the aim of providing resistance against side-channel attacks while minimizing area footprint, making it an ideal candidate for low-cost embedded applications. Next, we apply the state-of-the-art leakage detection method, namely the TVLA test introduced in [12], to practically verify the claimed first-order resistance of our design. To that end, our contribution is two-fold:

- We present a bit-serialized implementation of the lightweight block cipher Speck. This implementation style yields a highly area-efficient hardware implementation on FPGAs. Further, compared to previous bit-serialized implementations, our design has much better throughput at virtually same area cost.
- We further show that the bit-serialized implementation of Speck can be protected against first-order side-channel analysis using the Threshold Implementation technique. The design has been thoroughly tested using state-of-the-art leakage detection methods, yet has a smaller area footprint than many *unprotected* symmetric ciphers. As such, the bit serialized Threshold Implementation of Speck (named SPECTRE) provides a more secure crypto core for embedded scenarios while still maintaining the goal of a low-cost implementation.

It is surprising that a FPGA implementation of Speck, which was optimized for software, requires only slightly more area than Simon which was optimized for hardware. Meanwhile, SPECTRE achieves more than double the throughput of Simon. Our Threshold Implementation design occupies only 92 slices on an entry level FPGA, i.e. the Xilinx Spartan 3, while generating output at 10.25 Mbps, making it suitable for lightweight applications like wireless sensor networks, RFIDs, etc. We also prove the security of our design against first-order side-channel attacks by performing leakage detection tests on the SPECTRE core.

The paper is organized as follows. Section 2 provides background information on Speck block cipher, masking countermeasure and Threshold Implementations. Section 3 details the bit-serialized implementation of Speck on FPGAs. Section 4 shows how the Threshold Implementation of Speck is designed and implemented. Section 5 compares the implementation results against other ciphers. Section 6 discusses the experimental setup and the leakage detection test along with the result of evaluating the protected core. The paper is concluded in Sect. 7.

2   Background

We introduce the Speck cipher and give some background on side-channel analysis and how they can be mitigated.

2.1   Speck Cipher

Speck is a family of lightweight block ciphers publicly released by the NSA in June 2013 [2]. Speck has been optimized for performance in software implementations. Like other common block ciphers, Speck supports a range of key and block size options ranging from 64 bits to 256 bits and 32 bits to 128 bits, respectively. Speck is commonly notated by the block size $(2n)$ and key size (mn), where n is the word size. For example, Speck32/64 has a word size of 16 bits and works with input block size of 32 bits and key size of 64 bits. Depending on both the key and the block size, the number of rounds range from 22 rounds to 34 rounds.

As shown in Fig. 1, the input is split into two words, each of size n. Each round of Speck consists of bitwise XOR, an addition modulo 2^n, and left and right circular shift operations. These operations enable high throughput and efficient implementation on most microprocessors. As we will later show, the design also lends itself to efficient implementation in hardware. The round function can be represented as:

$$
\begin{aligned}
x_{i+1} &= (S^{-\alpha}(x_i) + y_i) \oplus k_i \\
y_{i+1} &= S^{\beta}(y_i) \oplus x_{i+1}
\end{aligned}
\tag{1}
$$

where S^j is left circular shift by j bits. Note that $\alpha = 8$ and $\beta = 3$, except for the Speck32/64 toy cipher, where $(\alpha, \beta) = (7, 2)$. Notably, the exact same round function is also used for the key scheduling. The key schedule of Speck takes

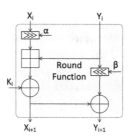

Fig. 1. Block diagram of the Speck cipher showing the round function

the key as input and outputs a round key for each round of the encryption by applying the round function. In the key schedule, differently than the encryption, the left word is XOR'ed with a constant representing the round number starting from 0.

According to [2], Speck with block and key sizes of 128-bits requires 1396 GE (Gate Equivalent) and produces 12.1 Kbps throughput compared to 2400 GE and 56.6 Kbps throughput of the AES 128. In most applications, this smaller circuit size translates into lower power consumption and more portability at lower cost. Note that even though the throughput/area ratio of the Speck is lower than the AES for 128-bits, it still has the advantage of being lightweight in addition to supporting smaller block sizes.

In [3], the authors of the Simon and Speck implemented both ciphers on a commercially available, 8-bit AVR micro-controller and compared the performance results to other block ciphers. The results show that the both ciphers perform well on the 8-bit test platform. Also, the Speck cipher has the best overall performance among all tested block ciphers *in software.*

To the best of our knowledge, Speck cipher was never studied against side-channel attacks. Only fault attack against Speck was proposed in FTDC'14 [25], without any recommended countermeasures. Although the proposed Threshold Implementation can improve resistance against fault attacks due to the introduction of fresh noise at each round of the algorithm, full protection against fault attack is not addressed in this version of the paper. This will be a direction for future research.

2.2 Differential Power Analysis and Masking Countermeasure

Differential Power Analysis (DPA) is an implementation attack that targets the underlying implementation of a crypto algorithm rather than its mathematical structure. DPA exploits the fact that learning even minimal information about intermediate states of a cryptographic algorithm can result in key recovery and hence a full break of the cryptosystem.

In this attack, the adversary measures the power consumption (or electromagnetic emanation) of the targeted platform while it performs cryptographic operations. Based on a guess on a small part of the secret key (subkey), the adversary can compute the hypothetical values of an intermediate cipher state, and thus predict changes in the power consumption. Finally, the predicted changes in power consumption are compared against the measured power traces, where the correct subkey that results in the best match. A detailed introduction to DPA is given in [15]. These attacks have been widely studied, apply to virtually any implementation of cryptography, and are very difficult to prevent [17].

One of the popular methods to thwart this attack is masking. Masking depends on using a fresh random variable to blind all the intermediate variables, hence prevents the ability to estimate correct hypothetical traces. Masking is typically achieved by splitting the input data (plaintext and/or key) into d shares using a random variable. This countermeasure is notated as t-order masking if it can resist t-th order side channel attacks. Each share is processed independently to produce an output. The outputs are then combined to retrieve the original output (ciphertext). The effect of linear functions within a crypto algorithm can easily be re-expressed in terms of the input shares. However, re-expressing non-linear functions is typically a challenging task and every crypto algorithm needs a special solution.

The adversary can still break a t-order secure implementation by higher-order DPA. If leakage from a single point in time is present, the attack is called univariate higher-order DPA. However, if the attacker uses leakage from different points in time, the attack is called multivariate DPA [18].

2.3 Threshold Implementation

Threshold Implementation (TI) is a popular method of applying masking countermeasure that is provably secure against first-order side-channel attacks. TI applies the concepts of XOR-secret sharing based multiparty computation with some basic requirements [20]. In addition to a straightforward XOR secret sharing, TI requires that any sub functions operating on the shares to be *correct*, *non-complete* and *uniform*. That is: the combination of the output shares must always return the correct result, inputs to each sub-function must always exclude at least one share, and the output shares must be uniformly distributed if the input shares were uniform. Non-completeness enforces that the secret state is not processed by any function within the embedded module (at least one share will be always missing). Uniformity enforces that all the intermediate variables within the new masked module have the same entropy of the original secret state. This last requirement is typically the most difficult to achieve. However, it can be achieved by introducing fresh randomness into the output state.

There are quite a few designs in the literature with Threshold Implementation countermeasure, including TI-AES [6], TI-Keccak [5] and TI-Simon [24]. Moreover, higher-order Threshold Implementations, where each sub-function excludes at least $n \geq 2$ shares, can also be realized [21].

3   A Bit-Serialized Speck Hardware Core

One goal of lightweight cryptography in hardware is to minimize the area footprint of a block cipher implementation. However, in most scenarios, the block size and key size enforce a lower bound for a given configuration, since each key and state bit needs to be stored. One exception is Ktantan [10], where the authors out-sourced the key storage to reduce the area footprint even further in case where the key is fixed. The authors of [22] showed that the combinational parts (i.e. the cryptographically critical part of the cipher) of their most serialized (and hence smallest) implementation of Present consumed only about 5% of the area. In general, ciphers that are fully bit-serializable can achieve the best area footprint for a given state and key size. In [1], a-bit-serialized design of the Simon block cipher was proposed to achieve a compact implementation. Besides being fully bit-serialized, the implementation stores key and cipher state in shift registers which can be efficiently implemented in FPGA slices.

Following the same concept for the Speck cipher, the arithmetic addition between two n-bit words can be implemented as n serialized one-bit full additions between the two corresponding-bits and the carry-bit from prior-additions. This approach sacrifices the performance while achieving small design size since only one-bit full adder is used instead of an n-bit adder.

Figure 2 shows the structure of the bit-serialized round function for the unprotected Speck128/128 (128-bit block and 128-bit key size). The structure runs for 32 rounds, where each round requires 64 clock cycles (a total of 2048 cycles). The 128-bit input plaintext is stored into two separate 64-bit shift registers. The left shift register represents x in Eq. 1, and the right register represents y.

The left register (x) is split into two parts to expose bit number α (=8 in Speck128/128), which eliminates the need for a dedicated cyclic shift operation. Instead, we directly feed the α-th-bit into the feedback function. Here, the feedback function of the left register accepts one bit from register x (starting from bit number α), one bit from register y, one key bit to perform a 1-bit full adder and an XOR. During the first α clock cycles of each round, the feedback function feeds the least significant part of the register. Meanwhile, the old values of this part are sequentially feed into the most-significant part waiting for their turn to activate the feedback function. After α clock cycles, the feedback function feeds the most significant part directly preparing the state register for the next round (putting bit number α in the lead).

While processing register x, we did not use any extra storage. This was possible because each bit of the x register is used only once. However, each bit of the y register is used two times, one in the left feedback function (that of register x) and one in the right feedback function (that of register y). Hence, we had to duplicate the β (=3 in Speck128/128) most significant bits of the register to hold the new and old values. Also, by exposing bit number $(64 - \beta = 61)$ and using it directly in the feedback function, we eliminated the need for a dedicated cyclic shift operation. Here, the feedback function of right register accepts the output of the left feedback function (that of register x) and one bit from register y (starting from bit number $(64 - \beta)$) to perform a single XOR. The output of this feedback function is feed to the most significant bit of register y. Note that one copy of β duplicated bits is used to hold the old values of register y, while the other copy holds the new values. This role is revered in the beginning of each round.

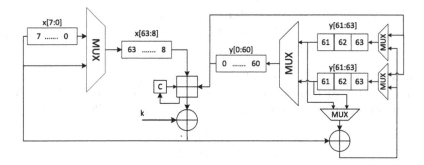

Fig. 2. Structure of one round of bit-serialized Speck

The key schedule applies the same round function and is performed in parallel to the encryption round function. Note that, since the round function is highly area optimized, this does not introduce any significant area overhead.

4   Threshold Implementation of Speck

In order to minimize the cost of design while fulfilling the three properties of Threshold Implementation, we chose to split the secrets, both the key and the plaintext blocks, into three shares. In the following, we show how *Correctness*, *Non-completeness* and *Uniformity* are achieved using three shares.

In 3-share Speck implementation, the key k and the plaintext p are split into three shares. This can be done in software in a secure platform. Two of the shares are chosen uniformly at random while the third share is the XOR-sum of k (or p) with the two random shares

$$p_1 \xleftarrow{\$} \{0,1\}^n \,; p_2 \xleftarrow{\$} \{0,1\}^n \,; p_3 = p_1 \oplus p_2 \oplus p$$
$$k_1 \xleftarrow{\$} \{0,1\}^n \,; k_2 \xleftarrow{\$} \{0,1\}^n \,; k_3 = k_1 \oplus k_2 \oplus k \tag{2}$$

where $(\xleftarrow{\$})$ denotes selecting at random from the given set. This yields a uniform and correct XOR-shared representation of the state p and key state k:

$$p = p_1 \oplus p_2 \oplus p_3$$
$$k = k_1 \oplus k_2 \oplus k_3 \tag{3}$$

In each round operation, both *cyclic rotation* and $\oplus$ are linear operations which can be performed on each share separately. The only nonlinear operation is the full addition between two n-bit words. We used the following equations to implement a valid TI 3-share addition. Moreover, we used-bit-serialized addition as shown in [23] where 1-bit addition is performed in one clock cycle. Hence a n-bit full addition will only cost a single addition circuit and n clock cycles. Suppose, at the i-th clock cycle, the i-th-bit addition, $i \in \{0, 1, \dots n - 1\}$, is performed between two plaintext-bits a and b and one carry bit c as follows:

$$a_i = a_{i,1} \oplus a_{i,2} \oplus a_{i,3}$$
$$b_i = b_{i,1} \oplus b_{i,2} \oplus b_{i,3} \qquad (4)$$
$$c_i = c_{i,1} \oplus c_{i,2} \oplus c_{i,3}$$

Where a_i and b_i are i-th-bit of the two words, c_i is the i-th carry-bit and subscript $j \in \{1, 2, 3\}$ indicates the j-th share of each-bit. Then the three shares of the sum-bit s_i and the carry-bit c_{i+1} can be written as follows:

$$s_{i,1} = a_{i,1} \oplus b_{i,1} \oplus c_{i,1}$$
$$s_{i,2} = a_{i,2} \oplus b_{i,2} \oplus c_{i,2} \qquad (5)$$
$$s_{i,3} = a_{i,3} \oplus b_{i,3} \oplus c_{i,3}$$

$$
\begin{aligned}
c_{i+1,1} = \; & (a_{i,2} \cdot b_{i,2}) \oplus (a_{i,2} \cdot b_{i,3}) \oplus (a_{i,3} \cdot b_{i,2}) \oplus \\
& (a_{i,2} \cdot c_{i,2}) \oplus (a_{i,2} \cdot c_{i,3}) \oplus (a_{i,3} \cdot c_{i,2}) \oplus \\
& (b_{i,2} \cdot c_{i,2}) \oplus (b_{i,2} \cdot c_{i,3}) \oplus (b_{i,3} \cdot c_{i,2}) \\
c_{i+1,2} = \; & (a_{i,3} \cdot b_{i,3}) \oplus (a_{i,3} \cdot b_{i,1}) \oplus (a_{i,1} \cdot b_{i,3}) \oplus \\
& (a_{i,3} \cdot c_{i,3}) \oplus (a_{i,3} \cdot c_{i,1}) \oplus (a_{i,1} \cdot c_{i,3}) \oplus \qquad (6)\\
& (b_{i,3} \cdot c_{i,3}) \oplus (b_{i,3} \cdot c_{i,1}) \oplus (b_{i,1} \cdot c_{i,3}) \\
c_{i+1,3} = \; & (a_{i,1} \cdot b_{i,1}) \oplus (a_{i,1} \cdot b_{i,2}) \oplus (a_{i,2} \cdot b_{i,1}) \oplus \\
& (a_{i,1} \cdot c_{i,1}) \oplus (a_{i,1} \cdot c_{i,2}) \oplus (a_{i,2} \cdot c_{i,1}) \oplus \\
& (b_{i,1} \cdot c_{i,1}) \oplus (b_{i,1} \cdot c_{i,2}) \oplus (b_{i,2} \cdot c_{i,1})
\end{aligned}
$$

Correctness requirement of the threshold cryptography holds true and can be verified using following equations.

$$s_i = s_{i,1} \oplus s_{i,2} \oplus s_{i,3}$$
$$c_{i+1} = c_{i+1,1} \oplus c_{i+1,2} \oplus c_{i+1,3} \qquad (7)$$

Also, it can be easily seen that each output share is independent of at least one share of each input, hence satisfying the *non-completeness* requirement. As pointed in [23], the three shares of c_{i+1} are *uniformly distributed* and can thus be sufficiently fulfill the uniformity of the scheme.

The actual TI implementation of the above equations can be constructed using three copies of the bit-serialized Speck shown in Fig. 2 with a slight modification. Note that the linear operations involve only one share of any input such as rotation, computing the sum bit and exclusive OR. However, computation of each share of the carry bit requires two shares of inputs a_i, b_i, c_i. Hence, the regular arithmetic adder which takes three input bits a_i, b_i, c_i in Fig. 2 is replaced with a TI adder according to Eqs. (5) and (6). As pointed out in [23], to preserve uniformity of the shared carry computation, each initial carry bit should be split as well while keeping the sum of all shares as zero. In order to do so, first carry bits of each execution of the adder are constructed using two randomly generated bits such that $c_0 = 0 = c_{0,1} \oplus c_{0,2} \oplus c_{0,3}$ and $c_{0,1}, c_{0,2}$ are uniformly random. In our design, we have used an LFSR outside the crypto core as the source of randomness for $c_{0,1}, c_{0,2}$.

5 FPGA Implementation Results

The unprotected and the TI versions of Speck as introduced in Sects. 3 and 4 are realized using Verilog. Detailed results are shown in Table 1. For the experiments, we implemented four versions of the Speck cipher: Speck48/96, Speck64/128, Speck128/128 and Speck128/256. These versions have 23, 27, 32 and 34 encryption rounds respectively. The designs are synthesized using Xilinx ISE 14.7. As for the hardware platform we chose the outdated Spartan 3 FPGA to enable better comparability to related lightweight cipher designs. This comparison is given in Table 2.

Our results show that the most comparable version of the Speck, the 128/128, requires 30 FFs, occupies 39 slices and runs at 164 MHz. The protected TI version on the other hand requires 66 FFs, occupies 92 slices and runs at 152 MHz resulting in 9.5 Mbps throughput. Note that unlike some other block cipher implementations on FPGAs, we did not use any block RAMs or any other type of storage.

After obtaining the implementation results, we compared our Speck implementations to other lightweight block cipher implementations. The most comparable implementations to Speck and TI-Speck are the Simon variants. As expected, Simon was optimized for hardware and therefore is smaller than Speck. However, Speck achieves more than double the throughput of Simon for a minor increase in the area (3 slices for the unprotected core, and 5 for the protected one). Due to the lower number of rounds (about half of that of Simon), Speck also has a much lower delay. In addition, the synthesis result in Table 1 shows the max frequency of TI-Speck is about 1.5 times greater than that of TI-Simon and thus it achieves higher throughput (about 3X) compared to TI-Simon. It should be noted that a throughput optimized TI-Simon can have higher throughput compared to TI-Speck but at the cost of area. Even then, additional number of

Table 1. Resource usage and performance of unprotected and protected TI-Speck. The slices in parentheses are used as shift registers.

Cipher	Regs	LUTs (ShiftRegs)	Slices	Speed [MHz]
Unprotected Implementation				
Speck48/96	32	68(15)	39	150
Speck64/128	32	71(18)	40	150
Speck128/128	30	70(22)	39	164
Speck128/256	33	80(30)	44	144
Threshold Implementation				
TI-Speck48/96	72	148(45)	87	132
TI-Speck64/128	72	157(54)	89	132
TI-Speck128/128	66	164(66)	92	152
TI-Speck128/256	75	192(90)	105	138

Table 2. Comparison of area requirements and throughput on FPGAs of various block and stream ciphers.

Cipher	Slices	Throughput [Mbps]	Platform
Threshold Implementation;			
TI-Speck 128/128	**92**	**9.5**	**xc3s50**
TI-Simon 128/128 [24]	87	3.0	xc3s50
Unprotected Block Ciphers;			
Speck 128/128	**39**	**10.25**	**xc3s50**
Speck 128/128 [4]	36	5.0	Spartan-3
Simon 128/128 [4]	28	5.7	Spartan-3
Simon 128/128 [1]	36	3.6	xc3s50
AES [8]	184	36.5	xc3S50-5
PRESENT [26]	117	28.4	xc3s50-5
Tiny XTEA-1 [14]	266	19	xc3s50-5
Stream Ciphers;			
GRAIN 128 [13]	50	196	xc3s50-5
TRIVIUM [13]	50	240	xc3s50-5

rounds would still reduce the throughput in comparison to TI-Speck. Also note that our implementation is heavily optimized in terms of both area and speed while the only available TI-Simon implementation [24] was optimized for area. The conclusion remains the same that the bit-serialized implementations of both ciphers can be protected against side-channel attacks using the TI countermeasure at a reasonable overhead. In terms of comparison to other TI implementations, while there are some previous publications [5,6,24] and all of them have been applied to FPGAs for side-channel evaluation, only the Simon paper [24] reported synthesis results for FPGAs, making this the only design we can compare to.

When compared to other block ciphers, especially AES, but also lightweight versions such as Present, it is remarkable that Speck is significantly smaller. In fact, the side-channel protected implementation of Speck128/128 is about the same size as a Present 64/80 core without side-channel protection. Hence, Speck (and Simon as well) make great choices for a wide range of embedded security solutions (Fig. 3).

When considering size and throughput, stream ciphers such as Grain and Trivium also achieve remarkable results on FPGAs. As can be seen in Table 2, both ciphers need slightly larger area, 50 slices instead of 39 for Speck128/128 while giving a throughput increase of a factor of 19 and 23 respectively. Although this is correct asymptotically, stream ciphers like Trivium suffer from a warm-up phase. The design must be clocked for up to 1124 cycles before the first bit can be encrypted, resulting in high delays. This makes the use of stream ciphers

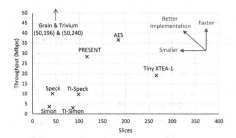

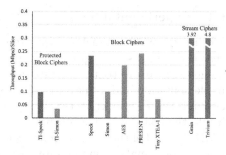

(a) Area and Throughput of various ciphers

(b) Throughput per Slice

Fig. 3. Area and performance results of various ciphers.

Table 3. Energy cost per encryption of Speck and Simon on Virtex 5

	Power Consumption (mWatts)	Throughput Mbps	Energy per Encryption (nJoules)
Speck128/128	422.46	10.25	5.275
TI-Speck128/128	530.35	9.5	7.145
Simon128/128	529.87	3.6	18.839
TI-Simon128/128	531.08	3	22.659

unattractive in most IoT scenarios where payloads are small and infrequent. In addition to that, IoT devices generally operate asynchronously, making the use of stream ciphers highly inefficient.

Finally, Table 3 shows the estimated power consumption per encryption of TI-Speck as well as some other reference designs. Our results show that TI-Speck is better in terms of power per encryption compared to Simon and TI-Simon. On the other hand, in comparison to the unprotected Speck, due to the larger circuit area, the power consumption increases by 35%. Note that this increase in power consumption is acceptable and still much lower than that of Simon variants both protected and unprotected.

6 Leakage Analysis

In this section, we show the results of leakage detection tests as applied to the protected TI-Speck128/128 implementation following the test suite proposed in [12]. Unlike traditional side-channel attacks, leakage detection tests are statistical tests that are designed to measure the influence of secret intermediate variables on side-channel traces. In other words, we are not interested in full recovering of the secret key but only validating first-order side-channel resistance. To this goal, we show that all the intermediate variables have no significant influence on the power consumption.

6.1 Experimental Setup

We use the Side-channel Attack Standard Evaluation Board G-II (SASEBO) that is designed specifically to measure side-channel leakage of FPGA hardware designs. The board contains a Virtex-5 XC5VLX30 FPGA used for cryptographic implementation and a Spartan-3A XC3S400A FPGA for control. The analyzed design is the TI-Speck128/128. We re-synthesize the design for Virtex-5 and port it into the board which is controlled via PC connection. The board is clocked at 3 MHz instead of the maximum frequency given in Table 1. In the future work, we may perform analysis on measurements from the same design clocked with higher frequency. We use Tektronix DPO 5104 to measure the power consumption of the cryptographic engine with sampling rate of 100 Mega-samples per second.

6.2 Leakage Detection Tests

In order to evaluate the side-channel leakage of both the unprotected and the TI-Speck designs, we used a test suite [12] that is commonly used to detect leakage of systems [7,16,24]. The concept of leakage detection depends on separating the collected traces into two groups based on any specified criteria. Then, use statistical tools trying to invalidate the null hypothesis that the two groups have equal means i.e. the two groups cannot be distinguished from each other at the first-order analysis. There are two scenarios to define the separation criteria;

- Fixed versus Random (FvR)
- Random versus Random (RvR)

The first scenario, FvR, takes two sets of leakage traces as input: one set of traces collected with a fixed plaintext while the other set collected with random plaintexts. Note that the same key is used for all encryptions. The two sets are collected in an interleaved fashion using a uniform binary random variable. Then we examine the null hypothesis using the Welchs t-test. Here, we compute the sample mean (μ) and the sample standard deviation (σ) for each group, and find the t metric as:

$$t = \frac{\mu_a - \mu_b}{\sqrt{((\sigma_a^2/N_a) + (\sigma_b^2/N_b))}} \tag{8}$$

where, a and b denote the two data sets and N_i the number of traces in set $i \in \{a, b\}$. For perfect secrecy, the two groups should have equal means, and the t metric should be zero. However, due to the random nature of the experiment, we allow t to slightly deviate from zero up to a critical threshold of ± 4.5, similar to what is commonly used in previous works [12]. This threshold is equivalent to a confidence level of >99.999% at a degree of freedom >100, which is typical in our experiments where the number of power traces is counted in thousands. This test examines first-order leakages. Higher order leakages can also be addressed by raising the traces to a higher power prior to applying the Welch's t-test.

The FvR test tries to invalidate the hypothesis that processing a fixed input generates a power trace that has the same mean as processing any random input. This test is non-parametric and assumes no particular knowledge about the running algorithm or the underlying module. Hence, it examines the leakage of all the intermediate variables along the algorithm.

The second scenario (RvR), uses the same analysis method but all the traces are collected with random plaintexts and the same key. In this scenario, traces are separated according to a chosen binary intermediate variable. This test resembles a profiled attack using the original 1-bit DPA of Kocher [15]. The test tries to invalidates the hypothesis that knowledge of any internal variable does not help in identifying leakage traces (following the first-order model) i.e. does not give any advantage to the adversary. The RvR test assumes knowledge of the key and the target algorithm (in order to compute the intermediate variable). Although the test does not assume any power consumption model, knowledge of the underlying implementation determines if the leakage should depend on the current state only, or on the transition between two states.

We would like to note that the FvR and RvR tests are stronger and far more sensitive to side-channel leakage than SPA and DPA attacks. Their ability to distinguish points in a leakage trace may not even result in partial or full recovery. In these types of attacks, the adversary must be able to distinguish a key dependent internal state from noise to actually carry out an attack and recover partial or full information about the secret. Having said that, SPA and DPA can be used to test the side-channel resistance of the proposed TI-Speck and can be conducted as future research.

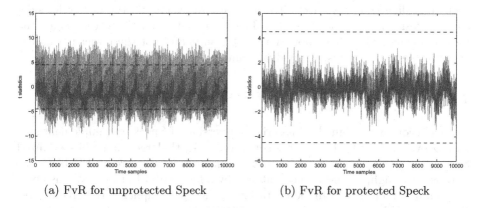

(a) FvR for unprotected Speck   (b) FvR for protected Speck

Fig. 4. Side-channel leakage results. The leakage detection clearly indicates leakage with 1,000 traces if masking is turned off, and indicates absence of leakage with 10 million traces with masking.

6.3 Results

In order to fairly compare between the two proposed designs, we used the TI-Speck to realize both the protected and unprotected implementations. For the unprotected implementation, we set the value of one share to the input secret (plaintext or key) and the value of the other shares to zero. In this scenario, 1000 encryptions are performed half of which are fixed inputs while the other half random inputs. For the protected implementation, all the three shares are set randomly and 10 million traces are obtained. This way, we can use the exact same script for collecting and analyzing traces. Note that we only perform the FvR test in this experiment due to its simplicity and effectiveness in validating the first-order resistance.

The unprotected core is expected to leak and serves as a reference to show that the leakage detection actually works properly in the given setup. As for the protected core, the masks are properly randomized and no leakage should be detected even for a high number of observations.

Figure 4(a) and (b) shows the FvR tests for unprotected and protected implementation respectively. Note that for practicality reasons, we have only measured the leakage in the first 6 rounds rather than the whole encryption. This is why we have 10K time samples in one trace. However, this is sufficient to observe the leakage in the crypto core since all rounds behave the same way. With unprotected implementation, t values at most time moments exceed the predefined threshold with only 1000 measurements indicating that the leakage caused by fixed input can be easily distinguished from the one of random inputs and the leakage is dependent on the sensitive intermediate values in the unprotected core. In contrast, the lesser t values in the protected implementation show the first-order leakage caused by fixed inputs and random inputs cannot be distinguished with 10 million traces and exploited for a key recovery, and the first-order side-channel resistance of the protected TI core is validated. Note that since the measurements in Fig. 4(b) show the t-test results and not the power trace, it is not possible to distinguish individual rounds.

7 Conclusion

In conclusion, we designed a bit-serialized version of Speck and implemented it on FPGA. The bit-serialized Speck core is only slightly larger that a bit-serialized Simon core—the current record-holder in smallest crypto core on FPGAs—but improves throughput and reduces latency by a factor of 3.16 times. We also proposed a novel Threshold Implementation of the Speck cipher with three shares. We analyzed the power consumption of SPECTRE and verified that the three-share TI-Speck is resistant to first-order side-channel attacks. Area-wise, our SPECTRE design did not create a significant overhead and stayed true to the cipher's essence. Also, speed-wise we observed only marginal slowdown compared to the unprotected version.

Acknowledgments. This work is supported by the National Science Foundation under grants CNS-1314770 and CNS-1261399.

References

1. Aysu, A., Gulcan, E., Schaumont, P.: SIMON says: break area records of block ciphers on FPGAs. IEEE Embed. Syst. Lett. **6**(2), 37–40 (2014)
2. Beaulieu, R., Shors, D., Smith, J., Treatman-Clark, S., Weeks, B., Wingers, L.: The Simon and Speck families of lightweight block ciphers. IACR Cryptology ePrint Archive 2013, 404 (2013)
3. Beaulieu, R., Shors, D., Smith, J., Treatman-Clark, S., Weeks, B., Wingers, L.: The SIMON and SPECK block ciphers on AVR 8-bit microcontrollers. In: Eisenbarth, T., Öztürk, E. (eds.) LightSec 2014. LNCS, vol. 8898, pp. 3–20. Springer, Cham (2015). doi:10.1007/978-3-319-16363-5_1
4. Beaulieu, R., Shors, D., Smith, J., Treatman-Clark, S., Weeks, B., Wingers, L.: Simon and Speck: block ciphers for the internet of things. In: NIST Lightweight Cryptography Workshop, vol. 2015 (2015)
5. Bilgin, B., Daemen, J., Nikov, V., Nikova, S., Rijmen, V., Van Assche, G.: Efficient and first-order DPA resistant implementations of KECCAK. In: Francillon, A., Rohatgi, P. (eds.) CARDIS 2013. LNCS, vol. 8419, pp. 187–199. Springer, Cham (2014). doi:10.1007/978-3-319-08302-5_13
6. Bilgin, B., Gierlichs, B., Nikova, S., Nikov, V., Rijmen, V.: A more efficient AES threshold implementation. In: Pointcheval, D., Vergnaud, D. (eds.) AFRICACRYPT 2014. LNCS, vol. 8469, pp. 267–284. Springer, Cham (2014). doi:10.1007/978-3-319-06734-6_17
7. Bilgin, B., Gierlichs, B., Nikova, S., Nikov, V., Rijmen, V.: Higher-order threshold implementations. In: Sarkar, P., Iwata, T. (eds.) ASIACRYPT 2014. LNCS, vol. 8874, pp. 326–343. Springer, Heidelberg (2014). doi:10.1007/978-3-662-45608-8_18
8. Chu, J., Benaissa, M.: Low area memory-free FPGA implementation of the AES algorithm. In: 2012 22nd International Conference on Field Programmable Logic and Applications (FPL), pp. 623–626. IEEE (2012)
9. Daemen, J., Rijmen, V.: AES proposal: Rijndael (1999)
10. De Cannière, C., Dunkelman, O., Knežević, M.: KATAN and KTANTAN — a family of small and efficient hardware-oriented block ciphers. In: Clavier, C., Gaj, K. (eds.) CHES 2009. LNCS, vol. 5747, pp. 272–288. Springer, Heidelberg (2009). doi:10.1007/978-3-642-04138-9_20
11. Eisenbarth, T., Kumar, S., Paar, C., Poschmann, A., Uhsadel, L.: A survey of lightweight-cryptography implementations. IEEE Des. Test Comput. **6**, 522–533 (2007)
12. Gilbert Goodwill, B.J., Jaffe, J., Rohatgi, P., et al.: A testing methodology for side-channel resistance validation. In: NIST Non-Invasive Attack Testing Workshop (2011)
13. Hwang, D., Chaney, M., Karanam, S., Ton, N., Gaj, K.: Comparison of FPGA-targeted hardware implementations of eSTREAM stream cipher candidates. In: The State of the Art of Stream Ciphers, pp. 151–162 (2008)
14. Kaps, J.-P.: Chai-Tea, cryptographic hardware implementations of xTEA. In: Chowdhury, D.R., Rijmen, V., Das, A. (eds.) INDOCRYPT 2008. LNCS, vol. 5365, pp. 363–375. Springer, Heidelberg (2008). doi:10.1007/978-3-540-89754-5_28
15. Kocher, P., Jaffe, J., Jun, B., Rohatgi, P.: Introduction to differential power analysis. J. Cryptographic Eng. **1**(1), 5–27 (2011)
16. Leiserson, A.J., Marson, M.E., Wachs, M.A.: Gate-level masking under a path-based leakage metric. In: Batina, L., Robshaw, M. (eds.) CHES 2014. LNCS, vol. 8731, pp. 580–597. Springer, Heidelberg (2014). doi:10.1007/978-3-662-44709-3_32

17. Mangard, S., Oswald, E., Popp, T.: Power Analysis Attacks: Revealing the Secrets of Smartcards. Springer, New York (2007)
18. Moradi, A., Mischke, O.: How far should theory be from practice? – Evaluation of a countermeasure. In: Prouff, E., Schaumont, P. (eds.) CHES 2012. LNCS, vol. 7428, pp. 92–106. Springer, Heidelberg (2012). doi:10.1007/978-3-642-33027-8_6
19. Moradi, A., Poschmann, A., Ling, S., Paar, C., Wang, H.: Pushing the limits: a very compact and a threshold implementation of AES. In: Paterson, K.G. (ed.) EUROCRYPT 2011. LNCS, vol. 6632, pp. 69–88. Springer, Heidelberg (2011). doi:10.1007/978-3-642-20465-4_6
20. Nikova, S., Rechberger, C., Rijmen, V.: Threshold implementations against side-channel attacks and glitches. In: Ning, P., Qing, S., Li, N. (eds.) ICICS 2006. LNCS, vol. 4307, pp. 529–545. Springer, Heidelberg (2006). doi:10.1007/11935308_38
21. Reparaz, O., Bilgin, B., Nikova, S., Gierlichs, B., Verbauwhede, I.: Consolidating masking schemes. In: Gennaro, R., Robshaw, M. (eds.) CRYPTO 2015. LNCS, vol. 9215, pp. 764–783. Springer, Heidelberg (2015). doi:10.1007/978-3-662-47989-6_37
22. Rolfes, C., Poschmann, A., Leander, G., Paar, C.: Ultra-lightweight implementations for smart devices – security for 1000 gate equivalents. In: Grimaud, G., Standaert, F.-X. (eds.) CARDIS 2008. LNCS, vol. 5189, pp. 89–103. Springer, Heidelberg (2008). doi:10.1007/978-3-540-85893-5_7
23. Schneider, T., Moradi, A., Güneysu, T.: Arithmetic addition over boolean masking – towards first- and second-order resistance in hardware. In: Malkin, T., Kolesnikov, V., Lewko, A.B., Polychronakis, M. (eds.) ACNS 2015. LNCS, vol. 9092, pp. 559–578. Springer, Heidelberg (2015). doi:10.1007/978-3-319-28166-7_27
24. Shahverdi, A., Taha, M., Eisenbarth, T.: Silent Simon: a threshold implementation under 100 slices. In: 2015 IEEE International Symposium on Hardware Oriented Security and Trust (HOST), pp. 1–6. IEEE (2015)
25. Tupsamudre, H., Bisht, S., Mukhopadhyay, D.: Differential fault analysis on the families of SIMON and SPECK ciphers. In: 2014 Workshop on Fault Diagnosis and Tolerance in Cryptography (FDTC), pp. 40–48, September 2014
26. Yalla, P., Kaps, J.-P.: Lightweight cryptography for FPGAs. In: International Conference on Reconfigurable Computing and FPGAs, ReConFig 2009, pp. 225–230. IEEE (2009)

Concealing Secrets in Embedded Processors Designs

Hannes Gross$^{(\boxtimes)}$, Manuel Jelinek, Stefan Mangard, Thomas Unterluggauer, and Mario Werner

Institute for Applied Information Processing and Communications (IAIK), Graz University of Technology, Inffeldgasse 16a, 8010 Graz, Austria
hannes.gross@iaik.tugraz.at

Abstract. Side-channel analysis (SCA) attacks pose a serious threat to embedded systems. So far, the research on masking as a countermeasure against SCA focuses merely on cryptographic algorithms, and has either been implemented for particular hardware or software implementations. However, the drawbacks of protecting specific implementations are the lack of flexibility in terms of used algorithms, the impossibility to update protected hardware implementations, and long development cycles for protecting new algorithms. Furthermore, cryptographic algorithms are usually just one part of an embedded system that operates on informational assets. Protecting only this part of a system is thus not sufficient for most security critical embedded applications.

In this work, we introduce a flexible, SCA-protected processor design based on the open-source V-scale RISC-V processor. The introduced processor design can be synthesized to defeat SCA attacks of arbitrary attack order. Once synthesized, the processor protects the computation on security-sensitive data against side-channel leakage. The benefits of our approach are (1) flexibility and updatability, (2) faster development of SCA-protected systems, (3) transparency for software developers, (4) arbitrary SCA protection level, (5) protection not only for cryptographic algorithms, but against leakage in general caused by processing sensitive data.

Keywords: Protected CPU · Domain-orientend masking · Masking · Side-channel protection · Threshold implementations · RISC-V · V-scale

1 Introduction

The resistance of security-critical systems against the broad field of passive physical attacks is a fundamental requirement of todays embedded devices and smart cards. If an attacker has direct or indirect physical access to an unprotected device, the observation of side-channel information (like power consumption [10] or electromagnetic emanation [14]) leaks information on the processed data. The security of such devices is then no longer guaranteed even if state-of-the-art cryptography is in place, because sensitive information like the used key material leaks through side-channel information.

K. Lemke-Rust and M. Tunstall (Eds.): CARDIS 2016, LNCS 10146, pp. 89–104, 2017.
DOI: 10.1007/978-3-319-54669-8_6

The history of countermeasures against side-channel analysis attacks (SCA) is as old as the first paper targeting differential side-channel analysis by Kocher *et al.* [10]. Hereby, masking has become the first-choice measure to defeat SCA. The first masking approach was introduced by Goubin et al. [4], but many schemes followed like the Trichina gate [19] approach and the works of Ishai *et al.* [8], who introduced the concept of private circuits. However, many masking schemes have shown to be insecure in the presence of glitches that occur within the combinatorial logic of hardware implementations.

To overcome the inherent issue of glitches of these masking schemes, Nikova *et al.* [12] introduced the first-order secure threshold implementation (TI) masking scheme. However, in comparison with software masking schemes, the original TI requires a higher number of random shares to handle glitches. A higher demand for fresh random shares goes hand in hand with increased hardware costs and higher randomness requirements, especially for implementations secure against higher-order attacks.

Most recently many works were published on the implementation of masked hardware implementations with reduced number of shares [1,2,6,13,16]. The work of Gross *et al.* [6] introduced the so-called domain-oriented masking scheme that requires only $d + 1$ shares, $d(d + 1)/2$ fresh randomness, and allows easy generalization to arbitrary protection orders.

Even though the trend to reduce the amount of shares to $d + 1$ made protected hardware implementations more efficient and resulted in generic higher-order implementations, the efficient protection against SCA is still cumbersome, requires a lot of expertise for both implementation and evaluation, and is error-prone. Furthermore, the reduction of shares introduces additional register stages due to the decomposition of complex functions into a couple of algebraically simpler subfunctions [1]. This circumstance of additional delay cycles naturally brings implementations based on hardware masking schemes closer to software masking schemes in terms of throughput.

The aforementioned issues when implementing efficiently masked applications motivated our work. In particular, we investigate the interesting question: Is it possible to construct a general-purpose processor that is inherently secure against side-channel analysis without giving up the benefits and flexibility of software-driven design? As far as we know, there exist only a few works that targets the protection of processors against SCA [5,15,18] which, however, only focused on first-order protection.

Our Contribution. In this work, we introduce a side-channel protected general-purpose CPU based on the RISC-V open instruction-set architecture [20] using the open-source V-scale [11] core. Therefore, we use the findings of domain-oriented masking [6] to modify the open-source V-scale CPU to be resistant against passive physical attacks.

The benefits of our approach compared to custom-made protected hardware implementations are, (1) more flexibility in terms of the selection of algorithms and updatability, (2) faster development of secure systems, (3) hardware-level protection that is transparent for both the running software and the designer,

(4) the CPU can be synthesized for arbitrary protection orders by just changing one parameter, (5) a CPU is part of most security-critical systems and therefore requires SCA protection for security-sensitive data processed by the CPU anyway (which are not necessarily cryptographic operations).

2   Efficient Masking in Hardware

Side-channel attacks such as differential power analysis or chip probing attacks typically exploit data dependencies within the observed side-channel informa-tion. Therefore, the intuition behind masking is to make security-critical com-putations independent of the underlying data. Many masking schemes achieve this data independence by representing variables in a so-called shared represen-tation which ensures independence up to a certain protection order d. One of the most popular formal models to investigate the security of masking schemes is the so-called d-probing model introduced by Isha et al. [8]. In this probing model, the protection order d equals the number of needles an attacker can utilize in parallel. A circuit that resists probing attacks with up to d needles is said to be d-secure.

The implementation costs for masking schemes, like chip area and random-ness requirements, are strongly related to the number of used shares. In the domain-oriented masking scheme (DOM), the primary goal is to minimize the number of required shares to $d + 1$ to reduce the implementation costs. Hereby, a variable x is represented as the sum of $d + 1$ shares in $GF(2)$. Each of these shares is associated with a specific share domain that we denote with capital letters (see Eq. 1) with the associated variable in the index. If the sharing itself is referenced we use a bold capital letter as abbreviation for writing each share of x explicitly.

$$x = \underbrace{A_x + B_x + C_x + \ldots}_{d+1} = \mathbf{X} \tag{1}$$

The intuition behind DOM is to prevent a protected circuit from combining shares associated with different domains in the same signal path. Therefore, any function that is intended to be performed on the unshared variable x is instead applied on the shares of x following the same principle of domain separation. As a result, any linear function $\mathrm{F}(x)$ is split up in $d + 1$ domain functions as shown in Eq. 2 and Fig. 1, respectively.

$$\mathrm{F}(x) = \underbrace{\mathrm{F_A} + \mathrm{F_B} + \mathrm{F_C} + \ldots}_{d+1} \tag{2}$$

The realization of any non-linear functions—$\mathrm{G}(x, y, \ldots)$ in Fig. 1—, however, requires the shares to cross the domain borders. A share that is used in a dif-ferent domain therefore needs to be blinded before it can be safely integrated in the target domain. The blinding is performed by adding a randomly picked

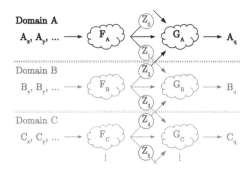

Fig. 1. DOM concept for protection order $d = 2$ and two shared functions

share Z to the cross-domain share. To keep the hardware cost low, more complex functions are decomposed into a cascade of simpler linear and non-linear functions.

In the original DOM paper [6], different designs of $GF(2^n)$ multipliers were introduced which serve as the basis for realizing protected logic functions. In particular, two different variants of DOM multipliers were introduced. The first multiplier (DOM-*dep*) does not have any restrictions on the shared inputs regarding the independence of their sharings. As a consequence, it is even allowed to use the same sharing of the same variable x for both inputs. Because the assumption of share independence is trivially given in some cases, a more efficient implementation of the multiplier (DOM-*indep*) was introduced, which requires less randomness and standard cells than the DOM-*dep* realization. The main difference between these two multipliers is that the DOM-*indep* variant does not require one input to be blinded before the multiplication is performed. Instead, only the partial products of the multiplier are remasked before the terms are summed up (for more detailed information please see [6]).

Besides efficiency, one main advantage of DOM is its genericity. This allows any hardware design being implemented according to the DOM scheme to be realized for any protection order d without any redesigning effort. In particular, it leads to hardware designs that use a security parameter d to automatically generate protected circuits for arbitrary protection order without touching the design.

3 Targeted Processor Platform

This work builds upon the V-scale processor that implements the RISC-V instruction-set architecture (ISA), which was originally developed at the University of California, Berkely. RISC-V is a customizable, modular, free and open RISC ISA which suits research perfectly. The architecture is highly flexible, meaning that the register size (32, 64, or 128 bit), their number (16 or 32), the number of privilege levels (1 to 4), and the supported instructions can be chosen according to the desired use case.

The ISA defines the mandatory base integer instruction set (I or E) which contains the most basic memory, arithmetic, logic, and control-flow instructions. Optionally, more complex instructions can be implemented and are defined via various standard extensions. These extensions include, for example, instructions for integer multiplication/division (M), atomic (A) operations, as well as single- (F) and double-precision (D) floating-point computations. The instructions in the base instruction set and the mentioned extensions are all encoded in 32 bits. However, both shorter and longer instructions are supported too. The extension for compressed instructions (C), for example, defines 16-bit instructions, which map to the base instruction set, to increase code density. Furthermore, RISC-V also supports the addition of fully-custom instructions as so called non-standard extensions (X).

The fact that RISC-V, unlike for example the AVR, x86, and the ARM ISA, has no status flags (carry, overflow, zero, ...) is noteworthy too, given that it simplifies the masking efforts. Carry propagation as well as comparisons are performed with dedicated instructions instead.

Like the ISA, also the V-scale processor core has been developed in Berkely. V-scale is a Verilog implementation of the RV32IM instruction set, i.e., it is a RISC-V processor with 32 registers with 32 bit width featuring the base integer instruction set and the integer multiplication extension. The core itself relies on a single-issue in-order 3-stage pipeline comprising a fetch, a combined decode+execute, and a write back stage. Additionally, the data dependencies between consecutive instructions can be resolved using a bypass of the write back stage which permits to maximize the utilization of the core. Communication with memory relies on separated AHB-Lite memory interfaces for instructions and data, permitting to build Harvard and von Neumann architectures.

4 Protected Implementation of V-scale

Our protected implementation of V-scale addresses the problem that data processed by the processor is subject to side-channel attacks. In this work we solely protect the instructions of the base RV32I instruction set as it is the most versatile. Nevertheless, the multiplication/division (M) extension of the original V-scale processor has been kept to maintain compatibility but is still unprotected.

Therefore, the register file, the majority of the ALU and the data memory interface of the V-scale processor have been protected using the DOM scheme. Other parts, like the instruction memory interface and the decoder have been left unprotected. The reason for this split is that in any case the implemented code must be written such that it does not leak information about the processed data over the instruction sequence because different instructions show different power signatures in leakage traces as also mentioned in [5]. Otherwise, even on a fully shared processor, timing attacks would for example be possible.

The resulting processor's architecture is depicted in Fig. 2. One major difference to the original V-scale processor is that the protected core now has four

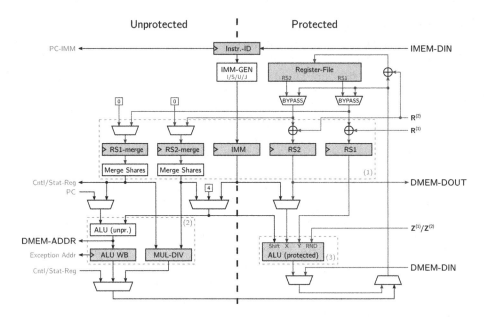

Fig. 2. Overview of the V-scale core. Grey blocks are registers or use a register stage internal. Shared data connections are illustrated in red, unshared in black and the randomness in blue. (Color figure online)

pipeline stages. The additional pipeline stage (see (1) in Fig. 2) splits the previously combined decode+execute stage and is necessary to prevent leakage due to glitches when data shares are merged. This aspect is described in more detail in Sect. 4.1.

From another perspective, the processor is split into a part that operates on DOM-shared data and a part operating with merged data shares. Accordingly, the ALU itself has been split into a protected and an unprotected part. The unprotected ALU (see (2) in Fig. 2) implements multiplication/division, address calculation, and data comparison for conditional jumps. Performing comparisons for conditional jumps in an unprotected way is legitimate as code is not allowed to branch on secure data anyway to avoid timing attacks. More details on the logic to securely merge the different DOM shares and on the unprotected ALU itself can be found in Sect. 4.2. All the remaining functionality being part of the base instruction set (*e.g.* AND, OR, XOR, ADD, ...) is implemented in the protected ALU in a DOM-protected way. The protected ALU is visualized in Fig. 2 at (3) and is thoroughly described in Sect. 4.3.

4.1 Additional Pipeline Stage

The major change to the unprotected processor are the additional source registers shown in Fig. 2 at (1). The main purpose of these buffer registers is to prevent glitches in the merging units connected to *RS1-merge* and *RS2-merge*. These merging units recombine the shares to the original value as shown in Eq. 1.

Without the registers *RS1-merge* and *RS2-merge*, (de-)activation of the merging units can result in data dependent glitches. This is illustrated using two basic scenarios. First, the output of the register file switches to sensitive data. This requires the merging units to be disabled by detaching their inputs from the source register. However, if the sensitive data is selected faster than the merging unit is disabled, sensitive data propagates into the merging unit and results in the leakage of sensitive data. Second, the output of the register file switches from sensitive data to data to be merged. This enables the merging unit by switching the multiplexer to the output of the register file. Here, if the multiplexer switches faster than the register file output is selected, the sensitive data from before glitches into the merging units which leaks information. Both scenarios are prevented by the additional buffer registers *RS1-merge* and *RS2-merge*. These effectively decouple the merging units from the register file selector by setting the input to the merging units to zero if not required. To adapt the delay of the protected to the unprotected data path, further buffer registers *RS1* and *RS2* are needed.

Another change to the processor design is the addition of fresh randomness to the processed values before the ALU result is written back to the register file and before the registers *RS1* and *RS2* are used as the operands for the protected ALU. This allows to restore the independence of the sharings after unprotected operations and shifts operations which generate zeros or duplicate the most significant bit, respectively. Furthermore, the addition of fresh randomness is required right before operating on identical operand registers for protected ALU operations.

4.2   Unprotected Operations

Figure 2 shows at (2) the modules *MUL-DIV* and *ALU (unpr.)* providing the unprotected operations of our core. These modules operate natively with 32-bit word size and use the merged data as described in Sect. 4.1. The *MUL-DIV*-module is the unprotected hardware multiplication and division unit from the original V-scale processor design and kept to maintain compatibility.

The unprotected ALU implements different compare operations, i.a., for branch instructions. However, the comparison results can also be written back to a register. While all branch instructions use two source register inputs, instructions storing the comparison result allow to alternatively use an immediate value as the second source. Note that the compare functionality could have been implemented without merging the data, but branching on protected data must anyway be avoided due to possible timing attacks [9]. This design decision should be kept in mind as it makes it necessary to avoid compare operations on protected data.

Furthermore, the unprotected ALU provides an adder to perform address calculations within load and store operations. Note however that the required merging of source register before the actual address computation does not reduce security. As the second operand is constant and determined by a known software implementation, the value of the source register can always be reconstructed, also if a masked adder was used and the shares of the memory address were merged afterwards. Besides, the unprotected adder is also used within two further instructions. First, the adder is used in the jump and link instruction to increment the program counter in the computation of the address of the following instruction. Second, in the add upper immediate to program counter instruction both the program counter and the immediate input are publicly known making a masked adder obsolete.

4.3 Protected ALU

The protected ALU is shown in Fig. 3 which provides the masked functionality for bit-wise logic operations and arithmetic operations. Both input sharings $\mathbf{X}$ and $\mathbf{Y}$ are composed of $d+1$ independent shares (see Eq. 3), where d is the protection order of the DOM implementation. For resharing purposes, the protected ALU has two additional inputs $\mathbf{Z}^{(1)}$ and $\mathbf{Z}^{(2)}$ holding the required fresh random shares. The data width of the input shares and the fresh random Z shares is 32 bits each.

$$\mathbf{X} = \underbrace{(A_x, B_x, C_x, \dots)}_{d+1} \qquad\qquad \mathbf{Y} = \underbrace{(A_y, B_y, C_y, \dots)}_{d+1} \qquad (3)$$

$$\mathbf{Z}^{(1)} = \underbrace{(Z_0^{(1)}, Z_1^{(1)}, Z_2^{(1)}, \dots)}_{d(d+1)/2} \qquad \mathbf{Z}^{(2)} = \underbrace{(Z_0^{(2)}, Z_1^{(2)}, Z_2^{(2)}, \dots)}_{d(d+1)/2} \qquad (4)$$

DOM-AND. The basis for all implemented non-linear operations is the so-called DOM-*indep* $GF(2)$ multiplier variant (see [6]) which corresponds to a logic *AND* gate with two one-bit inputs. The DOM-*indep* *AND* gate is illustrated

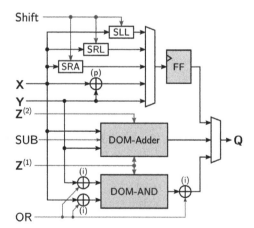

Fig. 3. Protected ALU using a single DOM-AND for AND and OR operation. Shown XOR operations used in different manner: (p)airwise XOR operation of inputs shares (e.g. $A_x + A_y$; $B_x + B_y$; $\dots$); (i)nverting the operand XORing the signal OR with every element of the corresponding first share.

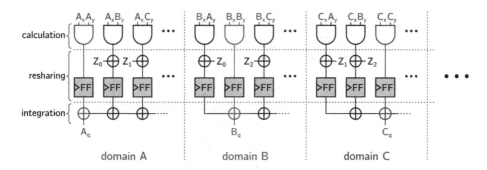

Fig. 4. Overview of the DOM-AND.

in Fig. 4. A basic requirement of the DOM-*indep* multipliers is that the two inputs
X $(A_x, B_x, C_x, \dots)$ and **Y** $(A_y, B_y, C_y, \dots)$ are independently shared which is
ensured by design of the protected core.

The construction of the *DOM-AND* is generic and can thus be extended
to arbitrary protection orders by adding additional shares. For the protection
order d, $d+1$ shares per variable are required giving $d+1$ independent share
domains. Every domain consists of $d+1$ AND gates and flip-flops which results
in a quadratical growth of the chip area accordign to the protection order. The
three steps (calculation, resharing, and integration) of the DOM implementation
are applied independently for every bit position of the 32-bit shares. Therefore,
a 32-bit AND gate consists of 32 *DOM-AND* gates.

In the *calculation* step the terms resulting from the calculation of **X** × **Y**
$(A_x A_y,\ A_x B_y,\ A_x C_y,\ B_x A_y \dots)$ are calculated separately. In the next step
(*resharing*) all terms that contain shares which are not associated with the
respective domain are reshared by using a fresh random Z share. The subsequent register ensure that no early propagation effects occur which could result
in glitches that would effect the SCA resistants of the gate. To keep the timing
of the masked *AND* synchronous the register is also inserted in inner-domain
paths of the domains (e.g., $A_x A_y$ or $B_x B_y$). The last step reduces the number
of shares again to $d+1$ by integrating the freshly masked cross-domain terms
into the inner-domain terms and hence generates the output **Q** $(A_q, B_q, C_q \dots)$.

DOM-Adder. The protected adder is based on a Kogge-Stone similar to the
construction of Schneider *et al.* [17]. The adder is a carry lookahead type adder
using a tree-like structure separating the addition into propagation and carry
generation. Figure 5 shows the secure DOM adder. It is composed of two *DOM-
ANDs*, two bit shifts, and multiple XORs. The XOR as well as the shift operations can be performed independently for each share domain and each input.
The nonlinear parts of the adder are formed by two *DOM-AND* gates. To make
the illustration of the adder in Fig. 5 more concise, the three steps for calculating
the DOM-AND are only indicated by the respective function (see Fig. 4 for more
details). The *DOM-AND*'s internal registers together with the **G** are used as the

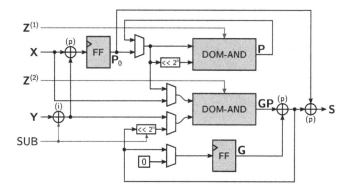

Fig. 5. Masked adder using two DOM-AND. Shown XOR operations used in different manner: (p)airwise XOR operation of inputs shares (e.g. $A_x + A_y; B_x + B_y; \ldots$); (i)nverting the operand by XORing the signal SUB with every element of the first share of **Y** (A_y).

working registers for the iterative calculation of the sum. The $DOM\text{-}AND$'s internal registers are indicated by **GP** which belongs to the carry generation path and **P** which belongs to the propagation path.

For the carry generation path the register **G** is used to store the previous value of the generation step as it is required in the next iteration. An important requirement of the used $DOM\text{-}AND$ gate is an independent sharing both inputs. This independence is ensured for both AND gates because the bit position of one operand is always shifted by at least one position. With the same argument the random Z shares in each cycle are applied for both AND gates without violating the independence requirement.

The subtraction operation can easily be performed by calculating the twos-complement of the subtrahend. The subtraction is controlled by the SUB input. Therefore, the input signal SUB is XORed with every bit of the first share of **Y** (A_y). Incrementing the result by one is done by connecting the carry-in of the adder with SUB which is active on a subtraction. This is done in the shifter of the generation path by appending the carry bit below the least significant bit of the first share and shifting it into the carry generation path. The following equations uses the $\ll$ operation to indicate a left shift performed independently on every input share supporting only shifts with 2^n where $n \geq 0$. The calculation of the sum is performed in three steps called preprocessing, processing, and postprocessing.

An addition is started with the initial preprocessing step initializing the registers **G**, **P**$_0$ and **GP** according to Eq. 5.

$$\mathbf{G_0} = 0 \qquad \mathbf{P_0} = \mathbf{X} + \mathbf{Y} \qquad \mathbf{GP_0} = \mathbf{XY} \qquad (5)$$

The processing step is performed five times in a row ($n = 1 \ldots 5$). The first and last steps are diverging form the normal processing operation. In the first step the input register **P** is replaced by **P**$_0$. In the last processing step the register update of **P** is omitted (see Eqs. 6–8).

$$\mathbf{G}_n = \mathbf{G}_{n-1} + \mathbf{GP}_{n-1} \qquad\qquad n = 1 \ldots N \qquad\qquad (6)$$

$$\mathbf{P}_n = \mathbf{P}_{n-1} \left(\mathbf{P}_{n-1} \ll 2^{n-1}\right) \qquad\qquad n = 1 \ldots N - 1 \qquad\qquad (7)$$

$$\mathbf{GP}_n = \mathbf{P}_{n-1}(\mathbf{G}_n \ll 2^{n-1}) \qquad\qquad n = 2 \ldots N \qquad\qquad (8)$$

In the final postprocessing step the resulting sum is simply computed by a single XOR operation as shown in Eq. 9.

$$\mathbf{S} = \mathbf{P}_0 + (\mathbf{G}_N \ll 1) \qquad\qquad\qquad (9)$$

Resharing of ALU Inputs and Outputs. To reduce the required fresh randomness the two resharing values $\mathbf{R}^{(1)}$ and $\mathbf{R}^{(2)}$ in Fig. 2 are generated from the random Z shares. Furthermore, the merged value of both $\mathbf{R}$ shares is always zero so that an addition of the shares with a sharing of the register file input or output always result in a resharing without changing the underlying value. For first-order protection the resharing value is generated by duplicating a single random share as shown in Eq. 10.

$$\mathbf{R}^{(1)} = (Z_0^{(1)}, Z_0^{(1)}) \qquad \mathbf{R}^{(2)} = (Z_0^{(2)}, Z_0^{(2)}) \qquad\qquad (10)$$

For other protection orders, the randomness is composed as shown in Eqs. 11 and 12.

$$\mathbf{R}^{(1)} = (Z_0^{(1)}, Z_0^{(1)} + Z_1^{(2)}, Z_2^{(1)} + Z_1^{(2)}, Z_2^{(1)} + Z_3^{(2)}, Z_4^{(1)} + Z_3^{(2)}, \ldots) \qquad (11)$$

$$\mathbf{R}^{(2)} = (Z_0^{(2)}, Z_1^{(1)} + Z_0^{(2)}, Z_1^{(1)} + Z_2^{(2)}, Z_3^{(1)} + Z_2^{(2)}, Z_3^{(1)} + Z_4^{(2)}, \ldots) \qquad (12)$$

To guarantee the independence of both resharing values, the first sharing $\mathbf{R}^{(1)}$ uses the shares of $\mathbf{Z}^{(1)}$ with even and shares of $\mathbf{Z}^{(2)}$ with odd indexes, whereas the second sharing $\mathbf{R}^{(2)}$ uses the remaining shares of $\mathbf{Z}^{(1)}$ and $\mathbf{Z}^{(2)}$. This combination of both Z shares is necessary to prevent adding of two shares which are also used in the *DOM-AND* for the integration step. For example, if the second term of $\mathbf{R}^{(1)}$ uses the same random Z share $(Z_0^{(1)} + Z_1^{(1)})$ it could be used to eliminate two random values in domain A as shown in Fig. 4. This reduces the number of signals an attacker has to probe to reveal an unshared intermediate.

Other ALU Operations. The remaining operations of the protected ALU (see Fig. 3) are the shift operations, the logic operations XOR and OR, and the pass-through path. The shift operations are represented by the blocks SLL, SRL and SRA, which perform logical left or right shift or an arithmetic right shift. The *Shift* operand uses a separate unshared input for selecting the shift width which is generated outside the module as shown in Fig. 2. This is necessary to prevent an unwanted merging of the default used shift operand $\mathbf{Y}$. The shifts are performed independently on every share of $\mathbf{X}$. For the arithmetic right shift the most significant bit of every share is duplicated. The logical shift operations add zeros to the shares. Therefore, the shares must be refreshed which is done before writing back the result into the register file or the buffer registers adding fresh randomness (see Fig. 2).

The XOR operation is done in a straight-forward way by adding the input shares of **X** and **Y** share wise. This leads to a zero result using the same input values. Again the results are reshared using fresh randomness before storing them in the buffer registers *RS1* and *RS2* to guarantee independence of the shares.

The pass-through applies the second input **Y** unmodified to the output. To prevent a duplication of the sharing of **Y** in different registers, the sharing is again refreshed before writing it to a register.

The OR operation is combined with the AND operation formed by the *DOM-AND* to reduce the logic overhead. This is done by transforming the logical OR into an AND by inverting both inputs and the output. If the OR operation is used, the input *OR* is set which inverts the first share of both input operands as well as the resulting output of the *DOM-AND* by adding to all bits the *OR* signal.

5   Hardware Results

The hardware results are gathered for a Xilinx Kintex-7 FPGA with the Xilinx Vivado Design Suite 2014.3. Therefore, the synthesis was done for the unprotected core as well as for the protected V-scale core with protection orders from 1 up to 4. Figure 6 shows the evolution of required look up tables (LUTs) (left) as well as the required registers (right) for increasing protection order. The overall area seems to grow only linearly with the protection order. The design of the DOM-AND gates which are part of the nonlinear modules of the protected ALU increase quadratically which, however, contribute only marginally to the overall size for lower protection orders. Table 1 shows the area result in numbers. Additional the required randomness is shown which increases quadratically with the protection order. In particular the randomness required for the protected ALU is $32 \times d(d+1)$ bits in each cycle. The last column shows the maximum clock frequency which is higher for the protection orders 1 up to 3 as for the

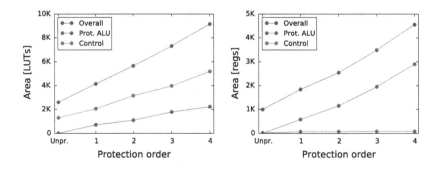

Fig. 6. Required LUT (left) and registers (right) on an FPGA.

Table 1. V-scale core implementation results.

Prot. order	FPGA logic		Randomness	Max. clock
d	*[LUTs]*	*[regs]*	*[Bits]*	*[MHz]*
Unpr.	2,607	996	0	45.6
1	4,143	1,842	64	61.0
2	5,626	2,551	192	59.5
3	7,259	3,484	384	58.3
4	9,244	4,561	640	41.0

unprotected implementation. This results from the additional pipeline stage of the protected implementation which reduces the critical path but increases the delay on the other hand.

6 Side-Channel Evaluation

We have discussed the security of our DOM implementation of the V-scale core in the d-probing model in Sect. 4. In this section we practically evaluate the resistance of our implementation. To show the first-order resistance of our protected V-scale design, the Welch's t-test is used according to the recommendations of Goodwill et al. [3]. The idea of this test is to collect two sets of traces. One set with completely random inputs and another set with constant inputs—the shares and random input bits for the non-linear are of course still random. The null-hypothesis is that both sets cannot be distinguished from each other, meaning they have identical means.

To make our leakage assessment as reproducible as possible, a SASEBO-GIII [7] based FPGA board, the SAKURA-X is used. The board is especially designed for side-channel evaluation and provides special measurement connectors for measuring the power consumption. The SAKURA-X board consists of a Xilinx Spartan-6 FPGA device working as controller connected to the measurement PC and the Xilinx Kintex-7 FPGA implements the device under attack (DUA)—the protected V-scale core in our case. The leakage traces are collected by a Picoscope 6404C oscilloscope at 312.5 Ms sampling rate for a 8 MHz DUA clock. As the targeted software implementation we implemented the round transformations of an authenticate encryption scheme (ASCON) together with additional code that triggers particular instructions and instruction sequences that were considered critical.

Random Number Generators Turned Off. The first-order t-test is performed according to Eq. 13 for the two trace sets A and B. In particular, for the two trace sets with random and constant inputs the difference of the mean traces X_A and X_B is calculated. The result is then scaled according to the estimated

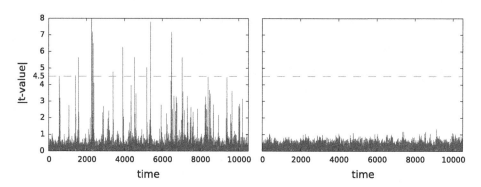

Fig. 7. T-test value of protected ALU operations with inactive random generator with $2M$ traces (left) and active random generator with $100M$ traces (right)

standard deviations S_A and S_B with respect to the size of the trace sets denoted by N_A and N_B, respectively.

$$t = \frac{X_A - X_B}{\sqrt{\frac{S_A^2}{N_A} + \frac{S_B^2}{N_B}}} \tag{13}$$

If the t-value exceeds the confidence interval of ± 4.5 the null-hypothesis is rejected with confidence greater than 99.99% for large sizes of N.

For validating the functionality of our measurement setup, we first deactivated the used random number generator and performed the t-test which is shown in Fig. 7 (left). As expected the t-test showed significant peaks over the ± 4.5 border which indicates first-order side-channel leakage for 2 million traces.

Random Number Generator Turned On. We repeated the t-test with the random number generators turned on and collected 100 million traces. Even with 50 times more traces compared to the first t-test the leakage evaluation does not show any significant peaks any more. We thus consider the side-channel countermeasures to work as expected.

7   Conclusions

In this work implemented a side-channel protected V-scale core following the DOM scheme. The implemented core is fully scalable in terms of protection order, and allows to protect informational assets that are processed by the protected V-scale core. As our results show the overhead for the side-channel protection of the core is only a factor of roughly 1.5 for the first-order implementation. We synthesized the processor up to protection order four. Up to this point the size of the core seems to grow only linearly. This results from the fact that the protected ALU (that contains non-linear modules which grow quadratically) is relatively small compared to other parts of the processor.

To show the resistance of our implementation against side-channel analysis attacks, we performed a first-order t-test of our core on a SAKURA-X FPGA evaluation board. The practical evaluation even with 100 million leakage traces does not show any statistical significance. However, a practical evaluation is of course never complete nor a complete argument for the security of an implementation. The formal analysis of our implementation is thus considered as part of future work. Furthermore, the security of our design is in general only given for software that does not introduce any control flow changes based on the asset one tries to protect (timing attacks). However, we do not consider this much of a drawback since constant runtime implementations are a basic requirement of protected software and hardware.

Acknowledgements. This work has been supported by the Austrian Research Promotion Agency (FFG) under grant number 845589 (SCALAS). This work was partially supported by the TU Graz LEAD project "Dependable Internet of Things in Adverse Environments". The HECTOR project has received funding from the European Union's Horizon 2020 research and innovation programme under grant agreement No 644052. This project has received funding from the European Research Council (ERC) under the European Union's Horizon 2020 research and innovation programme (grant agreement No 681402).

References

1. Chen, C., Farmani, M., Eisenbarth, T.: A tale of two shares: why two-share threshold implementation seems worthwhile—and why it is not. In: Cheon, J.H., Takagi, T. (eds.) ASIACRYPT 2016. LNCS, vol. 10031, pp. 819–843. Springer, Heidelberg (2016). doi:10.1007/978-3-662-53887-6_30. http://eprint.iacr.org/2016/434
2. De Cnudde, T., Reparaz, O., Bilgin, B., Nikova, S., Nikov, V., Rijmen, V.: Masking AES with $d+1$ shares in hardware. In: Gierlichs, B., Poschmann, A.Y. (eds.) CHES 2016. LNCS, vol. 9813, pp. 194–212. Springer, Heidelberg (2016). doi:10.1007/978-3-662-53140-2_10. http://eprint.iacr.org/2016/631
3. Goodwill, G., Jun, B., Jaffe, J., Rohatgi, P.: A testing methodology for side-channel resistance validation. In: NIST Non-Invasive Attack Testing Workshop (2011)
4. Goubin, L., Patarin, J.: DES and differential power analysis the "Duplication" method. In: Koç, Ç.K., Paar, C. (eds.) CHES 1999. LNCS, vol. 1717, pp. 158–172. Springer, Heidelberg (1999). doi:10.1007/3-540-48059-5_15
5. Gross, H.: Sharing is caring—on the protection of arithmetic logic units against passive physical attacks. In: Mangard, S., Schaumont, P. (eds.) RFIDSec 2015. LNCS, vol. 9440, pp. 68–84. Springer, Cham (2015). doi:10.1007/978-3-319-24837-0_5
6. Gross, H., Mangard, S., Korak, T., Masking, D.-O.: Compact masked hardware implementations with arbitrary protection order. Cryptology ePrint Archive, Report 2016/486 (2016). http://eprint.iacr.org/2016/486

7. Hori, Y., Katashita, T., Sasaki, A., Satoh, A.: SASEBO-GIII: a hardware security evaluation board equipped with a 28-nm FPGA. In: The 1st IEEE Global Conference on Consumer Electronics 2012, pp. 657–660, October 2012
8. Ishai, Y., Sahai, A., Wagner, D.: Private circuits: securing hardware against probing attacks. In: Boneh, D. (ed.) CRYPTO 2003. LNCS, vol. 2729, pp. 463–481. Springer, Heidelberg (2003). doi:10.1007/978-3-540-45146-4_27
9. Kocher, P.C.: Timing attacks on implementations of Diffie-Hellman, RSA, DSS, and other systems. In: Koblitz, N. (ed.) CRYPTO 1996. LNCS, vol. 1109, pp. 104–113. Springer, Heidelberg (1996). doi:10.1007/3-540-68697-5_9
10. Kocher, P., Jaffe, J., Jun, B.: Differential power analysis. In: Wiener, M. (ed.) CRYPTO 1999. LNCS, vol. 1666, pp. 388–397. Springer, Heidelberg (1999). doi:10.1007/3-540-48405-1_25
11. Lee, Y., Ou, A., Magyar, A.: V-scale (2013). https://github.com/ucb-bar/vscale
12. Nikova, S., Rechberger, C., Rijmen, V.: Threshold implementations against side-channel attacks and glitches. In: Ning, P., Qing, S., Li, N. (eds.) ICICS 2006. LNCS, vol. 4307, pp. 529–545. Springer, Heidelberg (2006). doi:10.1007/11935308_38
13. Del Pozo, S.M., Standaert, F.-X.:. A note on the security of threshold implementations with $d+1$ input shares. Cryptology ePrint Archive, Report 2016/420 (2016). http://eprint.iacr.org/2016/420
14. Quisquater, J.-J., Samyde, D.: ElectroMagnetic Analysis (EMA): measures and counter-measures for smart cards. In: Attali, I., Jensen, T. (eds.) E-smart 2001. LNCS, vol. 2140, pp. 200–210. Springer, Heidelberg (2001). doi:10.1007/3-540-45418-7_17
15. Regazzoni, F., Cevrero, A., Standaert, F.-X., Badel, S., Kluter, T., Brisk, P., Leblebici, Y., Ienne, P.: A design flow and evaluation framework for DPA-Resistant instruction set extensions. In: Clavier, C., Gaj, K. (eds.) CHES 2009. LNCS, vol. 5747, pp. 205–219. Springer, Heidelberg (2009). doi:10.1007/978-3-642-04138-9_15
16. Reparaz, O., Bilgin, B., Nikova, S., Gierlichs, B., Verbauwhede, I.: Consolidating masking schemes. In: Gennaro, R., Robshaw, M. (eds.) CRYPTO 2015. LNCS, vol. 9215, pp. 764–783. Springer, Heidelberg (2015). doi:10.1007/978-3-662-47989-6_37
17. Schneider, T., Moradi, A., Güneysu, T.: Arithmetic addition over boolean masking. In: Malkin, T., Kolesnikov, V., Lewko, A.B., Polychronakis, M. (eds.) ACNS 2015. LNCS, vol. 9092, pp. 559–578. Springer, Cham (2015). doi:10.1007/978-3-319-28166-7_27
18. Tillich, S., Kirschbaum, M., Szekely, A.: Implementation and evaluation of an SCA-Resistant embedded processor. In: Prouff, E. (ed.) CARDIS 2011. LNCS, vol. 7079, pp. 151–165. Springer, Heidelberg (2011). doi:10.1007/978-3-642-27257-8_10
19. Trichina, E.: Combinational logic design for AES subbyte transformation on masked data. IACR Cryptology ePrint Archive 2003, p. 236 (2003)
20. Waterman, A., Lee, Y., Patterson, D.A., Asanovic, K.: The RISC-V Instruction Set Manual, vol. I: User-Level ISA, Version 2.1. Technical report UCB/EECS-2016-118, EECS Department, University of California, Berkeley, May 2016

The Hell Forgery
Self Modifying Codes Shoot Again

Abdelhak Mesbah[1]([✉]), Leo Regnaud[2], Jean-Louis Lanet[3],
and Mohamed Mezghiche[1]

[1] LIMOSE Laboratory, Computer Science Department, Faculty of Sciences,
University Mohamed Bougara of Boumerdes, Boumerdes, Algeria
{abdelhak.mesbah,mohamed-mezghiche}@univ-boumerdes.dz
[2] University of Limoges, 123 Av. A. Thomas, 87000 Limoges, France
leo.reynaud@etu.unilim.fr
[3] INRIA-RBA, LHS-PEC, Campus de Beaulieu, 263 Avenue du Général Leclerc,
35042 Rennes, France
jean-louis.lanet@inria.fr

Abstract. We present in this paper a new approach to gain access to
assets of a smart card. It is based on the concept of reference forgery
and array extension. We characterize the metadata of the objects and
we use a weakness in the system to retrieve these data. We are able to
generate arbitrary but well formed references which allow us to execute
self modifying Java program inside the card. This hostile program is able
to dump the complete Non Volatile Memory (NVM) memory segment.

Keywords: Java Card · Logical attack · Reference forgery · Self modifying code

1 Introduction

Smart cards store several assets like PIN, keys and cryptographic algorithms.
Most of the cards are based on a tiny Java virtual machine and some of these
Java Cards are able to load and execute applets after post issuance. Due to the
possibility to load applets, these devices are prone to attacks in order to retrieve
these assets using hostile applets. Many efforts have been made by the smart
card industry to increase the security of cards to mitigate such attacks.

We believe that an adversary can gain access to different assets of the system
using a black box approach (without access even to the binary code) and to infer
enough information on the system internals. We propose in this paper to reverse
the data representation of a smart card and to use it in order to gain more
information about the internals of the card. The cards used in this paper are
freely available on web store and probably do not reflect the state of the art of
security for cards sell only to institutional customers.

A previous version of the firmware of this smart card has already been
attacked, as presented in the beginning of Sect. 3. The new version of the firmware

K. Lemke-Rust and M. Tunstall (Eds.): CARDIS 2016, LNCS 10146, pp. 105–121, 2017.
DOI: 10.1007/978-3-319-54669-8_7

patches the previous attack and we discover a new attack path based on array extension. We need several steps before accessing to a complete dump of the NVM. First, we develop the concept of well formed forge of references. A reference must satisfy a set of constraints related to the structure of the metadata.

The array extension attack provides us access to objects that belong to a graph of reachable objects. A reachable object is an object created by an applet. Each package manages a linked list (or any similar mechanism) of reachable objects such that the un-install of a package can occur quickly and it is also used for the garbage collector service. The set of linked lists defines the graph of reachable objects. Objects that have been garbage collected are unreachable objects but are resident in the memory. Then, we try to have access to objects outside the reachable graph developing arbitrary but well formed references. This step allows us to read and write already embedded executable code. Then, we can revisit a previous attack based on self modifying code. This attack leads to the dump of the content of the NVM memory. We evaluate the probability to discover a fragment of memory that can be considered by the system as valid metadata, and thus can be used legally. We confirm with experiments our model and apply this technique on another card from another smart card manufacturer to evaluate if this attack is generic or not.

We used on the first card a grey box approach to develop the attack. Then, we applied it to all the cards available on the web successfully in a pure black box approach without any knowledge about their internals. This attack is not specific to Java Card and can be applied to any device. The weakness comes from the object oriented paradigm.

The paper is organized as follows: the second section provides an overview on the different attacks on smart cards that can be split into control flow modification or array extension. The third section is our main contribution, where we develop the concept of reference forgery which leads to execute self modifying code in Java. In the last section, we propose an evaluation of probability to get arbitrary data similar to metadata and we confirm this probability with a set of experiments. Then we conclude with some research directions for gaining access to system assets of the evaluated card.

2   State of the Art of the Logical Attacks

Logical attacks rely mainly on the absence of the Byte Code Verifier (BCV) verification process. Nevertheless, the designers add a second line of defense by executing run time tests.

2.1   Modifying the Control Flow Graph

Misleading the application's control flow can lead to execute a shellcode stored somewhere in the memory. The aim of EMAN1 attack [11], explained by Iguchi-Cartigny *et al.*, is to abuse the Firewall mechanism with the unchecked static instructions (as `getstatic`, `putstatic` and `invokestatic`) to call malicious byte codes, this behavior is allowed by the Java Card specification. In a malicious CAP file, the parameter of an `invokestatic` instruction may redirect the Control Flow Graph (CFG) of another installed applet in the targeted smart card. The EMAN2 [5] attack was related to the return address stored in the Java Card stack. They used the unchecked local variables to modify the return address, while Faugeron in [9] uses an underflow on the stack to get access to the return address.

When a BCV is embedded, the install of an ill-formed applet is impossible. To bypass an embedded BCV, new attacks exploit the idea to combine software and physical attacks. Barbu *et al.* presented and performed several combined attacks such as the attack [3] based on the Java Card 3.0 specification leading to the circumvention of the Firewall application. Another attack [2] consists in tampering the Application Protocol Data Unit (APDU) which leads to access the APDU buffer array at any time. They also discussed in [1] about a way to disturb the operand stack with a combined attack. It also gives the ability to alter any method regardless of its Java context or to execute any byte code sequence, even if it is ill-formed. This attack bypasses the on-card BCV [4]. In [5], Bouffard *et al.* described how to change the execution flow of an application after loading it into a Java Card.

Razafindralambo *et al.* [13] introduced a combined attack based on fault enabled viruses. Such a virus is activated by hitting with a laser beam, a precise location in the memory, where the instruction of a program is stored. Then, the targeted instruction mutates from one instruction with one operand into an instruction with no operand. Then, the operand is executed by the Java Card Virtual Machine (JCVM) as an instruction. They demonstrated the ability to design a code in such a way that a given instruction can change the semantics of the program. And then a well-typed application is loaded into the card but an ill-typed one is executed.

2.2 Array Extension

The idea of [10] is to abuse shareable interfaces to obtain a type confusion without the need to load an ill typed Converted APplet (CAP) file. To do that, the authors create two applets which communicate using the shareable interface mechanism. To create a type confusion, each applet uses a different type of array to exchange data with two different interfaces. During compilation there is no way for the BCV to detect a difference in the typing of the exchanged array.

In the article [4], the authors remark the possibility that after a type confusion an instance can be manipulated as an instance but also as an array. On the tested card, if the first field of the instance is a short, it corresponds to the size of the array. So increasing the value of this field allows the authors to artificially increase the array size and then to have access in read and write capability to more byte than those contained in the initial array.

Transient arrays have been addressed by [6]. A transient array is an array where the data are stored in RAM and its descriptor is stored in EEPROM, precisely in the owner's heap area. They characterized on a card how the transient array are structured and in particular their metadata. Using the `getstatic` and `putstatic` instructions they modified the size and the address field of the metadata allowing them to access different memory segments with larger sizes.

3   Forging References

On an already expertized Java Card but with a novel firmware, we applied the EMAN2 attack to dump the NVM memory. Surprisingly, while trying this attack on the new version of the card we kill at each attempt the samples. We use this new attack to discover that the instruction `getstatic` has some novel and unknown countermeasures.

3.1   Characterizing an Object

In the paper [7], the authors have characterized how an array is stored in memory, in the previous version of this card. It can be divided into two parts, a metadata part which holds all the details about this array: its type, its size, its context and sometimes even references to memory. The second part contains the data of the array.

After several experiments, using different applets with various classes, fields and objects, we characterized the value of the different fields as in Listing 1.1, where the length represent the physical length of the array. The byte that represents the type requires values such as: 0x81 for the type byte, 0x82 for the type short and 0x83 for the type boolean. The context is represented with one byte. It is used by the firewall to separate different packages. All applet instances within a single package share the same context. In the evaluated card, the context of the first installed package has the value 0x08, and the context increases by two for each new installed package. There is one specific context which is the system context having the value 0x00.

```
structure array {
    u2 length
    u1 type
    u1 context
    u1 data[length]
}
```

Listing 1.1. The array representation

We want now to go further and characterize the instance objects. Changing or creating our own metadata provides us an access to perform otherwise unauthorized, arbitrary memory reads and writes from the modified object. To study the metadata we exploited the type confusion explained in [8]. We used the type confusion in order to reach the instance `this` and return it as an array.

We used a type confusion using the method `arrayCopyNonAtomic`. The signature of this method is as following `arrayCopyNonAtomic(byte[] src, short srcOff, byte[] dest, short destOff, short length)`. This method copies the content of source array `src` which is of type reference on a byte array into another one of the same type `dest`. The virtual machine relies on the BCV to ensure the type correctness of the parameters. If this verification is not done and the type of `src` is of another branch of the type system and in particular an instance, it becomes possible to copy the content of an instance into the APDU buffer as shown in the Listing 1.2.

```
1 short theAddress = getMyThis();
2 aByteArray  = trans2Ref(theAddress);
3 Util.arrayCopyNonAtomic(aByteArray, (short) 0,
4         apdu.getBuffer(), (short)0, (short)0x100);
5 apdu.setOutgoingAndSend((short) 0x00, (short) 0x100);
```

Listing 1.2. Recovering the instance `this`

Once we retrieve the address of the instance `this` at line 1, we use it as a parameter of a method at line 2, to transform it as an array reference. The reference is assigned to the array `aByteArray`. The `aByteArray` now points to the instance `this`, and we can copy the data of this array to the output buffer and return it. The raw data of the instance `this` is presented in the Listing 1.3.

```
0x0BCC  :                                           00 00 0D 20
0x0BD0  : 02 88 00 00 00 00 F8 07 0C 08 0C 14 0C 5C 0C A4
0x0BE0  : 0C B0 0D 08 0D 10 00 00 00 00 0B CC 11 11 22 22
0x0BF0  : 00 24 81 08 33 00 00 00 17 17 18 18 19 19 20 20
```

Listing 1.3. The data of the instance `this`

This instance is located at the address @0x0BCC. We are able to locate all objects and arrays declared as an instance field, and the initial values of the instance fields of primitive types declared in the class of this instance. The reversed version of the data of the instance `this` is shown in Listing 1.4.

With these references, we can locate the beginning of each array and object declared on the class of the instance `this`. The set of references can be represented as a directed graph of all objects created in the applet with the instance `this` as the root of the graph of reachable objects.

For instance, the array referenced with the value @0x0C08, points to the data field which starts at @0x0C04. Figure 1-A, illustrates this behavior. Figure 1-B presents an object (instance of class) referenced by the address @0x0C14.

A reference to an object (array or instance) does not refer to the header but to the first data for an instance of object, and surprisingly to the fourth byte of data for an array. This homogeneous representation explains why type

```
0x0BCC  :
            00 00 0D 20 // unknown data
0x0BD0  :
            02 88 00 00 00 00 F8 07 // unknown data
            0C 08 0C 14 0C 5C 0C A4 //References
0x0BE0  :
            0C B0 0D 08 0D 10 00 00 00 00 0B CC //References
            11 11 22 22 //initial values primitive fields
0x0BF0  :
            00 24 81 08 33 00 00 00 //initial values primitive fields
            17 17 18 18 19 19 20 20 //initial values primitive fields
```

Listing 1.4. The data reverse of the instance **this**

confusion works with this firmware. Both kind of objects share the same beginning of header, an object has four more bytes of header, but the reference is always pointing to a fixed offset from the beginning. The firmware does not check dynamically the value of the field type leading to the attack using the arrayCopyNonAtomic() function. Then, the countermeasure becomes obvious.

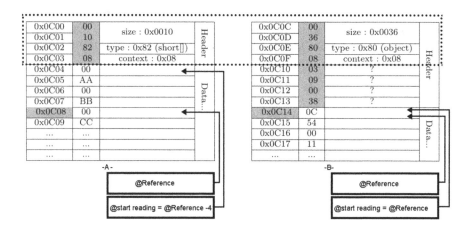

Fig. 1. Header and the data area

We propose a more formal representation of the instance **this** as presented in the Listing 1.5. The eight first bytes represent the header with the first four bytes common with a representation of an array. The next four bytes are yet unknown. The type of the object has been refined into two nibble. The high nibble reflects the nature of the memory used : transient (b4=1) or persistent (b4=0). In case of transient memory, b3 defines if the object is of type clear_on_deselect or clear_on_reset.

```
structure instance this {
    u2 length
    u1 bitfield {
        bit [4] nature
        bit [4] type
    }
    u1 context
    u4 unknown meta-data
    u12 unknown data
    u2 reference_instance_field_table[]
    u2 primitiv_instance_field_table[]
}
```

Listing 1.5. The instance this representation

This attack allows us to have access to different objects if the reference is known requiring only to have access to the root of graph *i.e.* the instance this. Then, once a root is known, the different reachable objects can recursively be obtained.

3.2   Access to Random References

In this section, we want to get access to the objects that do not belong to the reachable graph. We repeated the same experiments as before, but with arbitrary values of references. But **Each invalid address throws an exception**.

We can analyze a successful reference at the address @0x0BF8 with a length equals to 0x0024 as presented in Listing 1.6.

```
0x0BF8 :                      33 00 00 00 17 17 18 18
0x0C00 : 19 19 20 20 00 06 82 08 00 AA 00 BB 00 CC 00 00
0x0C10 : 00 36 80 08 03 09 00 38 0C 54 00 11
```

Listing 1.6. Obtained data from the address @0x0BF8

The first point to note about the two Listings 1.3 and 1.6, is that the first bytes of the data at the address @0x0BF8 correspond to a fragment of the data of the instance this. We can observe in the data of the instance this in the Listing 1.3 that there is a value 0x0024 which occurs before the beginning of the data of the structure stored at the address @0x0BF8. We hypothesize this can be the size of the structure.

To confirm this assumption, we change the value 0x0024, which is the initial value of an instance field of primitive type declared in the class of the instance this (public short x = 0x0024). We give another value to this field

0x0080 (`public short` x = 0x0080). Then, if we dump the content of the address @0x0BF8, we obtain an array with a size of 0x0080. Repeating this experiment with different values of the instance field provides an array with a size of the expected value. This confirms our hypothesis we can control the size of an arbitrary reference of an object. It allows us to read all the remaining part of the applet starting from the address @0x0BF8, the maximum size accepted is 0x7FFF.

This experiment clarifies the previous unexpected behavior. The system considers some data as an object, because these data have a form of well-formed header as explained before, including the constraints about types and contexts.

3.3 Forging Metadata

In the previous sections, we have analyzed the structure of arrays and objects, and understood the metadata. In this section, we forge our own structure (arrays and objects), using the instance fields of the applet. The objective is to force the card to treat data as metadata to get unauthorized access to the memory even if the forged reference does not belong to the graph of reachable objects. We can generate the data to be exploited as metadata in the attack either with instance fields or with data contained in arrays. We chose the instance fields because it gives us a faster access as we use the instance `this`. Using an array requires to add an indirection. The data must fulfill a set of constraint for a successful forge:

size ≤ 0x7FFF ∧ type ∈ {0x80, 0x81, 0x82, 0x83 ... } ∧ context ∈ {current context, system context}

The context can only be the context of the current package or the system context. For the moment, all the other values fail to recover data through the forge. Something unexplained yet is that the value of the size can be greater than the current offset plus the maximum size. The recovered data are meaningful. It seams that the size of the memory is greater than 64 kbyte such that we can access to other parts of the memory. The scenario followed to forge a header is described below :

Add the instance fields in the applet: when creating the applet we add the instance fields, which are considered latter as metadata. We need to select the value according to the constraints. In the following example in Listing 1.7, a header of an array of type byte 0x81 is forged, with a size of 0x7FFF, and a context of 0x08, which means that this array is usable by applets with the same context *i.e.* applets of the first installed package. The value of the context is constrained by the system and out of our control, each new package increases the value of the context by two.

```
public class ForgeArray extends javacard.framework.Applet {
    ...
    short size = (short) 0x7FFF;  //size of the array
    byte type = (byte) 0x81; // persistent byte array
    byte ctx  = (byte) 0x08; // current context
    ...
}
```

Listing 1.7. Forging Header's Array

Dump of the instance this: we load the applet and recover the data and the address of the instance this. We obtain the results listed in the Table 1.

Table 1. Instance this, the forged header

0x0BCC	...			
0x0BCD	...			
...	...			
0x0BD8	7F	size : 0x7FFF	Forged Header	
0x0BD9	FF			
0x0BDA	81	type = 0x81: byte[]		Instance this
0x0BDB	08	context : 0x08		
0x0BDC	...		Data ...	
0x0BDD	...			
0x0BDE	...			
0x0BDF	...			
0x0BE0	...			
0x0BE1	...			

Locate and calculate the forge address: in the data of the instance this located at the address @0x0BCC as defined in Table 1, we find the beginning of our forged header located at the address @0x0BD8. We need now, for using this header, to point the right address. We must add eight to the address where the first byte of the header is located, so we have to use the reference @0x0BE0. If we use this address, we can read 32 kbyte of data.

Thanks to this attack, we are able to recover all the memory of the NVM from the address of the first forge. This attack gives us access to objects that are unreachable from the instance this. The only limit is that, we can not read the memory before the first forged reference, *i.e.* before the this.

3.4 EMAN1 Revisited: Self Modifying Code

Thanks to the forges, it is possible to get the content of the NVM and in particular the area where the code is stored, from the address where the first forge is located. However, we want to have access to the code located before this forge.

For this reason, we revisit the EMAN1 attack, since the original attack does not work anymore on this card due to a countermeasure on the `Reference Location` component. The EMAN1's attack has been the first attack that generates a self modifying code inside a smart card. The authors [11] modified the statically resolved link of the instruction `invokestatic`. They first removed an entry into the component `Reference Location` and replace the original token by the reference of a static array. Dynamically, instead of invoking a method, the system invokes an array. If the array has the form of the metadata of a method and a set of byte code, the Java Card interpreter executes an array. In one hand, the program modifies the content of the array and on the other hand it executes the modified array, leading to a self modified code.

We redesign the attack in three steps. The first action is to locate the method table of the installed package. This table points the different methods and we want to modify the argument of the `getstatic` instruction located in the method `getMystatic()`. A search on the dump, allows us to locate it. This table is stored before the instance `this` of the package as shown in the Fig. 2. We can remark that we can not have access directly to this table from the applet itself because it is placed before the first forge. The revisited EMAN1 implies two packages and involves the following steps :

Step 1: We load a first package which contains an accessible forge from a second package. The forge must have a compatible context with the second package (context of the second package, or system context 00), and with a sufficient size to reach the code of the methods of the second package. Two packages are needed because the aim is to modify the code of a method, which contains the instruction used to read the memory `getstatic`. This instruction is located in the second package as shown in the Fig. 2.

Step 2: Once the two packages are installed, the forged array of the first package is used to get the code of the second package, and locate the code of the method which uses the `getstatic`. We also deduce the index of the argument of the `getstatic` instruction in the forged array, as presented in Fig. 3.

Step 3: We can execute the hostile code, we send to the second package, the address of the forged array, and the index of the first argument *i.e.* 0x199 of the `getstatic` instruction.

With this revisited attack, we gain access to all the memory segments that were previously unreachable from the forge's attack. The `Reference Location` component is not modified, then EMAN1 will bypass the embedded countermeasure. The general approach of this attack is to use an array to gain access to the data, thus the firewall can not play its role if the forged reference uses the same context as the applet which manipulates it.

The addresses used by the instruction `getstatic` are resolved with an indirection table, therefore the dump is an unstructured information hard to exploit which lacks of abstraction. We identify in the dump the different objects: arrays or instances. We can discriminate the objects belonging to the system and those belonging to the applications.

Begin Pack1 App1
...
Methods Table
...
Instance **this** App1
@Compatible forge with the App2
...
End Pack1 App1
Begin Pack2 App2
...
Methods Table
...
getMystatic()
...
...
Instance **this** App2
End Pack2 App2

Fig. 2. Methods table position

			Begin Pack1 App1
	...		
	20		
	00	Forged reference Header	
	81		
	00		
forge[0x0000]	...		
forge[0x0001]	...		
forge[0x0002]	...		
...	...		End Pack1 App1
...	...		Begin Pack2 App2
forge[0x0196]	01	Header getMyStatic	
forge[0x0197]	10		
forge[0x0198]	7C	getstatic_b	
forge[0x0199]	28	index_byte1	
forge[0x019A]	16	index_byte2	
forge[0x019B]	78	sreturn	
...	...		
forge[0x0199]	...		
	...		End Pack2 App2

Fig. 3. Revisited Eman 1

Having a more abstract representation of the memory allows us to recognize linked list of objects, arrays of linked lists *etc.* All those object belong to the system and become the new material for reverse engineering functionalities of the system *e.g.* the memory management algorithm.

4   Discovering Forges in the NVM

We consider an array of N bytes whose content is modeled as N independent and uniformly distributed random variables $\mathcal{X}_0, ..., \mathcal{X}_{N-1}$. We define below the local notion of a match which corresponds to some particular property that must fulfill any four consecutive bytes to give the attacker the opportunity to get forge. This section then derives the expectation of the number of matches over the array, and explain how to compute the probability that at least one match occurs in the array.

Definitions and Notations. We consider $A_0, ..., A_3$ four sets of bytes, $A_i \subset \{0, ..., 255\}$ ($i = 0, ..., 3$). For any $n = 0, ..., N-4$, given $(x_n, x_{n+1}, x_{n+2}, x_{n+3})$ a realization of $(\mathcal{X}_n, \mathcal{X}_{n+1}, \mathcal{X}_{n+2}, \mathcal{X}_{n+3})$, we define a match at position n the event $M_n = (x_n \in A_0 \wedge x_{n+1} \in A_1 \wedge x_{n+2} \in A_2 \wedge x_{n+3} \in A_3)$.

Notice that M_n and M_{n+1} are not independent since both quadruplets share three bytes which must satisfy $(x_{n+1} \in A_1, x_{n+2} \in A_2, x_{n+3} \in A_3)$ and $(x_{n+1} \in A_0, x_{n+2} \in A_1, x_{n+3} \in A_2)$. Similarly, M_n is not independent of M_{n+2} nor of M_{n+3}. We thus introduce the notions of state and of transition matrix which are necessary in the computation of the probability to obtain at least one match.

We define the state s_n as the set of 10 binary conditions related to the quadruplet $(x_n, x_{n+1}, x_{n+2}, x_{n+3})$ that have influence on all $M_n, \ldots, M_{n+3}$. Namely,

$$
\begin{aligned}
s_n = (x_n &\in A_0, \\
x_{n+1} &\in A_0, x_{n+1} \in A_1, \\
x_{n+2} &\in A_0, x_{n+2} \in A_1, x_{n+2} \in A_2, \\
x_{n+3} &\in A_0, x_{n+3} \in A_1, x_{n+3} \in A_2, x_{n+3} \in A_3).
\end{aligned}
$$

As an example, $s_n = 507 = (0111111011)_2$ in the case where all above conditions are true except that $x_n \notin A_0$ and $x_{n+3} \notin A_1$. We also denote by $\mathcal{M}$ the set of all states that match:

$$
\begin{aligned}
\mathcal{M} = \{(1, & \\
x_{n+1} &\in A_0, 1, \\
x_{n+2} &\in A_0, x_{n+2} \in A_1, 1, \\
x_{n+3} &\in A_0, x_{n+3} \in A_1, x_{n+3} \in A_2, 1)\}
\end{aligned}
$$

From the sets $A_0, \ldots, A_3$ we can construct the transition matrix $T = (T_{i,j})_{i,j}$ $(i, j = 0, \ldots, 2^{10} - 1)$ with $T_{i,j} = \Pr(s_{n+1} = j | s_n = i)$.

Expectation of the Number of Matches. Notice that the probability $\Pr(M_n)$ of a match at position n does not depend on n. Indeed we have:

$$
\begin{aligned}
\Pr(M_n) &= \Pr(x_n \in A_0 \wedge x_{n+1} \in A_1 \wedge x_{n+2} \in A_2 \wedge x_{n+3} \in A_3) \\
&= \Pr(x_n \in A_0) \cdot \Pr(x_{n+1} \in A_1) \cdot \Pr(x_{n+2} \in A_2) \cdot \Pr(x_{n+3} \in A_3) \\
&= \frac{\#(A_0)}{2^8} \cdot \frac{\#(A_1)}{2^8} \cdot \frac{\#(A_2)}{2^8} \cdot \frac{\#(A_3)}{2^8} \tag{1}
\end{aligned}
$$

Let $\mathcal{Y}$ be the random variable defined by the number of matches over the array, and $\mathcal{Y}_n = 1_{M_n}$ the random variables equal to 1 if a match occurs at position n and 0 otherwise. We obviously have $\mathcal{Y} = \mathcal{Y}_0 + \mathcal{Y}_1 + \cdots + \mathcal{Y}_{N-4}$, from which:

$$
\begin{aligned}
E(\mathcal{Y}) &= E(\mathcal{Y}_0) + E(\mathcal{Y}_1) + \cdots + E(\mathcal{Y}_{N-4}) \\
&= \Pr(M_0) + \Pr(M_1) + \cdots + \Pr(M_{N-4}) \\
&= (N - 3) \cdot \Pr(M)
\end{aligned}
$$

where $\Pr(M)$ is the probability of match given by (1).

Probability of at Least One Match. We want to compute the probability of the event denoted by G of at least one match in the array. Let F_n be the event of a first match at position n (a match at position n with no match at any position $k < n$). Notice that the collection of all F_n for $0 \leqslant n \leqslant N - 4$ forms a partition of G, so we have

$$
\Pr(G) = \sum_{n=0}^{N-4} \Pr(F_n).
$$

To compute $\Pr(F_n)$ we introduce $q_{n,j} = \Pr(s_0 \notin \mathcal{M} \wedge \ldots \wedge s_{n-1} \notin \mathcal{M} \wedge s_n = j)$ the probability of being in the state j at position n while never being in a state that matches before. We have $\Pr(F_n) = \sum\limits_{j \in \mathcal{M}} q_{n,j}$ where $q_{n,j}$ can be computed iteratively by $q_{n,j} = \sum\limits_{i \notin \mathcal{M}} q_{n-1,i} \cdot T_{i,j}$. Notice that $q_{0,i} = \Pr(s_0 = i)$ can be easily computed based on the sets A_i. As with our previous example, for $i = 507$ we have:

$$
\begin{aligned}
\Pr(s_0 = 507) &= \Pr(s_0 = (0111111011)_2) \\
&= \Pr(x_0 \notin A_0) \\
&\times \Pr(x_1 \in A_0 \wedge x_1 \in A_1) \\
&\times \Pr(x_2 \in A_0 \wedge x_2 \in A_1 \wedge x_2 \in A_2) \\
&\times \Pr(x_3 \in A_0 \wedge x_3 \notin A_1 \wedge x_3 \in A_2 \wedge x_3 \in A_3) \\
&= \frac{\#(\overline{A_0})}{2^8} \cdot \frac{\#(A_0 \cap A_1)}{2^8} \cdot \frac{\#(A_0 \cap A_1 \cap A_2)}{2^8} \cdot \frac{\#(A_0 \cap \overline{A_1} \cap A_2 \cap A_3)}{2^8}.
\end{aligned}
$$

For the evaluated card we have the following constraints: A_0= 0.. 0x7F, A_1= 0..0xFF, A_2= 0..0xFF, A_3= 0x0, 0x8, 0x10, 0x12, 0x14, 0x16, 0x18, 0x1A, 0x1C, 0x1E, 0x20, 0x22, 0x24, 0x26, 0x28. The probability of a match is greater than 0.99.

We experiment the search for forges on the evaluated card. Figure 4 shows the number of exploitable forges discovered into the first 42 kbyte of memory. In the first 2 kbyte we found 257 forges.

4.1 Application to Other Card

We repeat the experience on another model of card from a different smart card manufacturer. But the targeted card checks properly the type of the objects, disallowing to retrieve data from the instance this. To get access to the memory we modify slightly the process. We seek as an entry point an array instead of an instance. As expected, we can not use directly the forge's method described previously, because the metadata that represent a header are not the same. We have to find the metadata used by this card to forge our own, and get the access to the memory.

We install several packages, where the applet's class contains various instance fields. Once the packages are installed, we get the reference of the instance this. We use this reference to search around a successful reference. As done before in Sect. 3.2, we provide an arbitrary address. As for the previous card, most of given references fail to return a content, throwing an exception.

After several attempts we find a successful reference at the address @0x3A0E which gives a dump in the Listing 1.8. Thanks to this reference, we have access to the memory, where we can distinguish our different objects in the Listing 1.8. As we can see the step that can take a little time (two days for the first card) is the characterizations step of objects, where we have to install several applets and various classes and objects in order to increase the probability to find a usable address. Once we find such an address we can begin the characterization which gives us the hand to forge our own objects and have access to all the NVM which can be done in few minutes.

```
0x3A0E :                                                  32 32 44 44
0x3A10 : 55 55 66 66 77 77 88 88 99 99 AA AA BB BB CC CC
0x3A18 : DD DD EE EE FF FF
...     : 00 2B 30 59 00 01  //Header's array
          7F FF 00 81 40 00 00 81 30 00 00 82 10 00 00
          91
          02 00 E1 00 0C D0 99 00 00 00 00 00 FF FF 99
          00
          00 00 00 00  //Data

          00 0D 30 59 00 02 //Header's array
          00 AA 00 BB 00 CC //Data

          00 3D 10 59 B8 46  //Header's instance
          3A 88 00 11 67 67 34 34 45 45 56 67 67 78 78
          89
          89 9A 9A F0 10 F1 11 F2 12 F3 13 F4 14 F5 15
          F6
          16 F7 17 F8 18 F9 19 F0 20 F1 21 //Data
          ...
```

Listing 1.8. The data reverse of a dump

The metadata used by this card differ from the previous card, where the header of objects in this card is coded with 6 bytes as shown in Listing 1.9.

```
structure objects {
    u2 length
    bit[4] conftype
    bit[2] nature
    bit[10] context
    u2 type
}
```

Listing 1.9. The object representation

The field length represents the physical length of the object including the size of the header. The **conftype** specifies if the object is an instance or an array (0x1:instance or 0x3: array). The **nature** specifies a persistent or a transient object. The **context** is used by the firewall, if b8 and b9 of the context are set to 1, then we have a global object and the **type** is used to specify the type of an array (0: boolean, 1: byte...). The **conftype** ensures the type verification of the object. Then we can search for forges, even on a card which verifies the type of an object, by introducing a well formed forge with an valid **conftype** (0x3).

The probability to get a valid header has new constraints: $A\_0 = 0..0x7F$, $A\_1 = 0..0xFF$, $A\_2 = 0x20, 0x21, 0x22, 0x23, 0x24, 0x25, 0x26, 0x27 ...$, $A\_3 = 0x10, 0x11, 0x12, 0x13, 0x14, 0x15, 0x16, 0x17, ...$. Then the probability to get a match in the first 2 kbyte is 0.857078 while the probability to get a match in the first 42 kbyte is 0.99999. We validate it with the search the forges as shown in Fig. 5.

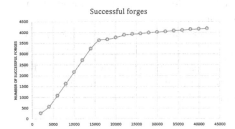

Fig. 4. Number of forges in the first card

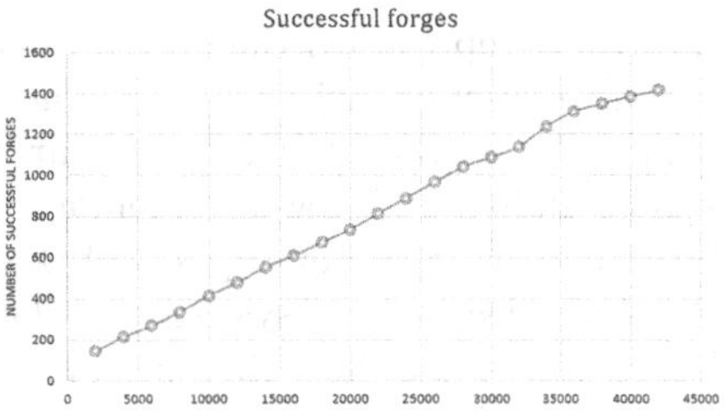

Fig. 5. Number of forges in the second card

In the first 2 kbyte on memory, we found only 142 valid forges which is coherent with the computed probability. This card exhibits much less forges than the first one.

4.2 Mitigating This Attack

The success of this attack is related to the possibility of loading an ill-typed applet in the card. For that purpose, it requires to use one of the attacks already published. Of course, on a product that does not allow post issuance downloading it can not work. These are the limits of this attack.

The possibility to consider any data as a potential meta data offers the possibility to dump the memory. Once a header is considered as an array, we can read and write in the memory. In particular we can inject new valid metadata to read more. This opportunity to consider arbitrary data as meta data can be mitigated with two approaches.

The first one requires to check if the current object belongs to the linked list of reachable object of the package declared in the metadata. This needs to walk through the complete list and can be costly for a simple read access and could be not affordable. The second approach would be to separate the metadata and the data using a pointer in the metadata to get access to the data. This solution is less costly but still requires another indirection.

5 Conclusion

In this paper, we have presented our methodology to gain access to hidden information on a secure embedded system. We characterized the metadata of objects and arrays using an already published attack. We set up a new attack based on the construction of well formed references that satisfy a set of constraints. We revisited a previous attack using the forged references to have access to the complete memory space of the NVM. This revisited attack is more simple than the original one, requires less hypothesis and allows to bypass the firewall protection.

We have been able to build the instance graph of the object belonging to any application but more interesting the instance graph of system objects. The access to a more abstract representation of the elements of the system is an important step toward the system reverse process.

Future works consist in gaining access to the other memory segments *i.e.* the Read Only Memory (ROM), that are currently out of scope of our attack. We need to understand how the memory allocation is managed inside the card. For this reason, we will develop a tool that provides graphical representation of the different objects of the system and their relationship. In particular we expect to clearly understand how the pages for static objects are managed.

References

1. Barbu, G., Duc, G., Hoogvorst, P.: Java Card operand stack: fault attacks, combined attacks and countermeasures. In: Prouff [12], pp. 297–313
2. Barbu, G., Giraud, C., Guerin, V.: Embedded eavesdropping on Java Card. In: Gritzalis, D., Furnell, S., Theoharidou, M. (eds.) SEC 2012. IFIP AICT, vol. 376, pp. 37–48. Springer, Heidelberg (2012). doi:10.1007/978-3-642-30436-1_4
3. Barbu, G., Hoogvorst, P., Duc, G.: Application-replay attack on Java Cards: when the garbage collector gets confused. In: Barthe, G., Livshits, B., Scandariato, R. (eds.) ESSoS 2012. LNCS, vol. 7159, pp. 1–13. Springer, Heidelberg (2012). doi:10.1007/978-3-642-28166-2_1
4. Barbu, G., Thiebeauld, H., Guerin, V.: Attacks on Java Card 3.0 combining fault and logical attacks. In: Gollmann, D., Lanet, J.-L., Iguchi-Cartigny, J. (eds.) CARDIS 2010. LNCS, vol. 6035, pp. 148–163. Springer, Heidelberg (2010). doi:10.1007/978-3-642-12510-2_11
5. Bouffard, G., Iguchi-Cartigny, J., Lanet, J.-L.: Combined software and hardware attacks on the Java Card control flow. In: Prouff [12], pp. 283–296
6. Bouffard, G., Lackner, M., Lanet, J.-L., Loinig, J.: Heap ... Hop! heap is also vulnerable. In: Joye, M., Moradi, A. (eds.) CARDIS 2014. LNCS, vol. 8968, pp. 18–31. Springer, Cham (2015). doi:10.1007/978-3-319-16763-3_2
7. Bouffard, G., Lanet, J.: Reversing the operating system of a Java based smart card. J. Comput. Virol. Hacking Tech. **10**(4), 239–253 (2014)
8. Farhadi, M., Lanet, J.L.: Chronicle of a Java Card death. J. Comput. Virol. Hack. Tech., 1–15 (2016)
9. Faugeron, E.: Manipulating the frame information with an underflow attack. In: Francillon, A., Rohatgi, P. (eds.) CARDIS 2013. LNCS, vol. 8419, pp. 140–151. Springer, Heidelberg (2014). doi:10.1007/978-3-319-08302-5_10
10. Hubbers, E., Poll, E.: Transactions and non-atomic API calls in java card: specification ambiguity and strange implementation behaviours. University of Nijmegen, Technical report (2004)

11. Iguchi-Cartigny, J., Lanet, J.L.: Developing a Trojan applets in a smart card. J. Comput. Virol. **6**(4), 343–351 (2010)
12. Prouff, E. (ed.): CARDIS 2011. LNCS, vol. 7079. Springer, Heidelberg (2011)
13. Razafindralambo, T., Bouffard, G., Lanet, J.-L.: A friendly framework for hidding *fault enabled virus* for Java based smartcard. In: Cuppens-Boulahia, N., Cuppens, F., Garcia-Alfaro, J. (eds.) DBSec 2012. LNCS, vol. 7371, pp. 122–128. Springer, Heidelberg (2012). doi:10.1007/978-3-642-31540-4_10

Logical Attacks on Secured Containers of the Java Card Platform

Sergei Volokitin[1]([✉]) and Erik Poll[2]

[1] Riscure B.V., Delft, The Netherlands
volokitin@riscure.com
[2] Digital Security Group, Radboud University Nijmegen, Nijmegen, The Netherlands
erikpoll@cs.ru.nl

Abstract. The Java Card platform provides programmers with API classes that act as containers for cryptographic keys and PIN codes. This paper presents a first systematic evaluation of the security that these containers provide against logical attacks, for a number of cards from different manufacturers.

Most cards we investigated do not appear to implement any integrity and confidentiality protection for these containers. For the cards that do, this paper presents new logical attacks that bypass these security measures. In particular, we show that the encryption of keys and PINs by the platform can be defeated using decryption functionality that the platform itself offers, so that logical attacks can still retrieve plaintext keys and PINs.

We also investigate the possibilities for type confusion to access the global APDU buffer and the presence of undocumented bytecode instructions.

1 Introduction

Like any smart card, a Java Card smart card can be subjected to logical attacks that exploit software flaws or to side-channel attacks, such as power analysis, glitching or other forms of fault injection [1,12,15]. In addition to the usual security risks posed by the possibly hostile environment, there is the risk of potentially malicious Java Card code on the card itself. Many Java Card cards do not have an on-card bytecode verifier, due to the resource constraints, which allows malformed code to be installed. Such code can break the security guarantees of the Java(Card) platform, notably memory-safety. Even on cards with a bytecode verifier, well-formed bytecode may still exhibit unwanted behaviour because of bugs in the platform implementation (e.g. in the transaction mechanism [11]) or through fault injection [2].

Some cards do runtime checks as a defence against malformed code. In principle, doing lots of runtime checks – effectively doing full runtime type checking – would prevent all ill-formed code from executing, but the overhead is prohibitively high.

The Java Card API provides several classes for security-sensitive data, notably the subclasses of `Key` for storing cryptographic keys and the `OwnerPIN`

© Springer International Publishing AG 2017
K. Lemke-Rust and M. Tunstall (Eds.): CARDIS 2016, LNCS 10146, pp. 122–136, 2017.
DOI: 10.1007/978-3-319-54669-8_8

class for PIN objects. The platform could – and maybe should – implement security measures for these objects against logical and/or physical attacks, to protect integrity and confidentiality of keys and PINs and integrity of PIN try counters. Indeed, applications may deliberately store data in Key objects, even though the data is not a key, just to benefit from any platform-level protection of these containers [16].

This paper investigates the security measures provided for these containers against logical attacks on various cards. Most cards we analysed do not seem to provide any such measures. On the cards which do protect keys and PINs, notably by encrypting them, we present new attacks which break this protection.

Section 2 presents related work on logical attacks on Java Card. Section 3 presents our security analysis of key and PIN containers against logical attacks using malicious code. It also presents a new attack on the global APDU buffer exploiting type confusion, and the results of the study of undocumented opcodes. Section 4 summarizes the evaluation of five Java Cards from different manufacturers. More details about the attacks can be found in the first author's Master thesis [17]. Finally, Sect. 5 discusses countermeasures presumably implemented on some cards and proposes improvements.

2   Background and Related Work

In logical attacks, malicious inputs are sent to a Java Card applet to exploit flaws in the implementation of the applet or the underlying platform. Logical attacks are also possible with malicious code rather than malicious input: installing malicious, ill-typed code can break the security guarantees of the Java Card platform provided, notably type- and memory-safety: a malicious (or buggy) applet can then compromise the integrity or confidentiality of data belonging to other applets or the platform itself, or even compromise the integrity of their code.

Since the first paper to discuss logical attacks on the Java Card platform [18], and the first systematic overview of logical attacks and countermeasures that various cards implement [11], there is now a considerable amount of literature on logical attacks on Java Cards, e.g. [1,6,7,9]. We do not discuss all this literature here, but focus on the related work that presents tricks that we also used in our attacks.

The simplest logical attacks just rely on ill-typed code and exploit the resulting type confusion to get illegal access to memory. The bytecode verifier is optional (except on the Java Card 3 Connected editions), and on cards without a bytecode verifier ill-typed code can in principle be installed. However, this does make very strong assumptions about the attacker and the card: many cards do include a bytecode verifier, and even if a card does not, installing applets will be tightly controlled with digital signatures using Global Platform. If ill-typed code can be installed, it can break the platform security guarantees of type- and memory-safety. Note that also the runtime measures of the firewall can be completely bypassed by ill-typed code. Additional runtime checks by a defensive platform implementation can mitigate this, and some cards do take such measures, as experiments with cards confirm [11].

A more subtle variant of ill-typed code is to use incompatible shareable interfaces [18]; this involves a pair of applets, each of which is well-typed in isolation. Another way to create type confusion is to exploit flaws in platform implementation, e.g. flaws in the implementation of the transaction mechanism [11], or flaws in the on-card bytecode verifier [10].

Once illegal memory access can be achieved, modifying meta-data of objects is a standard trick to escalate the impact of the attack. The classic example is to change the length field of an array, which is recorded as metadata in the representation of array objects, to get access to more data than allowed. Other tricks include pointer arithmetic to corrupt or spoof references and the use of the `getstatic_b` instruction. This last instruction allows malicious code to access arbitrary memory locations [8], as it bypasses the runtime checks of Java Card firewall. The ultimate goal of a memory attack is to obtain a full memory dump [4,7].

A more advanced way to escalate the impact of illegal memory access is to modify the code of other applets. Iguchi-Cartigny and Lanet present a Trojan applet which scans the memory and replaces instructions in the code of other applets to modify their behaviour [9]. To bypass bytecode verification, the authors use a byte array which contains the correct byte-level representation of a method body for a method with malicious code. As this byte array is data, not code, its content is not inspected by the bytecode verifier. However, by obtaining the address of the array and modifying the CAP file, the linker can be made to resolve method invocations to execute the data as a code.

Bouffard and Lanet present a way to execute 'shellcode' on the card and access the ROM memory of the card [4]. They also present a tool to identify native and Java Card bytecode in a memory dump.

Apart from attacking heap memory, attacks can also try to corrupt the stack. Faugeron presented a stack underflow attack on a Java Card VM [6]. The attack uses the instruction `dup_x`, which copies up to four words from the top of the stack. If the implementation of this instruction does not check for stack underflow, which is the case on some cards, the instruction can read outside the current stack frame, which allows access to data belonging to other methods located on the stack.

The only paper in the literature that looks at secure containers is by Farhadi and Lanet [5]. Here an attack is presented to access the plaintext value of a 3DES key belonging to another applet. The authors use a novel method to exploit type confusion, using the API method `arrayCopyNonAtomic`. The authors propose a number of countermeasures in the paper. In particular, they suggest encrypting the key container using the secret key which is not stored in non-volatile memory. The authors suggest that some cards do in fact use this protection. This is indeed the case, as we confirm in this paper, but we also show that it may be possible to bypass such protection.

3   Logical Attacks on Secure Containers

This section presents new logical attacks on secure containers that the Java Card platform provides for cryptographic keys and for PIN objects. The goal of these attacks is for one (malicious) applet to get illegal access to the content of such secure containers of another applet, with an ultimate aim to obtain the plaintext keys and PINs, or to reset the PIN try counter, which enables brute-force guessing of PINs.

These attacks assume that the attacker is able to install his own applet on a card. Using the techniques discussed in Sect. 2 the attacker can then try to illegally access memory, but here the attacker can be stopped by runtime countermeasures. For the secure containers the attacker may run into counter-measures designed to protect the confidentiality of keys and PINs, the integrity of the PIN try counter, and possibly also the integrity of keys and PINs.

The attacks described below require an attacker to get knowledge about secure container implementations and their representation in memory. For this, an attacker can install an applet which uses the containers he wants to study on a card and then use techniques as described in Sect. 2 to access the raw memory, which will reveal the internal memory representation of these containers. The attacker can then reverse-engineer the memory representation of the containers and try to locate such objects in the memory belonging to other applets.

Of course, if the platform does not provide any countermeasures to protect the confidentiality of PINs and keys – by storing the plaintext – or to protect the integrity of try counters, then it is clear that such attacks are possible. Indeed, it turns out that many cards store PINs and keys in plaintext format, unencrypted, and try counters without any redundancy or integrity checks.

The attacks presented in Sects. 3.1–3.3 below bypass defensive measures we found implemented in cards, namely simple integrity checks of try counters and encryption of keys and PIN with an unknown platform key.

Section 3.4 introduces the attack on APDU buffer which allows an attacker to store and reuse a reference to a global array, and Sect. 3.5 discusses the investigation of unspecified opcodes that some VMs turn out to support. An overview of all attacks on the different cards is given in Sect. 4.

3.1   Changing PIN Try Counters

The API class OwnerPIN offers applet developers a standard implementation for PIN objects, which store PIN codes and then provide all the associated functionality, including the administration of the number of tries left for guessing the PIN in a so-called try counter.

Providing this implementation of PIN codes in the platform is not only con-venient, it also avoids the risk of insecure ad-hoc implementations. Moreover, the API implementation can take into account platform level weaknesses or coun-termeasures, also regarding physical attacks. Indeed, the API specs say that the implementation of the OwnerPIN class should be secure against some attacks, including attacks that try to abuse the transaction mechanism.

					Max. number of tries		Number of tries left			
0x00	0x00	0x00	...	0x3C	0xFC	0x03	0xFD	0x02	...	0x24
46 bytes										

Fig. 1. Memory representation of an `OwnerPIN` object on `card_a`

Of the five cards we evaluated, only on one card, `card_a`, could we confirm that it implemented integrity checks of the `OwnerPin` try counter. However, as explained below, this integrity check could be reverse-engineered and bypassed.

Implementation of the Attack. Our attack used a malicious applet to access an arbitrary memory location by manipulating metadata of array objects, as described in [11]. We could then observe the raw memory representation of an `OwnerPIN` object, which is presented in Fig. 1.

It is clear that the data structure does not contain the PIN in a plaintext. Since the Java Card platform does not specify this, it is not easy to say where the PIN is actually stored. However, it is easy to see four bytes in the data structure that record the maximum number of tries and the number of tries left.

The card uses a redundant representation for the these counters, using two bytes for each of these counters to implement an integrity check. The second byte stores the counter value itself and the first byte stores its bit-level compliment, so that XORing the two bytes always yields `0xFF`.

This technique is widely used to prevent fault injections. Faults that change a memory cell to a random value are clearly dangerous for these counter values used in PIN objects, as setting them to random values is likely to result in more tries than intended. Indeed, we found that if we changed any of these bytes and broke this integrity check, then the card stops responding permanently.

These integrity checks are very effective against fault attacks, but not against the logical attacks we consider: once the attacker knows how the checks work, it is easy to use a logical attack to corrupt the counter values. Indeed, by adapting our malicious applet to reset the try counter to maximum values, we could easily brute force the PIN, by repeatedly guessing the PIN and then invoking our malicious applet to reset the try counter. Creating an applet with an `OwnerPIN` object and an interface allowing to input a PIN a four digit PIN could be brute forced within 15 min.

3.2 Retrieving Plaintext DES Keys

The Java Card API also provides classes to store and use cryptographic keys, e.g. the class `DESKey` for DES keys. Methods of this class include `setKey(byte[] keyData, short kOff)` and `getKey(byte[] keyData, short kOff)` for setting and getting value of the key. When setting a key, it is possible to supply the key in encrypted form[1]. Note that *supplying* a key in encrypted form does not say anything about whether keys are *stored* in an encrypted form: whether an API implementation chooses to store keys in an encrypted form is not specified, and indeed the user of the API cannot tell.

The method `getKey` always returns the plaintext key. From a security perspective, supporting this operation at all can be criticised [16], and indeed, we use it in our attack.

Using a malicious applet, one can inspect raw memory to see if keys are stored in plaintext format. Of the cards, we evaluated, only one card, `card_a`, stored keys in encrypted form. However, we could craft an attack which allows a malicious applet to retrieve the plaintext DES key of another applet, as described below.

Implementation of the Attack. To perform the attack, the malicious applet reads the raw byte representation of an encrypted DES key from the memory of another applet and copies it to a DES key object of its own. Once the encrypted key is copied, the attacker can then simply call the `DESKey.getKey()` method to get the plaintext. Figure 2 sketches this attack. So apparently on this card the same card encryption key is used to encrypt all DES keys of all the applets.

Note that we have to copy the content of the victim applet's key object to one owned by the malicious applet because the firewall prevents the malicious applet from invoking the `getKey()` method on a Key object belonging to another applet.

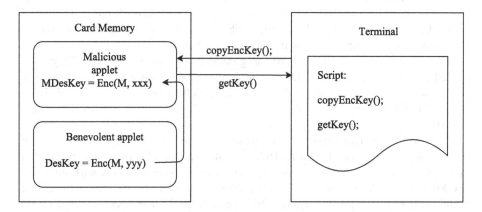

Fig. 2. `DESKey` decryption attack: from the terminal we invoke two operations on the malicious applet, the first to copy the encrypted key to a `MDesKey` object owned by the malicious applet, and a second to extract the plaintext key.

---

[1] The factory method `KeyBuilder.buildKey` for creating `Key` objects provides support for this, for those `Key` subclasses that implement the `javacardx.crypto.KeyEncryption` interface.

A – relatively simple – countermeasure against this attack would be to diversify the keys used for key encryption for different applets. A simple and cheap diversification operation, say XORing the master key with the AID of the applet, would already make the attack unfeasible. We did confirm that different cards of the same type use different encryption keys, so at least the platform implementation does not hardcode the same key on all cards.

As noted in [5], ideally the encryption key would be stored in memory that would be hard or impossible for an attacker to access (e.g. in ROM or memory of the crypto co-processor). We did not reverse engineer the card to the point that we could tell that this key is indeed not stored anywhere in non-volatile memory, but using the attack above we do not need to know this key anyway.

3.3   Retrieving Plaintext PINs

As described in Sect. 3.1, with illegal memory access we could modify the try counter and then find out a PIN by brute force guessing, even though the PIN was apparently stored encrypted. However, this attack is quite slow.

The class `OwnerPIN` does not provide a method `getPIN()`, similar to the `getKey()` of `DESKey` class, to retrieve plaintext PINs. From the point of view of security, providing such a method is clearly a bad idea, and from the point of functionality there is no sensible reason for having it. If such a `getPIN()` method was available, we might undo the encryption of PINs in the same way that we undid the encryption of DES keys in Sect. 3.2, by copying the raw encrypted byte representation of the PIN to another PIN object and invoking `getPIN()`.

Still, as the content of both PIN and key objects stored encrypted on the card, one possibility is that the same algorithm is used in both cases. Indeed, it is easy to notice that both 8 byte long DES keys and 8 byte long PIN are stored as 10 bytes, which suggests this may indeed be the case.

This suggested an attack where the `getKey()` operation of the `DESKey` class is used to retrieve plaintext PINs: a malicious applet copies the encrypted representation of a PIN belonging to another applet to one of his own DES key objects, and then invokes `getKey()` to retrieve the plaintext. Figure 3 sketches this attack.

We found this attack worked. So apparently the same encryption key is used not only for all keys but also for all PINs, for all applets. This provides an attacker with the ability to encrypt and decrypt any values using this key, without actually knowing it. Again, some key diversification would thwart this attack: just using a different key for encrypting PINs than is used for encrypting keys would suffice.

3.4   Illegal Access to APDU Buffer Array Reference

As part of the firewall functionality, the Java Card runtime environment restricts storing references to so-called global arrays, because they are potentially shared amongst applets. The APDU buffer is such a global array, and the runtime environment specification states:

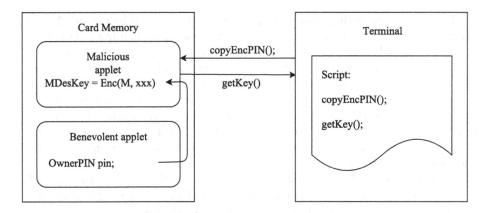

Fig. 3. OwnerPIN decryption attack

"All global arrays are temporary global array objects. These objects are owned by the JCRE context, but can be accessed from any context. However, references to these objects cannot be stored in class variables, instance variables or array components. The JCRE detects and restricts attempts to store references to these objects as part of the firewall functionality to prevent unauthorised re-use." [14, Sect. 6.2.2]

This means that references to global arrays cannot be stored in persistent memory on the heap (which is where class and instance variables are stored). Such references can only be stored in local variables, i.e. on the stack, which is in transient memory. (Moreover, to avoid data leakage between applets, the JCRE and API specs state that the APDU buffer must be cleared to zeroes whenever an applet is selected [14, Sect. 6.2.2].)

However, if an attacker can (illegally) cast a reference to a short value and back, then by storing that short value he can bypass the restriction on storing references to global arrays. We found that this was possible on all the cards we analysed. This effectively breaks the requirement quoted above.

The illegal access to the APDU buffer this allows and the attacks that this in turn enables are extensively discussed by Barbu et al. [2].

Implementation of the Attack. In order to bypass the restriction on storing references to global objects, a malformed applet was developed. The core functionality of the applet is given by the functions below:

```
public static short addr( byte[] ptr ) {
    return (short)ptr;
}

public static byte[] ptr( short addr ) {
    return (byte[]) addr;
}
```

The code in the listing above is clearly ill-typed, so it will be rejected by any compiler, but a CAP file for this code can be created by hand, and this CAP file can be installed on a card if it does not have an on-card bytecode verifier.

Once the code is installed, the method addr() allows a reference to any array, including a global array, to be turned into a short, and the platform will not prevent this short from being stored in a class or instance variable. At any point in time later, the method ptr() can be used to turn this stored short back into a reference, so this is functionally equivalent to storing the reference to the global array in a class or instance variable. This is illustrated in more detail in the code samples below.

First, the code below illustrates how the firewall will disallow storing a reference to a global array, the APDU buffer, in a class variable buffClassCopy, but will allow storing it in a local variable buffLocalCopy:

```
public class App extends Applet {
    byte[] instance;
    ...
    public void process(APDU apdu) {
        byte[] local;
        byte[] buffer = apdu.getBuffer();
        local = buffer; // allowed by the firewall
        instance = buffer; // forbidden by the firewall
    }
}
```

However, using the operations addr() and ptr() we can obtain equivalent functionality without breaking the firewall rules:

```
public class App extends Applet {
    short instanceShort;
    ...
    public void process(APDU apdu) {
        byte[] buffer = apdu.getBuffer();
        instanceShort = addr(buffer); // allowed by firewall
    }
}
```

In any method where we would want to use instanceShort as a reference to a byte array, we can declare a local byte array variable and use ptr() to convert the short back to a reference: C

```
byte[] localVar;
localVar = ptr(instanceShort); // allowed
...// localVar can now be used, and points to the global array
```

It is worth mentioning that we observed some non-trivial countermeasures on card_a to prevent references to global arrays being stored in class or instance variables. If we attempt to store ptr(instanceShort) in an instance variable of type byte[], the card terminates the session. There appears to be a runtime check so that when any class or instance variable is set to point to the APDU buffer, the card terminates the session.

Obviously, such a check uses resources and it is completely useless against the attack presented here: storing the reference as a short in a class variable is just as good as storing it as a reference.

3.5   Execution of 'illegal' Opcodes

According to the Java Card virtual machine specification, [13] correct Java byte-code must include only instruction bytes from 0x00 to 0xB8, 0xFE and 0xFF. The first range of opcodes is reserved for the standard bytecode operations. The last two opcodes are reserved for internal use by a virtual machine implementation, for any implementation-specific functionality.

Execution of illegal code on the cards revealed that one of the studied cards, namely card_a, supported opcodes which are outside of the range above, which we will call 'illegal' opcodes, for unspecified operations of the Java Card virtual machine.

Like the known and specified opcodes, illegal opcodes may be followed by zero or more byte parameters in the code (i.e. in the CAP file), and they can pop parameters from the top of the operand stack. In the case of the legal opcodes, the number of the code and stack parameters is defined in the specification. Finding out the number of parameters required by each of the illegal opcodes is the first challenge on the way to understanding the purpose of the illegal opcodes. We tackle this by executing an illegal opcode followed by a number of instructions pushing a constant on the operand stack and analyzing the state of the stack after execution. It is possible to analyse the stack state after execution of an illegal opcode by popping remaining words from the stack and saving to local variables. Unfortunately, just knowing the number of the parameters an illegal opcode uses does not provide a lot of clues for understanding its purpose.

Luckily, there is an emulator provided by the manufacturer of the card which also supports execution of the illegal opcodes. Comparison of the execution traces of the emulator executing illegal and legal bytecodes provided an understanding of the purpose of the opcodes since some of the illegal opcodes result in exactly the same or very similar execution traces as legal ones. Table 1 presents legal code corresponding to some of the illegal instructions. It suggests that these additional opcodes are just convenient shorthand, presumably for more compact bytecode. The idea to use the unused opcodes as abbreviations for common patterns is already discussed in [3].

A study of the illegal opcodes seemed to be promising, but it turned out to be very time-consuming and did not result in a successful attack. Still, a single bytecode instruction can be very dangerous, as illustrated by the power that getstatic_b gives to malicious code, so any additional opcodes deserve close

Table 1. Corresponding legal instructions to illegal opcodes

Illegal opcode	Equivalent instruction
0xBD	sload 4
0xBE	sload 5
0xBF	sload 6
0xC0	sload 7

attention in any security evaluation. The use of the emulator turned out to be a great tool in hands of an attacker to help understand the internal design of the Java Card implementation.

4 Evaluation

We tried out our attacks on five different cards from different manufacturers. Table 2 lists the version numbers of Java Card and Global Platform the cards provide. The outcome of the attacks is summarised in Table 3. Here ✓ indicates that an attack was successful, and ✗ that the attack failed. So the fewer ✗s a card has, the better its security is.

The techniques we used in our attacks, apart from those discussed in Sect. 3, were known techniques discussed in Sect. 2, namely

– modifying metadata (esp. of arrays),
– 'spoofing' references (by doing some pointer arithmetic),

Table 2. Specification of the cards

Card	Global Platform	Java Card
card_a	GP 2.1.1	JC 2.1.2
card_b	GP 2.1.1	JC 2.2.1
card_c	GP 2.2.1	JC 3.0.4
card_d	GP 2.1.1	JC 2.2.1
card_e	GP 2.1.1	JC 3.0.1

Table 3. The results of the attacks on the various cards.

Attack	Card				
	card_a	card_b	card_c	card_d	card_e
Changing a PIN trycounter	✓	✓	✗	✗	✓
Retrieving a plaintext PIN	✓	✓	✗	✗	✓
Retrieval a plaintext DES key	✓	✓	✗	✗	✓
APDU buffer array reference	✓	✗	✓	✓	✓

- using `getstatic_b`,
- using 'illegal' opcodes, in a variation of the attack of [9], and
- accessing arbitrary objects as if they were arrays (effectively a generalisation of the attack with `arrayCopyNonAtomic` used in [5][2]).

For `card_a`, the only card on which we found countermeasures to protect secure containers, we used the techniques described in Sect. 3 to bypass these.

On `card_b` and `card_e` no countermeasures were implemented and all the data and metadata were stored in a plain text. As a result, the keys and PINs were easily recovered without using the more complex attacks described in Sect. 3.

Most attacks failed on `card_c` and `card_d` because it was not possible to get unauthorised access to the memory of another applet. Although it was possible to install and run malicious code, type confusion was not possible, which might be a result of comprehensive defensive runtime type checks that these cards perform.

The APDU buffer attack failed on card `card_b` because this card refuses to install CAP files that contain library packages, which we use in this attack. Clearly, the APDU buffer reference attack worked on the largest number of cards. This underlines the observation in [2], that an applet developer should be aware of the risk that the APDU buffer may be compromised by other applets.

5 Countermeasures

The most obvious countermeasure against logical attacks with malicious code is of course to have an on-card bytecode verifier. Note that even on a card with an on-card verifier, bugs in the platform may still allow an attacker to bypass the protection it offers (as shown in [10, 11]).

In addition to a bytecode verifier, if the card's hardware provides a memory management unit to control access to memory areas, that can be used as additional line of defence against logical attacks.

Runtime checks can make logical attacks harder. Doing full type checking at runtime would stop any ill-typed code, but this is prohibitively expensive. In practice, cards do some checks at runtime. On two of the cards we studied, `card_c` and `card_d`, all our attempts to access secure containers with malicious code failed due to defensive runtime checks by the platform. When experimenting with attacks cards will sometimes mute because integrity checks are violated. In all, 24 cards permanently muted in the course of our experiments. Of course, which integrity checks are performed is unknown, and can only be figured out by trial and error: The Java Card specifications do not prescribe any such countermeasures, and this is completely up to the implementation. Many of the papers mentioned in Sect. 2 speculate about countermeasures that were encountered.

---

[2] We found that the attack using `arrayCopyNonAtomic` did not work on any of the cards we had, so this seems an implementation-specific weakness of the particular card studied in [5].

One implementation choice in a platform that can have a big impact on the capabilities of ill-formed code is how references are represented. Some implementations simply use pointers (i.e. memory addresses) for references. However, most modern cards use indirect referencing using an indirection table. Here a reference is an index in some table that stores the real pointer value (i.e. the memory address where the data is located). Using an indirection table makes attacks that corrupt or spoof references harder: it prevents an attacker from performing arithmetic operations on references in order to get access to the random location of the memory. Some of the manufacturers that implement indirect referencing store the metadata of an array next to data, instead of storing it in the reference table. Since array metadata has a fixed size it does not seem to be too difficult to store it in the table. Storing metadata in the reference table would make it much harder for an attacker to corrupt this data. For example, modifying memory outside the array bounds would not hit metadata of adjacent array objects in memory.

According to Java Card virtual machine specification memory addresses of a virtual machine are 16 bits. This means only 64 KB of non-volatile memory can be addressed by an applet using Java Card instructions. Nowadays many Java Cards have bigger non-volatile memory than 64 KB. This means there is unaddressable memory, that cannot be accessed by a malicious applet unless it can execute native code. Although it has been shown to be possible to execute native code on some Java Cards [4], this is not an easy task. Clearly, storing the reference table with object metadata in such memory that is not addressable by (non-native) code running on the virtual machine would be a good countermeasure to make logical attacks harder.

The reason we could retrieve plaintexts of data in the secured containers for card_a was that the same encryption key was used for all containers, i.e. both keys and PINs, and for all applets. This vulnerability could be avoided by using key diversification in such a way that for each applet, or even each object, a different key is used. There are many options for such a diversification scheme. For example, the AID of an applet could be used diversify a master encryption key to obtain a key for protecting objects of that applet. Of course, relying on the AID for the key diversification assumes that the attacker cannot manipulate the AID of his attack applet. An even stronger solution would be to use the memory address of the object as a parameter to diversify a key to obtain a unique key to protect a specific object. However, this measure would complicate re-allocation of objects; it would therefore not be a good choice if you want the platform to support memory compaction as part of garbage collection.

Protecting the integrity of try counters from logical attacks seems harder than protecting the confidentiality of keys or PIN. Whatever integrity measure is implemented (say a cryptographic integrity check with a keyed MAC using the same key used to encrypt the PIN), an attacker with access to memory may simply be able to restore an earlier value of a try counter together with all the right integrity measures. The integrity check could of course be made a lot harder to reverse-engineer, and spreading out the data involved to represent these counters and any associated integrity checks in memory would make life much harder for an attacker.

The reason that the global array reference attack is possible on most cards is that the operand stack on the cards is untyped and it is quite difficult to prevent the attack without runtime type checks. A possible solution could be to use a typed operand stack (but that comes with a big performance overhead) or separate stacks for references and other data types.

As noted by Barbu et al. [2], who extensively discuses attacks involving illegal access to the APDU buffer, here the applet developer should take into account that the APDU buffer can be compromised by other applets. It would seem to us that the risk this introduces (if any, as it assumes the presence of malicious applets) is greater on the new JavaCard 3 Connected Edition, because that supports multi-threading, which increases the possibilities for another applet to simultaneously access the shared APDU buffer.

6   Conclusions

Apart from explicitly specified security mechanisms such as the applet firewall and transaction mechanism, there are a number of additional countermeasures that can be implemented on Java Card smartcards. But, as it was shown in this paper, not all the countermeasures are equally effective. This underlines the importance of a bytecode verifier and the control on applet installation using digital signatures with Global Platform as lines of defence.

Our study showed that most cards we analyzed do not implement any special protection mechanism to protect secure containers from logical attacks with malicious, as they simply store keys and PINs in a plaintext. Even on cards which encrypts secret keys, we found that attackers can easily decrypt the ciphertexts by (ab)using the decryption functionality offered by the API itself through the getKey() method. The cards we had access to for our evaluation are engineering samples, so we cannot exclude the possibility that cards used in the field have different countermeasures.

It is worth mentioning that the encryption of the keys and PINs and the simple integrity check on try counters that we encountered may be aimed at preventing side-channel attacks rather than logical attacks. Against fault injections, these mechanisms would be very effective, both against fault attacks where the attacker tries to corrupt the try counter and against fault attacks where the attacker tries to modify PINs or keys to predictable values. (The latter requires stuck-at fault attacks where the attacker can predict that the value of a memory location after the attack will be a fixed value, e.g. all zeroes or all ones.)

As discussed in Sect. 5, a simple tweak of the scheme for encrypting keys and PINs – namely, adding some key diversification – would make the protection much stronger. Securing PIN try counters from logical attacks seems the harder problem.

References

1. Barbu, G., Duc, G., Hoogvorst, P.: Java card operand stack: fault attacks, combined attacks and countermeasures. In: Prouff, E. (ed.) CARDIS 2011. LNCS, vol. 7079, pp. 297–313. Springer, Heidelberg (2011). doi:10.1007/978-3-642-27257-8_19
2. Barbu, G., Giraud, C., Guerin, V.: Embedded eavesdropping on java card. In: Gritzalis, D., Furnell, S., Theoharidou, M. (eds.) SEC 2012. IAICT, vol. 376, pp. 37–48. Springer, Heidelberg (2012). doi:10.1007/978-3-642-30436-1_4
3. Bizzotto, G., Grimaud, G.: Practical java card bytecode compression. In: Proceedings of RENPAR14/ASF/SYMPA (2002)
4. Bouffard, G., Lanet, J.L.: Reversing the operating system of a java based smart card. J. Comput. Virol. Hacking Tech. **10**(4), 239–253 (2014)
5. Farhadi, M., Lanet, J.L.: Chronicle of a Java Card death. J. Comput. Virol. Hacking Tech. 1–15 (2016). doi:10.1007/s11416-016-0276-0. ISSN: 2263–8733
6. Faugeron, E.: Manipulating the frame information with an underflow attack. In: Francillon, A., Rohatgi, P. (eds.) CARDIS 2013. LNCS, vol. 8419, pp. 140–151. Springer, Heidelberg (2014). doi:10.1007/978-3-319-08302-5_10
7. Hogenboom, J., Mostowski, W.: Full memory read attack on a java card. In: 4th Benelux Workshop on Information and System Security Proceedings (WISSEC 2009) (2009)
8. Hyppönen, K.: Use of cryptographic codes for bytecode verification in smartcard environment. Master's thesis, University of Kuopio (2003)
9. Iguchi-Cartigny, J., Lanet, J.L.: Developing a trojan applet in a smart card. J. Comput. Virol. **6**(4), 343–351 (2010)
10. Lancia, J., Bouffard, G.: Java card virtual machine compromising from a bytecode verified applet. In: Homma, N., Medwed, M. (eds.) CARDIS 2015. LNCS, vol. 9514, pp. 75–88. Springer, Heidelberg (2016). doi:10.1007/978-3-319-31271-2_5
11. Mostowski, W., Poll, E.: Malicious code on java card smartcards: attacks and countermeasures. In: Grimaud, G., Standaert, F.-X. (eds.) CARDIS 2008. LNCS, vol. 5189, pp. 1–16. Springer, Heidelberg (2008). doi:10.1007/978-3-540-85893-5_1
12. Rothbart, K., Neffe, U., Steger, C., Weiss, R., Rieger, E., Mühlberger, A.: Power consumption profile analysis for security attack simulation in smart cards at high abstraction level. In: Proceedings of the 5th ACM International Conference on Embedded Software, pp. 214–217. ACM (2005)
13. Sun Microsystems: Java Card 2.1.1 Virtual Machine Specification (2000)
14. Sun Microsystems: Java Card 2.2.2 Runtime Environment Specification (2006)
15. Vermoen, D., Witteman, M., Gaydadjiev, G.N.: Reverse engineering java card applets using power analysis. In: Sauveron, D., Markantonakis, K., Bilas, A., Quisquater, J.-J. (eds.) WISTP 2007. LNCS, vol. 4462, pp. 138–149. Springer, Heidelberg (2007). doi:10.1007/978-3-540-72354-7_12
16. Vétillard, E.: Should we deprecate DESKey.getKey()? (2007). http://javacard.vetilles.com/2007/06/19/should-we-deprecate-deskeygetkey/, blogentry
17. Volokitin, S.: Good, bad and ugly design of java card security. Master's thesis, Radboud University Nijmegen (2016)
18. Witteman, M.: Java card security. Inf. Secur. Bull. **8**, 291–298 (2003)

Single-Trace Side-Channel Attacks on Scalar Multiplications with Precomputations

Kimmo Järvinen[1](✉) and Josep Balasch[2]

[1] Department of Computer Science, University of Helsinki, Helsinki, Finland
kimmo.u.jarvinen@helsinki.fi
[2] KU Leuven ESAT/COSIC and imec, Leuven, Belgium
josep.balasch@esat.kuleuven.be

Abstract. Single-trace side-channel attacks are a serious threat to elliptic curve cryptography in practice because they can break also cryptosystems where scalars are nonces (e.g., ECDSA). Previously it was believed that single-trace attacks can be avoided by using scalar multiplication algorithms with regular patterns of operations but recently we have learned that they can be broken with correlation tests to decide whether different operations share common operands. In this work, we extend these attacks to scalar multiplication algorithms with precomputations. We show that many algorithms are vulnerable to our attack which correlates measurements with precomputed values. We also show that successful attacks are possible even without knowledge of precomputed values by using clustering instead of correlations. We provide extensive evidence for the feasibility of the attacks with simulations and experiments with an 8-bit AVR. Finally, we discuss the effectiveness of certain countermeasures against our attacks.

1 Introduction

Elliptic curve cryptography (ECC) [36,39] has gained huge popularity in secure embedded systems because it offers high cryptographic security with short key sizes and relatively low computational requirements. The most important operation in ECC is the *scalar multiplication* $Q = kP$ where Q and P are points on an elliptic curve and k is an integer. The scalar k is typically secret and must remain unknown to attackers in order to maintain the security.

Side-channel attacks on ECC have gained significant amounts of research interest [17,18]. We focus on *passive attacks* where an attacker only observes a cryptographic device under its normal operation. They can be categorized into two classes: *single-trace attacks*, which use measurements from only one scalar multiplication, and *multi-trace attacks*, which utilize statistical methods onto multiple scalar multiplications sharing the same scalar. Single-trace attacks are much more serious threats because in most ECC protocols (e.g., ECDSA [44]) scalars are nonces, i.e., short-term secrets that change at each protocol execution. This prevents the attacker from obtaining multiple traces with the same scalar and nullifies multi-trace attacks. However, the attacker may still often launch a

© Springer International Publishing AG 2017
K. Lemke-Rust and M. Tunstall (Eds.): CARDIS 2016, LNCS 10146, pp. 137–155, 2017.
DOI: 10.1007/978-3-319-54669-8_9

repeated single-trace attack where she can acquire multiple traces with different scalars. We focus on (repeated) single-trace attacks in this paper.

The simplest algorithm for computing scalar multiplications is the *double-and-add*, where a *point doubling* $(2Q)$ is computed for every bit of k but a *point addition* $(Q + P)$ only when a bit is one. The double-and-add succumbs even to *simple power analysis* (SPA) where measurement traces are observed visually. It is relatively easy to protect against these attacks by adopting the so-called *atomicity* principle. An atomic implementation has a *regular pattern of operations* which does not depend on k. This can be achieved, e.g., by using dummy operations (e.g., double-and-add-always [13]), a regular scalar multiplication algorithm (e.g., Montgomery's ladder [35,41]), balancing point addition and doubling formulae (e.g., [9,25]), or using a unified point addition and doubling formula (e.g., [7]). Prior to recent advanced single-trace attacks, these principles were considered sufficient to protect against single-trace attacks.

The history of *advanced single-trace attacks* began in 2001 with Walter's *Big Mac attack* [52] on exponentiations, where the attacker targets partial multiplications computed in each long integer multiplication of an exponentiation. In 2010, Clavier et al. [11] introduced a single-trace attack on a larger class of exponentiation algorithms called *horizontal correlation analysis* by utilizing ideas from the Big Mac attack together with correlation power analysis. Correlation power analysis was originally introduced against secret-key cryptography by Brier et al. [8] in 2004 and it was already earlier applied in multi-trace attacks on public-key algorithms by Amiel et al. [1] in 2007. In 2013, Bauer et al. [4] (see [5] for an extended version) combined the ideas of [11] with Moradi et al.'s collision correlation analysis [42] and obtained a very powerful single-trace attack which thwarts many of the state-of-the-art countermeasures. Recently, further works have built on the ideas of improving Big Mac [15] and collision correlations [29]. Another trend of attacks uses clustering algorithms to launch a single-trace attack on ECC. A clustering attack was shown to break an ECC hardware implementation without any profiling or leakage models by Heyszl et al. [31]; Sprecht et al. [49] later improved this attack. In addition to these, also local electromagnetic measurements have been shown to offer means to launch successful single-trace attacks, e.g., by Heyszl et al. [32].

Precomputations based on P are commonly used to speed up scalar multiplications, but they play a role also in side-channel security. Even if SPA can distinguish point additions from point doublings, it is incapable of distinguishing operands used in point additions. For this reason, the double-and-add algorithm with, e.g., the width-w non-adjacent form (w-NAF), where digits are from $\{0, \pm 1, \pm 3, \dots, \pm(2^{w-1}-1)\}$ (see, e.g., [28]), offers better protection against side-channel attacks than a binary expansion, where digits are from $\{0, 1\}$. Nevertheless, direct use of, e.g., w-NAF still leaks a lot of information about the scalar and cannot be considered side-channel secure. Fully regular patterns of operations can be achieved with atomic scalar multiplication algorithms with precomputations which typically combine side-channel security with efficiency (see, e.g., [19,30,45,46]). Such algorithms have been recently used for side-channel protected lightweight hardware implementations, e.g., in [47,48] as well as fast software, e.g., in [14]. In the light of new advanced single-trace attacks, there have been doubts about the security offered by these algorithms (see, e.g., [3,31,47]).

We show that these doubts are well grounded, at least for processors with small word sizes. Hence, our paper has significance, in particular, for lightweight implementations of ECC. Such implementations typically implement ECC on 8-bit or 16-bit processors (see, e.g., [10,27,37,38,43,50]) or utilize datapaths with small multipliers (e.g., 16-bit multipliers used in [47,48]). The contributions of this paper can be summarized as follows:

- We extend existing correlation-based single-trace attacks (in particular, [4,5, 15,29,52]) to scalar multiplications with precomputations. While this type of correlation attacks have been conjectured to form a serious threat to scalar multiplication algorithms with precomputations already before, we are not aware of any works that would have studied this in depth before this paper.
- We show that a clustering-based attack allows the attacker to successfully attack these algorithms even without relying on a specific leakage model and with unknown precomputed values.
- We provide comprehensive evidence about the practicability of these attacks through simulations and experiments with an 8-bit AVR (ATMega163).
- We present a summary of countermeasures.

The paper is organized as follows: Sect. 2 discusses scalar multiplication algorithms that we target with our attacks. Section 3 describes the attack and its two variants. Section 4 presents simulation results and Sect. 5 presents experiments with the 8-bit AVR. Section 6 discusses countermeasures against the attacks. Finally, we draw conclusions and discuss topics for future research in Sect. 7.

2   Preliminaries

We assume that $Q = kP$ is computed so that k is a secret nonce and P may or may not be known by the attacker. Let $E(\mathbb{F}_q)$ be an additive abelian group of points on an elliptic curve, where $\mathbb{F}_q$ is the finite field of q elements. The group $E(\mathbb{F}_q)$ is formed by the points that satisfy the curve equation either including or appended with the point-at-infinity ∞, which is the zero element of the group.

We consider scalar multiplication algorithms that compute kP by using precomputations on P. We show the general structure of these algorithms in Algorithm 1. The secret scalar is converted by using a *recoding* transformation $\Delta(k)$ into ℓ digits $d = (d_0, d_1, \ldots, d_{\ell-1})$, where $d_i \in \mathcal{D}$ with $|\mathcal{D}| = n$. Let T be a table of n precomputed points[1]: $T_t \in E(\mathbb{F}_q)$ for all $t \in \mathcal{D}$. The table T is computed from the base point P via a *precomputation* transformation $\Pi(P)$. The bulk of the scalar multiplication is performed in a for-loop that iterates a *target* transformation $\Psi(R, T, d_i)$, where a static T is used depending on the value of d_i.

---

[1] For simplicity and without loss of generality, we consider one-to-one mapping between digit values d_i and points in T. In practice, the precomputed table may not include all values; e.g., the values for negative digits can be derived on-the-fly, etc.

Input: Scalar $k \in \mathbb{Z}_+$, base point $P \in E(\mathbb{F}_q)$
Output: Result point $Q = kP$
1 $d = (d_0, d_1, \ldots, d_{\ell-1}) \leftarrow \Delta(k)$
2 $T = (T_0, T_1, \ldots, T_{n-1}) \leftarrow \Pi(P)$
3 $R \leftarrow \infty$
4 **for** $i = 0, 1, \ldots, \ell - 1$ **do**
5    $R \leftarrow \Psi(R, T, d_i)$

6 **return** $Q = R$

Algorithm 1. The structure of targeted scalar multiplication algorithms

The attacker focuses only on transformation Ψ and aims to find the value of d_i by utilizing the fact that Ψ uses the precomputed table T according to the digit value d_i; i.e., most typically it adds T_{d_i} to R. The attacker does not need access to the precomputation; e.g., the table T can be stored in a ROM as in [47].

While Algorithm 1 depicts an abstract structure, it captures many commonly used algorithms with precomputations. The most interesting algorithms for our attack are algorithms which utilize a regular pattern of operations and are, thus, immune to basic single-trace attacks such as SPA. In this paper, we consider Okeya et al.'s *SPA-resistant width-w non-adjacent form* (w-NAF) scalar multiplication [45] as an example of a vulnerable algorithm, but the attack applies to a large number of scalar multiplication algorithms (see below). For the SPA-resistant w-NAF, the precomputation $\Pi(P)$ computes odd multiples of P:

$$T = (-(2^w - 1)P, \ldots, -3P, -P, P, 3P, \ldots, (2^w - 1)P). \tag{1}$$

In practice, only positive multiples can be precomputed and negative multiples computed as a part of Ψ, but this does not have an effect on the attacks. The recoding $\Delta(k)$ finds d with $d_i \in \mathcal{D} = \{\pm 1, \pm 3, \ldots, \pm(2^w - 1)\}$ such that $k = \Delta^{-1}(d) = \sum_{i=0}^{\ell-1} d_{\ell-i-1} 2^{iw}$; details about $\Delta(k)$ are available in [45]. The target transformation is $\Psi(R, T, d_i) = 2^w R + T_{d_i}$.

If the attacker knows the precomputed points that were used in Ψ in all iterations of the for-loop, then she learns all d_i and the secret value of k simply with $k = \Delta^{-1}(d)$. Section 3 presents how she can find out d_i if she (a) knows T and (b) even if T is unknown. In both cases, the attacker must know the algorithm and its parameters (e.g., w, ℓ and n), Δ^{-1}, and certain implementation details of Ψ (see Sects. 3–5).

A large number of scalar multiplication algorithm can be captured by Algorithm 1 and are at least potentially vulnerable to our attacks. These include many non-regular algorithms such as double-and-add, (sliding) window (NAF) methods, etc. However, we are more interested about regular algorithms which are protected from SPA but can be vulnerable to our attacks. These include, e.g., regular w-NAF and m-ary methods [20,34,40,45,51], regular width-w τ-adic NAF method for Koblitz curves [46], the regular signed-digit comb methods [21,30], and scalar multiplications on curves with fast endomorphisms that use multi-scalar multiplications with precomputations (e.g., GLV [24] and GLS [23] methods and, in particular, the recent regular algorithm [19]). Some of these methods have been recently utilized in lightweight ECC implementations to achieve protection against single-trace attacks: e.g., [30] was used in [46,47] in [48], and [19] in [14]. All deterministic countermeasures inside Ψ such as atomicity of point addition and point doubling, unified addition formulae, etc., do not work against the attack and are, thus, also in the list of vulnerable methods when used in a scalar multiplication algorithm that utilizes precomputations in the above sense. Montgomery's ladder [41], Joye's regular algorithms [33], and other algorithms, where for-loops iterate only on non-static values, are not vulnerable because there is no static T that would be used in Ψ which is required by our attacks. However, other similar types of single-trace attacks have recently identified similar weaknesses also in such algorithms (e.g., [4,5,31]).

Because k is a nonce, we focus only on single-trace attacks. However, the attacker is often able to retrieve t side-channel traces with different scalars (e.g., by observing t ECDSA signature generations). This allows her to carry out a repeated single-trace attack where she trials successive single-trace attacks until one of them succeeds. The probabilities work for the attacker. Let p_{sta} be the success probability of a single-trace attack. Then, the success probability of a repeated single-trace attack as a function of t is given by:

$$p_{\text{r-sta}}(t) = 1 - (1 - p_{\text{sta}})^t. \tag{2}$$

E.g., if $p_{\text{sta}} = 2\%$, the repeated single-trace attack succeeds with over 50% probability only after 35 traces and with over 99% probability after 228 traces. These numbers are completely realistic in many practical scenarios.

3 Description of the Attack

We extend the previous advanced single-trace attacks and, in particular, Walter's Big Mac [52] and Clavier et al.'s horizontal correlation [11] attacks on exponentiations to scalar multiplications with precomputations. Contrary to collision correlation attacks [4,5], which make a decision of which operation was computed by correlating multiple values of a side-channel trace to find out whether the operations used the same operands, our attack relies on distinguishing which particular static precomputed value was used in an operation.

Our attack targets the transformation Ψ and, especially, field multiplications in Ψ which use values from T as operands. We assume that the word-length W of the processor is small ($W \ll \log_2 q$, e.g., $W = 8$ or $W = 16$) so that elements of $\mathbb{F}_q$ split into multiple words. The words of an element $a \in \mathbb{F}_q$ are $a_0, a_1, \ldots, a_{N-1}$ where $N = \lceil \log_2 q/W \rceil$. In particular, we are interested in *partial multiplications* of a *long integer multiplication* (multiprecision multiplication) similarly to, e.g., [4,5,11,52]. Let $a, b \in \mathbb{F}_q$. Then, $a \times b$ requires N^2 $W \times W$-bit partial multiplications $a_i \times b_j$ with all $0 \leq i, j < N$. Although we focus on $W \times W$-bit partial multiplications of an integer multiplication, the attack can be straightforwardly generalized to binary fields $\mathbb{F}_{2^m}$ or asymmetric $W_1 \times W_2$-bit partial multiplications. It may also be possible to use other leakage sources including, e.g., memory addresses, register loads and stores, and multiprecision additions.

We assume that the attacker can identify all partial multiplications from a side-channel trace that belong to a long integer multiplication which uses a value from the precomputed table T as one of the operands (say, a). The other operand (b) is considered random[2]. The attacker collects samples from the partial multiplications. Let $s_{i,j}$ be a *sample* collected from the partial multiplication $a_i \times b_j$. The hypothesis is that $s_{i,j}$ depends on the properties of a_i and b_j (e.g., on their Hamming weights) and that utilizing this information allows the attacker to find out which value from T was used as the operand a.

Following Walter's example [52], most of the effects of the unknown b can be filtered out by computing an average over all samples that use a_i:

$$\hat{s}_i = \frac{1}{N} \sum_{j=0}^{N-1} s_{i,j}. \tag{3}$$

Even if b_j blinds a_i in $s_{i,j}$ (e.g., because of a particularly low or high Hamming weight), computing the average efficiently reduces the dependence on the (unknown) value of b. The averaging acts also as a low-pass filter for filtering out measurement noise.

A single execution of Ψ typically includes several multiplications with values from T_{d_i} and information from all of them should be utilized in the attack. Let M denote the number of such multiplications in Ψ. The attacker collects $\hat{s}_0^{i,m}, \hat{s}_1^{i,m}, \ldots, \hat{s}_{N-1}^{i,m}$ where i is the index of d_i and $m = 0, 1, \ldots, M-1$ is the index of the multiplication. She concatenates them into a *sample vector* that consists of MN averaged samples (MN^2 if not averaged):

$$S_i = \left(\hat{s}_0^{i,0}, \hat{s}_1^{i,0}, \ldots, \hat{s}_{N-1}^{i,0}, \hat{s}_0^{i,1}, \ldots, \hat{s}_{N-1}^{i,1}, \ldots, \hat{s}_0^{i,M-1}, \ldots, \hat{s}_{N-1}^{i,M-1} \right). \tag{4}$$

The attacker repeats the procedure for all ℓ executions of Ψ, after which she possesses $S_0, S_1, S_2, \ldots, S_{\ell-1}$ corresponding to digits $d_0, d_1, \ldots, d_{\ell-1}$, respectively. Next, we show two alternatives for finding out d_i from the sample vectors.

3.1   Correlation Attack with Known Precomputations

We assume that the attacker knows P and Π which allows her to compute the precomputed table T. Ideally, the attacker would be able to profile a similar device and use the profile to produce accurate estimates for each value in T, i.e., to launch a template attack (see, e.g., [2,16] for template attacks against ECC). In the following, we consider a model where the attacker only knows T and is able to produce the sample vectors $S_0, S_1, S_2, \ldots, S_{\ell-1}$ from the measurements. The knowledge of T is typically a weak assumption because P is public in many protocols.

---

[2] If R is not randomized in the beginning of Algorithm 1, b is not random and even more powerful attacks are possible by considering also its value recursively during Algorithm 1.

The attacker computes the table T. Based on its values, she calculates an *estimate vector* E^t for each $t \in \mathcal{D}$. In this paper, we consider E^t which are based on the Hamming weights of the words in T, but other methods can be used in a straightforward manner. As discussed above, Ψ uses values from T in M multiplications. Let T_t^m be the value that is used in multiplication m if $d_i = t$. Let $H(T_{t,i}^m)$ denote the Hamming weight of the ith word of T_t^m. We set $e_i^{t,m} = H(T_{t,i}^m)$ and concatenate them with $i = 0, \ldots, N-1$ and $m = 0, \ldots, M-1$ into an estimate vector corresponding to digit value $d_i = t$:

$$E^t = \left(e_0^{t,0}, e_1^{t,0}, \ldots, e_{N-1}^{t,0}, e_0^{t,1}, \ldots, e_{N-1}^{t,1}, \ldots, e_0^{t,M-1}, \ldots, e_{N-1}^{t,M-1} \right). \tag{5}$$

The attacker treats each sample vector S_i individually by computing correlations between S_i and E^t with all $t \in \mathcal{D}$. Her *digit guess* δ_i for the value of d_i is the value t receiving the highest correlation:

$$\delta_i = \arg\max_{t \in \mathcal{D}} (\text{cor}(S_i, E^t)). \tag{6}$$

When all $i = 0, 1, \ldots, \ell-1$ have been analyzed similarly, the attacker has a *scalar guess* $\delta = (\delta_0, \delta_1, \ldots, \delta_{\ell-1})$ and she can compute a trial scalar multiplication $Q' = \kappa P$ with $\kappa = \Delta^{-1}(\delta)$. The attack is successful iff $Q' = Q$.

3.2 Clustering Attack with Unknown Precomputations

We assume that the attacker is not able to construct T, e.g., because she does not know P, or Π produces a randomized table T. Thus, she cannot calculate the estimates E^t and is unable to launch the correlation attack of Sect. 3.1. We assume that the unknown table T remains static for the entire scalar multiplication (e.g., randomization of T happens only in Π). In that case, the same value from T is used in Ψ for two iterations i and j if $d_i = d_j$.

The attacker begins by acquiring sample vectors $S_0, S_1, S_2, \ldots, S_{\ell-1}$ according to (4). She then uses a *clustering algorithm*, which puts each of them into a cluster in $\mathcal{C} = \{1, 2, \ldots, n\}$, and obtains a cluster vector $C = (c_0, c_1, \ldots, c_{\ell-1})$ where $c_i \in \mathcal{C}$. If the clustering was made correctly, then $c_i = c_j$ iff S_i and S_j used the same value from T and, thus, $d_i = d_j$. In this paper, we use unsupervised k-means clustering, but other clustering algorithms can be straightforwardly used and some may lead to better results in practice.

Each cluster in $\mathcal{C}$ represents a digit value in $\mathcal{D}$, but the mapping $\pi : \mathcal{C} \to \mathcal{D}$ is unknown to the attacker. There are in total $n!$ possible mappings and if n is small, the attacker can trial all of them. She iterates over all possible π, finds $\delta = (\pi(c_0), \pi(c_1), \ldots, \pi(c_{\ell-1}))$, and checks if $\kappa = \Delta^{-1}(\delta)$ is equal to k until one of them is successful. If the clustering is correct, this process always returns the correct π. The attacker does not need to know specifics about the implementation of long integer multiplications in order to launch the clustering attack, because she can directly cluster sample vectors without the averaging of (3).

Clustering is a viable attack strategy only when n, the number of possible digits (clusters), is small. First, $n!$ quickly becomes very large which eventually makes finding the correct π impossible. E.g., $n! = 16! \approx 2^{44.25}$ is hard, but possible, to brute-force, but $32! \approx 2^{117.66}$ is already completely impractical. Second, ℓ, the number of digits in d, gets smaller when n and w grow. Hence, n becomes close to ℓ and each digit value appears only few times (or not at all) in d and clustering cannot gain much information about d. While the clustering attack is in general weaker than the correlation attack, it does not make any assumptions about the leakage of a device under attack. Hence, if the leakage model used for constructing E^t is inaccurate, then the clustering attack may outperform the correlation attack.

Clustering has been previously used in side-channel attacks on ECC by Heyszl et al. in [31]. They used it for launching an attack without any profile about the device (a hardware implementation) by clustering repeating patterns in a power trace; i.e., they would cluster the entire trace of Ψ. In our case, the attacker is expected to have more information about the device and its operation as described above, which allows her to use clustering on processed samples.

4   Simulations

We consider the following simulation setup to study the feasibility of the attacks. The simulations were performed with Matlab R2015b. We consider scalar multiplications on NIST P-256 curve with the base point from [44]. We assume that the SPA-resistant w-NAF method from [45] is used so that one precomputes odd multiples $\pm P, \pm 3P, \ldots, \pm(2^w - 1)P$. We experiment with window widths $w = 2, 3, 4, 5$ and word sizes $W = 8, 16$. Because we consider negative points as part of T, the number of points in T is $n = 2^w$ and the table consists of $T_t = tP = (x_t, y_t)$ with $t \in \mathcal{D} = \{\pm 1, \pm 3, \ldots, \pm(2^w - 1)\}$. Digits d_i are drawn uniformly at random from $\mathcal{D}$. The number of digits is $\ell = \lceil 256/w \rceil = 128, 86, 64, 52$ for $w = 2, 3, 4, 5$, respectively.

The transformation Ψ consists of w point doublings followed by a point addition. The point addition $R \leftarrow R + T_{d_i}$ is the interesting part of Ψ. We assume that it is computed using mixed affine-Jacobian coordinates using the algorithm from [28], which is given in Appendix A. This algorithm includes two multiplications, $x_2 \times t_1$ and $y_2 \times t_2$, where x_2 and y_2 are values from T; i.e., $M = 2$.

In the simulations, we construct the sample vectors by deriving a sample value $s_{i,j} = s_{i,j}^{(s)} + s_{i,j}^{(n)}$ for each partial multiplication $a_i \times b_j$. The operand a_i is a W-bit word of a coordinate selected from T by using d_i (x-coordinate for the first multiplication and y-coordinate for the second). The operand b_j is selected uniformly at random from $[0, 2^W - 1]$. The signal part is given by $s_{i,j}^{(s)} = H(a_i \times b_j)$, normalized to zero mean and unit variance ($\sigma_s^2 = 1$). The measurement noise $s_{i,j}^{(n)}$ is white Gaussian noise with variance σ_n^2. The noise level σ_n is incremented in steps of 0.1. The noisy samples $s_{i,j}$ are averaged to $\hat{s}_i$ by using (3). The averaged samples from the two multiplications are concatenated into a sample vector S_i corresponding to digit d_i by using (4). The length of a sample vector S_i is $MN = 2 \cdot \lceil 256/W \rceil$ which gives either 64 or 32 samples for $W = 8$ and $W = 16$, respectively.

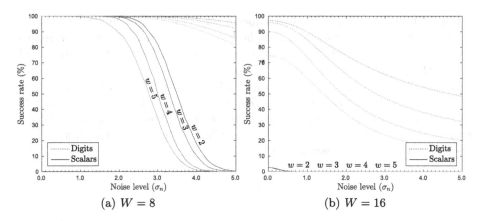

Fig. 1. Results of the simulated correlation attack ($W = 8$ and $W = 16$), averaged from 10,000 scalar multiplications for each noise level.

4.1 Simulated Correlation Attack

The correlation attack is simulated directly as described in Sect. 3.1.

The estimates E^t are constructed by setting

$$E^t = (H(x_{t,0}), H(x_{t,1}), \ldots, H(x_{t,N-1}), H(y_{t,0}), H(y_{t,1}), \ldots, H(y_{t,N-1})), \quad (7)$$

where $x_{t,i}$ and $y_{t,i}$ are i^{th} word of the x and y coordinate of T_t, after which they are normalized to zero mean and unit variance. We use Pearson's linear correlation coefficient as the correlation function in (6).

Figure 1 plots the results of the simulated correlation attack as a function of the noise level σ_n. It shows the *success rates* for individual digits d_i and entire scalars d; i.e., which percentage of digits and ℓ-digit scalars were guessed correctly. The digit success rates are only for evaluating the results of simulations, because in practice the attacker cannot verify the correctness of individual digits. The results are averages from 10,000 scalar multiplications (52,000–128,000 digits depending on the width w) for each noise level.

Figure 1(a) shows that the correlation attack is extremely powerful with $W = 8$ when noise is small: the attack works with 100% success rates for all w. Even high noise does not prevent an attack completely and allows a successful repeated single-trace attack as a consequence. The window width w has a surprisingly small effect on the success rates. This is partly explained by the fact that ℓ gets smaller for larger w which mitigates the effect of a lower digit success rate. On the other hand, Fig. 1(b) shows that the attack almost completely collapses when $W = 16$. We see that attacks are successful only with low noise and, even then, with rather low success rates. However, even low success rates are enough to launch a successful repeated single-trace attack.

The leakage model $s_{i,j}^{(s)} = H(a_i \times b_j)$ used in Fig. 1 is quite pessimistic because the input operands do not have a direct contribution to the leakage, but only through the result of $a_i \times b_j$. Our experiments (see Sect. 5) hint that a has a significantly stronger contribution to the leakage in practice. This motivated us to experiment with a different leakage model. We selected the following model $s_{i,j}^{(s)} = H(a_i \times b_j) + \omega(H(a_i) + H(b_j))$; in this model, the term $H(a_i \times b_j)$ still dominates but a has also a direct contribution through $H(a_i)$ with a weight ω. Results with the alternative leakage model are shown in Fig. 2 for $\omega = 0.5, 0.1$. They show that if $H(a_i)$ contributes to the leakage directly even with a small weight, the correlation attack succeeds with high success rates for all w even if $W = 16$ (except $w = 5$ when $\omega = 0.1$).

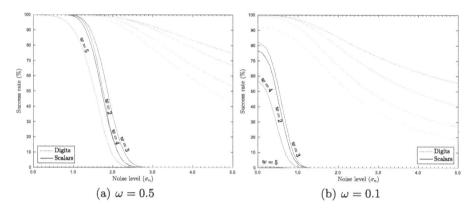

(a) $\omega = 0.5$ (b) $\omega = 0.1$

Fig. 2. Results of the simulated correlation attack ($W = 16$) using the alternative leakage model with (a) $\omega = 0.5$ and (b) $\omega = 0.1$, averaged from 10,000 scalar multiplications for each noise level.

4.2 Simulated Clustering Attack

Simulations of the clustering attack proceed similarly with the simulations of the correlation attack except that instead of computing correlations, we follow the blueprints of Sect. 3.2. In the simulation, we clustered ℓ sample vectors to n clusters by using k-means clustering. We evaluated results of clustering in two ways. For $w \leq 3$, we performed a brute-force search through all $n!$ possible π (see Sect. 3.2). Even if this failed in finding the correct scalar (clustering was erroneous), we found the best π by counting the number of correct digits. For $w = 4$, brute-force is expensive and, hence, we only checked whether clustering was correct, i.e., whether all digits with the same values were clustered into same clusters (if this is the case, then the correct scalar can be found via brute-force). Because we lacked the best π, we did not provide digit success rates for $w = 4$. In reality, the attacker needs to brute-force through $n!$ possibilities in order to find whether the attack was a success. Figure 3 collects results from simulations of 10,000 scalar multiplications per noise level σ_n (in steps of 0.1) for $w = 2, 3, 4$ and $W = 8, 16$. Width $w = 5$ was not simulated because then $n = 32$ and $n!$ prevents the attack in practice (see Sect. 3.2).

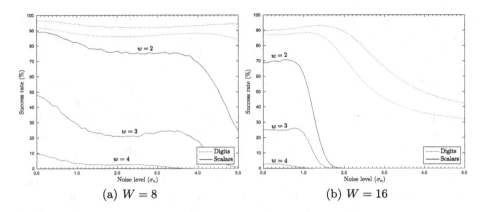

Fig. 3. Results of the simulated clustering attack ($W = 8$ and $W = 16$), averaged from 10,000 scalar multiplications for each noise level.

Figure 3(a) presents the results for $W = 8$ and shows that the clustering attack is successful for every w but w has a significantly larger effect than in the case of the correlation attack. Nevertheless, success rates are non-negligible for all w (excluding $w = 4$ and extreme noise) and (repeated) single-trace attacks are a threat. Noise has a significantly lower effect on the results compared to the correlation attack and the success rates remain flat for much of the noise spectrum. Despite being inferior to the correlation attack with low noise levels, the clustering attack outperforms correlation attack with high noise.

Figure 3(b) shows that the clustering attack succeeds with relatively high success rates even when $W = 16$ if noise is small. Most importantly, it outperforms the correlation attack with a large margin. As discussed in Sect. 4.1, the correlation attack fails to correlate leakage of the form $H(a_i \times b_j)$ with estimates E^t based on the Hamming weights. On the other hand, clustering, which does not rely on a specific leakage model, is significantly more robust in this case. Although success rates of $W = 16$ are surprisingly close to those of $W = 8$ with low noise, higher noise levels prevent a successful attack significantly earlier.

5   Experiments

We selected for our experiments an 8-bit AVR microcontroller in a smart card body, a well-known platform commonly used in academic works to evaluate side channel attacks and countermeasures. Our particular model is an ATMega163 clocked at 4 MHz and containing an 8×8-bit hardware multiplier that executes in two clock cycles. We implemented a semi-unrolled operand-scanning based multi-precision multiplication algorithm in assembly code, but the same results would be obtained, e.g., with product-scanning or operand-caching. Our code runs in constant-time and operates at byte level, i.e. for a word-length $W = 8$. We monitored the power consumption via a 50 Ω shunt resistor in the ground path. The sampling rate of the oscilloscope was set at $250\,\mathrm{MS/s}$. We used the I/O communication interface for triggering and synchronizing measurements.

We recorded traces from 256×256-bit multiplications, where one operand was random and the other was selected from the values of $T = (\pm P, \pm 3P, \pm 5P, \ldots, \pm 15P)$, where P is the NIST P-256 base point [44]. The power measurement traces were pre-processed to extract the points of interest, i.e. the intervals in which partial multiplications $a_i \times b_j$ were computed, by extracting the second cycle of each call to the MUL instruction. We further compressed data by taking the peak value of each clock cycle as a sample $s_{i,j}$ from a partial multiplication.

We emulated scalar multiplications with $w = 2, 3, 4, 5$ using the following procedure. We first selected d by taking $\ell = \lceil 256/w \rceil$ digits uniformly at random from $\mathcal{D} = \{1, 3, \ldots, (2^w - 1)\}$. Then, for all d_i, we constructed a trace representing an emulated point addition $R + T_{d_i}$ so that we randomly drew one trace which used x_{d_i} as an operand from the set of measurements and another which used y_{d_i} as an operand. These represented the interesting operations in Ψ that our attack targets to (see Appendix A). Our emulated trace for one scalar multiplication thus consisted of ℓ such point addition traces built from two multiplication traces. We constructed traces for 200 emulated scalar multiplications using the above procedure by additionally ensuring that one multiplication trace was never used more than once in any of the emulated scalar multiplication traces.

The results of the experiments with emulated scalar multiplications are collected in Table 1. We provide the results of the clustering attack with and without sample averaging of (3). The latter reflects the situation where the attacker does not know the algorithm used for the long integer multiplication (and, thus, cannot use the averaging of (3)). The correlation attack works perfectly for all window widths: it is always capable of finding all 200 scalars d correctly. The clustering attack is also able to find correct scalars with high success rates in every case when samples are averaged with (3). Even without this averaging the clustering attack is able to find at least a few correct scalars from 200 scalar multiplications for every w. Hence, a repeated single-trace attack would succeed in every case with few traces (see Sect. 2).

Table 1. Success rates from 200 emulated scalar multiplications using multiplication traces from the 8-bit AVR.

Window width	n	Correlation attack Digits (%)	Scalars (%)	Clustering attack[a] Digits (%)	Scalars (%)	Clustering attack[a,b] Digits (%)	Scalars (%)
$w = 2$	4	100.00	100.00	97.79	93.50	87.79	61.00
$w = 3$	8	100.00	100.00	96.38	75.00	83.11	11.00
$w = 4$	16	100.00	100.00	n/a	41.50	n/a	2.00
$w = 5$	32	100.00	100.00	n/a	n/a	n/a	n/a

[a] Success rates for $w = 4$ are for correct clustering only
[b] No sample averaging in use (i.e., without (3))

One distinctive observation from the results of Table 1 is that the clustering attack experiments outperform the simulated results shown in Fig. 3(a) even when simulations were performed with zero noise. A logical explanation for this is that the leakage model used in the simulations, where $s_{i,j}^{(s)} = H(a_i \times b_j)$, is too pessimistic. In practice a appears to have a significantly larger effect on the leakage at least in the case of an 8-bit AVR (ATMega163).

6   Countermeasures

Given the results from the simulations and experiments, it is clear that both the correlation and clustering attack are potential threats also in practice. As discussed, e.g., in [5], Coron's three countermeasures against DPA attacks [13] do not offer protection against these single-trace attacks. Hence, more efficient countermeasures are needed in practice. Our attacks can be made significantly more difficult with the same countermeasures as other attacks of the same trend [3,5]. We survey existing countermeasures based on hiding and masking (particularly, from [5,11]) and discuss their effectiveness in the case of our attacks.

6.1   Hiding

The attacks require that the order of partial multiplications (a) is known by the attacker or (b) remains the same for the entire scalar multiplication for the correlation attack and the clustering attack, respectively. Randomizing this order serves as an effective countermeasure against both attacks (and other similar types of attacks). The order can be randomized in multiple ways (see [5] for different options) and the number of permutations can grow up to $N^2!$ [5]. To avoid our attacks, it is essential to randomize the order of a_i in the partial multiplications. This can be done up to $N!$ permutations.

Randomizing the order of partial multiplications can lead to difficulties in efficient implementation of long integer multiplication because of carry propagation when accumulating different partial multiplications. E.g., randomizing the order prevents from using efficient long integer multiplication algorithms such as Comba's product-scanning algorithm [12]. If only the order of partial multiplications corresponding to a specific result word is randomized, then the low number of possible orders for low and high words may still allow successful attacks. Also, the amount of randomness may become a practical problem because the number of multiplications that needs to be randomized in one scalar multiplication is often large. Some of these technical issues were solved in [3].

6.2   Masking

Both attacks require that the table T is static for one scalar multiplication (i.e., it does not change during the for-loop in Algorithm 1). The correlation attack requires that T is known by the attacker, which can be prevented by randomizing the entries of T in $\Pi(P)$, e.g., by randomizing the base point by using Coron's countermeasure from [13]. However, the clustering attack will not be prevented with this because the table remains static for the for-loop and the computations of Ψ. The following masking thwarts both variants of the attack.

Let r be a random value in $\mathbb{F}_q$. Then, we get the (additively) masked precomputed value by computing $a' = a + r$. Multiplications are then computed by first computing $c' = a' \times b$ and second $c = c' - r \times b$. Masking prevents the correlation attack because the attacker does not know the value of a'. The precomputed values must be remasked for every multiplication (or at least several times in each scalar multiplication) to thwart the clustering attack. We must also ensure that b is random; otherwise $r \times b$ may leak sensitive information. This can be achieved, e.g., by randomizing the base point.

Clavier et al. [11] considered a scheme where both operands are masked: $a' = a + r_1$ and $b' = b + r_2$. Then, $c' = a' \times b'$ and $c = c' - a \times r_2 - b \times r_1 - r_1 \times r_2$. This countermeasure does not apply in the case of our attacks: if fresh randomness is used for each multiplication, then it is possible to attack $a \times r_2$ and, if randomization of a is done only in the beginning of a scalar multiplication (in $\Pi(P)$), then there is again no protection against the clustering attack.

Masking comes with a significant performance penalty because M additional multiplications are required in each execution of Ψ. However, M is often small (e.g., two). Another disadvantage is that the countermeasure requires large amounts of randomness ($\ell \cdot M \cdot \lceil \log_2 q \rceil$ bits per scalar multiplication).

7   Conclusions and Future Work

We studied single-trace side-channel attacks against scalar multiplications with precomputations. We presented two alternative approaches: one based on correlations and the other on clustering. We showed that they both pose a practical threat to scalar multiplication algorithms previously considered secure against single-trace attacks. In particular, implementations that use small word sizes are at risk. We demonstrated that it is possible to retrieve secret scalars from multiplications performed with an 8-bit AVR microcontroller (ATMega163). Our simulation results also show that at least implementations on 16-bit processors are potentially at risk. The future work includes studying the practical feasibility of the attacks with experiments on 16-bit and 32-bit processors ($W = 16, 32$).

The simulations show that the correlation attack is sensitive to the type of leakage from the device. Consequently, leakage from integer multiplication should be studied more thoroughly in order to validate the feasibility of the (correlation) attack in processors with larger word sizes.

We considered the correlation and clustering attacks separately but they can be used also as a combination. E.g., the result from a correlation attack can be used as an initial clustering for a clustering attack or used in searching the correct mapping π between clusters and digit values faster than brute-forcing through all possibilities.

If the attacker can select the base point P, then she can make sure that different entries in the table T have distinctive fingerprints (e.g., very low Hamming weights for different words). Such an attack could be seen as an extension of refined power analysis [26] or doubling attack [22] to scalar multiplications with precomputations.

Future work includes research on methods that can find long-term secrets by utilizing partial information about the nonces, similarly to, e.g., [6]. For instance, how could the results of clustering help the attacker, when she knows which digits had same values with high probability (but with some errors in them). The case with correlations seems more straightforward because she can simply fix digits with the highest correlations and use methods similar to [6].

Acknowledgments. Parts of the work of Kimmo Järvinen were done when he was an FWO Pegasus Marie Curie Fellow in KU Leuven ESAT/COSIC and a postdoctoral researcher in Aalto University, Department of Computer Science. Parts of his work were supported by the INSURE project (303578) of Academy of Finland. This work was supported in part by the Research Council KU Leuven (C16/15/058), by the Flemish Government through FWO G.0550.12N, and by the Hercules Foundation AKUL/11/19. We thank Pekka Marttinen from Aalto University for discussions about clustering methods.

A   Point Addition Algorithm

Input: $P_1 = (X_1, Y_1, Z_1)$ and $P_2 = (x_2, y_2)$
Output: $P_3 = (X_3, Y_3, Z_3) = P_1 + P_2$

1 $t_1 \leftarrow Z_1^2$

2 $t_2 \leftarrow t_1 \times Z_1$

3 $t_1 \leftarrow \boxed{x_2 \times t_1}$

4 $t_2 \leftarrow \boxed{y_2 \times t_2}$

5 $t_1 \leftarrow t_1 - X_1$

6 $t_2 \leftarrow t_2 - Y_1$

7 $Z_3 \leftarrow Z_1 \times t_1$

8 $t_3 \leftarrow t_1^2$

9 $t_4 \leftarrow t_3 \times t_1$

10 $t_3 \leftarrow t_3 \times X_1$

11 $t_1 \leftarrow 2t_3$

12 $X_3 \leftarrow t_2^2$

13 $X_3 \leftarrow X_3 - t_1$

14 $X_3 \leftarrow X_3 - t_4$

15 $t_3 \leftarrow t_3 - X_3$

16 $t_3 \leftarrow t_3 \times t_2$

17 $t_4 \leftarrow t_4 \times Y_1$

18 $Y_3 \leftarrow t_3 - t_4$

19 **return** (X_3, Y_3, Z_3)

Algorithm 2. Point addition over $E(\mathbb{F}_p) : y^2 = x^3 - 3x + b$ in affine-Jacobian coordinates [28]. The targeted multiplications are boxed.

References

1. Amiel, F., Feix, B., Villegas, K.: Power analysis for secret recovering and reverse engineering of public key algorithms. In: Adams, C., Miri, A., Wiener, M. (eds.) SAC 2007. LNCS, vol. 4876, pp. 110–125. Springer, Heidelberg (2007). doi:10.1007/978-3-540-77360-3_8

2. Batina, L., Chmielewski, Ł., Papachristodoulou, L., Schwabe, P., Tunstall, M.: Online template attacks. In: Meier, W., Mukhopadhyay, D. (eds.) INDOCRYPT 2014. LNCS, vol. 8885, pp. 21–36. Springer, Cham (2014). doi:10.1007/978-3-319-13039-2_2

3. Bauer, A., Jaulmes, E., Prouff, E., Wild, J.: Horizontal and vertical side-channel attacks against secure RSA implementations. In: Dawson, E. (ed.) CT-RSA 2013. LNCS, vol. 7779, pp. 1–17. Springer, Heidelberg (2013). doi:10.1007/978-3-642-36095-4_1

4. Bauer, A., Jaulmes, E., Prouff, E., Wild, J.: Horizontal collision correlation attack on elliptic curves. In: Lange, T., Lauter, K., Lisoněk, P. (eds.) SAC 2013. LNCS, vol. 8282, pp. 553–570. Springer, Heidelberg (2014). doi:10.1007/978-3-662-43414-7_28

5. Bauer, A., Jaulmes, E., Prouff, E., Reinhard, J.R., Wild, J.: Horizontal collision correlation attack on elliptic curves. Crypt. Commun. **7**(1), 91–119 (2015)

6. Benger, N., Pol, J., Smart, N.P., Yarom, Y.: "Ooh aah.. just a little bit": A small amount of side channel can go a long way. In: Batina, L., Robshaw, M. (eds.) CHES 2014. LNCS, vol. 8731, pp. 75–92. Springer, Heidelberg (2014). doi:10.1007/978-3-662-44709-3_5

7. Bernstein, D.J., Birkner, P., Joye, M., Lange, T., Peters, C.: Twisted Edwards curves. In: Vaudenay, S. (ed.) AFRICACRYPT 2008. LNCS, vol. 5023, pp. 389–405. Springer, Heidelberg (2008). doi:10.1007/978-3-540-68164-9_26

8. Brier, E., Clavier, C., Olivier, F.: Correlation power analysis with a leakage model. In: Joye, M., Quisquater, J.-J. (eds.) CHES 2004. LNCS, vol. 3156, pp. 16–29. Springer, Heidelberg (2004). doi:10.1007/978-3-540-28632-5_2

9. Chevallier-Mames, B., Ciet, M., Joye, M.: Low-cost solutions for preventing simple side-channel analysis: Side-channel atomicity. IEEE Trans. Comput. **53**(6), 760–768 (2004)

10. Chu, D., Großschädl, J., Liu, Z., Müller, V., Zhang, Y.: Twisted Edwards-form elliptic curve cryptography for 8-bit AVR-based sensor nodes. In: Proceedings of the 1st ACM Workshop on Asia Public-key Cryptography – AsiaPKC 2013, pp. 39–44. ACM (2013)

11. Clavier, C., Feix, B., Gagnerot, G., Roussellet, M., Verneuil, V.: Horizontal correlation analysis on exponentiation. In: Soriano, M., Qing, S., López, J. (eds.) ICICS 2010. LNCS, vol. 6476, pp. 46–61. Springer, Heidelberg (2010). doi:10.1007/978-3-642-17650-0_5

12. Comba, P.G.: Exponentiation cryptosystems on the IBM PC. IBM Syst. J. **29**(4), 526–538 (1990)

13. Coron, J.-S.: Resistance against differential power analysis for elliptic curve cryptosystems. In: Koç, Ç.K., Paar, C. (eds.) CHES 1999. LNCS, vol. 1717, pp. 292–302. Springer, Heidelberg (1999). doi:10.1007/3-540-48059-5_25

14. Costello, C., Longa, P.: FourQ: Four-dimensional decompositions on a $\mathbb{Q}$-curve over the Mersenne prime. In: Iwata, T., Cheon, J.H. (eds.) ASIACRYPT 2015. LNCS, vol. 9452, pp. 214–235. Springer, Heidelberg (2015). doi:10.1007/978-3-662-48797-6_10

15. Danger, J.L., Guilley, S., Hoogvorst, P., Murdica, C., Naccache, D.: Improving the big mac attack on elliptic curve cryptography. Cryptology ePrint Archive, Report 2015, 819 (2015)

16. Dugardin, M., Papachristodoulou, L., Najm, Z., Batina, L., Danger, J.-L., Guilley, S.: Dismantling real-world ECC with horizontal and vertical template attacks. In: Standaert, F.-X., Oswald, E. (eds.) COSADE 2016. LNCS, vol. 9689, pp. 88–108. Springer, Cham (2016). doi:10.1007/978-3-319-43283-0_6

17. Fan, J., Verbauwhede, I.: An updated survey on secure ECC implementations: attacks, countermeasures and cost. In: Naccache, D. (ed.) Cryptography and Security: From Theory to Applications. LNCS, vol. 6805, pp. 265–282. Springer, Heidelberg (2012). doi:10.1007/978-3-642-28368-0_18

18. Fan, J., Gao, X., De Mulder, E., Schaumont, P., Preneel, B., Verbauwhede, I.: State-of-the-art of secure ECC implementations: a survey on known side-channel attacks and countermeasures. In: Proceedings of the 2010 IEEE International Symposium on Hardware-Oriented Security and Trust – HOST 2010, pp. 76–87 (2010)

19. Faz-Hernández, A., Longa, P., Sánchez, A.H.: Efficient and secure algorithms for GLV-based scalar multiplication and their implementation on GLV-GLS curves (extended version). J. Cryptographic Eng. **5**(1), 31–52 (2015)
20. Feix, B., Verneuil, V.: There's something about m-ary. In: Paul, G., Vaudenay, S. (eds.) INDOCRYPT 2013. LNCS, vol. 8250, pp. 197–214. Springer, Cham (2013). doi:10.1007/978-3-319-03515-4_13
21. Feng, M., Zhu, B.B., Zhao, C., Li, S.: Signed MSB-set comb method for elliptic curve point multiplication. In: Chen, K., Deng, R., Lai, X., Zhou, J. (eds.) ISPEC 2006. LNCS, vol. 3903, pp. 13–24. Springer, Heidelberg (2006). doi:10.1007/11689522_2
22. Fouque, P.-A., Valette, F.: The doubling attack – Why upwards is better than downwards. In: Walter, C.D., Koç, Ç.K., Paar, C. (eds.) CHES 2003. LNCS, vol. 2779, pp. 269–280. Springer, Heidelberg (2003). doi:10.1007/978-3-540-45238-6_22
23. Galbraith, S.D., Lin, X., Scott, M.: Endomorphisms for faster elliptic curve cryptography on a large class of curves. J. Cryptol. **24**(3), 446–469 (2010)
24. Gallant, R.P., Lambert, R.J., Vanstone, S.A.: Faster point multiplication on elliptic curves with efficient endomorphisms. In: Kilian, J. (ed.) CRYPTO 2001. LNCS, vol. 2139, pp. 190–200. Springer, Heidelberg (2001). doi:10.1007/3-540-44647-8_11
25. Giraud, C., Verneuil, V.: Atomicity improvement for elliptic curve scalar multiplication. In: Gollmann, D., Lanet, J.-L., Iguchi-Cartigny, J. (eds.) CARDIS 2010. LNCS, vol. 6035, pp. 80–101. Springer, Heidelberg (2010). doi:10.1007/978-3-642-12510-2_7
26. Goubin, L.: A refined power-analysis attack on elliptic curve cryptosystems. In: Desmedt, Y.G. (ed.) PKC 2003. LNCS, vol. 2567, pp. 199–211. Springer, Heidelberg (2003). doi:10.1007/3-540-36288-6_15
27. Gura, N., Patel, A., Wander, A., Eberle, H., Shantz, S.C.: Comparing elliptic curve cryptography and RSA on 8-bit CPUs. In: Joye, M., Quisquater, J.-J. (eds.) CHES 2004. LNCS, vol. 3156, pp. 119–132. Springer, Heidelberg (2004). doi:10.1007/978-3-540-28632-5_9
28. Hankerson, D., Menezes, A.J., Vanstone, S.: Guide to Elliptic Curve Cryptography. Springer, New York (2004)
29. Hanley, N., Kim, H.S., Tunstall, M.: Exploiting collisions in addition chain-based exponentiation algorithms using a single trace. In: Nyberg, K. (ed.) CT-RSA 2015. LNCS, vol. 9048, pp. 431–448. Springer, Cham (2015). doi:10.1007/978-3-319-16715-2_23
30. Hedabou, M., Pinel, P., Bénéteau, L.: Countermeasures for preventing comb method against SCA attacks. In: Deng, R.H., Bao, F., Pang, H.H., Zhou, J. (eds.) ISPEC 2005. LNCS, vol. 3439, pp. 85–96. Springer, Heidelberg (2005). doi:10.1007/978-3-540-31979-5_8
31. Heyszl, J., Ibing, A., Mangard, S., Santis, F., Sigl, G.: Clustering algorithms for non-profiled single-execution attacks on exponentiations. In: Francillon, A., Rohatgi, P. (eds.) CARDIS 2013. LNCS, vol. 8419, pp. 79–93. Springer, Cham (2014). doi:10.1007/978-3-319-08302-5_6
32. Heyszl, J., Mangard, S., Heinz, B., Stumpf, F., Sigl, G.: Localized electromagnetic analysis of cryptographic implementations. In: Dunkelman, O. (ed.) CT-RSA 2012. LNCS, vol. 7178, pp. 231–244. Springer, Heidelberg (2012). doi:10.1007/978-3-642-27954-6_15
33. Joye, M.: Highly regular right-to-left algorithms for scalar multiplication. In: Paillier, P., Verbauwhede, I. (eds.) CHES 2007. LNCS, vol. 4727, pp. 135–147. Springer, Heidelberg (2007). doi:10.1007/978-3-540-74735-2_10

34. Joye, M.: Highly regular m-ary powering ladders. In: Jacobson, M.J., Rijmen, V., Safavi-Naini, R. (eds.) SAC 2009. LNCS, vol. 5867, pp. 350–363. Springer, Heidelberg (2009). doi:10.1007/978-3-642-05445-7_22

35. Joye, M., Yen, S.-M.: The montgomery powering ladder. In: Kaliski, B.S., Koç, K., Paar, C. (eds.) CHES 2002. LNCS, vol. 2523, pp. 291–302. Springer, Heidelberg (2003). doi:10.1007/3-540-36400-5_22

36. Koblitz, N.: Elliptic curve cryptosystems. Math. Comput. **48**(177), 203–209 (1987)

37. Liu, Z., Seo, H., Großschädl, J., Kim, H.: Efficient implementation of NIST-compliant elliptic curve cryptography for 8-bit AVR-based sensor nodes. IEEE Trans. Inf. Forensics Secur. **11**(7), 1385–1397 (2016)

38. Liu, Z., Wenger, E., Großschädl, J.: MoTE-ECC: Energy-scalable elliptic curve cryptography for wireless sensor networks. In: Boureanu, I., Owesarski, P., Vaudenay, S. (eds.) ACNS 2014. LNCS, vol. 8479, pp. 361–379. Springer, Cham (2014). doi:10.1007/978-3-319-07536-5_22

39. Miller, V.S.: Use of elliptic curves in cryptography. In: Williams, H.C. (ed.) CRYPTO 1985. LNCS, vol. 218, pp. 417–426. Springer, Heidelberg (1986). doi:10.1007/3-540-39799-X_31

40. Möller, B.: Securing elliptic curve point multiplication against side-channel attacks. In: Davida, G.I., Frankel, Y. (eds.) ISC 2001. LNCS, vol. 2200, pp. 324–334. Springer, Heidelberg (2001). doi:10.1007/3-540-45439-X_22

41. Montgomery, P.L.: Speeding the Pollard and elliptic curve methods of factorization. Math. Comput. **48**(177), 243–264 (1987)

42. Moradi, A., Mischke, O., Eisenbarth, T.: Correlation-enhanced power analysis collision attack. In: Mangard, S., Standaert, F.-X. (eds.) CHES 2010. LNCS, vol. 6225, pp. 125–139. Springer, Heidelberg (2010). doi:10.1007/978-3-642-15031-9_9

43. Nascimento, E., López, J., Dahab, R.: Efficient and secure elliptic curve cryptography for 8-bit AVR microcontrollers. In: Chakraborty, R.S., Schwabe, P., Solworth, J. (eds.) SPACE 2015. LNCS, vol. 9354, pp. 289–309. Springer, Cham (2015). doi:10.1007/978-3-319-24126-5_17

44. National Institute of Standards and Technology (NIST): Digital signature standard (DSS). Federal Information Processing Standard, FIPS PUB 186-4, July 2013

45. Okeya, K., Takagi, T.: The width-w NAF method provides small memory and fast elliptic scalar multiplications secure against side channel attacks. In: Joye, M. (ed.) CT-RSA 2003. LNCS, vol. 2612, pp. 328–343. Springer, Heidelberg (2003). doi:10.1007/3-540-36563-X_23

46. Okeya, K., Takagi, T., Vuillaume, C.: Efficient representations on Koblitz curves with resistance to side channel attacks. In: Boyd, C., González Nieto, J.M. (eds.) ACISP 2005. LNCS, vol. 3574, pp. 218–229. Springer, Heidelberg (2005). doi:10.1007/11506157_19

47. Pessl, P., Hutter, M.: Curved tags – A low-resource ECDSA implementation tailored for RFID. In: Saxena, N., Sadeghi, A.-R. (eds.) RFIDSec 2014. LNCS, vol. 8651, pp. 156–172. Springer, Cham (2014). doi:10.1007/978-3-319-13066-8_10

48. Sinha Roy, S., Järvinen, K., Verbauwhede, I.: Lightweight coprocessor for Koblitz curves: 283-bit ECC including scalar conversion with only 4300 gates. In: Güneysu, T., Handschuh, H. (eds.) CHES 2015. LNCS, vol. 9293, pp. 102–122. Springer, Heidelberg (2015). doi:10.1007/978-3-662-48324-4_6

49. Specht, R., Heyszl, J., Kleinsteuber, M., Sigl, G.: Improving non-profiled attacks on exponentiations based on clustering and extracting leakage from multi-channel high-resolution EM measurements. In: Mangard, S., Poschmann, A.Y. (eds.) COSADE 2014. LNCS, vol. 9064, pp. 3–19. Springer, Cham (2015). doi:10.1007/978-3-319-21476-4_1

50. Szczechowiak, P., Oliveira, L.B., Scott, M., Collier, M., Dahab, R.: NanoECC: Testing the limits of elliptic curve cryptography in sensor networks. In: Verdone, R. (ed.) EWSN 2008. LNCS, vol. 4913, pp. 305–320. Springer, Heidelberg (2008). doi:10.1007/978-3-540-77690-1_19

51. Thériault, N.: SPA resistant left-to-right integer recodings. In: Preneel, B., Tavares, S. (eds.) SAC 2005. LNCS, vol. 3897, pp. 345–358. Springer, Heidelberg (2006). doi:10.1007/11693383_24

52. Walter, C.D.: Sliding windows succumbs to big mac attack. In: Koç, Ç.K., Naccache, D., Paar, C. (eds.) CHES 2001. LNCS, vol. 2162, pp. 286–299. Springer, Heidelberg (2001). doi:10.1007/3-540-44709-1_24

A Compact and Exception-Free Ladder for All Short Weierstrass Elliptic Curves

Ruggero Susella[1(✉)] and Sofia Montrasio[2]

[1] STMicroelectronics, Agrate Brianza, Italy
`ruggero.susella@st.com`
[2] Università degli Studi di Milano, Milan, Italy
`sofia.montrasio@gmail.com`

Abstract. The field of elliptic curve cryptography has recently experienced a deployment of new models of elliptic curves, such as Montgomery or twisted Edwards. Computations on these curves have been proven to be exception-free and easy to make constant-time. Unfortunately many standards define elliptic curves in the short Weierstrass model, where the above properties are harder to achieve. This is especially true when scalar blinding, a simple but widely deployed side-channel attacks countermeasure, is adopted. In this paper we analyze previously undisclosed exceptional cases of popular scalar multiplication algorithms, highlighting the need for proofs of correctness. Then, with the final goal of providing a compact ECC hardware accelerator for embedded platforms, suitable to offload computations on all elliptic curve models, we present a constant-time adaptation of the Montgomery ladder, leveraging addition formulas by Izu and Takagi, that we *prove* return the correct result for *any* input point, *any* scalar value, on *all* elliptic curves in Weierstrass form defined over $\mathbb{F}_p$ with $p \neq 2, 3$.

Keywords: Elliptic curve cryptography · ECC · Scalar multiplication · Montgomery ladder · Exception-free · Constant-time · Scalar blinding

1 Introduction

The main operation of Elliptic Curve Cryptography (ECC) is the scalar multiplication, it is used for Diffie-Hellman key exchange and for digital signature schemes. Despite being, from a theoretical standpoint, a simple operation consisting in adding a point to itself many times, practical implementations might present undesired properties. In recent times several types of side-channel and fault attacks have been deployed to recover from real devices the secret used in the computation. Side-channel attacks (SCA) work by measuring side-channel leakage such as execution time, power consumption or electromagnetic emissions during a cryptographic computation and thanks to statistical analysis are able to recover the secret key. Fault attacks exploit malicious introduction of errors in the cryptographic computation, for example through laser fault injection, to recover the secret [6,14]. This has manifested the importance of being resilient

© Springer International Publishing AG 2017
K. Lemke-Rust and M. Tunstall (Eds.): CARDIS 2016, LNCS 10146, pp. 156–173, 2017.
DOI: 10.1007/978-3-319-54669-8_10

to such attacks. Among the many proposed countermeasures for SCA, for example in [10,21], the simpler, less expensive, and thus more deployed, are: building constant-time implementation, using scalar blinding and/or randomization of the projective coordinates. To protect against fault attacks, common techniques require checking for invariant values during the computation, such as verifying that input and output points belong to the proper subgroup of the expected elliptic curve [6]. Among the various families of elliptic curve scalar multiplication algorithms, in this work we focused on single base algorithms scanning the scalar one bit at a time. The reason to stick to single base is that those using multiple bases are usually used for signature verification, where no secret is involved, thus not requiring protections against SCA and fault attacks. The reason to avoid the use of windowed ladders, those who scan the scalar in windows of more than one bit at a time, relates to the fact that they are more complex as they require a scalar recoding and precomputation phases which add, apart from greater memory requirements, more target points for attacks. It is in fact common practice for secure embedded implementations, such as those targeting smartcards, to use so called *regular ladders*. Most of these algorithms were deployed targeting prime order elliptic curves in short Weierstrass form, furthermore they usually restrict the set of allowed scalars to those smaller than the order of the curve, complicating the usage of the scalar blinding SCA countermeasure.

In recent times, the field of ECC, has seen a strong push for curves in other forms, such as Montgomery or Twisted Edwards. Among some beneficial properties introduced by these forms is the fact that, if properly chosen, Montgomery curves can rely on a very fast ladder proved to work exception-free [2]. Twisted Edwards curves on the other side can rely on a fast and exception-free addition law [4] which makes it easy to build exception-free and constant time scalar multiplication algorithms. One of the drawback of both forms is that they do not allow prime order curves. The issue of supporting these new forms, at least in secure embedded implementations, is that the designer needs at least one secure scalar multiplication algorithm for each form, thus adding complexity and area/code space requirements. An exception-free secure ECC hardware accelerator as generic as possible would be interesting for the implementor. The generic argument could simply mean to support short Weierstrass form, in this model in fact every Montgomery and (twisted) Edwards curve over prime fields can be represented, as well as any future model that might be proposed. Unfortunately, no scalar multiplication algorithm so far has been proved to work exception-free for short Weierstrass curves of any order and for any scalar.

Our Contributions. In this paper we first analyze commonly deployed scalar multiplication algorithms, like the Double-and-add always of Coron [10], the Montgomery ladder of Brier and Joye [8] and the fast Co-Z ladder of Goundar et al. [16], and show that in some cases, particularly when scalars are allowed to be of any size, they fail to compute the correct result. By finding that such commonly deployed algorithms fail to be exception-free, we want to underline the importance for researchers to look for proofs of correctness.

Then we propose a simple and regular ladder, suitable for secure compact hardware implementations, which works without exceptions for all short Weierstrass elliptic curves and any scalar. We also empirically verified this claim through systematic tests on several curves defined over small finite fields.

Specifically our algorithm is a composition of the Bernstein reformulation [3] of the Montgomery ladder [23] with x-only differential addition and doubling formulas by Izu and Takagi [19] followed by an y-recovery by Ebeid and Lambert [13]. We do not claim novelty for the ladder, even though it was never presented in this form, nor we compare its efficiency with the Montgomery ladder or with window-based ladders, but we prove, using a framework similar to Bernstein [2] that our ladder is exception-free.

We also show how our ladder can be used to compute exception-free scalar multiplications for Montgomery curves, thus providing a viable way to use a single implementation for all elliptic curves.

Related Work. A lot of work has been done in the search for a complete addition formula for elliptic curves which would allow to build exception-free scalar multiplication algorithms. A first attempt to a complete addition formula was made in 2002 by Brier and Joye [8, Sect. 3]. Unfortunately, Izu and Takagi found exceptional cases which they exploited in attacks, even on standardized curves [20]. Complete addition laws have been found for non-Weierstrass models, such as (twisted) Edwards [4], but this fact cannot be used to compute over curves of prime order, like the extensively deployed P-256. The most recent contribution is from 2016, when Renes et al. showed complete addition formulas for elliptic curves with odd order [26]. Their formulas are less efficient than incomplete homogeneous or Jacobian formulas and to compute, for example, on curve25519, they require special handling of the input point and the retrieval of the initial y-coordinate through an expensive square root computation.

To the best of our knowledge the first convincing attempt made to prove completeness of a constant-time scalar multiplication algorithm, instead of an addition formula, was done in 2006 by Bernstein [2] and although successful it is limited to Montgomery curves $y^2 = x^3 + Ax^2 + x$ with non-square $A^2 - 4$. Brier and Joye have presented an adaptation of the Montgomery ladder for short Weierstrass curves [8, Sect. 4], this has unknown exceptions that we will explore in Sect. 3. Another example of ladder which comes with a proof is from Bos et al. who in 2014 presented a complete scalar multiplication algorithm for *prime order* short Weierstrass curves [7, Algorithm 1]. Their method also restricts scalars to those smaller than the order of the curve, thus not allowing scalar blinding.

2   Preliminaries

In this paper we will consider only finite fields $\mathbb{K}$ with $char(\mathbb{K}) \neq 2, 3$. An elliptic curve over $\mathbb{K}$ is a non-singular curve defined by an equation E of the form:

$$E : \ y^2 = x^3 + ax + b \text{ with } a, b \in \mathbb{K} \tag{1}$$

Eq. 1, also called short Weierstrass form, is used to represent the most common curves used in ECC; other curves, using a different definition of elliptic curve, e.g. (twisted) Edwards curves have been shown to be birationally equivalent to short Weierstrass. This relation allows to create an invertible map to compute the scalar multiplication in their short Weierstrass equivalent.

$E(\mathbb{K})$, the set of points $(x, y) \in \mathbb{K} \times \mathbb{K}$ satisfying Eq. 1 along with a point at infinity represented by ∞, has an additive group structure where the neutral element is ∞ and the inverse of $P = (x, y)$ is $-P = (x, -y)$.

If $P_1 = (x_1, y_1)$, $P_2 = (x_2, y_2)$ with $P_2 \neq -P_1$, the sum $P_1 + P_2 = (x_3, y_3)$ is:

$$x_3 = \lambda^2 - x_1 - x_2 \text{ and } y_3 = \lambda(x_1 - x_3) - y_1 \tag{2}$$

with $\lambda = \frac{y_2 - y_1}{x_2 - x_1}$ if $P_2 \neq P_1$ and $\lambda = \frac{3x_1^2 + a}{2y_1}$ if $P_2 = P_1$.

In the scalar multiplication a point $Q = (x_Q, y_Q)$ is commonly represented in homogeneous projective coordinates as $(x_Q, y_Q, 1)$. In this way the computation of $n(x_Q, y_Q, 1) = (x, y, z)$ has the advantage of not requiring expensive field inversions, and only at the very end, with just a single field inversion, the affine result $nQ = (x/z, y/z)$ is recovered. The relation between homogeneous and affine coordinates is in fact: $x_Q = x/z$ and $y_Q = y/z$. In the situations where the notation is ambiguous the context will indicate if we are using affine or projective coordinates.

The order of a point divides the cardinality, $\#E(\mathbb{K})$, of the group $E(\mathbb{K})$ which is here the product of a large prime l and a very small *cofactor* h.

Among the countermeasures against Differential Power Analysis (DPA) we highlight here *Scalar blinding* and *Coordinates randomization*. The first one is the substitution of the scalar n with $n' = n + rl$, where l is the order of the input point and $r \in \mathbb{N}$ is a random integer of the form $r = 2^c \cdot o$, where o is odd. The second method uses the equivalence in homogeneous projective coordinates between (x, y, z) and (rx, ry, rz) and before each new scalar multiplication randomizes the coordinates of the input point using the random value $r \in \mathbb{K}^*$.

3   Review of Common Scalar Multiplication Algorithms

In this section we look at some well known and commonly deployed scalar multiplication algorithms: Coron's Double-and-add always, Brier and Joye's Montgomery ladder and Goundar et al. Co-Z Montgomery ladder. We will show that these algorithms are not exception-free. Note that to simplify the description, in this section, we define a point to be ∞ if its z-coordinate is 0 without caring about the other coordinates.

3.1   Double-and-Add Always

Coron in 1999 presented his famous Double-and-add always ladder [10], resistant against simple power analysis, shown here as Algorithm 1. Unfortunately addition laws for short Weierstrass curves have exceptional cases. The main issue of incomplete addition laws is that unexpectedly $P + \infty = \infty$, thus if the accumulating variable of the ladder ($R[0]$) becomes equal to ∞, the final result will be ∞.

Line 3 in fact will produce $R[0] = 2R[0] = \infty$ if $\mathrm{ord}(R[0]) = 2$ (or $R[0] = \infty$). Line 4 will produce $R[1] = R[0] + Q = \infty$ if $R[0] = \pm Q$ (or $R[0] = \infty$). We verified that these exceptions are present with all jacobian and homogeneous mixed additions formulas of [5]. These exceptions explain why Algorithm 1 initializes $R[0] = Q$ in line 1, instead of using ∞, thus a first exception of this ladder happens when $n = 0$ and the ladder incorrectly returns Q. This initialization also makes the execution time dependent on the number of leading zeros in the binary representation of n. It is common practice to solve this last issue by adding l or $2l$ to n, as suggested in [7,9], but we believe that this adds unneeded complexity to the algorithm.

We now consider the exceptions for points of small order. If Q has order 2 the ladder will fail for all odd $n > 1$, because line 3 will produce an $R[0] = \infty$, which is correct by itself, but then line 4 will subsequently fail, causing the error in the result. If, instead, Q has order 3 then line 4 will make $R[1] = \infty$, if in line 5 $R[1]$ is assigned to $R[0]$ the result will be ∞. This is an incorrect result for all n not multiple of 3 with Hamming weight greater than 1.

Finally, there are exceptions even for points of large prime order, although only when $n > l$ as in the case of applying scalar blinding (replacing n with $n' = n + rl$ with a random r writable as $r = 2^c o$), which was presented by Coron in the same paper, without any mention of exceptional cases. Algorithm 1 is exceptional when $n \in \{1, 2, \ldots, 2^c - 1\}$ for $c > 0$ because the most significant part of n' becomes $o \cdot l$ so $R[0]$ becomes ∞. It is also exceptional for $n \in \{2 \cdot 2^c, 2 \cdot 2^c + 1, \ldots, 3 \cdot 2^c - 1\}$ for all c because line 3 will eventually compute $R[0] = 2\left(\frac{o \cdot l + 1}{2}Q\right) = Q$ and line 4 will then add Q to it, causing the failure of the incomplete addition.

The only solution to make Algorithm 1 exception-free is to modify the addition to correctly handle exceptions. Unfortunately, since no complete addition formula is known to work for all short Weierstrass curves, possible solutions are to call the doubling when input points are equal or to use *masking* techniques like [7, Algorithms 18, 19]. The first method will break the constant-time property while the second one will introduce dummy operations which are vulnerable to some attacks [28]. It is therefore more secure to avoid both.

Algorithm 1. Double-and-add always ladder	**Algorithm 2.** Brier-Joye's ladder
Input: $Q \in E(\mathbb{F}_p)$, $n = (n_{t-1}, .., n_0)_2$ **Output:** nQ	**Input:** $Q \in E(\mathbb{F}_p)$ and $n = (n_{t-1}, ..., n_0)_2$ **Output:** $X(nQ)$
1: $R[0] = Q$ 2: **for** $i = t - 2$ down to 0 **do** 3: $R[0] \leftarrow 2R[0]$ 4: $R[1] \leftarrow R[0] + Q$ 5: $R[0] \leftarrow R[n_i]$ 6: **return** $R[0]$	1: $R[0] = Q; R[1] = 2Q$ 2: **for** $i = t - 2$ down to 0 **do** 3: **if** $(n_i = 0)$ **then** 4: $x(R[1]) \leftarrow x(R[0] + R[1])$ 5: $x(R[0]) \leftarrow x(2R[0])$ 6: **else** $x(R[0]) \leftarrow x(R[0] + R[1])$ 7: $x(R[1]) \leftarrow x(2R[1])$ 8: **return** $x(R[0])$

We want to underline that, when scalars are allowed to be larger than l, all Double-and-add algorithms with incomplete addition law suffer from the above issue, as some scalar values will force them to compute the addition (not through doubling) of $Q + Q$.

3.2   Brier and Joye Montgomery Ladder

Brier and Joye in 2002 presented a variant of the Montgomery ladder for short Weierstrass elliptic curve [8], shown here in Algorithm 2. The ladder, like the Double-and-add Always, would leak, through timing, the number of leading zeros of the scalar. But, unlike in the previous case, this ladder allows to be initialized with $R[0] = \infty; R[1] = Q$, so that it can iterate for a constant number of times, thus solving the issue without adding unneeded complexity.

Notice that the authors provide proofs of the validity of their addition law, and that furthermore the ladder is extensively believed to work exception-free, see for example [26, Sect. 1]. Unfortunately, their proof fails to consider the exceptional case when x_Q, the x-coordinate of Q is 0. This can be clearly seen from their formula for the x-coordinate differential addition:

$$x(R[0] + R[1]) = \frac{-4b(x_0 + x_1) + (x_0 x_1 - a)^2}{x_Q(x_0 - x_1)^2} \tag{3}$$

If $x_Q = 0$ the output of the differential addition will always have $z = 0$, causing the ladder to return ∞, for every scalar. In short Weierstrass curves, if b is a non-zero square in the field there are two points with $x = 0$; this happens even for standardized prime order elliptic curves such as NIST curves P-256, P-384 and P-521. The Brier-Joye ladder is therefore exceptional.

3.3   Co-Z Montgomery Ladder

In 2011 Goundar et al. presented several ladders using the Co-Z arithmetic originally proposed by Meloni. We focus our attention on algorithm 15 of [16, Sect. 5.2.1] named "Montgomery ladder with (X,Y)-only co-Z addition formulæ" because it is the asymptotically fastest ladder for short Weierstrass curves known today. As in the case of the Double-and-add Always, this ladder leaks the number of leading zeroes of the scalar, and must be modified in the same way to achieve constant-time execution. Moreover, like in the case of the Brier-Joye ladder, the Co-Z ladder is exceptional if $x_Q = 0$ because the recovered z is defined as $x_Q y(...)$ and in this case becomes automatically 0, giving as output ∞.

If we consider exceptions on scalar values, then in the range of $[0, l]$ the problems are $0, 1$ and $l - 1$. In fact, if $n = 0$ the ladder returns $2Q$, if $n = 1$ it returns $3Q$ and if $n = l - 1$ it returns ∞. The first two cases depend on the definition inside the function $DBLU'$ of the two initial points Q and $2Q$, while in the last one the problem is that $R[0] = (l - 1)Q$ has the same z as $R[1] = lQ = \infty$. The usage of scalar blinding creates additional exceptional cases. The Co-Z ladder in fact returns ∞ when $n \in \{1, 2, \ldots, 2^c - 1\}$ for all $c > 0$ and $n \in \{l - 1, \ldots, l - 2^c\}$ for all c. This ladder has therefore several exceptions.

4   Exception-Free Ladder

In this section we present Algorithm 3, our exception-free (x, y)-ladder, which is the core of this paper. This is divided in two parts: the Montgomery ladder and the y-recovery. The Montgomery ladder uses the additive x-only formulas derived by Izu and Takagi [19] which eliminate the exception $x_Q = 0$ of the formulas in Sect. 3.2 at basically the same cost. Then a procedure based on a formula of Ebeid and Lambert [13] is used to recover the y-coordinate.
Notice five aspects of Algorithm 3:

1. It takes in input and returns (x, y) *and* a flag f. The flag allows to distinguish a valid affine point from ∞. We note that Montgomery ladder on Montgomery curves encodes ∞ into $(0,0)$, which corresponds to a 2-torsion point and avoids to distinguish the two. But this cannot be done on generic curves and we need a flag to make the distinction with valid affine points.
2. It has no conditional branches and the loop is iterated a fixed number of times, independent of the scalar value.
3. In the presented form it has conditional assignments based on the scalar bit. However it is trivial to modify it to use the *cswap* function as done in [3] to make it constant-time even for software implementations.
4. The algorithm, written in this way, takes in input also a random value $r \in \mathbb{F}_p^*$ for coordinates randomization. If the user is not interested in this counter-measure he can spare the two field multiplications in the initialization.
5. Inside the main loop no dummy operation occurs. This avoids some type of safe-error attacks such those in [28]. Dummy operations occur after the main loop but these depend only on the result of the main loop, which is considered known to the attacker, thus no secret can be recovered through safe-error attacks on these dummy operations.

Using the same framework of [2, Appendix B] we state and prove that the Izu and Takagi formulas are exceptional only if both x and z input coordinates are 0. Then we will show in Theorem 3 that our ladder never satisfies such condition and thus provides the correct result for all input points and scalar values. Note that in this paper it x/it z means the quotient of x and z in $\mathbb{F}_p$ if $z \neq 0$; it means ∞ if $x \neq 0$ and $z = 0$; it is undefined if $x = z = 0$.

Theorem 1 (Doubling). *Let p be a prime number with $p \geq 5$. Define E as the non-singular short Weierstrass elliptic curve $y^2 = x^3 + ax + b$ over $\mathbb{F}_p$. Define $X : E(\mathbb{F}_{p^2}) \rightarrow \{\infty\} \cup \mathbb{F}_{p^2}$ as follows: $X(\infty) := \infty, X(x, y) := x$. Defining:*

$$x_2 := (x^2 - az^2)^2 - 8bxz^3 \qquad and \qquad z_2 := 4z(x^3 + axz^2 + bz^3)$$

for fixed $x, z \in \mathbb{F}_p$ with $(x, z) \neq (0,0)$. Then $X(2Q) = \frac{x_2}{z_2}$ and $(x_2, z_2) \neq (0,0) \in \mathbb{F}_p \times \mathbb{F}_p$ for all $Q \in E(\mathbb{F}_{p^2})$ s.t. $X(Q) = \frac{x}{z}$.

Algorithm 3. Proposed Montgomery Ladder

Input: $p, a, b, n, x_Q, y_Q, f, r, m$. Where: $p \geq 5$ is a prime of bit-size s.
$a, b \in \mathbb{F}_p$ define $E(\mathbb{F}_p)$. The scalar is $n = (n_{t-1}, ..., n_0)_2 = \sum_{i=0}^{t-1} 2^i n_i \in \mathbb{N}$.
$Q \in E(\mathbb{F}_p)$ is the input base point of the scalar multiplication.
f is a flag $\in \{0, 1\}$, s.t. if $f = 1$ then $Q = (x_Q, y_Q)$ with $x_Q, y_Q \in \mathbb{F}_p$ else $Q = \infty$.
r is an optional randomization value $\in \mathbb{F}_p^*$. The algorithm processes $m \in \mathbb{N}$ bits of n,
independently of the value of n, with the only requirement of m being $\geq t$.
Output: x, y, f s.t. if $f = 0$ then $nQ = \infty$ else $nQ = (x, y)$
$\qquad\qquad\qquad\qquad$ ▷ All operations, except lines 11, 16 are performed modulo p

1: **function** PROPOSED-LADDER$(p, a, b, n, x_Q, y_Q, f, r = 1, m = \lceil \log_2(\#E(\mathbb{F}_p)) \rceil)$
2: $\quad x_0, z_0, x_1, z_1 \leftarrow 1, 0, x_Q \cdot r, f \cdot r$
3: $\quad$ **for** $i = m - 1$ down to 0 **do** $\qquad\qquad$ ▷ Note: m can be arbitrary big
4: $\qquad d \leftarrow n_i$ $\qquad\qquad\qquad\qquad\qquad$ ▷ $n_i = 0$ for $i \in [m - 1, t - 1)$
5: $\qquad x_{\neg d}, z_{\neg d} \leftarrow 2(x_d z_{\neg d} + x_{\neg d} z_d)(x_d x_{\neg d} + a z_d z_{\neg d}) + 4b z_d^2 z_{\neg d}^2$
$\qquad\qquad\qquad\qquad -x_Q(x_d z_{\neg d} + x_{\neg d} z_d)^2, \; (x_d z_{\neg d} - x_{\neg d} z_d)^2$
6: $\qquad x_d, z_d \leftarrow (x_d^2 - a z_d^2)^2 - 8b x_d z_d^3, \; 4(x_d z_d(x_d^2 + a z_d^2) + b z_d^4)$
7: $\qquad y_0 \leftarrow -y_Q z_0$ $\qquad\qquad\qquad\qquad\qquad$ ▷ Notice that $y_0/z_0 = -y_Q$
8: $\qquad x_0' \leftarrow 2 y_Q x_0 z_1 z_0$ $\qquad\qquad\qquad$ ▷ Use formulas from Lemma 1 for y-recovery
9: $\qquad y_0' \leftarrow 2b z_1 z_0^2 + z_1(a z_0 + x_Q x_0)(x_Q z_0 + x_0) - x_1(x_Q z_0 - x_0)^2$
10: $\qquad z_0' \leftarrow 2 y_Q z_1 z_0^2$
11: $\qquad f \leftarrow \mathbb{Z}(2^s - 1 + z_1) \gg s$ $\qquad\qquad$ ▷ $f = 1 \iff z_1 \neq 0$ else $f = 0$
12: $\qquad x = x_0 - f(x_0 - x_0')$ $\qquad\qquad$ ▷ $x = x_0' \iff z_1 \neq 0$ else $x = x_0$
13: $\qquad y = y_0 - f(y_0 - y_0')$ $\qquad\qquad$ ▷ $y = y_0' \iff z_1 \neq 0$ else $y = y_0$
14: $\qquad z = z_0 - f(z_0 - z_0')$ $\qquad\qquad$ ▷ $z = z_0' \iff z_1 \neq 0$ else $z = z_0$
15: $\qquad x, y \leftarrow x z^{p-2}, y z^{p-2}$ $\qquad\qquad\qquad\qquad$ ▷ get affine values
16: $\qquad f \leftarrow \mathbb{Z}(2^s - 1 + z) \gg s$ $\qquad$ ▷ where $\mathbb{Z}(x)$ means that x is evaluated in $\mathbb{Z}$
17: $\qquad$ **return** x, y, f $\qquad\qquad$ ▷ $f = 0 \iff nQ = \infty$ else $(f = 1$ and $nQ = (x, y))$

Proof. As in [2] we analyze all possible cases:

Case 1. $z = 0$. This implies $x \neq 0$ because $(x, z) \neq (0, 0)$. We notice that $x_2 = x^4 \neq 0$ and $z_2 = 0$. Also $X(Q) = \frac{x}{0} = \infty$ so $Q = \infty$ and $2Q = \infty$. Then for definition of X, $X(2Q) = \infty = \frac{x_2}{0} = \frac{x_2}{z_2}$.

Case 2. $z \neq 0$. In this case $Q = (\frac{x}{z}, y)$ for some $y \in \mathbb{F}_{p^2}$ such that $y^2 = (\frac{x}{z})^3 + a(\frac{x}{z}) + b$. Multiplying this equation by $4z^4$, which is nonzero, we obtain $4y^2 z^4 = 4(x^3 z + a x z^3 + b z^4)$ which corresponds to z_2. Now we need to make a distinction between the cases $y^2 = 0$ and $y^2 \neq 0$.

Case 2.1. $z \neq 0$ and $y^2 \neq 0$. Knowing that $z_2 = 4y^2 z^4$ we need to verify if $x_2 = 4y^2 z^4 \cdot X(2Q)$ holds. Replacing $X(2Q)$ with Eq. 2 we get:

$$4y^2 z^4 \cdot X(2Q) = 4y^2 z^4 \cdot \left[\frac{(3(\frac{x}{z})^2 + a)^2 - 8(\frac{x}{z})y^2}{4y^2} \right] = z^4 \left[(3(\frac{x}{z})^2 + a)^2 - 8(\frac{x}{z})y^2 \right]$$

Solving and substituting y^2 with $y^2 = (\frac{x}{z})^3 + a(\frac{x}{z}) + b$ we obtain: $(x^2 - az^2)^2 - 8bxz^3$ which corresponds to our definition of x_2. It is interesting to note that $x = 0$ is not a special case.

Case 2.2. $z \neq 0$ and $y^2 = 0 \implies x^3 + axz^2 + bz^3 = 0 \implies z_2 = 0$. In this case $Q = (\frac{x}{z}, 0)$ has order two, i.e. $2Q = \infty$. If we show that $x_2 \neq 0$ then $X(2Q) = \infty = \frac{x_2}{0} = \frac{x_2}{z_2}$ and we are done. To prove that $x_2 \neq 0$, we first note that:

$$x^3 + axz^2 + bz^3 = 0 \implies bz^3 = -x^3 - axz^2$$

Replacing bz^3 in $x_2 := (x^2 - az^2)^2 - 8bxz^3$ we get $x_2 = (3x^2 + az^2)^2$ which is 0 iff $az^2 = -3x^2$, substituting az^2 with $-3x^2$ in $x^3 + axz^2 + bz^3 = 0$ we obtain: $\frac{x}{z} = \sqrt[3]{\frac{b}{2}}$. Hence by imposing $x_2 = 0$ and $y^2 = 0$, we have a point of the form $Q = (\sqrt[3]{b/2}, 0)$. Forcing Q to satisfy Eq. 1 we obtain the following relation between a and b: $\frac{b}{2} + a\sqrt[3]{\frac{b}{2}} + b = 0 \implies a = -\frac{3}{2}b\sqrt[3]{\frac{2}{b}} \implies 4a^3 = 4\left(-\frac{27}{8}b^3\frac{2}{b}\right) = -27b^2$. But this contradicts the non-singularity condition $\Delta = -16(4a^3 + 27b^2)$ of the curve, therefore there is no such point Q, so $x_2 \neq 0$.

Note that $x = 0$ presents no issues in this case too. In fact we would obtain $x_2 = a^2z^4$ which is null iff $a = 0$, but this would imply $y^2 = b = 0$, which would again violate the non-singularity condition. $\qquad\square$

Theorem 2 (Differential Addition). *Let p be a prime number with $p \geq 5$. Define E as the non-singular short Weierstrass elliptic curve $y^2 = x^3 + ax + b$ over $\mathbb{F}_p$. Define $X : E(\mathbb{F}_{p^2}) \to \{\infty\} \cup \mathbb{F}_{p^2}$ as follows: $X(\infty) := \infty$, $X(x, y) := x$. Fix $x, z, x', z', x_1, z_1 \in \mathbb{F}_p$ with $(x, z) \neq (0,0)$, $(x', z') \neq (0,0)$ and $z_1 \neq 0$. Define:*

$$x_3 := \left[2\left(xz' + x'z\right)\left(xx' + azz'\right) + 4b\left(zz'\right)^2\right]z_1 - x_1\left(xz' - x'z\right)^2$$

$$z_3 := z_1\left(xz' - x'z\right)^2$$

Then $X(Q + Q') = \frac{x_3}{z_3}$ for all $Q, Q' \in E(\mathbb{F}_{p^2})$ such that $X(Q) = \frac{x}{z}$, $X(Q') = \frac{x'}{z'}$, $X(Q - Q') = \frac{x_1}{z_1}$ and $(x_3, z_3) \neq (0, 0) \in \mathbb{F}_p \times \mathbb{F}_p$.

Proof. Let's again analyze all possible cases:

Case 1. $Q = Q'$. Then $X(Q - Q') = X(\infty) = \infty$, so $z_1 = 0$, contradiction.

Case 2. $Q = \infty$. Then $z = 0$ and $x \neq 0$; also $X(Q - Q') = X(-Q') = X(Q') = \frac{x'}{z'}$, so $\frac{x_1}{z_1} = \frac{x'}{z'}$ and consequently $z' \neq 0$. Under the assumption $z = 0$, $x_3 = 2\left(xz'\right)\left(xx'\right)z_1 - x_1\left(xz'\right)^2$ and $z_3 = z_1\left(xz'\right)^2$, then $\frac{x_3}{z_3} = 2\left(\frac{x'}{z'}\right) - \left(\frac{x_1}{z_1}\right) = \frac{x'}{z'} = X(Q') = X(Q + Q')$ as wanted.

Case 3. $Q' = \infty$. Then $z' = 0$ and $x' \neq 0$; also $X(Q - Q') = X(Q) = \frac{x}{z}$, so $\frac{x_1}{z_1} = \frac{x}{z}$ and consequently $z \neq 0$. Given that $z' = 0$ we have $x_3 = 2\left(x'z\right)\left(xx'\right)z_1 - x_1\left(x'z\right)^2$ and $z_3 = z_1\left(x'z\right)^2$. Then, similarly to the previous case: $\frac{x_3}{z_3} = 2\left(\frac{x}{z}\right) - \left(\frac{x_1}{z_1}\right) = \frac{x}{z} = X(Q) = X(Q + Q')$.

Case 4. $Q = -Q'$. Here $X(Q) = X(-Q') = X(Q')$, so $\frac{x}{z} = \frac{x'}{z'}$ and $xz' = x'z$. Assuming now both $z, z' \neq 0$, then $z_3 = 0$. Suppose that $x_3 = 0$, knowing that

$z_1 \neq 0$ it means $4\,(xz')\,(xx' + azz') + 4b\,(zz')^2 = 0$, which dividing by $4\,(zz')^2$ becomes $\left(\frac{x}{z}\right)^3 + \left(\frac{x}{z}\right)a + b = 0$. This implies $Q = \left(\frac{x}{z}, 0\right) = Q'$ and a contradiction as in Case 1. Thus $x_3 \neq 0$ and $\frac{x_3}{z_3} = \infty = X\,(\infty) = X\,(Q + Q')$.

Case 5. $Q \neq \infty$, $Q' \neq \infty$, $Q \neq Q'$ and $Q \neq -Q'$. Then $\frac{x}{z} \neq \frac{x'}{z'}$ so $z_3 \neq 0$. Also $Q = \left(\frac{x}{z}, y\right)$ and $Q' = \left(\frac{x'}{z'}, y'\right)$ for some $y, y' \in \mathbb{F}_{p^2}$ such that $y^2 = \left(\frac{x}{z}\right)^3 + a\left(\frac{x}{z}\right) + b$ and $(y')^2 = \left(\frac{x'}{z'}\right)^3 + a\left(\frac{x'}{z'}\right) + b$. We now define $\alpha := \frac{x'}{z'} - \frac{x}{z} \neq 0$ and $\beta := \frac{x'}{z'} + \frac{x}{z}$. Using Eq. 2 we obtain: $X\,(Q + Q') = \frac{(y'-y)^2}{\alpha^2} - \beta$ and $X\,(Q - Q') = \frac{(-y'-y)^2}{\alpha^2} - \beta$. So $X\,(Q + Q') + X\,(Q - Q') = 2\left(\frac{(y')^2 + y^2}{\alpha^2} - \beta\right)$. Replacing $(y')^2$ and y^2 we get:
$$X\,(Q + Q') + X\,(Q - Q') = \frac{2\left(xz' + x'z\right)\left(xx' + azz'\right) + 4b\left(zz'\right)^2}{(xz' - x'z)^2}.$$
The statement follows remembering that $X\,(Q - Q') = \frac{x_1}{z_1}$. □

Before proving the correctness of Algorithm 3, we present the y-recovery procedure used in lines 7–14 of Algorithm 3 which also deals, in constant time, with the exceptional case of z_1 being null at the end of the loop. Note that, although the hypotheses of Lemma 1 exclude points of order two, at the end of the proof of Theorem 3 we will show they will not cause exceptions.

Lemma 1 (y-recovery). *Define X as in previous theorems. Let $Q, R\,[0]\,, R\,[1] \in E(F_p) \setminus \infty$ s.t. $R\,[0] = nQ$, $R\,[1] = R[0] + Q$ with $Q = (x_Q, y_Q)$, $X\,(R[0]) = \frac{x_0}{z_0}$ and $X\,(R[1]) = \frac{x_1}{z_1}$. Defining:*
$$x'_0 := 2y_Q x_0 z_1 z_0$$
$$y'_0 := 2b z_1 z_0^2 + z_1(az_0 + x_Q x_0)(x_Q z_0 + x_0) - x_1(x_Q z_0 - x_0)^2$$
$$z'_0 := 2y_Q z_1 z_0^2$$
then $z'_0 \neq 0$ and $R[0] = \left(\frac{x'_0}{z'_0}, \frac{y'_0}{z'_0}\right)$.

See Appendix B for the proof of Lemma 1.

Theorem 3 (Algorithm 3 is Exception-Free). *Define $XY_1 : E(\mathbb{F}_p) \to \mathbb{F}_p \times \mathbb{F}_p \times \{0,1\}$ as $XY_1(\infty) := (0,0,0)$, $XY_1(x,y) := (x,y,1)$. Let $Q \in E(\mathbb{F}_p)$ be the input point of the scalar multiplication, let $f \in \{0,1\}$ be a flag s.t. if $f = 0$ then $Q = \infty$ otherwise $Q = (x_Q, y_Q)$, with $x_Q, y_Q \in \mathbb{F}_p$, then Algorithm 3 correctly returns $XY_1(nQ)$ for every $n \in \mathbb{N}$.*

Proof. It is convenient in the proof to keep the values of intermediate points calculated by the ladder, even if only the x and z coordinates are actually computed. Referring to Algorithm 3 we call $R\,[0]_0 = \infty$ and $R\,[1]_0 = Q$ the two initial points. Line 5 can be seen as $R\,[\neg d] = (R\,[d] + R\,[\neg d])$ with $XZ(R\,[\neg d]) := (x_{\neg d}, z_{\neg d})$ where $d \in \{0,1\}$ and line 6 as $R\,[d] = 2R\,[d]$ with $XZ(R\,[d]) := (x_d, z_d)$.

The loop on the sequence of bits composing the scalar n produces a sequence of couples: $(R\,[0]\,, R\,[1])_1\,, (R\,[0]\,, R\,[1])_2\,, ..., (R\,[0]\,, R\,[1])_m$.

We now prove, by induction on j, where $j = m - i$ represents the jth iteration of the loop, that with $f = 1$ the following conditions hold:

$$(x_{0,j}, z_{0,j}) = XZ(R[0]_j) = XZ(\text{MSB}_j(n)Q) \text{ with } (x_{0,j}, z_{0,j}) \neq (0,0)$$

$$\text{and } R[1]_j = R[0]_j + Q \; \forall j \in 1, 2, ..., m$$

where $\text{MSB}_j(n)$ indicates the j most significant bits of the scalar n, with $j \leq$ bit-size(n). Let's start by the first iteration, $j = 1$:

Case 1. $d = 0$. We first notice that $R[0]_1 = 2(R[0]_0) = \infty = 0Q = \text{MSB}_j(n)Q$ and $(x_{0,1}, z_{0,1}) = XZ(R[0]_1) = XZ(2R[0]_0) = (1,0)$ due to the definition of x_0, z_0; so $(x_{0,1}, z_{0,1}) \neq (0,0)$. Since $R[0]_1 = \infty$ it is trivial to see that $R[1]_1 = R[0]_1 + Q$ as in the second condition.

Case 2. $d = 1$. Here $R[0]_1 = R[0]_0 + R[1]_0 = Q = \text{MSB}_j(n)Q$ and by definition $(x_{0,1}, z_{0,1}) = XZ(R[0]_1) = (x_Q \cdot r, r) \neq (0,0)$. Then $R[1]_1 = 2R[1]_0 = 2Q$ so $R[1]_1 - R[0]_1 = 2Q - Q = Q$ as expected.

Now we suppose this holds for iteration j and prove it for $j + 1$. Again we have two cases, depending on the value of bit d in iteration j:

Case 1. $d = 0$. In this case $(x_{0,j+1}, z_{0,j+1}) = XZ(R[0]_{j+1}) = XZ(2R[0]_j) = XZ(2\text{MSB}_j(n)Q) = XZ(\text{MSB}_{j+1}(n)Q) \neq (0,0)$ by Theorem 1.
Using the second condition we also have $R[1]_{j+1} = R[1]_j + R[0]_j = 2R[0]_j + Q = R[0]_{j+1} + Q$.

Case 2. $d = 1$. Here $(x_{0,j+1}, z_{0,j+1}) = XZ(R[0]_{j+1}) = XZ(R[0]_j + R[1]_j) = XZ(2R[0]_j + Q) = XZ((2\text{MSB}_j(n) + 1)Q) = X(\text{MSB}_{j+1}(n)Q)$ with $(x_{0,j+1}, z_{0,j+1}) \neq (0,0)$ by Theorem 2, using the fact that the difference between the two points is always Q which has $z_Q \neq 0$.
Also here $R[1]_{j+1} = 2R[1]_j = 2R[0]_j + 2Q = R[0]_{j+1} + Q$ as expected.

In the end when $j = m$ (the output case) the conditions become:

$$(x_{0,m}, z_{0,m}) = XZ(R[0]_m) = XZ(\text{MSB}_m(n)Q) = XZ(nQ)$$

$$\text{with } (x_{0,m}, z_{0,m}) \neq (0,0)$$

We now simplify the naming removing the index m which is implied hereafter. In line 7 $y_0 = -y_Q z_0$ is calculated and in lines 8–10 x_0', y_0', z_0' are calculated as per Lemma 1. Then lines 11–14 select, in constant-time, based on the value of z_1 whether x, y, z take the value of x_0, y_0, z_0 (when $z_1 = 0$) or the value of x_0', y_0', z_0' (when $z_1 \neq 0$). After this, the algorithm uses x, y, z to compute $XY_1(nQ)$ where it returns $(0,0,0)$ if $z = 0$ else $(\frac{x}{z}, \frac{y}{z}, 1)$. This last step is done in lines 15–16. We still have to show that $z = 0 \iff nQ = \infty$ and otherwise $(\frac{x}{z}, \frac{y}{z}) = nQ$. We, as the algorithm, need to distinguish the following two cases on z_1:

Case 1. $z_1 \neq 0$ so $x, y, z = x_0', y_0', z_0'$. Here $R[1] = R[0] + Q \neq \infty$. If $R[0] \neq \infty$ also holds, then $(\frac{x}{z}, \frac{y}{z}) = nQ$ with $z \neq 0$ by Lemma 1. Otherwise if $z_0 = 0$ then $nQ = R[0] = \infty$ but also $z = z_0' = 0$ as expected.

Case 2. $z_1 = 0$ so $x, y, z = x_0, y_0, z_0$. In this case $z_1 = 0$ implies $R[1] = R[0] + Q = \infty$ and therefore $nQ = R[0] = -Q$, which also implies $R[0] \neq \infty$. Since $y = y_0 = -y_Q z_0 = -y_Q z$ going back to affine coordinates we get $\left(\frac{x}{z}, \frac{y}{z}\right) = nQ = -Q$ as expected.

A careful reader could also be worried about a possible point Q with $y_Q = 0$ as this would always make $z'_0 = 0$. This is not an exception. In fact such Q has order 2, so if n is even $R[0] = nQ = \infty$ and $R[1] = Q$, which imply $z_0 = 0, z_1 \neq 0$, thus Case 1 handles it correctly. Otherwise if n is odd $R[0] = nQ = Q$ but then $R[1] = 2Q = \infty$ so $z_0 \neq 0, z_1 = 0$ and Case 2 correctly returns $-Q = Q$.

Until now we supposed $f = 1$ but if $Q = \infty$, $f = 0$ and consequently $z_1 = 0$. Having both $z_0 = 0$ and $z_1 = 0$ for the initial points implies having always $z_{0,j} = 0$ and $z_{1,j} = 0$ in the loop. Therefore $z = z_{0,m} = 0$ and we end again in the situation where $z = 0$. The output will be $(0, 0, 0)$ i.e. ∞ as expected. □

4.1   Algorithm 3 as *x*-only Ladder and Equivalence with X25519

Algorithm 3 could also be used as an x-only ladder by computing nQ with any $y_Q \neq 0 \in \mathbb{F}_p$ (e.g. $y_Q = 1$) and ignoring the second value of the output. After line 6 the loop returns x_0, z_0, x_1, z_1. At this point if $z_1 = 0$ Algorithm 3 returns $\frac{x}{z} = \frac{x_0}{z_0}$, if on the other hand $z_1 \neq 0$ it returns $\frac{x}{z} = \frac{x'_0}{z'_0} = \frac{2y_Q x_0 z_1 z_0}{2y_Q z_1 z_0^2}$ which remembering that $y_Q \neq 0$ is equal to $\frac{x_0}{z_0}$ if $z_0 \neq 0$. $z_0 = 0$ implies $z = z'_0 = 0$ and so $nQ = \infty$ as expected.

It is important to underline that such a use of Algorithm 3 allows also input points $Q \in E(\mathbb{F}_{p^2}) \setminus \infty$ with $x_Q \in \mathbb{F}_p$, i.e. points on the quadratic twist of E. For a theoretical justification of this fact see Theorem 5 in Appendix A.

The following theorem shows the equivalence between our ladder as x-only ladder and X25519[1] proposed by Bernstein in [2].

Theorem 4 (Equivalence with Bernstein Montgomery Ladder).
  Let p be a prime with $p \geq 5$, for all Montgomery curves $E_M : y^2 = x^3 + Ax^2 + x$ over $\mathbb{F}_p$ with $A^2 - 4$ non-square in $\mathbb{F}_p$, defining:

$$x_{djb} = \text{BernsteinLadder}(p, A, x_1, n) \text{ as in [3]}$$

$$x, y, f = \text{Proposed-Ladder}\left(p, \frac{3 - A^2}{3}, \frac{2A^3 - 9A}{27}, n, x_1 + \frac{A}{3}, 1, 1, 1, 256\right)$$

Then $x_{djb} = x - f\frac{A}{3}$ for all $x_1 \in \mathbb{F}_p$ and for all $n \in \mathbb{Z}$.

Proof. $\forall x_1 \in \mathbb{F}_p, \exists Q \in E_M(\mathbb{F}_{p^2})$ such that $X_0(Q) = x_1$ and $\forall n \in \mathbb{Z}, \exists x_{djb} \in \mathbb{F}_p$ such that $x_{djb} = X_0(nQ)$ where $X_0 : E_M(\mathbb{F}_{p^2}) \to \mathbb{F}_{p^2}$ with $X_0(\infty) = 0$ and $X_0(x, y) = x$. E_M is isomorphic to the short Weierstrass elliptic curve $E(\mathbb{F}_{p^2})$ with $a = \frac{3 - A^2}{3}$ and $b = \frac{2A^3 - 9A}{27}$ through the isomorphism:

$$\phi : \begin{cases} \infty \to \infty \\ (x, y) \to (x + A/3, y) \end{cases}$$

---

[1] Montgomery ladder on the Montgomery curve Curve25519 with $A = 486662$, $B = 1$.

The two points $Q \in E_M(\mathbb{F}_{p^2})$ with $X_0(Q) = x_1$ are mapped through ϕ to $\tilde{Q} = \phi(Q) \in E(\mathbb{F}_{p^2})$. Two cases are now to be considered:

Case 1. $nQ = \infty$, then $X_0(nQ) = X_0(\infty) = 0 = x_{djb}$. Using the isomorphism $\phi(nQ) = \infty = n\phi(Q) = n\tilde{Q}$. In this case Algorithm 3 returns $XY_1(n\tilde{Q}) = (0, 0, 0)$. Therefore the statement holds: $x_{djb} = 0 = x - f\frac{A}{3}$

Case 2. $nQ \neq \infty$, then $X_0(nQ) = x_{djb}$. Algorithm 3 returns $XY_1(\phi(nQ)) = XY_1(n\tilde{Q}) = (x, y, 1)$, so we get through the isomorphism that $x = x_{djb} + \frac{A}{3}$ but then $x_{djb} = x - f\frac{A}{3}$ because $n\tilde{Q} \neq \infty \rightarrow f = 1$. $\square$

4.2 Performance Evaluation

Our formulas, as defined by Algorithms 4 and 5, require the computation and storage of $b4 = 4 \cdot b$ and have a total cost per iteration in the main loop of Algorithm 3 of $10M, 5S, 2Ma, 2Mb4, 13a$,[2] which can be simplified if $a = -3$ to $10M, 5S, 2Mb4, 17a$. This implementation requires 8 auxiliary variables.

Algorithm 4. Doubling		**Algorithm 5.** Differential Addition	
Input: $x, z, a, b4 = 4 \cdot b \in \mathbb{F}_p$		**Input:** $x, z, x', z', x_1, a, b4 = 4 \cdot b \in \mathbb{F}_p$	
Output: $x_2, z_2 \in \mathbb{F}_p$ s.t. $X(2Q) = \frac{x_2}{z_2}$		**Output:** $x_3, z_3 \in \mathbb{F}_p$ s.t. $X(Q + Q') = \frac{x_3}{z_3}$	
1: $r_1 \leftarrow x, r_2 \leftarrow$	11: $r_8 \leftarrow r_1 \times r_7$	1: $r_1 \leftarrow x, r_2 \leftarrow z$,	11: $r_7 \leftarrow r_7 + r_6$
$\quad z$	12: $r_8 \leftarrow r_8 + r_8$	$\quad r_3 \leftarrow x', r_4 \leftarrow z'$	12: $r_7 \leftarrow r_7 \times r_8$
2: $r_7 \leftarrow r_2^2$	13: $r_1 \leftarrow r_5 - r_8$	2: $r_6 \leftarrow r_1 \times r_4$	13: $r_5 \leftarrow r_5^2$
3: $r_5 \leftarrow a \cdot r_7$	14: $r_6 \leftarrow r_6 + r_6$	3: $r_7 \leftarrow r_1 \times r_3$	14: $r_6 \leftarrow b4 \times r_5$
4: $r_8 \leftarrow r_1^2$	15: $r_6 \leftarrow r_6 + r_6$	4: $r_5 \leftarrow r_2 \times r_4$	15: $r_7 \leftarrow r_7 + r_7$
5: $r_6 \leftarrow r_8 + r_5$	16: $r_6 \leftarrow r_6 + r_7$	5: $r_8 \leftarrow r_3 \times r_2$	16: $r_7 \leftarrow r_7 + r_6$
6: $r_5 \leftarrow r_8 - r_5$	17: $r_2 \leftarrow r_2 \times r_6$	6: $r_3 \leftarrow r_6 - r_8$	17: $r_3 \leftarrow r_7 - r_3$
7: $r_5 \leftarrow r_5^2$	18: $x_2 \leftarrow r_1$	7: $r_4 \leftarrow r_3^2$	18: $x_3 \leftarrow r_3, z_3 \leftarrow$
8: $r_6 \leftarrow r_1 \times r_6$	19: $z_2 \leftarrow r_2$	8: $r_3 \leftarrow x1 \times r_4$	$\quad r_4$
9: $r_7 \leftarrow b4 \times r_7$	20: **return** x_2, z_2	9: $r_8 \leftarrow r_8 + r_6$	19: **return** x_3, z_3
10: $r_7 \leftarrow r_7 \times r_2$		10: $r_6 \leftarrow a \cdot r_5$	

Alternatively the loop can be rewritten similarly as [15, Algorithm 14] using only 7 auxiliary variables, for a cost per iteration of $8M, 7S, 3Ma, 1Mb4, 24a$ making it more appealing in implementations where squaring is optimized or when $a = -3$ resulting in a cost of $8M, 7S, 1Mb4, 31a$ thus asymptotic to $16M$. Our performances are almost identical to the Brier-Joye ladder. Izu et al. merged the Izu and Takagi differential addition and doubling achieving a total $13M, 4S, 18a$ [18, Appendix A.4] but their formula has exceptions since the speed-up is achieved by mixing the z-coordinates of the two points in the ladder, thus creating effects similar to the Co-Z ladder shown in Sect. 3.3. The recovery of the y-coordinate requires a total of $11M, 1S, 1Ma, 1Mb, 10a$ including the evaluation at line 7 of y_0 but not considering the conditional assignments, which could be implemented in

---

[2] M:multiplication, S:squaring, $Ma, Mb, Mb4$:multiplication by constants, a:addition.

Table 1. Operations costs per scalar bit for regular ladders without pre-computations except the last one where $w = 4$ indicates a 4-bit window

Ladder	$a \neq -3$						$a = -3$				
	M	S	Ma	Mb	a	**M/loop**	M	S	Mb	a	**M/loop**
Algorithm 3	10	5	2	2	13	20.3	8	7	1	31	19.1
Brier-Joye [8, 19]	10	5	2	2	12	20.2	8	7	1	31	19.1
Improved Izu-Takagi [18]	10	4	2	1	18	18.8	10	4	1	23	17.3
(x,y) Co-Z [16, Algorithm 15]	8	6	0	0	43	18.3	8	6	0	43	18.3
x-only Co-Z [17, Algorithm 6]	10	5	0	0	13	16.3	10	5	0	13	16.3
Renes et al. [26] $w = 4$	11	3	3.75	2.5	20.75	22.33	11	3	2.5	28.25	19.33

*M/loop is calculated as $1S = 1Ma = 1Mb = 1M$ and $1a = 0.1M$

different ways. Table 1 compares our costs with the ones of other scalar multiplication algorithms including a windowed ladder which uses the complete formula for odd order curves by Renes et at. [26]. It presents exceptions although only when used on even order curves (e.g. curve25519).

4.3   Security Considerations

Due to the regular structure of the Montgomery ladder Algorithm 3 is protected against timing attacks and simple power analysis. To protect against DPA-like attacks our ladder can use both the randomization of projective coordinates and scalar blinding. Note that on a Montgomery ladder the randomization of the projective coordinates usually requires additional costs for each iteration step of the ladder as the formulas are derived assuming $z_Q = 1$. However Okeya et al. showed that randomizing x_1 and z_1 in line 2 is enough [25] and costs only $2M$. We underline the fact that scalar blinding has been claimed to be an ineffective countermeasure, but this happens only when r is chosen too small. If r is chosen accordingly to the form of $\#E(\mathbb{K})$ then scalar blinding is secure as expected [27]. Furthermore the combination of scalar blinding and coordinates randomization has been proved to provide resistance to some *horizontal* attacks, e.g. [12]. Horizontal attacks are more powerful than DPA as the attacker utilizes only a single trace. For some of these attacks ([1,11]) the only known countermeasures are internal to the multiplication algorithm. These are independent of the scalar multiplication structure and are thus out of scope here. In absence of fault attacks it is interesting to note that our proposed ladder does not require any check on the input point if used with a twist secure elliptic curve. When, on the contrary, the curve has a twist with weak order, Algorithm 3 can be modified to check if the output point lies indeed on the proper curve. This, combined with the y-recovery, acts as a fault countermeasure as described by Ebeid and Lambert [13]. We suggest to perform the check just after the y-recovery and also after the conversion to affine coordinates as the cost of point checking is very limited (for both checks the total cost is $5M, 7S$).

To handle with input/output points equal to ∞ Algorithm 3 makes use of a flag f, which might be target of faults. We claim that no additional information on the value of the scalar n could be obtained in this way. In fact f is used in 3 different occasions: (1) for the input point Q, (2) for the point $\frac{x_1}{z_1}$ at the end of the main loop and (3) for the result nQ. In case (1) if $Q \neq \infty$ the result will be ∞, independently of n, while the case where $Q = \infty$ is no different from the unfaulted case where the attacker chooses the input point. In case (2) the faulted result will be $-Q$ (when $nQ \neq -Q$), giving no information about n, or ∞ (when $nQ = -Q$), giving complete knowledge of n *exactly* as in the unfaulted scenario. In case (3) the output coordinates x and y will not change, while the resulting f will change. This might be exploited at protocol level but it will not reveal any information on n.

5   Conclusion

To the best of our knowledge this paper presented the first regular and constant-time scalar multiplication algorithm *proved* to work for *all* points on *all* short Weierstrass elliptic curves with *any* scalar value. This last point, as we showed in Sect. 3, is something that other state-of-the-art algorithms fail to achieve. The presented ladder has performances comparable with other regular ladders for short Weierstrass curves, it supports scalar blinding combined with projective coordinates randomization as countermeasure for side-channel attacks and, thanks to its internal structure of an x-only Montgomery ladder coupled with y-recovery, provides intrinsic protection against fault attacks.

All these properties make it appealing as possible low area hardware accelerator for secure microcontrollers where several ECC operations, on different elliptic curve models, might be required.

A   *X*-only Scalar Multiplication

We now state and prove an analogous version of Theorem 2.1 of [2] which holds for short Weierstrass curves (together with the function X_1). The definition of $X_1 : E(\mathbb{F}_{p^2}) \rightarrow \mathbb{F}_{p^2} \times \{0, 1\}$ is $X_1(\infty) = (0, 0), X_1(x, y) = (x, 1)$ and in the following lines we will indicate with δ the smallest non-square integer in $\mathbb{F}_p$. For an exact description of the operations on the extension field $\mathbb{F}_{p^2}$ see [2, Appendix A] but the addition law we will refer to, is the one described in Sect. 2.

First note that the following three sets are subgroups of $E(\mathbb{F}_{p^2})$:

- $\{\infty, \text{points of order two}\}$. Indeed if there is just one point of order two $\infty + \infty = \infty$; $(q_1, 0) + (q_1, 0) = \infty$; and $(q_1, 0) + \infty = (q_1, 0)$. If there are three points we have in addition that $(q_1, 0) + (q_2, 0) = (q_3, 0)$.

- $\{\infty\} \cup (E(\mathbb{F}_{p^2}) \cap (\mathbb{F}_p \times \mathbb{F}_p))$. Indeed, if $x, y, x', y' \in \mathbb{F}_p$ then the quantities λ, x_3, y_3 defined as in Eq. 2 are all in $\mathbb{F}_p$.
- $\{\infty\} \cup (E(\mathbb{F}_{p^2}) \cap (\mathbb{F}_p \times \sqrt{\delta}\mathbb{F}_p)$. This time λ is an element of $\sqrt{\delta}\mathbb{F}_p$ and therefore $x_3 \in \mathbb{F}_p$ while y_3 will be an element of $\sqrt{\delta}\mathbb{F}_p$.

Theorem 5. *Let n be an integer and $(q, f_0) \in \mathbb{F}_p \times \{0, 1\}$. Then there exists a unique couple $(s, f_1) \in \mathbb{F}_p \times \{0, 1\}$ such that $X_1(nQ) = (s, f_1)$ for all $Q \in E(\mathbb{F}_{p^2})$ such that $X_1(Q) = (q, f_0)$.*

Proof. We first, consider $f_0 = 0$. The only Q satisfying $\{Q \in \mathbb{F}_{p^2} : X_1(Q) = (0, 0)\}$ is ∞, so $nQ = \infty$ and $X_1(nQ) = (0, 0)$. If $f_0 = 1$ we define, as Bernstein did in [2], $\alpha := q^3 + aq + b$ and check different cases for α.

Case 1. $\alpha = 0$. The only square root of 0 in $\mathbb{F}_{p^2}$ is 0 and therefore we are speaking only of possible points of order two. A curve E could have no points of order two, in this case $\{Q \in \mathbb{F}_{p^2} : X_1(Q) = (q, 1)\} = \{\emptyset\}$. It could have just one single root q_1; then the point $(q_1, 0)$ would be contained in the group $\{\infty, (q_1, 0)\}$. This is a subgroup of $E(\mathbb{F}_{p^2})$ and therefore nQ will lie in it. Depending on the scalar n we will have $X_1(nQ) = (0, 0)$ or $X_1(nQ) = (q_1, 1)$. If the polynomial has two roots in $\mathbb{F}_p$ it has the third too and in this last case the set $\{\infty, (q_1, 0), (q_2, 0), (q_3, 0)\}$ is again a subgroup of $E(\mathbb{F}_{p^2})$. The output will be $X_1(nQ) = (0, 0)$ or one of the three points returning $X_1(nQ) = (q_i, 1)$. In all these cases $X_1(nQ) \in \mathbb{F}_p \times \{0, 1\}$.

Case 2. α nonzero square in $\mathbb{F}_p$. The square roots of α are $\pm r \in \mathbb{F}_p$. Therefore $\{Q \in \mathbb{F}_{p^2} : X_1(Q) = (q, 1)\} = \{(q, r), (q, -r)\}$. These are contained in the group $\{\infty\} \cup (E(\mathbb{F}_{p^2}) \cap (\mathbb{F}_p \times \mathbb{F}_p))$ and nQ too. Notice that $n(q, -r) = n(-(q, r)) = -n(q, r)$. The function X_1 considers only the x-coordinate and eventually the infinity, so $X_1(n(q, -r)) = X_1(n(q, r))$ which is equal, depending on the scalar n to $(s, 1)$ or $(0, 0)$. In both cases $X_1(nQ) \in \mathbb{F}_p \times \{0, 1\}$.

Case 3. α non-square in $\mathbb{F}_p$. By definition of δ, $\frac{\alpha}{\delta}$ is a nonzero square in $\mathbb{F}_p$ with roots $\pm r \in \mathbb{F}_p$; then the only square roots of α are $\pm r\sqrt{\delta} \in \mathbb{F}_{p^2}$. The two points $(q, r\sqrt{\delta}), (q, -r\sqrt{\delta})$ are contained in the group $\{\infty\} \cup (E(\mathbb{F}_{p^2}) \cap (\mathbb{F}_p \times \sqrt{\delta}\mathbb{F}_p)$ so it contains also $n(q, r\sqrt{\delta})$ and $n(q, -r\sqrt{\delta})$ which again are opposite and have the same $X_1(nQ) = (s, 1)/(0, 0)$ depending on n with s still in $\mathbb{F}_p$ as shown above. $\qed$

B   Proof of Lemma 1

The hypothesis $R[0], R[1] \neq \infty$ implies $y_Q \neq 0$. In fact if $y_Q = 0$ then Q would have had order 2 causing either $R[0]$ or $R[1] (= R[0] + Q)$ to be ∞. Since $y_Q, z_0, z_1 \neq 0$, then $z_0' \neq 0$. It is easy to see that $\frac{x_0'}{z_0'} = \frac{2y_Q x_0 z_1 z_0}{2y_Q z_1 z_0^2} = \frac{x_0}{z_0} = X(R[0])$. For the y-coordinate of $R[0]$, hereafter referred to as $y_{R[0]}$, we have two cases.

Case 1. $R[0] \neq Q$. Using Eq. 2 we have $\frac{x_1}{z_1} = \left(\frac{y_{R[0]} - y_Q}{x_0/z_0 - x_Q}\right)^2 - x_Q - \frac{x_0}{z_0} = \frac{-2y_Q y_{R[0]} + 2b + (a + x_Q \frac{x_0}{z_0})(x_Q + \frac{x_0}{z_0})}{(x_0/z_0 - x_Q)^2}$. Multiplying by $(x_0/z_0 - x_Q)^2 \neq 0$ and dividing by $2y_Q$ we obtain $y_{R[0]} = \frac{2b z_1 z_0^2 + z_1(az_0 + x_Q x_0)(x_Q z_0 + x_0) - x_1(x_0 - x_Q z_0)^2}{2y_Q z_1 z_0^2} = \frac{y_0'}{z_0'}$.

Case 2. $R[0] = Q$ (i.e. $n \equiv 1 \mod \text{ord}(Q)$). Applying the equivalence $x_0 = z_0 x_Q$ we get $\frac{y_0'}{z_0} = \frac{2bz_0^2 + 2x_Q z_0(az_0 + x_Q^2 z_0)}{2y_Q z_0^2} = \frac{x_Q^3 + ax_Q + b}{y_Q} = \frac{y_Q^2}{y_Q} = y_Q$ as expected. $\square$

References

1. Bauer, A., Jaulmes, É., Prouff, E., Reinhard, J.R., Wild, J.: Horizontal collision correlation attack on elliptic curves. Cryptogr. Commun. **7**(1), 91–119 (2015)
2. Bernstein, D.J.: Curve25519: new Diffie-Hellman speed records. In: Yung, M., Dodis, Y., Kiayias, A., Malkin, T. (eds.) PKC 2006. LNCS, vol. 3958, pp. 207–228. Springer, Heidelberg (2006). doi:10.1007/11745853_14
3. Bernstein, D.J.: Does the Curve25519 Montgomery ladder always work? CFRG Mailing List. https://www.ietf.org/mail-archive/web/cfrg/current/msg05004.html (2014). Accessed 22 Jan 2016
4. Bernstein, D.J., Lange, T.: Faster addition and doubling on elliptic curves. In: Kurosawa, K. (ed.) ASIACRYPT 2007. LNCS, vol. 4833, pp. 29–50. Springer, Heidelberg (2007). doi:10.1007/978-3-540-76900-2_3
5. Bernstein, D.J., Lange, T.: Explicit-Formulas Database (2016). http://hyperelliptic.org/EFD
6. Biehl, I., Meyer, B., Müller, V.: Differential fault attacks on elliptic curve cryptosystems. In: Bellare, M. (ed.) CRYPTO 2000. LNCS, vol. 1880, pp. 131–146. Springer, Heidelberg (2000). doi:10.1007/3-540-44598-6_8
7. Bos, J.W., Costello, C., Longa, P., Naehrig, M.: Selecting elliptic curves for cryptography: an efficiency and security analysis. J. Cryptographic Eng. **6**(4), 259–286 (2016). doi:10.1007/s13389-015-0097-y
8. Brier, E., Joye, M.: Weierstraß elliptic curves and side-channel attacks. In: Naccache and Paillier [24], pp. 335–345
9. Brumley, B.B., Tuveri, N.: Remote timing attacks are still practical. In: Atluri, V., Diaz, C. (eds.) ESORICS 2011. LNCS, vol. 6879, pp. 355–371. Springer, Heidelberg (2011). doi:10.1007/978-3-642-23822-2_20
10. Coron, J.-S.: Resistance against differential power analysis for elliptic curve cryptosystems. In: Koç, Ç.K., Paar, C. (eds.) CHES 1999. LNCS, vol. 1717, pp. 292–302. Springer, Heidelberg (1999). doi:10.1007/3-540-48059-5_25
11. Danger, J.-L., Guilley, S., Hoogvorst, P., Murdica, C., Naccache, D.: Improving the Big Mac attack on elliptic curve cryptography. In: Ryan, P.Y.A., Naccache, D., Quisquater, J.-J. (eds.) The New Codebreakers. LNCS, vol. 9100, pp. 374–386. Springer, Heidelberg (2016). doi:10.1007/978-3-662-49301-4_23
12. Dugardin, M., Papachristodoulou, L., Najm, Z., Batina, L., Danger, J.-L., Guilley, S.: Dismantling real-world ECC with horizontal and vertical template attacks. In: Standaert, F.-X., Oswald, E. (eds.) COSADE 2016. LNCS, vol. 9689, pp. 88–108. Springer, Heidelberg (2016). doi:10.1007/978-3-319-43283-0_6
13. Ebeid, N.M., Lambert, R.: Securing the elliptic curve montgomery ladder against fault attacks. In: Breveglieri, L., Koren, I., Naccache, D., Oswald, E., Seifert, J. (eds.) Sixth International Workshop on Fault Diagnosis and Tolerance in Cryptography, FDTC 2009, Lausanne, Switzerland, 6 September 2009, pp. 46–50. IEEE Computer Society (2009)
14. Fouque, P., Lercier, R., Réal, D., Valette, F.: Fault attack on elliptic curve Montgomery ladder implementation. In: Breveglieri, L., Gueron, S., Koren, I., Naccache, D., Seifert, J. (eds.) Fifth International Workshop on Fault Diagnosis and Tolerance in Cryptography, 2008, FDTC 2008, Washington, DC, USA, 10 August 2008, pp. 92–98. IEEE Computer Society (2008)

15. Goundar, R.R., Joye, M., Miyaji, A.: Co-Z addition formulæ and binary ladders on elliptic curves. In: Mangard, S., Standaert, F.-X. (eds.) CHES 2010. LNCS, vol. 6225, pp. 65–79. Springer, Heidelberg (2010). doi:10.1007/978-3-642-15031-9_5

16. Goundar, R.R., Joye, M., Miyaji, A., Rivain, M., Venelli, A.: Scalar multiplication on Weierstraß elliptic curves from Co-Z arithmetic. J. Cryptogr. Eng. 1(2), 161–176 (2011)

17. Hutter, M., Joye, M., Sierra, Y.: Memory-constrained implementations of elliptic curve cryptography in Co-Z coordinate representation. In: Nitaj, A., Pointcheval, D. (eds.) AFRICACRYPT 2011. LNCS, vol. 6737, pp. 170–187. Springer, Heidelberg (2011). doi:10.1007/978-3-642-21969-6_11

18. Izu, T., Möller, B., Takagi, T.: Improved elliptic curve multiplication methods resistant against side channel attacks. In: Menezes, A., Sarkar, P. (eds.) INDOCRYPT 2002. LNCS, vol. 2551, pp. 296–313. Springer, Heidelberg (2002). doi:10.1007/3-540-36231-2_24

19. Izu, T., Takagi, T.: A fast parallel elliptic curve multiplication resistant against side channel attacks. In: Naccache and Paillier [24], pp. 280–296

20. Izu, T., Takagi, T.: Exceptional procedure attack on elliptic curve cryptosystems. In: Desmedt, Y.G. (ed.) PKC 2003. LNCS, vol. 2567, pp. 224–239. Springer, Heidelberg (2003). doi:10.1007/3-540-36288-6_17

21. Joye, M., Tymen, C.: Protections against differential analysis for elliptic curve cryptography — an algebraic approach —. In: Koç, Ç.K., Naccache, D., Paar, C. (eds.) CHES 2001. LNCS, vol. 2162, pp. 377–390. Springer, Heidelberg (2001). doi:10.1007/3-540-44709-1_31

22. Kim, K. (ed.): ICISC 2001. LNCS, vol. 2288. Springer, Heidelberg (2002)

23. Montgomery, P.L.: Speeding the Pollard and elliptic curve methods of factorization. Math. Comput. 48(177), 243–264 (1987)

24. Naccache, D., Paillier, P. (eds.): PKC 2002. LNCS, vol. 2274. Springer, Heidelberg (2002)

25. Okeya, K., Miyazaki, K., Sakurai, K.: A fast scalar multiplication method with randomized projective coordinates on a montgomery-form elliptic curve secure against side channel attacks. In: Kim [22], pp. 428–439

26. Renes, J., Costello, C., Batina, L.: Complete addition formulas for prime order elliptic curves. In: Fischlin, M., Coron, J.-S. (eds.) EUROCRYPT 2016. LNCS, vol. 9665, pp. 403–428. Springer, Heidelberg (2016). doi:10.1007/978-3-662-49890-3_16

27. Schindler, W., Wiemers, A.: Efficient Side-Channel Attacks on Scalar Blinding on Elliptic Curves with Special Structure. NIST Workshop on ECC Standards (2015)

28. Yen, S., Kim, S., Lim, S., Moon, S.: A countermeasure against one physical cryptanalysis may benefit another attack. In: Kim [22], pp. 414–427

Inner Product Masking for Bitslice Ciphers and Security Order Amplification for Linear Leakages

Weijia Wang[1], François-Xavier Standaert[2], Yu Yu[1,3]($\boxtimes$), Sihang Pu[1],
Junrong Liu[1], Zheng Guo[1], and Dawu Gu[1]

[1] School of Electronic Information and Electrical Engineering,
Shanghai Jiao Tong University, Shanghai, China
{aawwjaa,yyuu,push.beni,liujr,guozheng,dwgu}@sjtu.edu.cn
[2] ICTEAM/ELEN/Crypto Group, Université catholique de Louvain,
Louvain-la-Neuve, Belgium
fstandae@uclouvain.be
[3] Westone Cryptologic Research Center, Beijing, China

Abstract. Designers of masking schemes are usually torn between the contradicting goals of maximizing the security gains while minimizing the performance overheads. Boolean masking is one extreme example of this tradeoff: its algebraic structure is as simple as can be (and so are its implementations), but it typically suffers more from implementation weaknesses. For example knowing one bit of each share is enough to know one bit of secret in this case. Inner product masking lies at the other side of this tradeoff: its algebraic structure is more involved, making it more expensive to implement (especially at higher orders), but it ensures stronger security guarantees. For example, knowing one bit of each share is not enough to know one bit of secret in this case.

In this paper, we try to combine the best of these two worlds, and propose a new masking scheme mixing a single Boolean matrix product (to improve the algebraic complexity of the scheme) with standard additive Boolean masking (to allow efficient higher-order implementations). We show that such a masking is well suited for application to bitslice ciphers. We also conduct a comprehensive security analysis of the proposed scheme. For this purpose, we give a security proof in the probing model, and carry out an information leakage evaluation of an idealized implementation. For certain leakage functions, the latter exhibits surprising observations, namely information leakages in higher statistical moments than guaranteed by the proof in the probing model, which we can connect to the recent literature on low entropy masking schemes. We conclude the paper with a performance evaluation, which confirms that both for security and performance reasons, our new masking scheme (which can be viewed as a variation of inner product masking) compares favorably to state-of-the-art masking schemes for bitslice ciphers.

1 Introduction

In the recent literature on masking schemes, increasing the algebraic complexity of the operation mixing the shares has been frequently used to improve the

© Springer International Publishing AG 2017
K. Lemke-Rust and M. Tunstall (Eds.): CARDIS 2016, LNCS 10146, pp. 174–191, 2017.
DOI: 10.1007/978-3-319-54669-8_11

resistance of cryptographic implementations in scenarios where limited noise is available in the adversary's measurements. Examples include inner product masking [1], polynomial masking [7,14] and affine masking [6]. For a comparable amount of shares, these masking schemes offer a (sometimes slightly) better security than the mainstream Boolean masking. Yet, this usually comes at the cost of (sometimes large) performance overheads.

In this paper, we therefore start from the observation that it would be interesting to design a hybrid masking scheme, where some of the shares are mixed based on a more complex operation (to guarantee some security in low noise contexts where the simplicity of Boolean masking is problematic), while the others are just mixed thanks to additive Boolean masking (which efficiently generalizes to higher-orders [15]). We instantiate a first proposal in this direction, that we denote as Boolean matrix product masking, and which is particularly well suited to block ciphers with efficient bitslice representation. In this masking scheme, we split the secret x into n shares $\boldsymbol{x} = (x_1, \ldots, x_n)$ and use a (public) random nonsingular Boolean matrix A, such that $x = A \times x_1 \oplus \bigoplus_{2 \leq i \leq n} x_i$ (see Sect. 2.1 for definitions and notations) and the public matrix A is fixed as a constant in each running of the masked block cipher. Intuitively, our masking scheme can therefore be seen as a variant of inner product masking specialized to bitslice ciphers (yet applicable to the AES), which we discuss in Sects. 2.6 and 2.7. Note that inner product masking is itself a particular case of the code-based masking recently introduced in [3,4]. Next, we show how to perform standard operations such as addition and multiplication (i.e. bitwise XOR and AND in GF(2)) securely. The standard operations can be composed to protect a complete bitslice cipher such as the recently introduced (X)LS-designs [8,11].

We then investigate the security of our masking scheme in the probing model [10], and prove that it guarantees dth-order security for $n \geq 2d + 1$. Further, we evaluate the concrete information leakage of our masking shares based on an information theoretic analysis [16]. As expected, the results show that they leak less than Boolean shares and comparably to inner product shares in low noise contexts. More surprisingly, the information theoretic analysis also reveals that in high noise contexts, Boolean matrix product masking (and, in fact, inner product masking in general) can lead to additional gains. Namely, their information leakages can be of higher order than what is guaranteed by the proof in the probing model. As in the context of low entropy masking scheme, we can justify that this gain can only be observed for linear leakage functions [9].

We finally complement these results with a performance evaluation, which allows us to complete the picture of our new masking scheme. In particular, the implementations of the masked LS-design Fantomas exhibit excellent performances, with only limited overheads compared to Boolean masking.

2   Our Construction

In this section, we give the construction of our masking scheme, including the encoding and decoding of the secret and different operations in masked domain.

2.1   Preliminaries

Let lowercases (e.g., i, x) denote any integral variables or binary vectors, and capital letters (e.g., A) be the Boolean matrices. $A(i, :)$ (or $A(i)$ for short) denotes the ith row of matrix A and $x(i)$ denotes the ith element of vector x. And $A(:, i)$ denotes the ith column of matrix A. Let $A(i : j, k)$ (resp., $A(k, i : j)$) be the elements of kth column (resp., kth row) and ith to jth row (resp., ith to jth column). Let the bold lowercases (e.g., $\boldsymbol{x} = (x_1, x_2, \ldots)$) denote the vectors whose elements are binary vectors, and let the bold capital letters be vectors of Boolean matrices (e.g., $\boldsymbol{X} = (X_1, X_2, \ldots))$). Finally, Let E denote the identity matrix and A^{-1} and A^{T} denote the inverse and transpose of the matrix A, respectively. We recall the tensor product (denoted as $\otimes$) between Boolean matrices. Suppose that two matrices are A, B with size $m_1 \times n_1$ and $m_2 \times n_2$ respectively, then the result is a matrix C with size $m_1 m_2 \times n_1 n_2$:

$$A \otimes B \stackrel{\text{def}}{=} \begin{bmatrix} A(1,1) & ,\ldots, & A(1, n_1) \\ \ldots & ,\ldots, & \ldots \\ A(m_1, 1) & ,\ldots, & A(m_1, n_1) \end{bmatrix} \otimes \begin{bmatrix} B(1,1) & ,\ldots, & B(1, n_2) \\ \ldots & ,\ldots, & \ldots \\ B(m_2, 1) & ,\ldots, & B(m_2, n_2) \end{bmatrix}$$

$$= \begin{bmatrix} A(1,1)B & ,\ldots, & A(1, n_1)B \\ \ldots & ,\ldots, & \ldots \\ A(m_1, 1)B & ,\ldots, & A(m_1, n_1)B \end{bmatrix} = C,$$

where $A(i, j)B = \begin{bmatrix} A(i,j)B(1,1) & ,\ldots, & A(i,j)B(1, n_2) \\ \ldots & ,\ldots, & \ldots \\ A(i,j)B(m_2, 1) & ,\ldots, & A(i,j)B(m_2, n_2) \end{bmatrix}.$

2.2   Encoding and Decoding of the Secret Variable

The encoding of an m-bit secret variable (say, x) is close to that of the Boolean masking but the first share is multiplied by a nonsingular matrix: $x = (A \times x_1) \oplus x_2 \oplus \ldots \oplus x_n$. Algorithms 1 and 2 are the pseudocode of encoding and decoding respectively. Note that the matrix A (and its inverse) is fixed in each running of the block cipher, thus in the remainder of this paper, we often omit the matrix A and use the shares $\boldsymbol{x} = (x_1, \ldots, x_n)$ to represent the encoding of x.

Algorithm 1. Enc

Require: m-bit secret variable x, invertible matrix A and its inverse A^{-1}
Ensure: $\text{Enc}(x) = \boldsymbol{x} = (x_1, \ldots, x_n)$ as the masked variables
 1: **for** $i = 1; i < n; i{+}{+}$ **do**
 2:    x_{i+1} is a randomly generated m-bit value
 3: **end for**
 4: $x_1 := A^{-1} \times (x \oplus \bigoplus_{i=2}^{n} x_i)$

Algorithm 2. Dec
___

Require: masked variables $\boldsymbol{x} = x_1, \ldots, x_n$
Ensure: $x = \text{Dec}(\boldsymbol{x})$ as the secret variable
1: $x := (A \times x_1) \oplus \bigoplus_{i=2}^n x_i$

2.3 Initialization for Masked Operations

In order to reduce the complexity of masked operations, an initialization step is necessary to pre-compute some variables. Algorithm 3 details the precomputation of the matrices (A, A^{-1}), $\hat{A}$, $\grave{A}$ and $\acute{A}$, where $\otimes$ is tensor product, ReRandMat() is the function that re-randomize the nonsingular matrix and its inverse (details deferred to Sect. 2.5), A_{old} and A_{old}^{-1} are the Boolean matrices of the last running (which can been replaced by the identity matrix for the first run), and E' consists of the $(i + m(i-1))$-th rows of the $m \times m^2$ identity matrix for all $i \in \{1, \ldots, m\}$. For example, we have: $E' = \begin{bmatrix} 1,0,0,0,0,0,0,0,0 \\ 0,0,0,0,1,0,0,0,0 \\ 0,0,0,0,0,0,0,0,1 \end{bmatrix}$ for $m = 3$.

Algorithm 3. Setup
___

Require: length of the masked variable m
Ensure: random nonsingular $m \times m$ matrix A (and its inverse A^{-1}) and some other pre-computed values
1: $(A, A^{-1}) := \text{ReRandMat}(A_{old}, A_{old}^{-1})$
2: $\hat{A} := A^{-1} \times (E' \times (A \otimes A))$
3: $\grave{A} := A^{-1} \times (E' \times (A \otimes E))$
4: $\acute{A} := A^{-1} \times (E' \times (E \otimes A))$

2.4 Operations in Masked Domain

Mask Refreshing. Mask refreshing is a re-randomized procedure to re-encode the secret variables. As we will introduce in Sect. 3.1, this procedure will be called n times at the beginning of block cipher to re-randomize the masking of the key. Algorithm 4 gives the details of this operation.

Addition (XOR) of Two Masked Variables. Algorithm 5 gives the masked addition of $\boldsymbol{x} = (x_1, \ldots, x_n)$ and $\boldsymbol{y} = (y_1, \ldots, y_n)$ that are encodings of two secret values x and y respectively.

Algorithm 4. Refresh

Require: masked variable $x = (x_1, \ldots, x_n)$
Ensure: refreshed encoding $x' = (x'_1, \ldots, x'_n)$
1: randomly generate a vector of m-bit variables $a = (a_1, \ldots, a_n)$ s.t. $(A \times a_1) \oplus a_2 \oplus \ldots \oplus a_n = 0$
2: **for** $i = 1;\ i \le n;\ i{+}{+}$ **do**
3:     $x'_i := x_i \oplus a_i$
4: **end for**

Algorithm 5. SecAdd

Require: two masked variables $x = (x_1, ..., x_n)$ and $y = (y_1, ..., y_n)$
Ensure: encoding of $x \oplus y$ (namely, $(\text{Enc}(x \oplus y) = z = (z_1, ..., z_n))$
1: **for** $i = 1;\ i \le n;\ i{+}{+}$ **do**
2:     $z_i := x_i \oplus y_i$
3: **end for**

Bitand of Two Masked Variables. The most basic nonlinear operation for bitslice S-box is the bitand. This operation in masked domain is given in Algorithm 6, where variables, x and y, are encoded as $x = (x_1, \ldots, x_n)$ and $y = (y_1, \ldots, y_n)$ respectively, and $\odot$ denotes bitand. The algorithm is similar in spirit to the ISW scheme [10] except for some additional adaptions to the matrix case. Note that $x_i \otimes y_i$ is of size $m^2 \times 1$ (by tensor product $\otimes$), and the (pre-computed) matrices $\hat{A}$, A and $\acute{A}$ are all of size $m \times m^2$ (see Algorithm 3). Thus $t_{i,j}$ is always of size $m \times 1$. We next sketch the proof of correctness for Algorithm 6. First we have:

$$
(A \times x_1 \oplus x_2 \oplus \ldots \oplus x_n) \odot (A \times y_1 \oplus y_2 \oplus \ldots \oplus y_n)
$$
$$
= ((A \times x_1) \odot (A \times y_1)) \oplus ((A \times x_1) \odot y_2) \oplus \ldots \oplus ((A \times x_1) \odot y_n)
$$
$$
\oplus (x_2 \odot (A \times y_1)) \qquad \oplus (x_2 \odot y_2) \qquad \oplus \ldots \oplus (x_2 \odot y_n)
$$
$$
\ldots
$$
$$
\oplus (x_n \odot (A \times y_1)) \qquad \oplus (x_n \odot y_2) \qquad \oplus \ldots \oplus (x_n \odot y_n).
$$

We handle the terms separately, let $u = (A \times x_1) \odot (A \times y_1)$, then we have: $u(i) = \bigoplus_{i,j \in (1,\ldots,m)} A(i,j) x_1(i) y_1(j) = (A(i,:) \otimes A(i,:)) \times (x_1 \otimes y_1)$. Thus we have $t_{i,j} = A^{-1} \times (A \times x_1) \odot (A \times y_1) = \hat{A} \times (x_1 \otimes y_1)$. Similar conclusions can be obtained for $A^{-1} \times (A \times x_1) \odot y_i$ and $A^{-1} \times x_i \odot (A \times x_1)$ when $i \in (2, \ldots, n)$. Therefore we can prove that $(A \times x_1 \oplus x_2 \oplus \ldots \oplus x_n) \odot (A \times y_1 \oplus y_2 \oplus \ldots \oplus y_n) = (\bigoplus_{i,j \in (2,\ldots,m)} t_{i,j}) \oplus (\bigoplus_{j \in (1,\ldots,m)} A \times t_{1,j}) \oplus (\bigoplus_{i \in (1,\ldots,m)} A \times t_{i,1})$. Finally the lines 6–19 are very similar to the ISW scheme and please refer to [10] for the remainder of correctness proof.

Note that Algorithm 6 includes the multiplication operation between a fix matrix (size of $m \times m^2$ or $m \times m$) and a scalar, which is not very efficient with the processors that don't support the 'popcnt' instruction.[1] Thus we present in

---

[1] 'popcnt' instruction counts the number of bits set to 1 in one cycle.

Algorithm 6. SecBitAnd

Require: $x = (x_1, \ldots, x_n)$, $y = (y_1, \ldots, y_n)$, $\hat{A}$, $\acute{A}$

Ensure: encoding of $x \odot y$ (i.e., $z = (z_1, \ldots, z_n)$)

1: **for** $i = 1$; $i \le n$; $i{++}$ **do**
2:    **for** $j = 1$; $j \le n$; $j{++}$ **do**
3:      $t_{i,j} := \begin{cases} \hat{A} \times (x_i \otimes y_j) & \text{if } i = j = 1 \\ \hat{A} \times (x_i \otimes y_j) & \text{if } i = 1 \\ \acute{A} \times (x_i \otimes y_j) & \text{if } j = 1 \\ x_i \odot y_j & \text{others} \end{cases}$
4:    **end for**
5: **end for**
6: Let a matrix of vectors $T = (t_{i,j})$
7: **for** $i = 1$; $i \le n$; $i{++}$ **do**
8:    $r_{i,i} := t_{i,i}$
9:    **for** $j = i + 1$; $j \le n$; $i{++}$ **do**
10:      Set $r_{i,j}$ to be a random $m \times 1$ vector
11:      $r_{j,i} := t_{j,i} + (r_{i,j} + t_{i,j})$
12:      **if** $i = 1$ **then**
13:        $r_{i,j} := A \times r_{i,j}$
14:      **end if**
15:    **end for**
16: **end for**
17: **for** $i = 1$; $i \le n$; $i{++}$ **do**
18:    $z_i := \bigoplus_j r_{j,i}$
19: **end for**

Algorithms 7, 8 and 9 different ways of computing the multiplication between a matrix A (size of $m_1 \times m_2$) and a scalar x for different situations. Algorithm 7 benefits from the 'popcnt' instruction and its time/memory complexities are $O(m_1 * m_2/w)/O(1)$, where w is the bit width of the processor and we only consider the case that $w|m_1$ and $w|m_2$. Algorithm 8 first operates the bitand between each line of A and x, resulting in a matrix V of size $m_1 \times m_2$, then it computes the product y in a bitslice manner by XORing the columns of V. Its time complexity is also $O(m_1 * m_2/w)$ but the memory complexity is $O(m_1 * m_2)$ for the storage of matrix V. Thus Algorithm 8 can obtain a same time complexity without the supporting of 'popcnt' instruction at the cost of some (but not much) memory complexity. As show in Fig. 1, Algorithm 9 first separates A and x into k equal sized parts (each of length is $l = m_2/k$) and creates the look-up table $M_i()$ for each part of scalar (i.e., $x((i-1)*l+1 : i*l)$) multiplied by the corresponding part of matrix (i.e., $A(:, (i-1) * l + 1 : i * l)$). As presented before, the matrix A should be fixed during each running of the encryption/decryption, thus these look-up tables can be pre-computed in the setup stage and stored in the memory or flash. Finally the multiplication can be done by XORing the result of k times table look-up. The time complexity of Algorithm 9 is $O(k * m_1/w)$ excluding the pre-computing of look-up tables, but the memory complexity is relatively larger: $O(k * m_1 * 2^{m_2/k})$. In particular, if we take $k = m_2$, we then have the same time complexity as Algorithm 8 but double the memory. Note that, thanks to the table look-up process, there are less variables operated in Algorithm 9, thus it can be more secure than the other two against multivariate side-channel attacks.

Algorithm 7. MatrixMul-popcnt

Require: an $m_1 \times m_2$ matrix A, an $m_2 \times 1$
  scalar x
Ensure: $y = A \times x$
1: **for** $i = 1$; $i \leq m_1$; i++ **do**
2:    $v = A(i,:) \odot x^T$
3:    $y(i) = \text{popcnt}(v)$
4: **end for**

Algorithm 8. MatrixMul-bitslice

Require: an $m_1 \times m_2$ matrix A
Ensure: $y = A \times x$
1: **for** $i = 1$; $i \leq m_1$; i++ **do**
2:    $V(i,:) = A(i,:) \odot x^T$
3: **end for**
4: $y = V(:,1)$
5: **for** $j = 2$; $j \leq m_2$; j++ **do**
6:    $y = y \oplus V(:,j)$
7: **end for**

Algorithm 9. MatrixMul-tabulate

Require: an $m_1 \times m_2$ matrix A, k that
  we have $k|m_2$
Ensure: pre-computed tables $M_{i \in \{1,\ldots,k\}}$
1: **Pre-computation Stage:**
2: $l = m_2/k$
3: **for** $i = 1$; $i \leq k$; i++ **do**
4:    create the loop-up table M_i for any
     l-bit value multiplied by the matrix
     $A(:,(i-1)*l+1:i*l)$, i.e., $\text{M}_i(v) = A(:,(i-1)*l+1:i*l) \times v$
5: **end for**

Require: an $m_2 \times 1$ scalar x, k and the
  pre-computed tables $M_{i \in \{1,\ldots,k\}}$
Ensure: $y = A \times x$
1: **Online Stage:**
2: $l = m_2/k$
3: $y = M_1(x(1:l))$
4: **for** $i = 2$; $i \leq k$; i++ **do**
5:    $y = y \oplus \text{M}_i(x((l-1)*i+1:l*i))$
6: **end for**

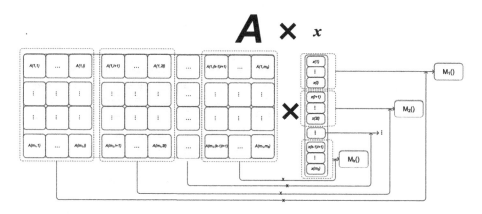

Fig. 1. Create the look-up table.

2.5 Nonsingular Matrix Re-randomization

We introduce in Algorithm 10 how to re-randomize a nonsingular matrix and its
inverse in an efficient manner. A random elementary matrix T is generated using
only rows switching from the identity matrix (lines 1, 2). It is obvious that this

matrix is orthogonal, i.e., $T^{-1} = T^{\mathsf{T}}$. In each iteration of the loop (lines 5–7), a random elementary matrix P is generated using only one row addition with random bits and the corresponding row of A is re-randomized by multiplying with P, i.e., $P \times A$. We also keep a record of its inverse $A^{-1} \times P^{-1} = A^{-1} \times P$ (since P's inverse is P itself) along the way so that Algorithm 10 needs no matrix inverse operations. We admit that the output of Algorithm 10 is not strictly uniform over the set of all Boolean nonsingular matrices. But this is not a problem in our setting where we anyway assume that the matrix is fixed and public in each run of the masked block cipher.

Algorithm 10. ReRandMat

Require: A_{old} and A_{old}^{-1}
Ensure: $m \times m$ random matrices A, A^{-1}
 1: $T := E$, $A := A_{old}$, $A^{-1} := A_{old}^{-1}$
 2: Randomly permute the rows of T
 3: $A := T \times A$, $A^{-1} := A^{-1} \times T^{\mathsf{T}}$
 4: **for** $i = 1; i \leq m; i{+}{+}$ **do**
 5:     $P := E$
 6:     generate $m - 1$ random bits, replace the zeros in $P(i)$ with the random bits
 7:     $A := P \times A$, $A^{-1} := A^{-1} \times P$
 8: **end for**

Based on the operations above, we can construct the masking scheme of bitslice block cipher. The description of masked (X)LS-design block ciphers is given in the full version due to lack of space.

2.6   Links with Inner Product Masking

Our masking scheme can be seen as a variant of inner product masking, specialized to bitslice ciphers for efficiency purposes. Recall that the inner product masking shares a secret variable as $x = l_1 \cdot x_1 + l_2 \cdot x_2 + \ldots + l_n \cdot x_n$, where $\cdot$ denotes the multiplication in a Galois field, the vector $(l_1, \ldots, l_n)$ is public, and every $(n-1)$-tuple of $\{x_1, \ldots, x_n\}$ is independent of x. As the multiplication (in a Galois field) of two variables $x \cdot y$ can be represent as y left-multiplied by the x's GF(2^m)-multiplication matrix X, i.e., $x \cdot y = X \times y$, where the first column of X is x and the other ones are generated by $X(,i) = 2^i \cdot x$, the inner product masking can been rewritten as $x = A_1 \times x_1 + \ldots + A_n \times x_n$, where $A_1, \ldots, A_n$ are GF(2^m)-muliplication matrices. Thus the inner product masking can been seen as a masking such that (1) each share is multiplied by a different Boolean matrix and, (2) the matrices are selected as corresponding to Galois field multiplication rather than simply as nonsingular Boolean.

2.7   Application to the AES

The application of our masking to the AES is also possible. As the Galois field multiplication of two variables $x \cdot y$ can be represented as $x \cdot y = X \times y$, we define a function $F_{GF} : \mathbb{F}_2^m \to \mathbb{F}_2^m \times \mathbb{F}_2^m$, which converts any value in $GF(2^m)$ to the corresponding Boolean matrix, i.e., $F_{GF}(x) = [2^0 \cdot x : 2^1 \cdot x : \ldots : 2^{m-1} \cdot x]$, where : concatenates the vectors (or matrices) of two sides thereof. Then the multiplication of two variables $\hat{x} = A_x \times x$ and $\hat{y} = A_y \times y$ equals:

$$
\begin{aligned}
z &= A_z^{-1} \times (\hat{x} \cdot \hat{y}) \\
&= A_z^{-1} \times (\hat{x} \cdot (A_y \times y)) \\
&= A_z^{-1} \times F_{GF(2^m)}(\hat{x}) \times A_y \times y \\
&= A_z^{-1} \times [F_{GF}(2^0) \times \hat{x} : \ldots : F_{GF}(2^{m-1}) \times \hat{x}] \times A_y \times y \\
&= [A_z^{-1} \times F_{GF}(2^0) \times A_x \times x : \ldots : A_z^{-1} \times F_{GF}(2^{m-1}) \times A_x \times x] \times A_y \times y.
\end{aligned}
$$

This process is precised in Algorithm 11. $G(,i)$ denotes the t-th column of binary matrix G, the list of matrices $(J_1, \ldots, J_m)$ can be hard-coded in the implementation and the corresponding $(H_1, \ldots, H_m)$ can be pre-computed in the setup phase. Therefore, the masked multiplication in Galois field can be constructed by modifying the line 3 of Algorithm 6 using Algorithm 11.

Algorithm 11. GFMul

Require: two variables x, y and the corresponding matrices A_x, A_y and A_z
Ensure: $z = A_z^{-1} \times ((A_x \times x) \cdot (A_y \times y))$
1: $(J_1, \ldots, J_m) := (F_{GF}(2^0), \ldots, F_{GF}(2^{m-1}))$
2: $(H_1, \ldots, H_m) := (A_z^{-1} \times J_1 \times A_x, \ldots, A_z^{-1} \times J_m \times A_x)$
3: **for** $i = 1$; $i <= m$; $i++$ **do**
4:    $G(,i) := H_i \times x$
5: **end for**
6: $temp := G \times A_y$
7: $z := temp \times y$

---

3   Security Analysis

3.1   Provable Security in the Probing Model

In this section, we give a security proof for our masking scheme in the probing model introduced in [10]. Recall that an m-bit variable x is encoded into n shares $(x_1, \ldots, x_n)$ with $x = (A \times x_1) \oplus x_2 \oplus \ldots \oplus x_n$ for a nonsingular public matrix A. We omit the leakage about A since it is public. We will show that our masking scheme is secure against d-probing adversary for $n \geq 2d + 1$. That is, every d-tuple of its intermediate variable is independent of any sensitive variables. In order to do this, we shall show that every d-tuple of its intermediate variable can be perfectly simulated without knowledge of any inputs.

Security for the Masking Operations. We start the security analysis of the masked operations with a security proof for Algorithm 6.

Theorem 1. *Let $x_1, \ldots, x_n$ and $y_1, \ldots, y_n$ be two encodings from the inputs of Algorithm 6 and let $n \geq 2d+1$. Then the distribution of every tuple of d intermediate variables in Algorithm 6 is independent of the distributions $x = A \times x_1 \oplus \bigoplus_{2 \leq i \leq n} x_i$ and $y = A \times y_1 \oplus \bigoplus_{2 \leq i \leq n} y_i$.*

Our proof follows and is very similar to the one outlined in [10]. We show that we can efficiently construct a $(n-1)$-tuple of random variables which is identically distributed to any d-tuple $(v_1, v_2, \ldots, v_d)$ of intermediate variables of Algorithm 6, independently of any statement about x and y. Therefore, we shall construct a set I of indices in $\{1, \ldots, n\}$ with cardinalities lower than or equal to $n-1$ and such that the distribution of any d-tuple $(v_1, v_2, \ldots, v_d)$ can be perfectly simulated from $x_{|I} \overset{\text{def}}{=} (x_i)_{i \in I}$ and $y_{|I} \overset{\text{def}}{=} (y_i)_{i \in I}$. This will prove the Theorem 1 since, $x_1, \ldots, x_n$ (and $y_1, \ldots, y_n$) being $(n-1)$-wise independent, $x_{|I}$ and $y_{|I}$ are jointly independent of $(x; y)$ as long as the cardinalities of I is strictly smaller than d, where I is constructed as follows:

1. Initially, I is empty and all v_h's are unassigned.
2. For every intermediate variables of the form x_i, y_i, $t_{i,i}$, $r_{i,j}$ (for any $i \neq j$), or a sum of values of above form (including z_i as a special case), add i to I. This covers all the intermediate variables except for ones corresponding to $t_{i,j}$ or $r_{i,j} + t_{i,j}$ for some $i \neq j$. For such variables, add both i and j to I.
3. Now that the set I has been determined, and cardinality of I can be at most $m = 2t$ since there are at most t intermediate variables. We show how to complete a perfect simulation of the values on intermediate variables using only values $x_{|I}$ and $y_{|I}$. Assign values to the $r_{i,j}$ as follows:
   - If $i \in I$ (regardless of j), then $r_{i,j}$ does not enter into the computation for any intermediate variables. Thus, its value can be left unassigned.
   - If $i \in I$, but $j \notin I$, then $r_{i,j}$ is assigned a random independent value. Analysis: Note that if $i < j$ this is what would have happened in the Algorithm 6. If $i > j$, however, we are making use of the fact that by construction, $r_{i,j}$ will never be used in the computation of any intermediate variables. Hence, we can treat $r_{i,j}$ as a uniformly random and independent value.
   - If both $i \in I$ and $j \in I$, then we have access to x_i, x_j, y_i and y_j. Thus, we compute $r_{i,j}$ and $r_{j,i}$ exactly as they would have been computed in the actual Algorithm 6.
4. For every intermediate variable of the form x_i, y_i, $x_i y_i$ (for any $i \neq j$), or a sum of values of the above form (including z_i as a special case), we know that $i \in I$, and all the needed values of $r_{i,j}$ have already been assigned in a perfect simulation. Thus, the intermediate variable can be computed in a perfect simulation.
5. The only types of intermediate variables left are $t_{i,j}$ or $r_{i,j} + t_{i,j}$. But by step 2, both $i, j \in I$, and by Step 3, $z_{i,j}$ has been assigned, thus the value of intermediate variable can be simulated perfectly.

6. Note that all z_i values for $i \in I$ can be simulated perfectly by the argument above. This completes the simulation and the argument of correctness.

Theorem 1 considers the probing of any variable in Algorithm 6 and Corollary 1 below states a result for the probing of the output variables.

Corollary 1. *Let $x_1, \ldots, x_n$ and $y_1, \ldots, y_n$ be two encodings from the inputs of Algorithm 6. Then the distribution of every tuple of $(n-1)$ outputs in Algorithm 6 is independent of the distributions $x = A \times x_1 \oplus \bigoplus_{2 \leq i \leq n} x_i$ and $y = A \times y_1 \oplus \bigoplus_{2 \leq i \leq n} y_i$.*

The proof of Corollary 1 follows from that of Theorem 1 by considering output z_i. To this end, we can add at most $n - 1$ indices into the set I, which correspond to $n - 1$ shares of output.

The security proofs of Algorithms 4 and 5 are quite simple and we give an informal one for Algorithm 5 (masked addition) with inputs $\boldsymbol{x} = (x_1, \ldots, x_n)$ and $\boldsymbol{y} = (y_1, \ldots, y_n)$ here. The intermediate variables in the algorithm are x_i, y_i and $x_i \oplus y_i$ for $i \in \{1, \ldots, n\}$. Thus any d-family variables of above correspond to at most d shares of $\boldsymbol{x}$ or $\boldsymbol{y}$, which are uniform and independent of $\boldsymbol{x}$ or $\boldsymbol{y}$. Therefore, Algorithm 5 is secure against a d-probing adversary for $n \geq d + 1$. Likewise, we can get the same conclusion for Algorithm 4.

Security of the General Masking Scheme. We now show the security of the general masking scheme. That is, we compose the proofs of individual masked operations to a general one, e.g., the masked (X)LS-design cipher.

Our analysis is similar to the work in [1,2,10]. Firstly we only provide an analysis that the composed masked operations have d-probing security. Namely, the distribution of any tuple of d or less intermediate variables in the masked cipher is independent of any plaintext or key. This requires that, for a sequence of operations, the adversary could learn d_i intermediate variables for each operation, as long as $\sum_i d_i \leq d \leq (n - 1)/2$. We consider w masked operations $\mathcal{F} = (f_1, \ldots, f_w)$ in sequence. As shown in Fig. 2, suppose that the adversary probes d_i intermediate variables in the i-th operation f_i and let ϕ_{w-1} be the input of the last operation f_w, then we can see that d_w probes of f_w are corresponding to at most $2d_w$ shares of ϕ_{w-1}. Since ϕ_{w-1} is in turn the output of f_{w-1} and by Corollary 1, the probing of d_w variables to f_w can be perfectly simulated from $2d_w$ shares of the input of f_{q-1}. By adding the probing of d_{w-1} variables of f_{w-1}, the probing of $(d_w + d_{w-1})$ variables of f_w and f_{w-1} can be perfectly simulated from $2(d_w + d_{w-1})$ shares of the input of f_{w-1}. At last, by induction we can conclude that the probing of $\sum_i d_i$ variables of the sequence of the operations can be perfectly simulated from $2\sum_i d_i$ shares of the inputs of the whole masked operations. As discussed in [1, Sect. 5.2], to handle the situation that adversary learns up to d variables in each execution of the masked cipher (and thus he probes many values in a multiple-run setting), the masking refreshing algorithm (i.e., Algorithm 4) should be carried out on the secret key

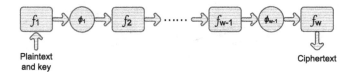

Fig. 2. The sequence of operations in consideration.

whenever the encryption/decryption starts over again. It should be noted that the refreshing algorithm should be called n times for nth-order masking against an $(n-1)$-probing adversary.

3.2 Practical Evaluation

In order to illustrate Boolean matrix product masking's resistance to higher-order side-channel attacks, we evaluate the information leakage of its shares and compare it to the one of Boolean masking and inner product masking shares. We focus on the $m = 4$ case (which allows us to limit the computational cost of the evaluations) and follow the evaluation framework of [16]. Namely, we compute the mutual information between a secret m-bit value and the leakage of its n shares. For this purpose, we follow the standard simulation setting with Hamming weight power model and Gaussian noise that has been used, e.g. in [1,17] for analyzing Boolean and inner product masking. That is, we model the leakage of shares $\boldsymbol{x} = (x_1, \ldots, x_n)$ for secret variable x as:

$$\text{Leakage}(\boldsymbol{x}) = \text{Leakage}((x_1, \ldots, x_n)) = (\text{HW}(x_1) + \epsilon_1, \ldots, \text{HW}(x_n) + \epsilon_n), \quad (1)$$

where $\text{HW}(\cdot)$ denotes the Hamming weight and each ϵ_i for $i \in \{1, \ldots, n\}$ is Gaussian noise. Figure 3 shows the mutual information in $\log_{10}$ scale for the leakages of different masking schemes of order $n = 2, 3$ for 4-bit secret variables. For better comparison, we also show the leakage of inner product masking (in both $\text{GF}(2^4)$ and $\text{GF}(2^8)$) [1]. For this first experiment, we picked up a public matrix $A = (1\,1\,0\,0; 0\,0\,1\,1; 1\,0\,1\,0; 1\,1\,0\,1)$ for Boolean matrix product masking, and took $(l_1 = 1, l_2 = 15)$, $(l_1 = 1, l_2 = 255)$ and $(l_1 = 1, l_2 = 13, l_3 = 15)$ for inner product masking of order $n = 2, 3$ (similar to the choices made in [1]). Based on these settings, our observations are threefold.

First, the mutual information of all settings decreases with the noise level and both inner product and Boolean matrix product masking leak consistently less than the Boolean masking (for all noise levels).

Second, and as expected, inner product masking has lower information leakage than our masking scheme in low noise region for $n = 3$, since in our case only one share is of higher algebraic complexity. This is the price to pay for the more efficient generalization of our scheme to the higher-order cases. That is, Boolean matrix product masking should be seen as a tradeoff between Boolean masking and inner product masking in low noise contexts.

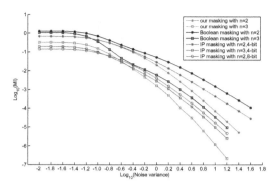

Fig. 3. Mutual information in function of the noise variance for different schemes.

Third, another important (and somewhat surprising) observation from Fig. 3 is that the slopes of the IT curves for our masking scheme exceed what is predicted by the probing proof of security. For example, for $n = 2$ we can see that this slope tends to -3, while it is only -2 for Boolean and inner product masking. This is naturally a very useful observation, since it implies larger (concrete) security levels for our shares. (As proven in [5] the mutual information metric is directly proportional to the success rate of a worst-case side-channel adversary). And similar observations hold for $n = 3$. Interestingly, these reductions of the information leakages can be directly connected to the results in [9] where it is shown that the information leakages can indeed be reduced in such a way for certain types of encodings and (linear) leakage functions. However, contrary to low entropy masking schemes (which loose their security properties in case of nonlinear leakages) the "security order amplification" we observe is only a bonus in our case (i.e. even for nonlinear leakage function, we at least keep the security guarantee of the probing model). To further confirm this observation, we computed the (noise-free) statistical moments of the share's leakages for our encodings, together with the Boolean ones. Recall that in [9], the statistical moments for nth-order masking are defined as $m = \prod_{i=1}^{n}(x_i - \mathrm{E}(x_i))^{o_i}$, where E is the expectation and $o_i \in \{0, 1, 2, \ldots\}$. Thus the degree of a statistical moment is $o = \sum_{i=1}^{n} o_i$. In Table 1, the degree of the lowest key-dependent statistical moments (denoted as o_{min}) for different matrices A are listed. We can see that the value of o_{min} relates to the choice of matrix A, and specifically the minimum Hamming weight of its (or its inverse's) rows (denoted as h and ih for A and A^{-1} respectively). This can be easily explained by considering the fact that if the leakage function is linear, it will manipulate the bits of an m-bit nibble independently, and therefore the matrix multiplication has the impact of XORing more independent shares together. As a result, for a Boolean matrix product masking with n shares, the degree of the lowest key-dependent statistical moment is $o_{min} = \min(2n, h+n-1, (n-1)*ih+1)$, where the $2n$ value comes from the fact that there is at least one moment of this order that is key-dependent, namely the one multiplying the square of all the shares. For completeness, we confirm

Table 1. Degree of the lowest secret variable-dependent statistical moments.

Type of masking and its degree	h, ih	o_{min}
Our masking, $n = 2$	1, 1	2
	2,3	3
	3,4	4
	$h \geq 4$ or $ih \geq 4$	4
Our masking, $n = 3$	2, 1	3
	2,2	4
	3,2	5
	4,2	6
	$h \geq 5$ or $ih \geq 3$	6
Boolean masking, $n = 2$		2
Boolean masking, $n = 3$		3

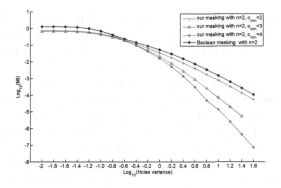

Fig. 4. Mutual information in function of the noise variance for Boolean matrix product masking using the matrices A for different degree of lowest key-dependent statistical moments.

these expectations on Fig. 4, where we plot the mutual information leakages of our masking scheme in function of the values of o_{min}.[2] For comparison we also add the curves of Boolean for $n = 2$.

The latter observation leads to two additional discussion points. First, by the links between inner product masking and ours in Sect. 2.6, the security order amplification in this section also holds for inner product masking. That is, by selecting the L vectors appropriately, we can also improve the statistical order inner product masking for linear leakage functions, which we could confirm experimentally. So by chance, the authors in [1] just picked up the worst possible L vectors for their information theoretic evaluations.

---

[2] We take the matrices A as $(1\,0\,0\,0; 1\,1\,1\,0; 0\,0\,1\,0; 1\,1\,1\,1)$, $(1\,1\,0\,0; 0\,0\,1\,1; 1\,0\,1\,0; 1\,1\,0\,1)$ and $(1\,1\,1\,0; 1\,1\,0\,1; 1\,0\,1\,1; 0\,1\,1\,1)$ respectively.

Second, as for low entropy masking schemes, such gains are not observed for non-linear leakage functions. Hence, it is an interesting scope for further research to investigate how they materialize in real-world devices. Most likely, the situation will be intermediate (i.e. lower gains than with perfectly linear leakage functions, but less informative leakages than with Boolean masking). Similarly, the order amplification observation in this section is only shown for the encoding parts of the schemes. We leave it as another interesting open question to find out if other parts of the computations maintain this property. Here as well, we conjecture that the situation will be intermediate (i.e. not all the tuples will allow order amplification for linear leakages but many of them will be less informative than with Boolean masking). So overall, this suggests inner product masking (in general) has interesting potential for reducing the number and informativeness of "tuples of interest" in masked implementations.

4   Performance Evaluation

In order to compare the efficiency of our proposed masking scheme with Boolean masking, we applied them to protect the LS-designs Fantomas [8]. The cipher uses 8-bit bitslice S-box and 16-bit L-box for 12 rounds. We implemented Boolean matrix product masking for $n = 2, 3, 4$ and $m = 4, 8$. For the part of matrix multiplication, we apply the Algorithm 9 and set the k to 1 and m for matrix of size $m \times m$ (for matrix A) and $m \times m^2$ (for matrices $\hat{A}$, $\acute{A}$ and $\grave{A}$) respectively [3]. Thus the (additional) memory for the pre-computed lookup tables is $2^m + m * 2^m * 3$ bytes, where the left side 2^m bytes come from the look-up table for $A \times x$ and the right side $m * 2^m * 3$ bytes come from the look-up takes for $\hat{A} \times x$, $\acute{A} \times x$ and $\grave{A} \times x$. As analyzed in Sect. 3.1, we run the masking refreshing algorithm n times on the key shares at the beginning of every execution of the cipher. We also implemented the Boolean masking [10] with the same number of shares. We wrote the codes in C language and ran them on a Atmega 2560 processor. Admittedly, the efficiency of our codes could be highly improved if rewritten in assembly language.

We summarize the performances of our implementations in Table 2. We can see that the penalty factors of our masking (using 8×8 matrix A) are not far from the ones of Boolean masking (with same n), which indicates that the efficiency of our masking scheme is comparable to Boolean masking. Note that it is counterintuitive that the performance of our masking for $m = 8$ is (slightly) better than that for $m = 4$. Yet, this is due to the fact that the smallest unit of variable in C language is the 8-bit 'char', and thus the operations on 4×4 matrices take more time than necessary.[4]

---

[3] Note that in this case we don't need to keep the memory for the matrices $\hat{A}$, $\acute{A}$ and $\grave{A}$.

[4] This problem could be solved by an optimized assembly implementation.

Table 2. Performances of our implementations.

Masking type	n	m	Clock cycles	Penalty factor
No masking			386048	1
Boolean	2		1112064	2.88
Boolean	3		2285568	5.92
Boolean	4		3743744	9.70
Our masking	2	8	2421760	6.27
Our masking	3	8	4670464	12.10
Our masking	4	8	7450624	19.30
Our masking	2	4	2428928	6.29
Our masking	3	4	5480448	14.1963
Our masking	4	4	9590784	24.84

5   Conclusion

In this paper, we have proposed Boolean matrix product masking as a variant of the inner product masking in [1]. It can be used as an efficient alternative to the commonly used Boolean masking to protect bitslice ciphers such as the (X)LS-designs, and leads to efficient implementations in software computing platforms. Our scheme is proven secure in the probing model. Besides, its information theoretic analysis reveals that inner product masking can generally exhibit information leakages reduced beyond the guarantees given by the probing security order for linear leakage functions. Thanks to our matrix descriptions, we can additionally provide a simple explanation of this phenomena, which relates to the minimum Hamming weight of the multiplication matrices used in inner product masking. It is therefore an interesting scope for further research to investigate the behavior of such masking schemes in the context of concrete (close to but not exactly linear) leakage functions, and to analyze how this security order amplification be in complete implementations (and not just encodings). Incidentally, this will require the development of new analysis models and tools - since highly multivariate side-channel (e.g. information theoretic) analysis is computationally hard, and this effect is not captured by probing security.

Besides, all our analyses considered the matrix used in our multiplication as fixed and public. Yet, since this matrix is not supposed to leave the device to protect, nothing prevents the designers to keep it secret. This would make the security analysis more involved (since it would then include some kind of reverse engineering problem), but has interesting potential to further improve the security of our masking scheme without any performance penalty, which we leave as another important scope for further research.

Acknowledgements. This work has been funded in parts by the European Commission through the ERC project 280141, the CHIST-ERA project SECODE, Major State Basic Research Development Program (973 Plan) (2013CB338004). François-Xavier

Standaert is a research associate of the Belgian Fund for Scientific Research (FNRS-F.R.S.). Yu Yu was supported by the National Natural Science Foundation of China Grant (Nos. 61472249, 61572192, 61572149) and International Science & Technology Cooperation & Exchange Projects of Shaanxi Province (2016KW-038). Zheng Guo was supported by the National Natural Science Foundation of China (No. 61402286) and Shanghai Minhang Innovation project (No. 2015MH069). Junrong Liu was supported by the National Natural Science Foundation of China (No. U1536103). Dawu Gu was supported by National Natural Science Foundation of China (No. 61472250).

References

1. Balasch, J., Faust, S., Gierlichs, B.: Inner product masking revisited. In: Oswald, E., Fischlin, M. (eds.) EUROCRYPT 2015. LNCS, vol. 9056, pp. 486–510. Springer, Heidelberg (2015). doi:10.1007/978-3-662-46800-5_19

2. Barthe, G., Belaïd, S., Dupressoir, F., Fouque, P.-A., Grégoire, B., Strub, P.-Y.: Verified proofs of higher-order masking. In: Oswald, E., Fischlin, M. (eds.) EUROCRYPT 2015. LNCS, vol. 9056, pp. 457–485. Springer, Heidelberg (2015). doi:10.1007/978-3-662-46800-5_18

3. Carlet, C., Guilley, S.: Complementary dual codes for counter-measures to side-channel attacks. Adv. Math. Commun. **10**(1), 131–150 (2016)

4. Castagnos, G., Renner, S., Zémor, G.: High-order masking by using coding theory and its application to AES. In: Stam, M. (ed.) IMACC 2013. LNCS, vol. 8308, pp. 193–212. Springer, Heidelberg (2013). doi:10.1007/978-3-642-45239-0_12

5. Duc, A., Faust, S., Standaert, F.-X.: Making masking security proofs concrete. In: Oswald, E., Fischlin, M. (eds.) EUROCRYPT 2015. LNCS, vol. 9056, pp. 401–429. Springer, Heidelberg (2015). doi:10.1007/978-3-662-46800-5_16

6. Fumaroli, G., Martinelli, A., Prouff, E., Rivain, M.: Affine masking against higher-order side channel analysis. In: Biryukov, A., Gong, G., Stinson, D.R. (eds.) SAC 2010. LNCS, vol. 6544, pp. 262–280. Springer, Heidelberg (2011). doi:10.1007/978-3-642-19574-7_18

7. Goubin, L., Martinelli, A.: Protecting AES with Shamir's secret sharing scheme. In: Preneel, B., Takagi, T. (eds.) CHES 2011. LNCS, vol. 6917, pp. 79–94. Springer, Heidelberg (2011). doi:10.1007/978-3-642-23951-9_6

8. Grosso, V., Leurent, G., Standaert, F.-X., Varici, K.: LS-Designs: bitslice encryption for efficient masked software implementations. In: Cid, C., Rechberger, C. (eds.) FSE 2014. LNCS, vol. 8540, pp. 18–37. Springer, Heidelberg (2015). doi:10.1007/978-3-662-46706-0_2

9. Grosso, V., Standaert, F.-X., Prouff, E.: Low entropy masking schemes, revisited. In: Francillon, A., Rohatgi, P. (eds.) CARDIS 2013. LNCS, vol. 8419, pp. 33–43. Springer, Heidelberg (2014). doi:10.1007/978-3-319-08302-5_3

10. Ishai, Y., Sahai, A., Wagner, D.: Private circuits: securing hardware against probing attacks. In: Boneh, D. (ed.) CRYPTO 2003. LNCS, vol. 2729, pp. 463–481. Springer, Heidelberg (2003). doi:10.1007/978-3-540-45146-4_27

11. Journault, A., Standaert, F.X., Varici, K.: Improving the security and efficiency of block ciphers based on LS-designs. In: 9th International Workshop on Coding and Cryptography, WCC 2015, Paris, France, April 2015

12. Oswald, E., Fischlin, M. (eds.): EUROCRYPT 2015. LNCS, vol. 9056. Springer, Heidelberg (2015)

13. Preneel, B., Takagi, T. (eds.): CHES 2011. LNCS, vol. 6917. Springer, Heidelberg (2011)

14. Prouff, E., Roche, T.: Higher-order glitches free implementation of the AES using secure multi-party computation protocols. In: Preneel, B., Takagi, T. (eds.) CHES 2011. LNCS, vol. 6917, pp. 63–78. Springer, Heidelberg (2011). doi:10.1007/978-3-642-23951-9_5

15. Rivain, M., Prouff, E.: Provably secure higher-order masking of AES. In: Mangard, S., Standaert, F.-X. (eds.) CHES 2010. LNCS, vol. 6225, pp. 413–427. Springer, Heidelberg (2010). doi:10.1007/978-3-642-15031-9_28

16. Standaert, F.-X., Malkin, T.G., Yung, M.: A unified framework for the analysis of side-channel key recovery attacks. In: Joux, A. (ed.) EUROCRYPT 2009. LNCS, vol. 5479, pp. 443–461. Springer, Heidelberg (2009). doi:10.1007/978-3-642-01001-9_26

17. Standaert, F.-X., Veyrat-Charvillon, N., Oswald, E., Gierlichs, B., Medwed, M., Kasper, M., Mangard, S.: The world is not enough: another look on second-order DPA. In: Abe, M. (ed.) ASIACRYPT 2010. LNCS, vol. 6477, pp. 112–129. Springer, Heidelberg (2010). doi:10.1007/978-3-642-17373-8_7

Squeezing Polynomial Masking in Tower Fields
A Higher-Order Masked AES S-Box

Fabrizio De Santis[1](✉), Tobias Bauer[1], and Georg Sigl[1,2]

[1] Technische Universität München (TUM), Munich, Germany
{desantis,tobias.bauer,sigl}@tum.de
[2] Fraunhofer Institute for Applied and Integrated Security (AISEC),
Munich, Germany
georg.sigl@aisec.fraunhofer.de

Abstract. Polynomial masking is a higher-order and glitch-resistant masking scheme to protect cryptographic implementations against side-channel attacks. Polynomial masking was introduced at CHES 2011, while a 1st-order polynomially masked AES S-box hardware implementation was presented at CHES 2013, and later on improved at TIs 2016. Polynomial masking schemes are advantageous in the way they can be easily adapted to every block-cipher and inherently scaled to any masking order using simple hardware design patterns. As a drawback, they typically have large area, time, and randomness requirements when compared to other masking schemes, e.g. threshold implementations. In this work, we show how tower fields can be perfectly committed to polynomial masking schemes, to reduce both area and randomness requirements of higher-order polynomially masked implementations, with application to AES. We provide ASIC synthesis results up to the 6th masking order and perform side-channel attacks on a Xilinx Spartan6 FPGA up to the 2nd masking order.

Keywords: Polynomial masking · Secret sharing · Multi-party computation · AES · Tower fields · Side-channel analysis

1 Introduction

Nowadays, the security of cryptographic devices does not only depend on the cryptographic properties of mathematical algorithms, but also, and mainly, on the physical security of their implementations. In fact, while the cryptographic security of standardized block ciphers, such as AES or PRESENT, currently provides adequate security margins for most applications, the physical security of their implementations is still far from yielding a satisfactory "security vs. costs vs. performance" trade-off in many practical situations, e.g. on resource constrained devices such as RFID or smart cards.

Since the seminal work of Kocher et al. in the late nineties [KJJ99], many countermeasures have been proposed to thwart side-channel attacks at different

© Springer International Publishing AG 2017
K. Lemke-Rust and M. Tunstall (Eds.): CARDIS 2016, LNCS 10146, pp. 192–208, 2017.
DOI: 10.1007/978-3-319-54669-8_12

levels of abstraction *e.g.*, protected logic styles at the cell level [PKZM07, Kir11, MKEP12], masking schemes at the algorithmic level [CJRR99b, RP10, PR11], and fresh re-keying schemes at the protocol level [MSGR10, BDH+14, DKM+15]. In particular, higher-order masking schemes represent one very effective and common way to protect block-cipher implementations against side-channel attacks at the algorithmic level. The basic idea of higher-order masking schemes is to split the computation of secret-dependent intermediate values into multiple random shares, as to randomize the information leaked by cryptographic computations and increase the attack complexity exponentially in the number of shares [CJRR99a].

Polynomial masking is based on Shamir's secret sharing scheme [Sha79] and secure multi-party computation protocols [BOGW88], and represents the first attempt to conceive both glitch-resistant and higher-order masking schemes in literature. It was originally introduced at CHES 2011 [PR11], while a 1st-order AES S-box implementation on FPGA was presented at CHES 2013 [MM13]. Subsequently, 1st-order and 2nd-order polynomially masked implementations of the PRESENT S-box on FPGA were published in [DCBRN15]. Finally, the CHES 2013 design was improved in [DBS16], where a shuffling countermeasure to hide higher-order univariate leakages was also proposed. Another approach to provide both glitch-resistant and higher-order masking schemes is given by Threshold Implementations (TIs) [BGN+14, DCBR+16]. While TIs are typically faster, smaller, and have considerably lower randomness requirements than polynomially masked implementations, these latter have the advantages that can be straightforwardly adapted to any block-cipher and inherently scaled to any masking order using regular hardware structures (which could be possibly implemented in full-custom secure logic). Additionally, they intrinsically provide more side-channel security than TIs in a standard setting, as they process each share individually over time, hence forcing the adversary to estimate the leakage distribution over more dimensions.

Originally presented in [Rij], tower fields have been successfully employed many times in literature to reduce the area requirements of both unprotected and protected AES hardware implementations [RDJ+01, WOL02]. In this work, we show how tower fields also perfectly commit to polynomial masking schemes (due to their algebraic structure) to reduce the area and randomness requirements of higher-order polynomially masked implementations. We present the design of a higher-order polynomially masked AES S-box in the tower field $GF((2^4)^2)$, built around a small shared $GF(2^4)$ multiplier. We provide ASIC synthesis results up to the 6th masking order and present side-channel collision attacks up to the 2nd masking order on a Xilinx Spartan6 FPGA.

Organization. Section 2 provide background information on polynomial masking schemes, while Sect. 3 summarizes the arithmetic of AES in the tower field $GF((2^4)^2)$. Section 4 details the hardware design and provides ASIC synthesis results together with a performance comparison with the state of art. Side-channel attacks on a Xilinx Spartan6 FPGA are presented in Sect. 5. Conclusions are given in Sect. 6.

2   Higher-Order Polynomial Masking

Let $\mathsf{GF}(2^n)$ denote a binary extension field. A dth-order masking scheme splits each secret intermediate value $x \in \mathsf{GF}(2^n)$ into m random shares, such that no subset of cardinality $d < m$ can reveal information about x. Polynomial masking [PR11,RP12] is a dth-order masking scheme ($m = 2d+1$) based upon Shamir's secret sharing scheme [Sha79] and multi-party computation protocols [BOGW88]. The basic operations of polynomial masking are summarized.

Initialization. At the beginning, m elements $(\alpha_i)_{1 \leq i \leq m} \xleftarrow{\$} \mathsf{GF}(2^n)^*$ are chosen at random, such that $\forall i \neq j \in [1,m]$, $\alpha_i \neq \alpha_j$, and made public. Then, the m elements $(\lambda_i)_{1 \leq i \leq m}$ on the first row of the inverse of the Vandermonde $(m \times m)$-matrix $(\alpha_i^j)_{1 \leq i,j \leq m}$ are computed, such that $\lambda_i = \prod_{k=1, k \neq i}^{m} -\alpha_k (\alpha_i - \alpha_k)^{-1}$.

Sharing and Reconstruction. Let $P_x(Y) = x + \sum_{j=1}^{d} r_j Y^j$ be a random polynomial instantiated using d random coefficients $(r_j \xleftarrow{\$} \mathsf{GF}(2^n))_{1 \leq j \leq d}$ and representing the secret intermediate value $x \in \mathsf{GF}(2^n)$. Then, the m random shares $(x_i)_{1 \leq i \leq m}$ are obtained by evaluating P_x at the public points $(\alpha_i)_{1 \leq i \leq m}$, such that $x_i = x + \sum_{j=1}^{d} r_j \alpha_i^j$, $i \in [1,m]$. Conversely, a secret x can be reconstructed using Lagrange's interpolation formula and the previously computed public values $(\lambda_i)_{1 \leq i \leq m}$, as: $x = \sum_{i=1}^{m} x_i \lambda_i$.

Shared Addition. The addition of two secrets $z = x + y$ can be performed independently on the shares $(x_i, y_i)_{1 \leq i \leq m}$ in a straightforward way, as: $z_i = (x_i + y_i) + \sum_{j=1}^{d} (r_j + r'_j) \alpha_i^j$, $i \in [1,m]$, where $P_x(Y) = x + \sum_{j=1}^{d} r_j Y^j$, $P_y(Z) = y + \sum_{j=1}^{d} r'_j Z^j$, and no fresh randomness is required.

Shared Multiplication by a Constant. Similarly to addition, the multiplication of a secret x by a constant value $c \neq 0$ can be performed independently on each share: $z_i = (c x_i) + \sum_{j=1}^{d} (c r_j) \alpha_i^j$, $i \in [1,m]$, where $P_x(Y) = x + \sum_{j=1}^{d} r_j Y^j$ and no fresh randomness is required.

Shared Multiplication. The multiplication of two secrets $z = xy$ can be performed in three steps using the method of Ben-Or, Goldwasser and Wigderson [BOGW88]:

$$\begin{cases} \text{Step 1.) } t_i = x_i y_i \\ \text{Step 2.) } q_{i,k} = t_i + \sum_{j=1}^{d} s_j \alpha_k^j, \quad i, k \in [1,m]. \\ \text{Step 3.) } z_i = \sum_{w=1}^{m} q_{w,i} \lambda_w \end{cases} \tag{1}$$

First, the shares are pairwise multiplied in a straightforward way (Step 1). Then, the result is re-shared using d freshly generated masks $(s_j)_{1 \leq j \leq d}$ for each share (Step 2). Finally, the resulting polynomial is reduced to the original degree d by Lagrange interpolation using the public values $(\lambda_i)_{1 \leq i \leq m}$ (Step 3).

3   AES Arithmetic in Tower Fields

3.1   The AES S-Box

The AES S-box is defined as the composition of two operations: an inversion in the field $\mathsf{GF}(2^8) \simeq \mathbf{F}_2[x]/(x^8+x^4+x^3+x+1)$ followed by an affine transformation in the field $\mathsf{GF}(2)$. Using Lagrange interpolation, the affine transformation can also be represented in the field $\mathsf{GF}(2^8)$ and the AES S-box can be expressed as:

$$y = \mathsf{S}(x) = \delta_0 + \sum_{k=1}^{8} \delta_k x^{255-2^{k-1}} = \delta_0 + \sum_{k=1}^{8} \delta_k (x^{-1})^{2^{k-1}}, \qquad (2)$$

where $(\delta_k)_{0 \le k \le 8}$ are the coefficients defined by the vector (0x63, 0x05, 0x09, 0xF9, 0x25, 0xF4, 0x01, 0xB5, 0x8F), cf. [DR02, p.192]. This algebraic representation of the AES S-box allows for a straightforward application of polynomial masking, as previously described.

3.2   Arithmetic in $\mathsf{GF}((2^4)^2)$

Tower fields represent a convenient way to reduce the area requirements of extension field arithmetic circuits in hardware, i.e. arithmetic in $\mathsf{GF}(2^8)$ can be performed in the tower field $\mathsf{GF}((2^4)^2)$ implementing small $\mathsf{GF}(2^4)$ arithmetic circuits in place of $\mathsf{GF}(2^8)$ circuits. Let $\Phi : \mathsf{GF}(2^8) \to \mathsf{GF}((2^4)^2)$ denote the isomorphic mapping, which bijectively maps the elements from $\mathsf{GF}(2^8)$ to $\mathsf{GF}((2^4)^2)$, and $\Phi^{-1} : \mathsf{GF}((2^4)^2) \to \mathsf{GF}(2^8)$ its inverse, where $\mathsf{GF}((2^4)^2) \simeq \mathbf{F}_{2^4}[y]/(y^2+y+\gamma)$.

Inversion. The inversion $b = a^{-1}$ of an element $a \in \mathsf{GF}(2^8)$ can be computed in the tower field $\mathsf{GF}((2^4)^2)$ as:

$$\begin{cases} b_H = a_H [a_H^2 \gamma + a_H a_L + a_L^2]^{-1} \\ b_L = (a_L + a_H)[a_H^2 \gamma + a_H a_L + a_L^2]^{-1} \end{cases}, \qquad (3)$$

where $a \mapsto_{\Phi} (a_H, a_L)$, $(b_H, b_L) \mapsto_{\Phi^{-1}} b$, and all operations are defined in $\mathsf{GF}(2^4)$.

Multiplication. The multiplication $c = ab$ of two elements $a, b \in \mathsf{GF}(2^8)$ can be computed in $\mathsf{GF}((2^4)^2)$ as:

$$\begin{cases} c_H = (b_H + b_L)(a_H + a_L) + b_L a_L \\ c_L = b_H a_H \gamma + b_L a_L \end{cases}, \qquad (4)$$

where $a \mapsto_{\Phi} (a_H, a_L)$, $b \mapsto_{\Phi} (b_H, b_L)$, $(c_H, c_L) \mapsto_{\Phi^{-1}} c$, and all operations are defined in $\mathsf{GF}(2^4)$.

Squaring. The squaring $b = a^2$ of an element $a \in \mathsf{GF}(2^8)$ follows immediately from Eq. (4):

$$\begin{cases} b_H = a_H^2 \\ b_L = a_H^2 \gamma + a_L^2 \end{cases}, \qquad (5)$$

where $a \mapsto_{\Phi} (a_H, a_L)$, $(b_H, b_L) \mapsto_{\Phi^{-1}} b$, and all operations are defined in $\mathsf{GF}(2^4)$.

3.3   Inversion in $\mathsf{GF}(2^4)$

Inversion in finite fields can be implemented in several ways. In this work, we implemented the inversion in $\mathsf{GF}(2^4)$ using addition chains, as they fit well to polynomial masking schemes.

Definition 1 (Addition Chain). *An addition chain for a positive integer q is a sequence of positive integers $(a_0 = 1, \ldots, a_\ell = q)$, such that $\forall 1 \leq i \leq \ell$, there exist $0 \leq j, k < i$ and $a_i = a_j + a_k$, where ℓ represents the length of the chain.*

Addition chains in the form $a_i = a_{i-1} + a_k$ are particularly relevant for hardware implementations, as the input a_{i-1} is directly available from the previous output. To compute the inversion $x^{-1} = x^{14} \in \mathsf{GF}(2^4)$, we used the addition chain $(1, 2, 3, 6, 7, 14)$ given in [DBS16]:

$$C_{14}: \quad x \xrightarrow{S} x^2 \xrightarrow{M} x^3 \xrightarrow{S} x^6 \xrightarrow{M} x^7 \xrightarrow{S} x^{14}.$$

This addition chain requires only 3 squarings and 2 multiplications. Notably, it does not require the storage of any intermediate result but the input x, hence allowing for minimal implementation costs.

4   Hardware Design

In this section, we present the design of a polynomially masked AES S-box in the tower field $\mathsf{GF}((2^4)^2)$ for any masking order $d = (m - 1)/2$. We denote $\mathsf{GF}(2^4) \simeq \mathbf{F}_2[z]/(z^4 + z + 1)$ polynomial basis multipliers by $\otimes$, while $\mathsf{GF}(2^4)$ adders are denoted by $\oplus$. The respective shared operations are denoted using the original symbols surrounded with boxes, e.g. the shared $\mathsf{GF}(2^4)$ multiplier is denoted by $\boxed{\otimes}$. The design basically consists of two hardware modules: a $\mathsf{GF}(2^4)$ shared multiplier (shamul) and a $\mathsf{GF}(2^4)$ shared multiplier by a constant equipped with a $\mathsf{GF}(2^4)$ shared adder (shamac). We proceed as follows: first, we describe the design of the shamul and shamac modules for any masking order. Then, we describe how to use such modules to perform a shared inversion and a shared affine transformation in $\mathsf{GF}((2^4)^2)$ to securely compute the AES S-box at any order. Finally, we present synthesis ASIC results up the 6th masking order.

4.1   The shamul Module

The shamul module implements the multiplication of two shared secrets in $\mathsf{GF}(2^4)$, according to Eq. (1). In order to minimize the area requirements, it is used to perform both shared $\mathsf{GF}(2^4)$ multiplications and $\mathsf{GF}(2^4)$ squaring operations, as needed by the inversion and the affine transformation in $\mathsf{GF}((2^4)^2)$. The shamul module instantiates $m^2 \times (d+1) + 2 \times m$ $\mathsf{GF}(2^4)$-multipliers, $m^2 \times (d+1) + m$ $\mathsf{GF}(2^4)$-adders, $m^2 + m \times d + 3 \times m$ 4-bit D-type Flip-Flops (DFFs) and a few multiplexers (MUXes). Note that all MUXes in the design are clocked using DFFs with enable in order to prevent glitches on the select lines [MM13]. Each shared multiplication requires a total of $4 \times m \times d$-bit randomness, whereas only $4 \times d$-bit are needed per clock cycle. To securely multiply two secrets it takes $2 \times m$ clock cycles in total. In the first m clock cycles, the input values are multiplied and re-masked according to (Step 1) and (Step 2) of Eq. (1). In each clock cycle, only the ith share is activated using the signals $(em_i)_{1 \leq i \leq m}$ and $(eout_i)_{1 \leq i \leq m}$. This helps providing a sufficient separation of the leakages of each share over time. The signals $(selm_i)_{1 \leq i \leq m}$ and $(selout_i)_{1 \leq i \leq m}$ are used to select the inputs to the multiplication. In the subsequent m clock cycles, the result is reconstructed according to (Step 3) of Eq. (1) activating one share at the time using the enable signals $(em_i)_{m+1 \leq i \leq 2m}$. Finally, the results are stored in the appropriate registers using the $(el_i)_{1 \leq i \leq m}$ and $(eh_i)_{1 \leq i \leq m}$ signals for the low and high part, respectively. The low part is stored in $(el_i)_{1 \leq i \leq m}$ and the high part is moved from $(em_i)_{1 \leq i \leq m}$ to $(eh_i)_{1 \leq i \leq m}$ at the clock cycles $11 \times m + 1$ (1st share is active) to $11 \times m + m$ (m^{th} share is active) (cf. Fig. 2). The shamul module is illustrated in Fig. 9 (cf. Appendix B) for the exemplary case of $(d,m) = (2,5)$. Note that the shamul module is additionally equipped with m $GF(2^4)$-multipliers, $2 \times m$ $GF(2^4)$-adders, and m 2-to-1 MUXes to perform also shared additions and shared multiplications by the constant 0xE. This allows to compute shared multiplications and shared additions in parallel and save m clock cycles in the first step of the inversion and in the last step of the shared $GF((2^4)^2)$ squaring.

4.2 The shamac Module

The shamac module implements the shared multiplication by a constant and the shared addition of two shared secrets in $GF((2^4)^2)$, as required by the affine transformation. Hence, the shamac module instantiates m circuits (shares), each one consisting of 3 $GF(2^4)$-multipliers, 5 $GF(2^4)$-adders, 5 4-bit DFFs, and a few MUXes, as illustrated in Fig. 1. The shamac module takes m clock cycles and does not require fresh randomness: in the ith clock cycle, only the ith share is activated using the $(ea_i)_{1 \leq i \leq m}$ signals, where the inputs are selected using the signals $(sela_i)_{1 \leq i \leq m}$ and (selconstleft, selconstmiddle, selconstright). The constant values, which are selected by the selconst* signals, are precomputed according to Table 2 (cf. Appendix A). The multiplication by a constant is performed according to Eq. (4), where $(b_H, b_L) = \Phi(\delta_i)$. More specifically, the signal (selconstleft) selects the constants obtained from the addition $\Phi(\delta_i)_H + \Phi(\delta_i)_L$, while the signal (selconstright) selects the constants obtained from the multiplication $\gamma \Phi(\delta_i)_H$. The values selected by (selconstmiddle) correspond to the values $\Phi(\delta_i)_L$. These pre-computations allow to save the area of 1 $GF(2^4)$-multiplier and 1 $GF(2^4)$-adder per each share. Finally, the $(eo_i)_{1 \leq i \leq m}$ signals are activated in the $54 \times m + 2$ clock cycle (1st share) to $55 \times m + 1$ clock cycle (m^{th} share) to output the result. Note that the shamac module can be easily adapted to perform also the initial sharing, the round key additions, and the AES MixColumns operation. All these operations require the shared multiplication by a constant and the shared addition of two shared secrets.

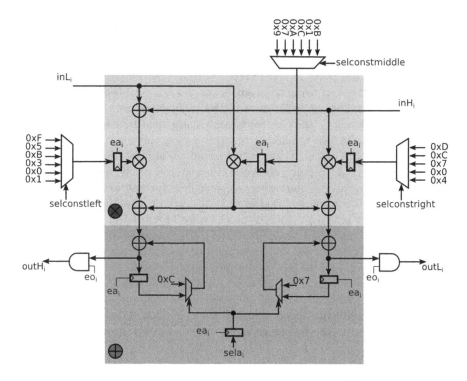

Fig. 1. Multiplication and shared addition module (i^{th} share).

4.3 Shared Tower Field AES S-Box

When using Lagrange interpolation for the affine transformation, the AES S-box $y = \mathsf{S}(x)$ in the tower field $\mathsf{GF}((2^4)^2)$ can be written as follows:

$$(y_H, y_L) = \left(\delta_{H,0} + \sum_{k=1}^{8} \delta_{H,k} z_H^{2^{k-1}}, \delta_{L,0} + \sum_{k=1}^{8} \delta_{L,k} z_L^{2^{k-1}} \right),$$

where $(\delta_{H,k})_{0 \le k \le 8}$ are the coefficients defined by the vector (0xC,0x4,0x4,0x7, 0x9,0x7,0x0,0x4,0xC), $(\delta_{L,k})_{0 \le k \le 8}$ are the coefficients defined by the vector (0x7, 0xB, 0x1, 0xC, 0xA, 0x7, 0x1, 0x7, 0x9), $(z_H, z_L) = \Phi(x^{-1})$ is the result of inversion in $\mathsf{GF}((2^4)^2)$, and all operations are defined in $\mathsf{GF}(2^4)$.

Shared Inversion. The shared inversion in $\mathsf{GF}((2^4)^2)$ is computed according to Eq. (3), where the inversion in $\mathsf{GF}(2^4)$ is computed using the addition chain $\mathcal{C}_{14}$ of Sect. 3.3. The shared inversion is illustrated in Fig. 2 ([Step I1] to [Step I10]) and consists of 9 shared multiplications, 1 shared addition, and 1 shared multiplication by a constant and addition. In [Step I1], a shared addition is performed in parallel to a shared multiplication, where the addition is performed during the first m clock cycles. The output of the first shared multiplication

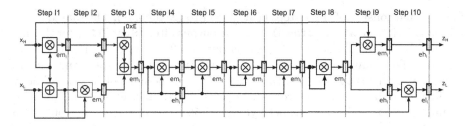

Fig. 2. Shared inversion in $\mathsf{GF}((2^4)^2)$.

is stored in the corresponding registers using the em_i signals. The result of the shared addition must be selected for [Step I2] and [Step I10] using the selm_i signal. The output of shared multiplication in [Step I2] is then stored in the em_i registers and the values of [Step I1] are moved to the eh_i registers. This means that in each clock cycle $1 \leq i \leq m$ of [Step I3], [Step I5] and [Step I10] the signal eh_i is enabled, in order to move the content of the registers em_i from the previous steps into the eh_i registers. For [Step I3], the output of the shared multiplication with the constant 0xE is selected using the selout_i signal, which is enable over the signal eout_i. Therefore only m clocks cycles are needed and the results are stored into the em_i registers. After [Step I3], the shared addition chain $\mathcal{C}_{14}$ is calculated in [Step I4] to [Step I8] and stored in the em_i registers. Therefore, the outputs of [Step I3] are stored in the eh_i registers, for [Step I7]. In the [Step I9] and [Step I10], the last two shared multiplications are calculated and the output values are stored in the eh_i and el_i register to perform the affine transformation. Overall the shared inversion takes $19 \times m = 38 \times d + 19$ clock cycles and requires $36 \times m \times d = 72 \times d^2 + 36 \times d$-bit of randomness to compute the inverse in the tower field $\mathsf{GF}((2^4)^2)$.

Shared Affine Transformation. The affine transformation consists of 7 squaring operations and 8 multiplications by a constant (cf. Fig. 3). The 7 squarings and the first 7 multiplications with the constants run in parallel. Each squaring operation consists of 2 shared $\mathsf{GF}(2^4)$ multiplications (squarings), 1 shared $\mathsf{GF}(2^4)$ multiplication by a constant and a final $\mathsf{GF}(2^4)$ addition (cf. Eq. (5)). The operations needed for one shared squaring operation in $\mathsf{GF}((2^4)^2)$ are illustrated

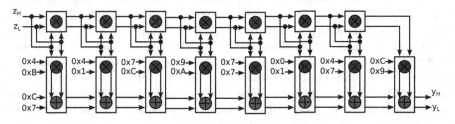

Fig. 3. Shared affine transformation in $\mathsf{GF}((2^4)^2)$.

in Fig. 4 and consists of three steps ([Step A1] to [Step A3]). The shared multiplication in [Step A1] uses the el_i register output after [Step I10] for the first squaring in $GF((2^4)^2)$ and the el_i register output after [Step A3] for the following ones. The computation of [Step A2] and [Step A3] are performed in the same way as in [Step I2] and [Step I3]. Hence, the multipliers and addition modules from shamul can be reused. In total, the shared affine transformation requires $36 \times m = 72 \times d + 36$ clock cycles and $56 \times m \times d = 112 \times d^2 + 56 \times d$-bit of randomness, where one squaring costs $5 \times m = 10 \times d + 5$ clock cycles and uses $8 \times m \times d = 16 \times d^2 + 8$-bit of randomness.

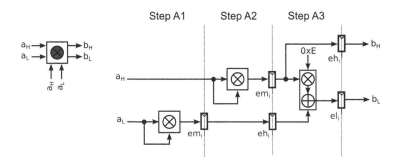

Fig. 4. Shared $GF((2^4)^2)$ squaring.

Isomorphic Mappings. All input values should be transformed using an isomorphic mapping $\Phi : GF(2^8) \rightarrow GF((2^4)^2)$ and, similarly, all the output values should be transformed back using the inverse isomorphic mapping $\Phi^{-1} : GF((2^4)^2) \rightarrow GF(2^8)$. As these transformations are defined over $GF(2)$, they might be problematic for polynomial masking schemes. However, we suggest to apply them directly on the input/output values (e.g. plaintexts, keys and ciphertexts) before/after each encryption, i.e. before sharing and after reconstructing secrets. In this way, no special consideration for these mappings is required in the masking scheme.

Performance Evaluation. We synthesized our design using Synopsys Design Compiler J-2014.09-SP3 and targeting a TSMC 45 nm standard technology library (tcbn45gsbwptc) at 1 MHz. Our gate equivalent (GE) estimations were obtained using the smallest 2-to-1 NAND gate available in the library (ND2D0BWP), whose area accounts for $0.7056\ \mu m^2$, and the compile command to enable a fair comparison of the results. The $GF(2^4)$ multiplier costs only 53 GE, while the $GF(2^4)$ adder costs 10 GE in our library. In total, the computation of a shared AES S-box requires $110 \times d + 55$ clock cycles and $184 \times d^2 + 92 \times d$-bit of fresh randomness. Table 1 provides an overview on the performance of our design as compared to the improved $GF(2^8)$ design described in [DBS16].

Table 1. $GF(2^8)$ vs $GF((2^4)^2)$ AES S-box Comparison.

$GF(2^8)$ [DBS16]	$d = 1$	$d = 2$	$d = 3$	$d = 4$	$d = 5$	$d = 6$
Area [kGE]	10.2	33.4	79.7	157.8	276	442.7
Speed [Clock cycles]	105	175	245	315	385	455
Random [Bit]	408	$1,360$	$2,856$	$4,896$	$7,480$	$10,608$
$GF((2^4)^2)$ [This work]	$d = 1$	$d = 2$	$d = 3$	$d = 4$	$d = 5$	$d = 6$
Area [kGE]	4.0	9.8	20.4	37.1	61.6	95.5
Speed [Clock cycles]	165	275	385	495	605	715
Random [Bit]	276	920	$1,932$	$3,312$	$5,060$	$7,176$

5   Side-Channel Collision Attacks

We synthesized the design using Xilinx ISE Webpack version 14.7 targeting a Xilinx Spartan-6 FPGA (xc6slx9-2-ftg256). We measured the variations of the Electro-Magnetic (EM) field on the front-side FPGA chip surface using an Agilent DSO9254A 2.5 GHz digital oscilloscope with a 10 mm diameter magnetic field coil (RF-R 50-1) and a 30 dB amplifier (PA303) from Langer EMV-Technik. This setup allowed us to: (1) exploit the full vertical resolution of the oscilloscope (due to the low EM field strength); (2) evaluate the worst-case scenario analysis. The oscilloscope sampled at 100 MSa/s and we clocked our design at 4 MHz, resulting in 25 MSa/s for all our experiments. We fixed the security level at $10,000,000$ measurements (where not otherwise specified) and performed univariate 1st- and 2nd-order side-channel correlation-collision attacks. These class of attacks have been shown to be practically effective against hardware polynomially masked implementations in previous works (cf. [MM13]). For the sake of evaluation, we fixed the public points $(\alpha_i)_{1 \leq i \leq m}$ and $(\lambda_i)_{1 \leq i \leq m}$ to $(0x2, 0x3, 0x4)$ and $(0x2, 0x5, 0x6)$ for $d = 1$ and to $(0x4, 0x5, 0x6, 0x0A, 0x0B)$ and $(0x6, 0xE, 0x4, 0x5, 0x8)$ for $d = 2$, respectively. Note that this is a worst-case assumption, as they do not need to be fixed in practice, hence reducing the effectiveness of our attacks in a real scenario. We proceeded as follows: (1) we considered a 1st-order implementation and verified the existence of 1st-order univariate leakage, when the masks were off; (2) we activated the masks and observed the presence of 2nd-order univariate leakage; (3) we activated the shuffling countermeasure of [DBS16] to hide the 2nd-order univariate leakage; (4) we verified the univariate security of a 2nd-order implementation without shuffling.

1st-Order Masking and Masks Off. We verified the existence of 1st-order univariate leakages, when the masks are off, using only 100,000 measurements. The results are reported in Fig. 5, clearly showing the existence of leakages during the whole S-box computations.

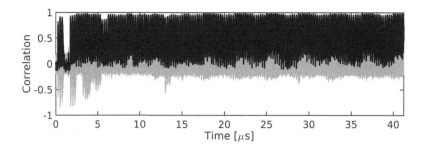

Fig. 5. 1st-Order masking, masks off, 1st-Order univariate attacks, 100,000 traces.

1st-Order Masking, Masks On and Shuffling Off. The results of 1st-order and 2nd-order univariate side-channel attacks are shown in Fig. 6. Even though the shamul and shamac modules are active at the same time, no leakage can be observed in the 1st-order moment. However, similarly to [MM13, DBS16], leakage information is present in the 2nd-order moment during the affine transformation.

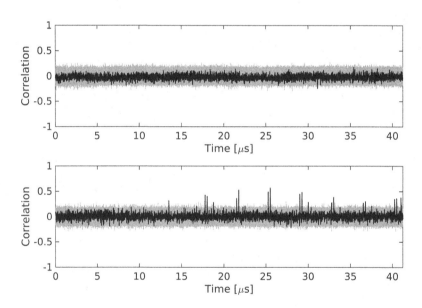

Fig. 6. 1st-Order masking, masks on, shuffling off, 1st-Order (top) and 2nd-Order univariate attacks (bottom), 10,000,000 traces.

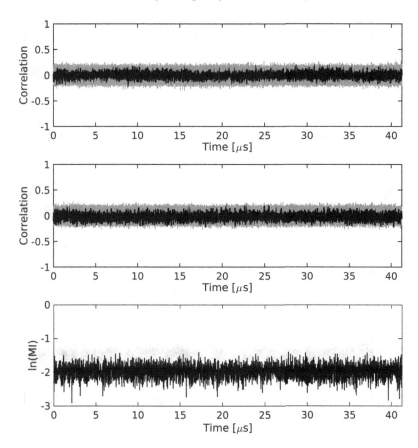

Fig. 7. 1st-Order masking, masks on, shuffling on, 1st-Order (top) and 2nd-Order univariate attacks (middle), mutual information (bottom), 10,000,000 traces.

1st-Order Masking, Masks On and Shuffling On. The results of the analysis is reported in Fig. 7, when the activation order of the secret shares is shuffled using the countermeasure described in [DBS16]. No leakage can be observed in any of the first four moments. Interestingly, also mutual information analysis[1] does not reveal the presence of any leakage.

---

[1] Mutual information was estimated using histograms.

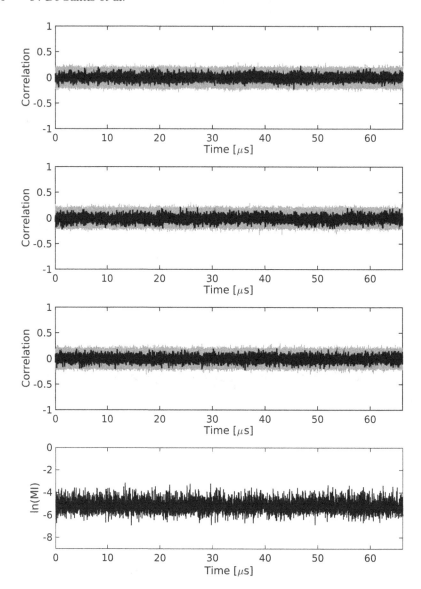

Fig. 8. 2nd-Order masking, masks on, shuffling off, 1st-Order (top), 2nd- and 3rd-Order univariate attacks (middle), mutual information (bottom), 10,000,000 traces.

2nd-Order Masking, Masks On and Shuffling Off. The results of 1st-order and 2nd-order univariate side-channel attacks against a 2nd-order implementation without shuffling are reported in Fig. 8. Also in this case, no univariate leakages can be observed either in any of the first four moments nor using mutual information analysis.

6 Conclusion

We showed how to reduce the area and randomness requirements of higher-order polynomial masking hardware implementations using tower fields. Our 1st-order and 2nd-order masked implementations of the AES S-box in $\mathsf{GF}((2^4)^2)$ cost 4.0 kGE and 9.8 kGE, respectively. Both can guarantee univariate side-channel security up to 10,000,000 measurements in a worst-case scenario analysis.

Acknowledgements. This work was partly funded by the German Federal Ministry of Education and Research (BMBF) in the project SIBASE under grant number 01IS13020A.

A Tables

Table 2. Isomorphic mapping $\Phi : \mathsf{GF}(2^8) \to \mathsf{GF}((2^4)^2)$ of the AES constants.

	Affine transformation									MixColumns			
δ_i	0x63	0x05	0x09	0xF9	0x25	0xF4	0x01	0xB5	0x8F	ψ_i	0x01	0x02	0x03
$\Phi(\delta_i)_H$	0xC	0x4	0x4	0x7	0x9	0x7	0x0	0x4	0xC	$\Phi(\psi_i)_H$	0x0	0x2	0x2
$\Phi(\delta_i)_L$	0x7	0xB	0x1	0xC	0xA	0x7	0x1	0x7	0x9	$\Phi(\psi_i)_L$	0x1	0x6	0x7

B   Figures

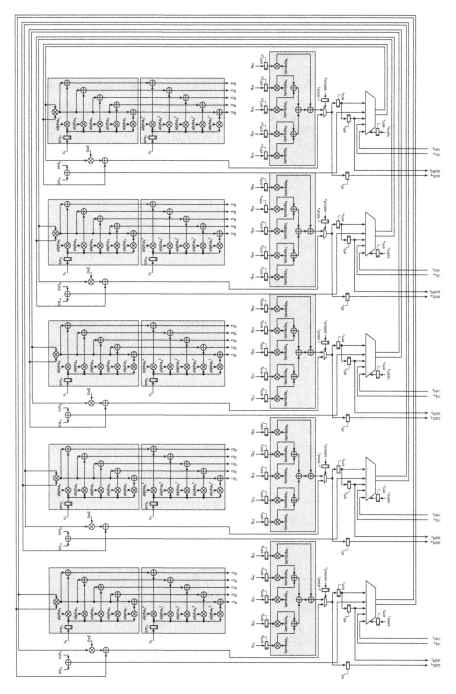

Fig. 9. Shared $\mathsf{GF}(2^4)$ multiplication module for $(d, m) = (2, 5)$.

References

[BDH+14] Belaid, S., De Santis, F., Heyszl, J., Mangard, S., Medwed, M., Schmidt, J.-M., Standaert, F.-X., Tillich, S.: Towards fresh re-keying with leakage-resilient PRFs: cipher design principles and analysis. JCEN **4**(3), 1–15 (2014)

[BGN+14] Bilgin, B., Gierlichs, B., Nikova, S., Nikov, V., Rijmen, V.: Higher-order threshold implementations. In: Sarkar, P., Iwata, T. (eds.) ASIACRYPT 2014. LNCS, vol. 8874, pp. 326–343. Springer, Heidelberg (2014). doi:10.1007/978-3-662-45608-8_18

[BOGW88] Ben-Or, M., Goldwasser, S., Wigderson, A.: Completeness theorems for non-cryptographic fault-tolerant distributed computation. In: 20th ACM Symposium on Theory of Computing, STOC, pp. 1–10. ACM (1988)

[CJRR99a] Chari, S., Jutla, C., Rao, J.R., Rohatgi, P.: A cautionary note regarding evaluation of AES candidates on smart-cards. In: 2nd Advanced Encryption Standard (AES) Candidate Conference (1999)

[CJRR99b] Chari, S., Jutla, C.S., Rao, J.R., Rohatgi, P.: Towards sound approaches to counteract power-analysis attacks. In: Wiener, M. (ed.) CRYPTO 1999. LNCS, vol. 1666, pp. 398–412. Springer, Heidelberg (1999). doi:10.1007/3-540-48405-1_26

[DBS16] De Santis, F., Bauer, T., Sigl, G.: Hiding higher-order univariate leakages by shuffling polynomial masking schemes. In: Theory of Implementation Security (TIs) ACM CCS Workshop (2016)

[DCBR+16] Cnudde, T., Bilgin, B., Reparaz, O., Nikov, V., Nikova, S.: Higher-order threshold implementation of the AES S-Box. In: Homma, N., Medwed, M. (eds.) CARDIS 2015. LNCS, vol. 9514, pp. 259–272. Springer, Cham (2016). doi:10.1007/978-3-319-31271-2_16

[DCBRN15] De Cnudde, T., Bilgin, B., Reparaz, O., Nikova, S.: Higher-order glitch resistant implementation of the PRESENT S-Box. In: Ors, B., Preneel, B. (eds.) BalkanCryptSec 2014. LNCS, vol. 9024, pp. 75–93. Springer, Cham (2015). doi:10.1007/978-3-319-21356-9_6

[DKM+15] Dobraunig, C., Koeune, F., Mangard, S., Mendel, F., Standaert, F.-X.: Towards fresh and hybrid re-keying schemes with beyond birthday security. In: Homma, N., Medwed, M. (eds.) CARDIS 2015. LNCS, vol. 9514, pp. 225–241. Springer, Cham (2016). doi:10.1007/978-3-319-31271-2_14

[DR02] Daemen, J., Rijmen, V.: The Design of Rijndael. Springer, New York Inc. (2002)

[Kir11] Kirschbaum, M.: Power analysis resistant logic styles - design, implementation, and evaluation. Ph.D. thesis (2011)

[KJJ99] Kocher, P., Jaffe, J., Jun, B.: Differential power analysis. In: Wiener, M. (ed.) CRYPTO 1999. LNCS, vol. 1666, pp. 388–397. Springer, Heidelberg (1999). doi:10.1007/3-540-48405-1_25

[MKEP12] Moradi, A., Kirschbaum, M., Eisenbarth, T., Paar, C.: Masked dual-rail precharge logic encounters state-of-the-art power analysis methods. IEEE Trans. VLSI Syst. **20**, 1578–1589 (2012)

[MM13] Moradi, A., Mischke, O.: On the simplicity of converting leakages from multivariate to univariate. In: Bertoni, G., Coron, J.-S. (eds.) CHES 2013. LNCS, vol. 8086, pp. 1–20. Springer, Heidelberg (2013). doi:10.1007/978-3-642-40349-1_1

[MSGR10] Medwed, M., Standaert, F.-X., Großschädl, J., Regazzoni, F.: Fresh re-keying: security against side-channel and fault attacks for low-cost devices. In: Bernstein, D.J., Lange, T. (eds.) AFRICACRYPT 2010. LNCS, vol. 6055, pp. 279–296. Springer, Heidelberg (2010). doi:10.1007/978-3-642-12678-9_17

[PKZM07] Popp, T., Kirschbaum, M., Zefferer, T., Mangard, S.: Evaluation of the masked logic style MDPL on a prototype chip. In: Paillier, P., Verbauwhede, I. (eds.) CHES 2007. LNCS, vol. 4727, pp. 81–94. Springer, Heidelberg (2007). doi:10.1007/978-3-540-74735-2_6

[PR11] Prouff, E., Roche, T.: Higher-order glitches free implementation of the AES using secure multi-party computation protocols. In: Preneel, B., Takagi, T. (eds.) CHES 2011. LNCS, vol. 6917, pp. 63–78. Springer, Heidelberg (2011). doi:10.1007/978-3-642-23951-9_5

[RDJ+01] Rudra, A., Dubey, P.K., Jutla, C.S., Kumar, V., Rao, J.R., Rohatgi, P.: Efficient rijndael encryption implementation with composite field arithmetic. In: Koç, Ç.K., Naccache, D., Paar, C. (eds.) CHES 2001. LNCS, vol. 2162, pp. 171–184. Springer, Heidelberg (2001). doi:10.1007/3-540-44709-1_16

[Rij] Rijmen, V.: Efficient Implementation of the Rijndael S-box

[RP10] Rivain, M., Prouff, E.: Provably secure higher-order masking of AES. In: Mangard, S., Standaert, F.-X. (eds.) CHES 2010. LNCS, vol. 6225, pp. 413–427. Springer, Heidelberg (2010). doi:10.1007/978-3-642-15031-9_28

[RP12] Roche, T., Prouff, E.: Higher-order glitch free implementation of the AES using secure multi-party computation protocols - extended version. J. Cryptogr. Eng. 2(2), 111–127 (2012)

[Sha79] Shamir, A.: How to share a secret. Commun. ACM 22(11), 612–613 (1979)

[WOL02] Wolkerstorfer, J., Oswald, E., Lamberger, M.: An ASIC implementation of the AES S boxes. In: Preneel, B. (ed.) CT-RSA 2002. LNCS, vol. 2271, pp. 67–78. Springer, Heidelberg (2002). doi:10.1007/3-540-45760-7_6

PRNGs for Masking Applications
and Their Mapping to Evolvable Hardware

Stjepan Picek[(✉)], Bohan Yang, Vladimir Rozic, Jo Vliegen, Jori Winderickx,
Thomas De Cnudde, and Nele Mentens

KU Leuven ESAT/COSIC and imec, Kasteelpark Arenberg 10,
3001 Leuven-Heverlee, Belgium
stjepan@computer.org

Abstract. This paper proposes the use of evolutionary computation
for the design and optimization of lightweight Pseudo Random Number
Generators (PRNGs). In this work, we focus on PRNGs that are suitable
for generating masks and secret shares. Such generators should be lightweight and have a high throughput with good statistical properties. As
a proof-of-concept, we present three novel hardware architectures that
have an increasing level of prediction resistance and an increasing level
of reconfigurability at run-time. We evaluate the three architectures on
Zynq, Virtex-6, and ASIC platforms and compare the occupied resources
and the throughput of the obtained designs. Finally, we use the Spartan-
6 platform for the evaluation of the masked implementation where the
masks are obtained via our PRNG.

1 Introduction

In cryptographic algorithms and protocols, Random Number Generators (RNGs)
are important for the generation of keys, nonces, one-time pads, and salts. Since
a few decades, PRNGs have gained novel application options in the field of
countermeasures against Side-Channel Analysis (SCA) [1], more specifically in
the generation of random masks, which are used to decorrelate the internally
processed data in a cipher from the actual secret data [2]. The statistical quality
of a PRNG is evaluated using standard test suites such as the NIST 800-22
statistical test suite [3].

For the generation of random masks, the throughput of the PRNG is an
important design criterion, especially when the cipher-to-be-masked is realized
as a high-throughput hardware implementation. Therefore, we focus on PRNGs
that are suitable for hardware implementation in embedded devices. We present

This work has been supported in part by Croatian Science Foundation under
the project IP-2014-09-4882. In addition, this work was supported in part by
the Research Council KU Leuven (C16/15/058), (CREA/14/005), and CORNET
project DynamIA (IWT 140389). It was also supported in part by the Flemish
Government through G.0130.13N and FWO G.0876.14N, the Hercules Foundation
AKUL/11/19, and through the Cathedral ERC Advanced Grant 695305.

© Springer International Publishing AG 2017
K. Lemke-Rust and M. Tunstall (Eds.): CARDIS 2016, LNCS 10146, pp. 209–227, 2017.
DOI: 10.1007/978-3-319-54669-8_13

an evolutionary framework that evolves the update function of the PRNG based on an architecture with a 128-bit state.

We present three methods for generating PRNGs. The first method is device-independent and consists of a single high-quality PRNG that is generated at design-time using the evolutionary framework. The second method focuses on FPGAs with partial reconfiguration capabilities. It consists of several high-quality PRNGs that are generated at design-time and that are randomly configured at run-time in order to confuse an attacker that tries to model the behavior of the PRNG. The third method relies on an evolvable hardware architecture driven by an embedded processor hosting the evolutionary framework, which is suitable for implementation on a System-on-Chip with a coarse-grained configurable ASIC architecture. We note that by high-quality PRNG we mean a PRNG that passes all the NIST statistical tests.

We emphasize that the PRNGs presented here are not intended for generating cryptographic keys; for this purpose a TRNG (True Random Number Generator) or a cryptographic PRNG, compliant to the AIS31 standard [4], should be used. Rather, the intention is to use the PRNG for generating masks. Masked and threshold implementations often require large quantities of random bits. Solutions presented in literature, for these applications, include LFSRs and PRNGs based on fully unrolled implementations of block ciphers, neither of which conform to the AIS31 standard. We aim to outperform these solutions in terms of area and throughput. Therefore, our design goals are:

1. proper statistical quality of the output (passing all NIST tests),
2. high throughput,
3. low area.

The quantity of interest is the throughput per area unit because the throughput can always be increased by implementing several PRNGs operating in parallel. The contributions of the paper are the following:

- A methodology for the generation of novel high-quality PRNG circuits: The evolutionary framework manages to evolve novel PRNG circuits that pass the full set of the NIST statistical test suite [3]. The framework is generic in the sense that it can be tuned to any optimization criterion. Furthermore, the framework can output PRNGs with a different number of operations, different types of operations and different input/output sizes.
- Two novel architectures with an increased prediction resistance:
  - An architecture that increases the prediction resistance by randomly configuring pre-designed high-quality PRNG state update functions at run-time.
  - An architecture that increases the prediction resistance by generating and configuring high-quality PRNG state update functions at run-time. This is achieved in an evolvable hardware architecture with the evolutionary framework running on an embedded processor.

2 Related Work

Evolutionary Computation (EC) techniques, in several forms, have been used for more than 50 years to solve various real-world problems. Today, there exist a plethora of different techniques, tuned to specific problems. When considering cryptography-related applications, we see that the dominant part of the papers concentrate on the optimization of Boolean functions [5,6] and S-boxes [7]. However, it is more interesting to consider evolutionary computation techniques through their representation specificities. If we consider a representation that is most suitable to represent a solution for hardware, then the natural choices are either Genetic Programming (GP) [8] or Cartesian Genetic Programming (CGP) [9]. Both of those techniques are devised with an idea on the natural representation of digital circuits since they use in their representation the same logical operations as found in circuits [8,10]. GP uses tree-like structures, while CGP can be considered as a more general form in which the solutions are represented as indexed graphs. GP has even been used to evolve PRNGs with the goal to be used in cryptographic systems [11]. However, the main problem of that approach was the choice of the cost function as well as the fact that GP can have only one output. Finally, Picek et al. use CGP in order to produce PRNGs that are small and fast in hardware [12]. We follow that line of work and extend it to several scenarios where the most advanced one works in the evolvable hardware setting.

Evolvable hardware deals with techniques to reconfigure hardware (FPGA or ASIC) at run-time in order to address new working conditions [13]. In general, there are two main techniques for circuit evaluation: extrinsic and intrinsic evolution [14]. In the extrinsic evolution, the circuits are evaluated using a circuit simulator, while in the intrinsic evolution, circuits are evaluated on physical reconfigurable hardware. Furthermore, if one uses CGP to reconfigure an FPGA, there are two methods: virtual reconfigurable circuits [15] and dynamic partial reconfiguration [16]. As far as the authors know, there are no applications of evolvable hardware in the form of virtual reconfigurable circuits in the area of cryptography.

Run-time adaptations have been used in cryptographic hardware for the purpose of side-channel analysis resistance [17–19]. In a way, SCA attacks are similar to modeling attacks on PRNGs, since a side-channel attacker also tries to extract secret information by modeling the side-channel behavior of an electronic device. In that case, adapting the implementation at run-time makes it more difficult for an attacker to combine consecutive side-channel measurements, since the implementation constantly changes. We are not aware of any previously designed run-time adaptable hardware architectures of PRNGs.

3 Preliminaries

3.1 PRNG Structure

In this section, we introduce the hardware architecture of the PRNG under consideration. It consists of a 128-bit state register and a combinatorial update function. The update function consists of a number of instantiations of binary and unary operations with two or one 32-bit values at the input, respectively, and one 32-bit value at the output. Our initial setting included AND, XOR, NOT, XNOR, rotate left/right, shift left/right, XOR with a constant, multiplication, and different types of permutation/surjection operations. Then, on the basis of the statistical results, we include the operations that appear most often while being as cheap as possible in hardware:

- AND: bitwise logical AND (binary)
- XOR: bitwise logical exclusive OR (binary)
- S: fixed surjection (binary)
- NOT: inversion (unary)
- P: fixed permutation (unary)
- RL: rotate left (unary)
- RR: rotate right (unary)
- XORC: exclusive OR with a fixed constant (unary)

We note that the developed framework is capable of hosting any binary or unary operation. Here, we work with the minimal set of operations we could find that provide enough diversity to result in PRNGs passing NIST statistical tests. The evolutionary framework determines which operations are instantiated in the update function and how many times each operation is used. Section 5 shows the way the functions are mapped onto specific hardware platforms in three different architectures. In Fig. 1 we display the basic structure of the generated PRNGs.

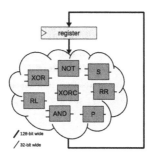

Fig. 1. General structure of the generated PRNGs

3.2   Quality Assessment

Two types of testing are needed in the presented evolutionary framework. The first type is used for computing the fitness function. This testing is performed in a loop on many candidates for many iterations. For this reason, it is necessary that this testing is not computationally intensive and that it operates on short bit strings. It also has to be sufficiently effective to produce good PRNGs. For this purpose we use a reduced version of the approximate entropy test from the NIST statistical test suite [3].

The second type of testing is used for the final evaluation of the obtained generators. This testing is performed only once after the generator has been developed. For this reason, this testing can be very thorough and complex and it can operate on long bit strings. For this testing we use the full set of the NIST statistical tests [3], using up to 100 MB of generated data.

Next to these two types of testing, that are performed on all 3 scenarios, we also do an experimental evaluation of the side-channel security of a masked cipher, based on random masks generated by one PRNG instance in scenario 1. Because the PRNGs in scenario 2 and 3 are generated using the same fitness function and the same offline evaluation based on the full NIST suite, we expect similar outcomes of this experiment for scenario 2 and 3.

4   Evolutionary Framework

Evolutionary Computation (EC) is a research area within computer science that draws inspiration from the process of natural evolution [20]. EC is a part of artificial intelligence and more particularly computational intelligence that involves continuous and combinatorial optimization. By EC methods we consider all algorithms that are based on a set of solution candidates which are iteratively refined [20]. Evolutionary algorithms (EAs) on the other hand belong to a subclass of EC in which algorithms draw inspiration from natural evolution (e.g. mutation, selection, survival of the fittest). Next, we concentrate on two forms of evolutionary algorithms, namely, Cartesian Genetic Programming (CGP) and Genetic Algorithms (GAs). Informally speaking, the main difference between them is the representation of solutions. We selected these two methods since they use encoding of solutions appropriate for our test cases but other techniques should also be able to perform similarly.

4.1   Basic Notions of Evolutionary Computation

In Algorithm 1 we present the pseudocode of any evolutionary algorithm.

Algorithm 1. Pseudocode for EA.

Input : Parameters of the algorithm
Output : Optimal solution set
$t \leftarrow 0$
$P(0) \leftarrow CreateInitialPopulation$
while $TerminationCriterion$ **do**
    $t \leftarrow t + 1$
    $P'(t) \leftarrow SelectMechanism \ (P(t-1))$
    $P(t) \leftarrow VariationOperators(P'(t))$
end while
Return OptimalSolutionSet(P)

The population is the set of individuals used during the optimization process [20]. An individual is the data structure that corresponds to an element in the search space, i.e. a single member of the population of solutions. A chromosome is a candidate solution to a problem and genes are the building blocks of chromosomes [20]. All individuals are encoded in a specific representation, which is the encoding of the genotype. The phenotype is a behavioral expression of the genotype in a specific environment. A generation represents the individuals in one iteration on an EC. The fitness function is a function that assigns a score to each potential solution [20]. The fitness function represents the definition of the problem to be solved with EC. Crossover is a process where a new individual (offspring, child) is created from the information contained within two or more solutions (usually called parents) [20]. Mutation operators are those that use only one parent and create one child by applying a randomized change to its genotype [20]. The parameter mutation probability P_c defines the rate of the mutation. A selection method is used to make a distinction between individuals based on their quality (fitness) [20].

4.2   Cartesian Genetic Programming for Scenario 1 and 2

Julian Miller introduced a new genetic programming paradigm in 1999 that represents programs as directed graphs instead of trees [21]. From that time on, CGP has been shown to be more computationally efficient on a number of problems.

In CGP, a program is represented as an indexed graph. The graph is encoded in the form of a linear string of integers [10]. Terminal set (inputs) and node outputs are numbered sequentially. Node functions are also numbered separately [10]. CGP has three parameters that are chosen by the user; **number of rows** n_r, **number of columns** n_c and **levels-back** l. Number of rows and number of columns make the two-dimensional grid of computational nodes. Their product gives the maximal number of computational nodes. The levels-back parameter controls the connectivity of the graph, i.e. it determines which columns a node can get its input from.

The genotype is a list of integers that represents the program primitives (functions and terminals) and the way they are connected. Genotypes are of fixed length while phenotypes have a variable length in accordance to the number of unexpressed genes. Unexpressed (inactive) genes are those of which the output is not connected to any input of some other gene or to the output of a circuit. The maximal length of the genotype is given by the following formula:

$$max\_length = n_r n_c (n_n + l) + n_o, \tag{1}$$

where n_n is the number of node input connections and n_o is the number of program output connections. For more details about CGP, we refer the interested reader to [10,21].

In our setting, we set the number of inputs and outputs to 4, the number of columns to 250, and the number of rows to 1. The operation set consists of AND, XOR, S, NOT, P, RL, RR, and XORC. We set the levels-back parameter to be equal to the number of columns in order to provide a maximal flexibility in the design. The number of evaluations is 5 000, which showed to be enough to produce good results. In the process of obtaining that number, we used the stagnation strategy where we looked after how many generations there is no more improvement in the fitness value. Since on average we obtained the result of 4 500 generations, we added 10% to that value as a security margin. The number of inputs and outputs is determined by the size of the PRNG we aim to evolve (128-bit state) while the other parameters are selected after a tuning phase. We aim to have as small as possible number of columns since that will result in faster evolution process as well as it will serve as an upper bound for the size of the evolved PRNG. Since our goal is to find small PRNGs, we want it to use as small number of nodes as possible. 250 columns is the smallest size where we observe that CGP consistently finishes with good PRNGs.

For the CGP individual selection we use a $(1 + 4)$-ES strategy (i.e. a type of evolutionary algorithm that uses only mutation) in which offspring is favored over parents when it has a fitness less than or equal to the fitness of the parents. The mutation type is probabilistic. This choice of the selection mechanism as well as the mutation operation is the standard one when working with CGP. The initial population is generated uniformly at random and the size of population equals 5 (since we use $(1 + 4)$-ES strategy). Since in CGP we use an encoding with logical operations, the mapping to hardware is a natural one. Furthermore, it allows us to estimate the size of the PRNG already in the evolution phase.

4.3 Genetic Algorithms for Scenario 3

Genetic Algorithms (GAs) are probabilistic algorithms whose search methods model some natural phenomena: genetic inheritance and survival of the fittest. GAs are a subclass of evolutionary algorithms (EAs) where the elements of the search space are arrays of elementary types like strings of bits, integers, floating-point values and permutations [20]. The usual variation operators in GAs are mutation and crossover. Crossover is considered by many to be one of the most important features of GAs. For further information about GAs, we refer to [20].

Differing from scenario 1 and 2, scenario 3 enforces a structure on the PRNGs, and that structure is a 4×8 matrix, denoted by the term Virtual Reconfigurable Circuit (VRC). Furthermore, we do not allow that a certain gate is connected to arbitrary gates, but only to gates that are maximally 1 column away (i.e. levels-back is set to 1). We decided to use a matrix of size 4×8 based on the results of the experiments in scenario 1. There, we observed that the average number of nodes used in PRNGs with good results after the NIST statistical tests equals 28.3 nodes. The number we select here is close to the minimal number of nodes we require in order to have sufficient diversity in the operations in our PRNGs. The number of rows is determined based on the number of inputs the PRNG has, which is equal to 4. Naturally, bigger matrices would also work, but a structure having many more columns would result in the decrease of the throughput of the generators. By doing so, we can encode our solutions as a matrix of dimension 4×8 where each value has a range between 0 and 511 since we need 9 configuration bits for each VRC cell. More details on the use of the configuration bits in the VRC cells, can be found in Sect. 5.3. In our GA, we use 3-tournament selection where 3 individuals are randomly selected and the worst one is discarded. Out of the two remaining ones we create one offspring with one-point crossover. One-point crossover splits both parents at the same randomly determined crossover point. Subsequently, a new child is created by appending the first part of the first parent with the second part of the second parent [20]. After the crossover, we use simple mutation where each gene is randomly changed with a probability of 1%. Selection procedure as well as the crossover and mutation operator we use are considered as common choices [20]. The population size equals 30 and the termination criterion is 2 500 generations. We use the same fitness function as for scenarios 1 and 2. Similarly, the initial population is generated uniformly at random. We note that in the scenarios 1 and 2 we obtained enough information about the necessary size of the matrix as well as the needed function set so in this scenario we can encode all required options with a bitstring representation which makes our evolution algorithm small with respect to the implementation size.

4.4   Fitness Function

Our design goal is to produce PRNGs that pass all statistical tests. To this end, we need a fitness function that can reliably lead the convergence process. We experimented with a number of different fitness functions derived from the NIST tests, starting with the simplest ones based on the bias and the frequency of ones within a block. However, using these simple fitness functions resulted in PRNGs that didn't pass the full set of NIST tests. The simplest function that resulted in PRNGs of good statistical quality was derived from the NIST approximate entropy test [3].

The fitness function is computed by measuring the relative frequencies of all 4-bit and 3-bit patterns and by estimating the entropy as:

$$Test(out\_value) = \sum_{i(m=3)} \frac{\nu_i}{n} log\frac{\nu_i}{n} - \sum_{i(m=4)} \frac{\nu_i}{n} log\frac{\nu_i}{n}, \qquad (2)$$

where ν_i is the number of occurrences of each bit pattern and n is the length of the sequence. The test function results in a number between 0 and 1.

In order to evaluate the diffusion properties of the state update function, we use this estimator to approximate the entropy-per-bit of a change caused by a single bit flip. Firstly, we choose a random 128-bit number r and compute the state update function $\phi(r)$. Then, we apply the state update function on all 128 $r \oplus c_i$ numbers, where c_i is a 128-bit number consisting of all zeroes and a single one at the i-th position. The test function is applied to all difference vectors $Test(\phi(r) \oplus \phi(r \oplus c_i))$.

In addition, we compute the state update values using all-zeros and all-ones input vectors (denoted by All_0 and All_1), we run the test for those values and the result is again sent to the Test function (note, now there are no pairs of output values to XOR before invoking the Test function).

Finally, all test results are added up to compute the fitness:

$$fitness = Test(\phi(All_0)) + Test(\phi(All_1)) + \sum_{i=0}^{127} Test(\phi(r) \oplus \phi(r \oplus c_i)). \quad (3)$$

In order to improve the quality of the results, in each evaluation we run the PRNG in a loop for a number of rounds, where the input in round $n+1$ is the output in the round n. The final fitness value equals the smallest of the round values with the number of rounds set to 2. By doing so, we ensure that the evolution mimics the actual working of a PRNG, where every output is the input to a new iteration and our PRNG behaves at least as good as in the worst evaluation round.

5 Hardware Architectures

In this section, we elaborate on the details of the three hardware architectures that have an increased level of resistance against modeling attacks.

5.1 Scenario 1

PRNG architecture. The first architecture consists of the implementation of a fixed PRNG, generated at design-time by Cartesian Genetic Programming (CGP), as explained in Sect. 4.2. The PRNG follows the structure given in Sect. 3.1 and is evolved with a fitness function consisting of the statistical tests explained in Sect. 3.2. We start with the C code of one of developed PRNGs:

```
typedef unsigned int uint;
void rngCGPFunc(uint x0, uint x1, uint x2, uint x3,
uint* z0, uint* z1, uint* z2, uint* z3){
    uint y4 = (x3 << 1) | (x3 >> (sizeof(uint)*8 - 1));
    uint y5 = x2 ^ y4;      uint y6 = p1(x3);
    uint y7 = y6 ^ y5;      uint y8 = y7 ^ x3;
    uint y9 = y5 ^ 2557891585;    uint y10 = p1(y8);
    uint y11 = p1(y9);      uint y12 = x1 ^ y5;
    uint y13 = x0 & y12;    uint y14 = y13 ^ y11;
    uint y15 = y14 ^ 2557891585; uint y16 = y10 ^ 2557891585;
    uint y17 = (y10 << 1) | (y10 >> (sizeof(uint)*8 - 1));
    uint y18 = (y17 >> 1) | (y17 << (sizeof(uint)*8 - 1));
    uint y19 = y16 ^ x3;
    uint y20 = (y19 >> 1) | (y19 << (sizeof(uint)*8 - 1));
    uint y21 = y17 ^ y20;
    uint y22 = y14 ^ y21;   uint y23 = x3 ^ y21;
    uint y24 = p1(y18);
    uint y25 = (y15 >> 1) | (y15 << (sizeof(uint)*8 - 1));
    uint y26 = (y23 << 1) | (y23 >> (sizeof(uint)*8 - 1));
    uint y27 = y21 ^ y24;   uint y28 = y25 ^ y27;
    *z0 = y26; *z1 = y16; *z2 = y28; *z3 = y22;}
```

To compare our design with other ones, we implement our solution as well as the Lamar PRNG (recall, this is a PRNG also obtained via evolutionary algorithms) in Verilog HDL. Moreover, we compare those two designs with the Mersenne Twister generator which is a widely used general-purpose PRNG [22].

We synthesize the algorithms with Xilinx ISE14.7 on a Virtex4 xc4vfx100-10ff1152 to draw a fair comparison with the reference implementation of the Mersenne Twister. The implementation results are given in Table 1. With the utilization of 188 slices, our design achieves a maximum working frequency of 286 MHz while the Lamar can reach a working frequency of 43 MHz with 645 slices. We note that designs can be parallelized to obtain a higher throughput. Therefore we use throughput per slice as the metric for implementation efficiency. As shown in the table, given the same footprint on FPGA, our design could be 90 times faster than the Lamar and 3 times faster than the Mersenne Twister design [22].

Table 1. Comparison of the hardware implementation results

	Slices	LUTs/FFs/BRAMs	Throughput/slice
CGP	188	317/128/0	**195 Mbps/slice**
Lamar [11]	645	1 045/238/0	2.16 Mbps/slice
Mersenne twister [22]	128	213/193/4	65.7 Mbps/slice

5.2   Scenario 2

Top-level Architecture. For scenario 2, high-quality PRNG circuits are generated using CGP in the same way as for scenario 1. Instead of implementing only one of the generated circuits, we use an FPGA platform to store the bitstreams of many PRNGs and we make a random implementation selection at run-time. Because the PRNGs are implemented through partial reconfiguration of the FPGA, we call the PRNG bitstreams "partial bitstreams". Figure 2 shows the top-level hardware architecture consisting of a core controlling the reconfiguration (RECONFIG), a re-configurable PRNG core, a TIMER, a True Random Number Generator (TRNG) and an FSM.

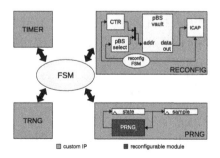

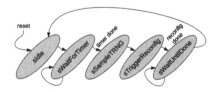

Fig. 2.   Top-level   architecture   for scenario 2

Fig. 3. Flowchart representation of the control sequence on the FSM

FSM, TIMER and TRNG. The FSM uses the TIMER value to set the reconfiguration frequency and the TRNG output to randomly select one of the PRNG configurations. Note that the throughput constraints on the TRNG are much more relaxed than on the PRNG, which counters the fact that the PRNG would become obsolete in the presence of a TRNG. Figure 3 depicts a flowchart of the control sequence running on the FSM.

PRNG. The reconfigurable PRNG core consists of a fixed 128-bit register and a reconfigurable update function. When the update function is reconfigured, the state of the PRNG is maintained. This means that the register only needs a random seed (coming from the TRNG) upon initialization. The purpose of the sample register is to make consistent snapshots of the state register.

RECONFIG. The RECONFIG core handles the dynamic partial reconfiguration of the update function. The Internal Configuration Access Port (ICAP) allows to access the configuration memory from the re-configurable fabric on Xilinx FPGAs. The reconfig FSM inside the RECONFIG core addresses one of the partial bitstreams in the Block RAM memory (called pBS vault in Fig. 2) through the pBS select signal. Because one partial bitstream resides on more than one position in the BRAM, a counter is used to perform the read-out of a complete partial bitstream. The ICAP receives a partial bitstream in chunks of 32 bits and updates the according part of the configuration memory in order to reconfigure the update function of the PRNG. In our proof-of-concept implementation, we use 8 partial bitstreams for the PRNG configurations, where each bitstream has a size of 58 836 bytes. The number of partial bitstreams in the pBS is arbitrarily chosen. In a real-life implementation this number would be the outcome of a balancing-act between the affordable cost (size on the FPGA, and Block RAMs in particular) and the prediction resistance. Because the ICAP is connected to a 100 MHz clock, which is the overall clock signal of the implementation, and accepts 32-bit words per clock period, the reconfiguration time is around 150 μs = 58836 $bytes * 8 / 32 * 10$ ns.

Bitstream Generation. The off-line tool flow for the generation of partial bitstreams at design-time is depicted in Fig. 4. A representation of a high-quality PRNG is generated through CGP in text format. Next, a parser transforms this representation into a Verilog file describing the hardware circuit of the PRNG update function. Next, a partial bitstream is generated from the Verilog file using the VIVADO 2014.4 tool of Xilinx. Finally, the data2mem tool is used to initialize the partial bitstream vault. The initialization of this vault can only be done after generation of the full and partial bitstreams. A C program converts the partial bitstreams in to standardized memory file (.mem), which is used by data2mem to initialize the partial bitstream vault after bitstream generation. The architecture for scenario 2 is designed for FPGAs with partial reconfiguration capabilities without the need for an embedded processor.

.

Fig. 4. Automated off-line tool flow, used at design time to generate partial bitstreams and include them in the partial bitstream vault.

5.3   Scenario 3

Top-level Architecture. Figure 5 shows the architecture of scenario 3. It consists of a Virtual Reconfigurable Circuit (VRC), which is a matrix of configurable cells, introduced by Vašíček and Sekanina in [15]. The functionality of the cells and the routing between the cells is controlled by configuration bits that are generated by a Genetic Algorithm (GA) hosted by an embedded microprocessor. The reconfiguration frequency is determined by a TIMER module and the seed for the GA is generated by a TRNG. This architecture can be realized on a coarse-grained reconfigurable ASIC. Although this would lead to the most optimal implementation in terms of resource usage, we implement our proof-of-concept on a Xilinx Zynq^{TM}-7000 SoC XC7Z020-CLG484-1, which holds an embedded ARM processor. The DDR3 memory serves as the data and program memory of the processor. We use a the PetaLinux full Linux distribution as operating system on the ARM to run the GA. The TIMER, the TRNG and the VRC communicate with the ARM over a 32-bit AXI bus. For this architecture, we do not use the partial reconfiguration facilities of the FPGA, since this would require the synthesis, place&route and bitstream generation tools to be embedded in the ARM. Instead, we build a virtual reconfiguration layer on top of the FPGA.

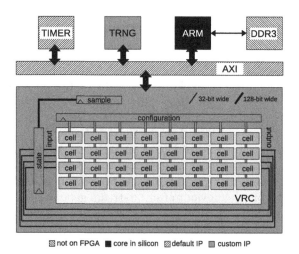

Fig. 5. Top-level architecture for scenario 3

VRC Cell. Each cell is capable of hosting one of the 8 functions explained in Sect. 3.1. The architecture of one cell is shown in Fig. 6. The functionality is determined by an 8-1 multiplexer controlled by 3 configuration bits. The 32-bit inputs of the cells come from outputs of cells of a previous column or one of the four 32-bit inputs of the overall matrix. Since the depth of a column is equal to 4 and the number of input values is also 4, we use an 8-1 multiplexer for each input. Therefore, we need 6 configuration bits to control the routing. In total this results in 9 configuration bits for each VRC cell.

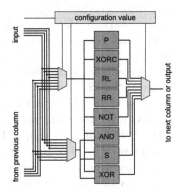

Fig. 6. Architecture of a VRC cell

6 Evaluation and Discussion

6.1 Implementation Results

First, to investigate the performance of our generators, we tested them with the full battery of NIST tests using sequences of 10^9 bits. Our results show that the vast majority of our generators are able to pass those tests. In fact, we evolved 50 PRNGs; 45 pass all NIST statistical tests with an average number of active genes equal to 28.3.

In order to discuss the three architectures, we summarize the most important implementation results in Table 2. Scenario 1 and scenario 3 are suitable for both ASIC and FPGA, although scenario 3 requires an embedded processor to run the GA. Therefore, we report on both the ASIC and the FPGA implementation properties for these scenarios. Scenario 2 can only be implemented on partially reconfigurable FPGAs. In order to compare the three scenarios, we need an FPGA with an embedded processor. We choose the Xilinx Zynq-7000 SoC XC7Z020-CLG484-1 for our experiment. Because scenario 2 can also run on an FPGA without an embedded processor, we also report on the implementation results on a Xilinx Virtex-6 C6VLX240T-1FFG1156 FPGA. For the designs suitable for ASIC implementation, we use the open source NanGate 45 nm standard cell library.

Table 2 clearly shows the trade-off between the efficiency in terms of small area and high throughput on the one hand and the reconfigurability of the implementation on the other hand. The architecture in scenario 1, consisting of a single, fixed PRNG, has the smallest area and the highest throughput on all the considered implementation platforms. It has no built-in countermeasures against modeling attacks in the form of dynamic reconfigurability at run-time. The architecture in scenario 2 has a larger area and a smaller throughput than the first architecture. It has an increased reconfigurability in the sense that it can randomly instantiate one of eight possible PRNG circuits. This makes a modeling attack more difficult since a certain PRNG circuit is only instantiated 1/8 of the time on average. In scenario 3, the architecture consists of a coarse-grained reconfigurable matrix, which introduces an overhead in both area and delay. It also needs an embedded processor to run the GA. This architecture results in the highest level of reconfigurability, since it generates high-quality PRNGs on-the-fly. Both scenarios 2 and 3 need a TRNG to initiate the state of the PRNG and to provide a seed for the evolutionary computation framework. The presence of the TRNG does not make the PRNG obsolete, since the throughput requirements of the PRNG are too high to be met by the TRNG.

As already mentioned, the quantity used to compare the performance of the different PRNGs is throughput per area unit. Cryptographic primitives often cannot reach a high throughput because they require many cycles to produce a result. The exceptions are single-cycle implementations that perform the whole encryption in one clock cycle. One can observe that our implementation for scenario 3 is relatively large (31 kGE), but we emphasize that this implementation is done as a proof of a concept and that area optimizations are possible. In the proposed architecture, each configurable cell utilizes eight operations as well as connections to all inputs and to all cells of the previous column. This solution offers high flexibility but it results in large multiplexers that consume a lot of area. This multiplexer area of a single cell can be reduced by using fewer operations and less connections in a matrix. For FPGA implementations, improvements are possible by switching from 32-bit architecture to a configuration that utilizes smaller cells, for example an architecture in which each cell maps into a single LUT or a single slice on the implementation platform. Exploring these optimization strategies is left for future work.

However, even without such optimizations, our implementation still outperforms single-cycle PRESENT80 [23] and SIMON64 [24]. For a unit area ($1GE$), the implemented scenarios 1 and 3 obtained 68.14 Mbit/s and 0.8355 Mbit/s, while PRESENT80 and SIMON64 only have 0.0686 Mbit/s and 0.0606 Mbit/s [25]. We note that all tested PRNGs (ours as well as those based on block ciphers) are used here without invertible functions (therefore, not conforming to the AIS31 standard). Nevertheless, adding such functions would increase the area and throughput for all configurations equally, so we consider our comparison fair. Furthermore, as far as we are aware, at this moment there is no definitive opinion in the cryptographic community whether such invertible functions are necessary when using PRNGs for masking purposes.

Table 2. Summary of the implementation results, where Zynq-7000 and Virtex-6 refer to a XC7Z020-CLG484-1 and a C6VLX240T-1FFG1156 on a ZedBoard and a ML605 Evaluation Board, respectively. The ASIC results for scenario 3 are based only on the VRC-based PRNG. GE stands for the number of equivalent NAND gates in the NanGate 45 nm library. The throughput is derived from the possible maximal working frequency. "-" indicates that the implementation is static, "+" stands for an implementation that can be reconfigured to a limited number of pre-stored reconfiguration instances, while "++" denotes an implementation that is reconfigured on-the-fly to an undetermined number of different reconfiguration instances.

Scenario	Target platform	Experimental platform	Area	Throughput	Reconfigurability
1	ASIC	NanGate 45 nm	1 717 GE	117 Gbit/s	–
	FPGA	Zynq-7000	86 slices	49.7 Gbit/s	–
		Virtex-6	94 slices	66.2 Gbit/s	–
2	partially reconfigurable FPGA	Zynq-7000	673 slices 117 BRAMs	13.5 Gbit/s	+
		Virtex-6	579 slices 117 BRAMs	11.2 Gbit/s	+
3	FPGA + embedded processor	Zynq-7000	2 413 slices	3.7 Gbit/s	++
	ASIC + embedded processor	NanGate 45 nm	31 kGE	25.9 Gbits/s	++

Although throughput is not an optimization criterion, the PRNGs need to fulfill certain throughput requirements, especially in hardware implementations where the PRNGs generate masks for block ciphers. The actual required throughput depends on the application and is in the range of 0.024-11.44 Gbit/s for TIs ranging from a first-order secure PRESENT implementation [26] to a second-order secure AES implementation [27]. Taking this throughput range into account, Table 2 shows that the generated PRNGs are suitable for practical usage.

6.2   Evaluation of a Masked Implementation

In order to examine the applicability of the PRNG for the generation of random masks, we integrated the PRNG obtained in scenario 1 with a masked cipher design on the Spartan-6 FPGA of the SAKURA-G evaluation board [28] and analyze the security of the implementation using the t-test leakage detection method [29,30]. We choose Poschmann's Threshold Implementation (TI) of PRESENT as our case study [26].

In Fig. 7, the result of the leakage detection test is shown for the implementation with a biased initial sharing. The t-test value exceeds the confidence

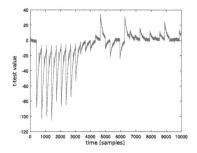
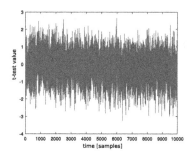

Fig. 7. Results of the leakage detection test for PRESENT-TI with biased masking, 20 000 traces

Fig. 8. Results of the leakage detection test for PRESENT-TI without biased masking, 20 000 traces

threshold of ±4.5 at multiple points in the corresponding power consumption trace, showing the implementation to be insecure. This is to be expected as masking schemes can not provide security without uniform masks. Figure 8, on the other hand, shows the result of the leakage detection test for the PRESENT-TI cipher, in which the initial sharing comes from our PRNG. The t-test value does not exceed the confidence threshold. This shows that our PRNG can be used in settings where side-channel resistance is provided using masking.

Although we do not conduct similar analysis for scenarios 2 and 3, we expect those results would be in accordance with the results obtained here. We emphasize that we use the same fitness function as well as the offline evaluations in all 3 scenarios and therefore we expect the results to be in conformance. Moreover, we tested a large number of PRNGs from scenario 1 and compared the average node number of nodes as well as the operations used and we could not detect any significant statistical difference from the designs obtained in scenarios 2 and 3.

7   Conclusions

This paper presents a novel way of generating high-quality Pseudo Random Number Generators (PRNGs) through the use of evolutionary computation. We implement three different implementation scenarios with an increasing level of run-time reconfigurability, aiming at an increasing level of resistance against modeling attacks. In the first scenario, we use Cartesian Genetic Programming (CGP) to generate PRNGs at design-time. We also provide a masked cipher implementation using one of the generated PRNGs, which passes the t-test. The second scenario also uses CGP to generate several PRNG bitstreams at design-time. At run-time, one of the pre-generated bitstreams can be randomly selected, increasing the resistance of the implementation against modeling attacks. The third scenario provides an even higher level of random reconfigurability by generating new high-quality PRNGs on-the-fly in an embedded processor using a

Genetic Algorithm (GA), of which the seed is generated by a True Random Number Generator (TRNG) with relaxed throughput constraints. We implement the three scenarios on the hardware platforms for which they are suitable and we evaluate and compare the implementation properties. We can clearly see the trade-off between small area and high throughput on the one hand and high configurability and resistance against modeling attacks on the other hand.

Future work consists of optimizing the architectures towards the targeted implementation platforms. For instance, the proof-of-concept implementation of scenario 3 consists of a virtual reconfigurable layer on an FPGA. A more efficient implementation can be achieved by building on the existing reconfiguration infrastructure of the FPGA, addressing the Look-up Tables directly. Further, the size and the routing of the reconfigurable structure in scenario 3 can be explored in order to optimize the results generated by the GA. Finally, the partial reconfiguration in scenario 2 introduces a down-time of the PRNG, which can be avoided using an interleaved design with two PRNGs.

References

1. Kocher, P.C., Jaffe, J., Jun, B.: Differential power analysis. In: Wiener, M. (ed.) CRYPTO 1999. LNCS, vol. 1666, pp. 388–397. Springer, Heidelberg (1999). doi:10.1007/3-540-48405-1_25
2. Akkar, M.-L., Giraud, C.: An implementation of DES and AES, secure against some attacks. In: Koç, Ç.K., Naccache, D., Paar, C. (eds.) CHES 2001. LNCS, vol. 2162, pp. 309–318. Springer, Heidelberg (2001). doi:10.1007/3-540-44709-1_26
3. Rukhin, A. et al.: A statistical test suite for random and pseudorandom number generators for cryptographic applications (August 2008)
4. Killmann, W., Schindler, W.: A proposal for: functionality classes for random number generators (2011). https://www.bsi.bund.de
5. Clark, J.A., Jacob, J.L., Stepney, S., Maitra, S., Millan, W.: Evolving Boolean functions satisfying multiple criteria. In: Menezes, A., Sarkar, P. (eds.) INDOCRYPT 2002. LNCS, vol. 2551, pp. 246–259. Springer, Heidelberg (2002). doi:10.1007/3-540-36231-2_20
6. Millan, W., Clark, A., Dawson, E.: Heuristic design of cryptographically strong balanced Boolean functions. In: Nyberg, K. (ed.) EUROCRYPT 1998. LNCS, vol. 1403, pp. 489–499. Springer, Heidelberg (1998). doi:10.1007/BFb0054148
7. Picek, S., Ege, B., Papagiannopoulos, K., Batina, L., Jakobovic, D.: Optimality and beyond: the case of 4x4 S-boxes. In: 2014 IEEE International Symposium on Hardware-Oriented Security and Trust (HOST), pp. 80–83 (2014)
8. Koza, J.R.: Genetic Programming: On the Programming of Computers by Means of Natural Selection. MIT Press, Cambridge (1992)
9. Miller, J.F. (ed.): Cartesian Genetic Programming. Natural Computing Series. Springer, Heidelberg (2011)
10. Miller, J.F., Thomson, P.: Cartesian genetic programming. In: Poli, R., Banzhaf, W., Langdon, W.B., Miller, J., Nordin, P., Fogarty, T.C. (eds.) EuroGP 2000. LNCS, vol. 1802, pp. 121–132. Springer, Heidelberg (2000). doi:10.1007/978-3-540-46239-2_9

11. Lamenca-Martinez, C., Hernandez-Castro, J.C., Estevez-Tapiador, J.M., Ribagorda, A.: Lamar: a new pseudorandom number generator evolved by means of genetic programming. In: Runarsson, T.P., Beyer, H.-G., Burke, E., Merelo-Guervós, J.J., Whitley, L.D., Yao, X. (eds.) PPSN IX 2006. LNCS, vol. 4193, pp. 850–859. Springer, Heidelberg (2006). doi:10.1007/11844297_86

12. Picek, S., Sisejkovic, D., Rozic, V., Yang, B., Jakobovic, D., Mentens, N.: Evolving cryptographic pseudorandom number generators. In: Handl, J., Hart, E., Lewis, P.R., López-Ibáñez, M., Ochoa, G., Paechter, B. (eds.) PPSN 2016. LNCS, vol. 9921, pp. 613–622. Springer, Heidelberg (2016). doi:10.1007/978-3-319-45823-6_57

13. Torresen, J.: An evolvable hardware tutorial. In: Becker, J., Platzner, M., Vernalde, S. (eds.) FPL 2004. LNCS, vol. 3203, pp. 821–830. Springer, Heidelberg (2004). doi:10.1007/978-3-540-30117-2_83

14. Sekanina, L. (ed.): Evolvable Components: From Theory to Hardware Implementations. Springer, Heidelberg (2004)

15. Vašíček, Z., Sekanina, L.: Hardware accelerator of cartesian genetic programming with multiple fitness units. Comput. Inform. 29(6+), 1359–1371 (2012)

16. Dobai, R., Sekanina, L.: Image filter evolution on the Xilinx Zynq platform. In: 2013 NASA/ESA Conference on Adaptive Hardware and Systems (AHS), pp. 164–171, June 2013

17. Mentens, N., Gierlichs, B., Verbauwhede, I.: Power and fault analysis resistance in hardware through dynamic reconfiguration. In: Oswald, E., Rohatgi, P. (eds.) CHES 2008. LNCS, vol. 5154, pp. 346–362. Springer, Heidelberg (2008). doi:10.1007/978-3-540-85053-3_22

18. Güneysu, T., Moradi, A.: Generic side-channel countermeasures for reconfigurable devices. In: Preneel, B., Takagi, T. (eds.) CHES 2011. LNCS, vol. 6917, pp. 33–48. Springer, Heidelberg (2011). doi:10.1007/978-3-642-23951-9_3

19. Sasdrich, P., Mischke, O., Moradi, A., Güneysu, T.: Side-channel protection by randomizing look-up tables on reconfigurable hardware. In: Mangard, S., Poschmann, A.Y. (eds.) COSADE 2014. LNCS, vol. 9064, pp. 95–107. Springer, Heidelberg (2015). doi:10.1007/978-3-319-21476-4_7

20. Eiben, A.E., Smith, J.E.: Introduction to Evolutionary Computing. Springer, Heidelberg (2003)

21. Miller, J.F.: An empirical study of the efficiency of learning boolean functions using a cartesian genetic programming approach. In: GECCO, pp. 1135–1142. Morgan Kaufmann (1999)

22. Tian, X., Benkrid, K.: Mersenne twister random number generation on FPGA, CPU and GPU. In: NASA/ESA Conference on Adaptive Hardware and Systems, AHS 2009, pp. 460–464, July 2009

23. Bogdanov, A., Knudsen, L.R., Leander, G., Paar, C., Poschmann, A., Robshaw, M.J.B., Seurin, Y., Vikkelsoe, C.: PRESENT: an ultra-lightweight block cipher. In: Paillier, P., Verbauwhede, I. (eds.) CHES 2007. LNCS, vol. 4727, pp. 450–466. Springer, Heidelberg (2007). doi:10.1007/978-3-540-74735-2_31

24. Beaulieu, R., Shors, D., Smith, J., Treatman-Clark, S., Weeks, B., Wingers, L.: The SIMON and SPECK Families of Lightweight Block Ciphers. Cryptology ePrint Archive, report 2013/404 (2013). http://eprint.iacr.org/

25. Maene, P., Verbauwhede, I.: Single-cycle implementations of block ciphers. In: Güneysu, T., Leander, G., Moradi, A. (eds.) LightSec 2015. LNCS, vol. 9542, pp. 131–147. Springer, Heidelberg (2016). doi:10.1007/978-3-319-29078-2_8

26. Poschmann, A., Moradi, A., Khoo, K., Lim, C., Wang, H., Ling, S.: Side-channel resistant crypto for less than 2,300 GE. J. Cryptol. 24(2), 322–345 (2011)

27. De Cnudde, T., Bilgin, B., Reparaz, O., Nikov, V., Nikova, S.: Higher-order threshold implementation of the AES S-box. In: Homma, N., Medwed, M. (eds.) CARDIS 2015. LNCS, vol. 9514, pp. 259–272. Springer, Heidelberg (2016). doi:10.1007/978-3-319-31271-2_16

28. Guntur, H., Ishii, J., Satoh, A.: Side-channel attack user reference architecture board SAKURA-G. In: 2014 IEEE 3rd Global Conference on Consumer Electronics (GCCE), pp. 271–274 (2014)

29. Coron, J.-S., Kocher, P., Naccache, D.: Statistics and secret leakage. In: Frankel, Y. (ed.) FC 2000. LNCS, vol. 1962, pp. 157–173. Springer, Heidelberg (2001). doi:10.1007/3-540-45472-1_12

30. Coron, J., Naccache, D., Kocher, P.C.: Statistics and secret leakage. ACM Trans. Embed. Comput. Syst. 3(3), 492–508 (2004)

Automated Detection of Instruction Cache Leaks in Modular Exponentiation Software

Andreas Zankl[1(✉)], Johann Heyszl[1], and Georg Sigl[2]

[1] Fraunhofer Research Institution AISEC, Munich, Germany
{andreas.zankl,johann.heyszl}@aisec.fraunhofer.de
[2] Technische Universität München, Munich, Germany
sigl@tum.de

Abstract. The shared instruction cache of modern processors is an established side-channel that allows adversaries to observe the execution flow of other applications. This has been shown to be a threat to cryptographic software whose execution flow depends on the processed secrets. Testing implementations for these dependencies, or *leaks*, is essential to develop protected cryptographic software. In this work, we present an automated testing methodology that allows to detect execution flow leaks in implementations of modular exponentiation, a key operation in schemes like RSA, ElGamal, and Diffie-Hellman. We propose a simple and effective leakage test that captures problematic properties of vulnerable exponentiation algorithms. The execution flow of an implementation is directly monitored during exponentiation using a dynamic binary instrumentation framework. This allows to efficiently detect leaking code with instruction-level granularity in a noiseless and controlled environment. As a practical demonstration, we test multiple RSA implementations of modern cryptographic libraries with the proposed methodology. It reliably detects leaking code in vulnerable implementations and also identifies leaks in a protected implementation that are non-trivial to spot in a code review. We present a fix for these leaks and strongly recommend to also patch the other implementations. Because instruction cache attacks have been shown to be a threat in practice, it seems advisable to integrate an automated leakage test in the software release process of cryptographic libraries.

Keywords: RSA · Granular leakage detection · Open-source crypto library · Non-trivial bug discovery · Noiseless evaluation environment · Automated software testing · DBI

1 Introduction

Using cryptographic algorithms securely in practice is challenging, because many implementations are vulnerable to the exploitation of side-channels. Execution time, power consumption, electromagnetic radiation, fault behavior, and the micro-architecture of processors have all been used to attack implementations

© Springer International Publishing AG 2017
K. Lemke-Rust and M. Tunstall (Eds.): CARDIS 2016, LNCS 10146, pp. 228–244, 2017.
DOI: 10.1007/978-3-319-54669-8_14

in practice. A subset of micro-architectural attacks focuses on the instruction cache, which is a high-speed memory close to the processing unit that is used to speed up code execution. Caches are typically transparent to applications, i.e. they work regardless of an application's awareness of the cache. Yet, an application can actively manipulate its cache usage. With sufficient details about the cache sub-system, code can actively be placed in a specific location in the instruction cache at a specific point in time. Because caches are also shared resources, an adversary can reconstruct an application's execution flow by cleverly replacing the application's code in the instruction cache and checking whether it has been reused after a while. This is a well-known threat to cryptographic software, because performance optimizations often shape the execution flow according to processed secrets. By observing the instruction cache, an adversary is then able to recover secret data or parts thereof. This spawned a number of instruction cache attacks that have been proposed over the past decade. As a consequence, execution flow dependencies that reveal, or *leak*, processed secrets should be removed from cryptographic software. In this work, we propose a testing methodology that allows to automatically detect execution flow leaks in implementations of modular exponentiation, a key operation in asymmetric ciphers such as RSA, digital signature schemes like DSA or ElGamal and key agreements protocols such as Diffie-Hellman.

In Sect. 2 we give an overview of related testing approaches and tools. We then briefly discuss common modular exponentiation algorithms and their general vulnerability to instruction cache attacks in Sect. 3. In short, vulnerable algorithms leak information about the exponent, because they optimize, e.g. skip, calculations depending on its value. These execution flow dependencies are the basis for instruction cache attacks. To automatically find them, we propose a simple and effective test in Sect. 4 that captures the optimization strategies of vulnerable algorithms such as square-and-multiply and sliding window exponentiation. The test assumes that leaking code is used more often, the more 1-bits occur in the exponent (or vice versa). Hence, the correlation of (1) the Hamming weight of the exponent and (2) the number of times an instruction is used during exponentiation systematically identifies vulnerable code. Testing this leakage model requires programs to be monitored during execution with instruction-level granularity. For this purpose we use the dynamic binary instrumentation framework Pin [13] known from software debugging and performance analysis. It is described in Sect. 5 and allows to take execution flow measurements in a controlled environment free from interferences from the processor, the operating system or other applications.

To practically demonstrate our methodology, we test the RSA implementations of nine open-source cryptographic libraries: BoringSSL [9], cryptlib [11], Libgcrypt [17], LibreSSL [21], MatrixSSL [12], mbed TLS [3], Nettle [19], OpenSSL [28], and wolfSSL [30]. The selection is briefly discussed in Sect. 6 and focuses on well known C-based cryptographic libraries. It is by no means exhaustive and does not follow any specific selection criteria other than the preferences of the authors. To verify our testing framework, we additionally test one self-written textbook implementation of RSA that is intentionally vulnerable to instruction cache attacks. Among the open-source libraries, not all use exponentiation algorithms that offer protection against instruction cache attacks. The test results discussed in Sect. 7 confirm this observation and, as a novelty, clearly state the extent of the leaks for each library. While MatrixSSL exhibits the most extensive leaks, the default implementations of OpenSSL and its forks as well as cryptlib do not leak at all. The tests also uncover leaks in the otherwise protected implementation of wolfSSL. In the analysis in Sect. 8 we show that these leaks are non-trivial to find and remove the responsible instructions with minor code changes that have negligible performance impact. In our conclusions in Sect. 9, we strongly recommend to fix all affected libraries and suggest to integrate automated leakage tests in the software release process of cryptographic libraries.[1] In summary, our main contributions are

- a simple and effective leakage test for implementations of modular exponentiation allowing to detect execution flow leaks that are the basis of instruction cache attacks,
- a testbench based on dynamic binary instrumentation that efficiently monitors the execution flow in a noiseless and controlled environment,
- a quantification and comparison of execution flow leaks in RSA implementations of a selection of modern cryptographic libraries, and
- an analysis and fix of leaks detected in the wolfSSL library demonstrating the necessity and benefits of the proposed leakage test.

2   Related Work

The detection of information leakage through a program's execution flow has been addressed in the context of static code analysis. Doychev et al. [7] as well as Doychev and Köpf [8] propose a static analysis tool called *CacheAudit*, which quantifies the amount of information leaked through cache observations. It takes a 32-bit x86 program binary and a cache configuration as inputs and reports the information leakage for different attacker models. Barthe et al. [4] propose a static analysis tool that checks whether implementations are constant-time, i.e. do not perform conditional jumps or memory accesses depending on secrets. The authors mainly evaluate symmetric ciphers with their tool, but also state that it successfully detects implementations of modular exponentiation that branch based on secrets. Rodrigues et al. [24] propose another static analysis tool called *FlowTracker*, which is directly incorporated into the compiler. With their tool, the authors detect not further specified time-based side-channels in the Montgomery exponentiation implementation of OpenSSL. In contrast to static analysis, we perform our leakage test based on runtime measurements for concrete inputs. This allows us to specifically observe only active code paths, which reduces the evaluation effort for large and complex software components.

---

[1] To facilitate the integration, the source code used in this work can be obtained from https://github.com/Fraunhofer-AISEC/cache-leak-detector.

Basic runtime detection of execution flows leaks has been performed by Molnar et al. [20]. The authors propose the so-called *program counter security model*, in which a program's execution flow must be independent of any secret input such that an adversary does not gain any information from observing its program counter. While the focus of their work is put on program, i.e. source-code, transformations to achieve program counter security, they also analyze example programs to detect code that potentially violates program counter security. For these measurements, the authors use *gcov*, a code coverage tool from the GNU Compiler Collection (GCC). It instruments code compiled with GCC and reports the code coverage, e.g. how often a line of source code has been executed. If different inputs cause different numbers of executions, a potential program counter security violation is detected. There is no further notion of whether the number of executions are statistically related to the inputs. In contrast to the work by Molnar et al., our leakage test specifically identifies linear relations between the number of executions and the Hamming weight of the exponents in modular exponentiation implementations. In addition, our measurement framework has fewer restrictions regarding the software under test. Unlike *gcov*, it does not require access to the source code of an implementation. It is also not limited to code compiled with GCC and does not require additional compiler flags. Hence, it is easier to deploy in practice.

Langley [18] proposes a dynamic analysis tool called *ctgrind*, which is an extension to the dynamic binary instrumentation framework Valgrind. The tool allows to mark secret data as uninitialized and then uses the existing capabilities of the memory error detector to warn if a branch is taken or a memory lookup is performed depending on the uninitialized (secret) data. With the tool, Langley identifies secret-dependent memory accesses in a modular exponentiation implementation of OpenSSL. Reparaz et al. [23] analyze whether an implementation is constant-time by processing fixed and random inputs and measuring the corresponding execution times. The authors then use Welch's t-test to determine whether an implementation is constant-time or not. In contrast to both approaches, we propose a leakage test specifically constructed to capture vulnerabilities in modular exponentiation implementations. Furthermore, we systematically evaluate multiple modern cryptographic libraries as well as quantify and compare the extent of their execution flow leaks.

3   Modular Exponentiation and Instruction Cache Attacks

Modular exponentiation with large integers is a key computation in multiple cryptographic ciphers and schemes. On computer systems with limited native word length, special algorithms are needed to implement arbitrary length integer arithmetic. A common choice for modular exponentiation of the form $b^e \bmod p$ are so-called m-ary algorithms. Binary variants ($m = 2$) process the exponent e bitwise, from most to least significant bit or vice versa. The square-and-multiply algorithm [16] executes a modular square operation for any bit e_l in the exponent, whereas a modular multiplication is performed only if $e_l = 1$. Obviously, this approach creates a highly irregular execution flow that directly depends on the bit values of the exponent. 2-ary algorithms with a more regular execution flow are the Montgomery ladder [14], which uses a square and a multiply step for any e_l, and the square-and-multiply-always algorithm [6], which simply adds dummy multiplication steps to balance the execution flow. Faster exponentiation with higher memory demand is achieved by fixed-window exponentiation (FWE) algorithms [10] ($m = 2^k$). They process the exponent in bit-windows of size k and use pre-computed powers of the current base $b^2, b^3, ..., b^{k-1}$. For every window, k modular square operations are performed together with an additional modular multiplication step using one of the pre-computed values. FWE algorithms exhibit a regular execution flow that is independent of the value of the exponent. Further optimizations are introduced in sliding-window exponentiation (SWE) algorithms [15], which for the same window size k require just half of the pre-computed values and fewer multiplications by skipping windows containing only zeros. Similar to the square-and-multiply algorithm this creates an irregular execution flow that again depends on the bit values of the exponent.

In the context of instruction cache attacks, which allow an adversary to observe the execution flow, traditional square-and-multiply as well as SWE implementations should be avoided, as previous literature shows. A practical instruction cache attack on square-and-multiply is shown by Yarom and Falkner [31]. With their attack the authors are able to recover over 90% of the private exponent. Percival [22] and Acıçmez [1] both demonstrate attacks on the SWE implementation used for fast RSA private key operations in the OpenSSL cryptographic library. By observing the exponent-dependent sequences of modular square and multiply operations, the authors are able to retrieve around 200 bits of each 512-bit Chinese remainder theorem (CRT) component used in the decryption. After the publication of Percival [22], OpenSSL refrained from using its SWE implementation for secret exponents [27]. Acıçmez et al. [2] and Chen et al. [5] further improve the work by Acıçmez [1] by relaxing instruction cache observation requirements and by proposing a better key recovery from SWE measurements.

Literature clearly shows that instruction cache observations can successfully be used to infer an application's execution flow. Because caches handle data in chunks, i.e. cache lines, adversaries can typically observe only groups of instructions that all fit on one cache line. The size of cache lines as well as other properties of the cache can vary in practice. To test software in worst case conditions, we assume an adversary is able to observe single instructions. If an implementation does not leak at instruction-level granularity, observations via the cache will not succeed, regardless of the cache configuration in practice.

4   Definition of the Leakage Test

Both square-and-multiply and sliding window exponentiation algorithms optimize the runtime by skipping calculation steps if there are 0-bits in the exponent.

When implemented in software, this causes some instructions, e.g. one function, to be executed more often, the more 1-bits the exponent contains. To systematically capture these execution flow variations in implementations of modular exponentiation, we correlate the Hamming weight (HW) of the exponent e with the number of times an instruction is executed during exponentiation. Note that the test also detects those instructions that are executed more often, the more 0-bits the exponent contains. This case would yield a negative correlation.

To test an implementation, N random bases are exponentiated with a corresponding number of random exponents $e_{n=1..N}$. This gives a sequence of Hamming weights $\mathbf{H} = \{\mathrm{HW}(e_1), ..., \mathrm{HW}(e_N)\}$. For all instructions i in the software, the number of executions $x_{i,n}$ is saved for each exponentiation. The sequences $\mathbf{X}_i = \{x_{i,1}, ..., x_{i,N}\}$ are then compared to $\mathbf{H}$ using Pearson's correlation coefficient, which yields

$$c_i = \frac{\sum_{n=1}^{N} \left(\mathbf{H}[n] - \overline{\mathbf{H}} \right) \cdot \left(\mathbf{X}_i[n] - \overline{\mathbf{X}}_i \right)}{\sqrt{\sum_{n=1}^{N} \left(\mathbf{H}[n] - \overline{\mathbf{H}} \right)^2} \cdot \sqrt{\sum_{n=1}^{N} \left(\mathbf{X}_i[n] - \overline{\mathbf{X}}_i \right)^2}}. \tag{1}$$

The correlation sequence $\mathbf{C} = \{c_1, ..., c_I\}$ finally contains the leakage results for all I instructions of the implementation. To check whether an instruction's leakage is significant, we use the standard significance test based on the approximated t-distribution of Pearson's correlation coefficient. The confidence level $(1 - \alpha)$ is set to 99.9999% and the degrees of freedom df are derived from the number of exponentiations N with $df = (N - 2)$. The significance threshold T is then defined as

$$T = \pm \sqrt{\frac{t_{1-\alpha}^2}{t_{1-\alpha}^2 + df}}. \tag{2}$$

All instructions with $c_i \geq T$ or $c_i \leq \text{-}T$ are considered to *leak* information about the exponent. In our practical experiments, the tests are done with $N = 5,000$ exponentiations. This number is derived empirically from initial tests of a vulnerable square-and-multiply implementation. In these tests it is sufficient to confidently distinguish leaking and non-leaking instructions. With 5,000 exponentiations, $t_{1-\alpha}$ becomes 4.7590 and the threshold T evaluates to ± 0.0672.

The advantage of the selected leakage test is that it allows to automatically and efficiently detect leaking code in vulnerable modular exponentiation implementations that have successfully been attacked in literature by observing the execution flow through the instruction cache.

5   Description of the Measurement Framework

The leakage test requires that the execution flow of a program is monitored with instruction-level granularity. In particular the numbers of executions $\mathbf{X}_i$ are needed for each instruction to compute the correlation coefficients. To retrieve these numbers we observe the instruction pointer (or program counter) over time, because it references all the instructions that are executed during runtime. This is an easy task for instrumentation tools that are normally used for debugging and performance analysis in software development. Instrumenting a compiled program during runtime is called dynamic binary instrumentation (DBI) and typically works by injecting analysis code into the original instruction stream.

For testing programs against instruction cache attacks, dynamic binary instrumentation is beneficial because it allows to monitor a program during runtime without interference from the processor, the operating system, and other applications, which are typical challenges for attacks in practice. DBI also provides greater control over the software under test and supports instruction-level instead of cache-line-level observation granularity. DBI is therefore able to evaluate software under a worst case instruction cache attack with high quality measurements and a cache line size of one instruction. Other, more general benefits are that DBI operates on binaries rather than source code, which might not always be available, especially when third party libraries are used. It avoids the impact of the compiler and its optimizations, because it instruments the actual instructions that are executed and that an adversary would observe during an attack. Compared to static analysis, dynamic instrumentation has the advantage that not all possible code paths must be followed, which quickly gets infeasible to handle for large software components. The analysis effort is reduced to the actual execution flow of a specific input, which is efficient and sufficient for the selected leakage test.

The question of which instrumentation framework to use for the leakage test is not critical. Observing the instruction pointer can be done with any major DBI framework available. We choose Pin [13], which is developed and supported by Intel, because it is a performance-oriented framework that efficiently handles the light-weight instrumentation tasks that we require. This reduces the evaluation time in practice and is especially beneficial for modular exponentiation, which is a costly computation to perform. We implement a custom extension to Pin, a so-called *Pintool*, that attributes the observed instruction pointer addresses to specific instructions within the executed program and its loaded shared libraries.

For the evaluation of the selected cryptographic libraries, we implement a test program that is able to interface and initialize different libraries. It invokes a modular exponentiation operation through the RSA cipher interface provided by each library. In every execution, the test program triggers one RSA decryption with a random exponent and ciphertext. The test program binary is then run by Pin and instrumented by our Pintool, which stores the number of executions of all instructions that were executed at least once. These are the measured X_i required by the leakage test. Note that the instrumentation is done only for the decryption operation. Library (de-)initialization is omitted, because it adds noise and may consequently prolong the measurement phase. This is achieved by performing the actual decryption in a separate thread and by leaving library setup and teardown to the main program thread. Within the Pintool the instrumentation can then precisely be limited to the decryption thread. In summary, the following steps are performed to generate the measurements and leakage test results for each RSA implementation:

1. Selection of the implementation under test and compilation of the test program.
2. Execution of the compiled binary with Pin and storage of the instructions' execution counts. This step is repeated N times.
3. Correlation of the exponents' Hamming weights $\mathbf{H}$ with the execution counts $\mathbf{X}_i$.
4. Significance test of the correlation coefficients $\mathbf{C}$ using the threshold T and documentation of the detected leaks.

6   Cryptographic Libraries Under Test

The practical demonstration of the leakage test and the measurement framework is done on an x86-64 system. A selection of nine open-source cryptographic libraries and one textbook implementation of RSA are tested using 2048-bit keys.

Table 1. Overview of the tested cryptographic libraries with corresponding version, usage of CRT components during decryption and the implemented exponentiation algorithm.

Library	Version	CRT	Algorithm
Textbook	-[a]	-	Sqr. & Mul.
wolfSSL	3.8.0	✓	Mont. Ladd.
MatrixSSL	3.7.2b	-	Sliding Win.
OpenSSL$_{sw}$	1.0.2g	-	Sliding Win.
LibreSSL$_{sw}$	2.2.5	-	Sliding Win.
Nettle	3.1.1	✓	Sliding Win.
mbed TLS	2.2.1	-	Sliding Win.
Libgcrypt	1.6.4	-	Sliding Win.
OpenSSL$_{fw}$	1.0.2g	-	Fixed Win.
LibreSSL$_{fw}$	2.2.5	-	Fixed Win.
BoringSSL	72f7e21[b]	-	Fixed Win.
cryptlib	3.4.2	✓	Fixed Win.

[a] Self-written implementation.
[b] Shortened git commit hash, because version number not available.

Table 1 displays information about all implementations under test. For each one, the version number (if applicable), the usage of CRT components during decryption (marked with a $\sqrt{}$) and the fundamental algorithm that is used to implement modular exponentiation is given. The textbook implementation is a self-written RSA decryption function based on the binary exponentiation algorithm described by Schneier in [25], Chap. 11.3. It processes the exponent bit-wise in a square-and-multiply fashion and intentionally exhibits execution flow leaks. We include this implementation for two reasons. First, it is useful to verify our testing approach, which should eventually detect leaking instructions. Second, it serves as a known reference for readers, as square-and-multiply is a common target in previous work. Across the other tested libraries, mainly sliding and fixed window exponentiation algorithms are used. OpenSSL and LibreSSL are listed twice, once with a sliding window (sw) and once with a fixed window implementation (fw). Fixed window exponentiation is used by default in both libraries. wolfSSL is the only library that implements exponentiation using a Montgomery ladder. From the discussion in Sect. 3 it is clear that the square-and-multiply and all sliding window algorithms are expected to contain execution flow leaks, whereas the fixed window and Montgomery ladder implementations should not exhibit leaks.

Before the libraries are compiled, most of them automatically adapt themselves to the current system with configuration scripts. In addition, we enable available side-channel countermeasures and other security options, if they are applicable to the RSA decryption functionality. For every library, we implement an interface that allows the test program to (de-)initialize the library, set random exponents and ciphertexts, and trigger decryptions. The majority of the selected libraries performs exponentiation using the private exponent d or provide it as an option. In these cases, a random value is set for d before a decryption is triggered. For all libraries that enforce the use of the CRT components d_p and d_q for exponentiation, a random value is set for d_p while d_q is set to zero. Zeroing the second exponent allows to perform the leakage test identically to the non-CRT case. Although this corrupts the overall decryption result, the first exponentiation is performed normally and the test results of the exponentiation code are not impaired. An alternative approach would be to set random values for both d_p and d_q and to compare the execution counts of the instructions with $\mathrm{HW}(d_p) + \mathrm{HW}(d_q)$. We do not further evaluate this strategy, because setting d_q to zero does not cause any erratic behavior of the libraries in the measurement phase. The choice of CRT or non-CRT exponentiation has no further impact on our tests and where possible we prefer non-CRT exponentiation to simplify interfacing with the cryptographic libraries. More details about the usage of the libraries and all manual configuration steps are provided in Appendix A.

7   Discussion of the Test Results

The output of the leakage test are correlation coefficients for all instructions that are used during RSA decryption. Listing 1.1 shows an excerpt of the test output obtained from MatrixSSL. Every instruction is identified by a hexadecimal offset into the program or shared library binary that is followed by the correlation coefficient.

```
0x0000faf6:   0.5702   (pstm_exptmod:   call   0x5a40)
0x0000fafb:   0.5702   (pstm_exptmod:   test   eax, eax)
0x0000fafd:   0.5702   (pstm_exptmod:   je     0xfaac)
0x0000fbec:  -0.9981   (pstm_exptmod:   sub    ax, 1)
0x0000fbf0:  -0.9981   (pstm_exptmod:   jne    0xfa8f)
```

Listing 1.1. Excerpt of the test output obtained for MatrixSSL.

If applicable, the corresponding function is given together with the assembly code of the instruction. Every instruction with a correlation coefficient exceeding the significance threshold of 0.0672 is a leak and a potential point of attack for an adversary observing the instruction cache. To compare the cryptographic libraries and the extent of their leakage, we provide three result metrics for each of them. First, the maximum correlation coefficient that is detected over all instructions is given. It indicates the strongest available leak that could potentially be exploited by an adversary. For example, the maximum correlation coefficient detected in the square-and-multiply textbook implementation is 1.0000, indicating a perfect linear relation to the Hamming weight of the private exponent. In contrast, the instructions in the fixed window implementation of cryptlib do not exceed a correlation of 0.0312. Their dependence on the bit values of the private exponent is insignificant in our leakage test. The second and third metric are the total number of leaks and the percentage of leaking instructions of all executed ones. Both indicate how big the attack surface of an implementation is. The more instructions leak, the easier it gets to implement an actual attack in practice.

Table 2 displays the leakage results of all tested implementations. Most importantly it shows that our proposed leakage test effectively detects execution flow leaks and is able to quantify the extent of the leakage. Libraries with sliding window exponentiation, namely MatrixSSL, OpenSSL$_{sw}$, LibreSSL$_{sw}$, Nettle, mbed TLS, and Libgcrypt, exhibit a considerable number of leaks and high maximum correlation coefficients. The risk they face from instruction cache attacks is clearly reflected in the test results. Libraries with fixed window exponentiation, namely OpenSSL$_{fw}$, LibreSSL$_{fw}$, BoringSSL, and cryptlib, have no leaks at all. This reflects their inherent protection against instruction cache attacks as discussed in Sect. 3. The significant differences between OpenSSL$_{sw}$ and OpenSSL$_{fw}$ as well as LibreSSL$_{sw}$ and LibreSSL$_{fw}$ clearly demonstrate the importance of choosing a protected modular exponentiation implementation. They also show that proper library configuration is vital to the secure usage of cryptographic libraries in practice. Note that the fixed window implementation (fw) is enabled by default in both OpenSSL and LibreSSL.

Among the vulnerable sliding window implementations, MatrixSSL has the largest number of leaks comprising over 50% of its executed instructions.

Table 2. Results of the leakage tests showing the maximum detected correlation coefficient, the number of leaking instructions and their percentage of all executed unique instructions during decryption. Libraries without leaks are highlighted in gray.

Library	Maximum Corr. Coeff.	Leaking Instructions	% of Exec. Instructions
Textbook	1.0000	1642	44.9
wolfSSL	-1.0000	2	0.1
MatrixSSL	-0.9981	5815	52.7
OpenSSL$_{sw}$	0.9907	505	6.4
LibreSSL$_{sw}$	0.9903	522	7.1
Nettle	0.7362	432	8.3
mbed TLS	-0.7061	343	10.1
Libgcrypt	0.5731	676	16.0
OpenSSL$_{fw}$	-0.0497	0	0.0
LibreSSL$_{fw}$	0.0430	0	0.0
BoringSSL	0.0426	0	0.0
cryptlib	0.0312	0	0.0

Together with a high maximum correlation coefficient, these results are disturbingly close to the trivial square-and-multiply implementation. Quite different and surprising results are obtained from wolfSSL. Although it implements a Montgomery ladder exponentiation, it exhibits a maximum correlation coefficient of -1.0000. The fact that only two instructions are above the significance threshold strongly suggests that this is a software bug. The source of the two leaks is discussed in more detail in the upcoming Sect. 8.

Another illustration of the test results is provided by Fig. 1. It displays the correlation coefficients of all executed instructions in MatrixSSL and OpenSSL$_{fw}$ over an increasing number of measurements. The positive and negative significance thresholds are displayed as dotted, red lines. All significant correlation coefficients are plotted in black, all others are colored in gray. The plots clearly visualize the extent of the leakage of the two implementations. The plots also indicate that stable test results are obtained well within 5,000 measurements, which agrees with our initial trials to derive an appropriate number of measurements for the tests. Monitoring 5,000 decryptions on our test system takes on average around 5.50 h. This is an acceptable time to produce the results for this work and reflects that the execution flow of a single decryption consists of roughly 10^6 to 10^7 executed instructions that must all be instrumented and counted. Note that this time can be significantly reduced by simple optimizations such as using smaller RSA keys, opting for exponentiation with CRT exponents, or parallelizing the measurements. Because each decryption is monitored in a separate Pin process, the parallelization of the measurements can be arbitrary. This shows that the proposed leakage test is not only effective but can also efficiently be adapted to one's computational resources and requirements.

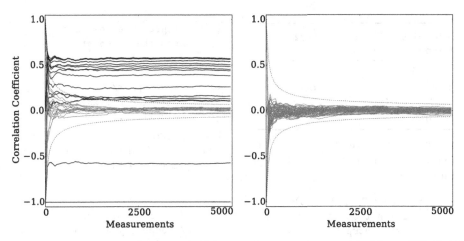

Fig. 1. Correlation coefficients of all executed instructions within MatrixSSL (left) and OpenSSL$_{fw}$ (right) over an increasing number of measurements. The significance threshold is displayed as dotted red lines. (Color figure online)

8   Analysis and Patch of wolfSSL

We recommend to patch cryptographic libraries that exhibit execution flow leaks, because these leaks are the basis of instruction cache attacks. Using the test output of wolfSSL, we practically demonstrate how such a patch can look like. To recap, the wolfSSL library implements a Montgomery ladder, which is shown in Algorithm 1. The regular execution flow is achieved with two helper variables R_0 and R_1. The basic idea is to always perform a multiplication and a squaring step, but choose the source and destination helper variables according to the bits of the exponent. Despite implementing this algorithm, two instructions in the wolfSSL library strongly correlate with the Hamming weight of the private exponent. To find the root cause, we start in function _fp_exptmod that implements the exponentiation routine. An excerpt of the Montgomery ladder loop body is shown in Listing 1.2. In each loop, the variable y contains one bit of the exponent. The multiplication of the helper variables R[0] and R[1] is done on line 1029 by calling the function fp_mul, which is defined in wolfcrypt/src/tfm.c. The result is written back to either R[0] or R[1], depending on the value of y. In fp_mul, the call is forwarded to the function fp_mul_comba, which is defined in the same source file. The problematic code within fp_mul_comba, which was discovered by our test, is shown in Listing 1.3. In general, the function multiplies big integers A and B and stores the result in C. The code in Listing 1.3 checks, whether the reference provided for C is equal to A or B. If this is the case, a temporary variable tmp is used to store the intermediate multiplication results. If C points to different memory, it is cleared and used to store the intermediate values directly. This is a simple and straightforward optimization to save time and memory.

Input: $g, k = (k_{t-1}, ..., k_0)_2$
Output: $y = g^k$

$R_0 \leftarrow 1;\ R_1 \leftarrow g$
for $j = t - 1$ downto 0 do
$\quad R_{\neg k_j} \leftarrow R_0 R_1;\ R_{k_j} \leftarrow (R_{k_j})^2$
return R_0

Algorithm 1: Montgomery ladder exponentiation proposed by Joye and Yen [14].

```
1024: /* grab the next msb
.....    from the exponent */
1025: y = <next msb>;

1028: /* do ops */
1029: fp_mul(&R[0], &R[1],
.....    &R[y^1]); ...
```

Listing 1.2. Code excerpt from the Montgomery ladder exponentiation in _fp_exptmod (wolfSSL).

```
453: if (A == C || B == C) {
454:     fp_init(&tmp);
455:     dst = &tmp;
456: } else {
457:     fp_zero(C);
458:     dst = C;
459: }
```

Listing 1.3. Leaking code in the fp_mul_comba multiplication routine (wolfSSL).

```
453:
454: // fix: always use
455: // temporary variable
456:
457: fp_init(&tmp);
458: dst = &tmp;
459:
```

Listing 1.4. Replacement for the leaking code in the multiplication routine shown in Listing 1.3.

The problem is that when fp_mul_comba is called from within the Montgomery ladder, the variable C contains either the reference to R[0] or R[1], depending on the exponent. If the current exponent bit is 1, C contains the reference to A. In this case, the if clause on line 453 in Listing 1.3 only evaluates the first condition (A == C), which is true and sufficient to enter the conditional code. If the current exponent bit is 0, C contains the reference to B. In this case, the if clause evaluates both conditions (A == C) and (B == C) until it enters the conditional code. In other words, the condition (B == C) is only evaluated, if the current exponent bit is 0. The instructions checking this second condition are exactly those two that correlate (negatively) with the Hamming weight of the private exponent (see Table 2).

A simple fix of this problem is given in Listing 1.4. It removes the if clause and always uses the temporary variable tmp. To verify the effectiveness of this fix, we repeated the leakage test for the patched wolfSSL library. The results are shown in Table 3. The patched version is completely free from leaks. Note that the maximum correlation coefficient is now less than 0.0000, which means that the instructions during decryption are either executed a constant number of times or simply do not exhibit a linear relation with the Hamming weight of the private exponent. Since the if clause was introduced to improve performance, we also tested the decryption speed of the patched version. As shown in Table 3, the patch decreases performance by 0.05%, which is a negligible slowdown.

In the spirit of responsible disclosure, wolfSSL was informed by the authors about the discovered leaks prior to publication of this paper.

Table 3. Comparison of the original and patched wolfSSL library. The speed comparison is based on 10^7 decryptions.

Library	Maximum Corr. Coeff.	Leaking Instructions	Speed (decr. / s)	Speed (relative)
original	-1.0000	2	129.87	1.0000
patched	< 0.0000	0	129.81	0.9995

9 Conclusion

The instruction cache is an established side-channel that allows an adversary to learn applications' secret data that is leaked through their execution flow. Numerous publications and practical attacks have been demonstrated in the past decade, many of which focus on implementations of modular exponentiation. Although robust algorithms for modular exponentiation are available, various cryptographic libraries use implementations that are inherently vulnerable to instruction cache attacks. To test cryptographic software for instruction cache leaks, we propose an effective leakage test that can be efficiently conducted with readily available dynamic binary instrumentation tools. With this test we detect and quantify leaks in multiple cryptographic libraries with instruction-level granularity. Since instruction cache leaks have been shown to be a threat in practice, we recommend libraries to carefully select the algorithm for modular exponentiation. Square-and-multiply-always, Montgomery ladder, and fixed window exponentiation are all practicable choices that limit the leakage an adversary can exploit via the instruction cache. Furthermore, we recommend testing any final library binary to ensure that no additional leaks are introduced in the software development process. The analysis and fix of a non-trivial execution flow leak in wolfSSL clearly demonstrates the necessity of this final check. For the future, the proposed leakage test may be applied to operations similar to modular exponentiation, e.g. scalar multiplication in elliptic-curve based schemes. Further work might also establish a systematic link between a detected execution flow leak and the number of exponent bits an adversary can learn from observing a given implementation via the instruction cache. For now, we consider every significant leak as a potential point of attack and therefore recommend to remove all of them.

A Configuration of Cryptographic Libraries

Most of the cryptographic libraries configure themselves with automatic scripts that adapt the library to the current processor, which is an Intel Xeon E5440 in our tests. The paragraphs beneath discuss all manual configuration steps and also list the functions and source code files containing the exponentiation code. This is important to verify and reproduce our results, because libraries often feature multiple implementations of modular exponentiation and pick one depending on their configuration.

wolfSSL. On our x86-64 test system, wolfSSL automatically speeds up public key operations by defining the `fastmath` option. In addition, we define the flag `TFM_TIMING_RESISTANT`, because it is recommended in the documentation [29]. The exponentiation function `_fp_exptmod` is defined in `wolfcrypt/src/tfm.c`.

MatrixSSL. For MatrixSSL no extra configuration steps are done. The exponentiation function `pstm_exptmod` is implemented in `crypto/math/pstm.c`.

Nettle. This library offers two functions for RSA decryption, `rsa_decrypt` and `rsa_decrypt_tr`. We use the latter one, because it implements base blinding to mitigate timing attacks and is therefore recommended in practice. For the required random numbers, we use the included implementation of the Yarrow PRNG. By default Nettle calls the external GNU multi precision arithmetic library (GMP) [26] to perform exponentiation. In particular, it relies on the function `mpn_powm` in the source file `mpn/generic/powm.c`. We compile GMP in version 6.1.0 with default configuration and link it with decryption program.

mbed TLS. The mbed TLS library is compiled with the flag `MBEDTLS_RSA_-NO_CRT` to enforce decryption without CRT components. Setting this flag does not affect the exponentiation code in function `mbedtls_mpi_exp_mod` defined in `library/bignum.c`. For the implemented base blinding countermeasure the `CTR_DRBG` random number generator is used.

Libgcrypt. The Libgcrypt library implements a secure memory feature that can be used for key storage. Because this is not required in our tests and does not change the exponentiation algorithm, we disable the feature during runtime. Exponentiation is done in function `_gcry_mpi_powm`, which is implemented in `mpi/mpi-pow.c`.

cryptlib. Before triggering the decryption in the cryptlib library, we set the `CRYPT_RANDOM_SLOWPOLL` and `CRYPT_OPTION_MISC_SIDECHANNELPROTECTION` options. A random slowpoll gathers entropy before the library actually needs it, which speeds up the retrieval of random numbers at a later point in time. The enabled side-channel protection activates a base blinding countermeasure, sanity checks in the code and the constant-time, fixed window exponentiation in function `BN_mod_exp_mont_consttime`, which is defined in `bn/bn_exp.c`.

OpenSSL and Forks. The OpenSSL library is compiled with the options `OPENSSL_BN_ASM_MONT` and `OPENSSL_BN_ASM_MONT5`, which activate assembly optimized Montgomery multiplication. By default, the base blinding countermeasure and the constant-time, fixed window exponentiation in function `BN_mod_-exp_mont_consttime` defined in `crypto/bn/bn_exp.c` are enabled. The LibreSSL and BoringSSL libraries are compiled and used with the default options, which enable a similar exponentiation implementation as in OpenSSL. Sliding window exponentiation can be manually enabled in OpenSSL and LibreSSL by setting the `RSA_FLAG_NO_CONSTTIME` flag during runtime.

References

1. Acıiçmez, O.: Yet another microarchitectural attack: exploiting i-cache. In: Proceedings of the 2007 ACM Workshop on Computer Security Architecture, CSAW 2007, pp. 11–18. ACM (2007)
2. Acıiçmez, O., Brumley, B.B., Grabher, P.: New results on instruction cache attacks. In: Mangard, S., Standaert, F.-X. (eds.) CHES 2010. LNCS, vol. 6225, pp. 110–124. Springer, Heidelberg (2010). doi:10.1007/978-3-642-15031-9_8
3. ARM Limited: mbed TLS (2016). https://tls.mbed.org/
4. Barthe, G., Betarte, G., Campo, J., Luna, C., Pichardie, D.: System-level non-interference for constant-time cryptography. In: Proceedings of the 2014 ACM SIGSAC Conference on Computer and Communications Security, CCS 2014, pp. 1267–1279. ACM, New York (2014)
5. Chen, C., Wang, T., Kou, Y., Chen, X., Li, X.: Improvement of trace-driven i-cache timing attack on the RSA algorithm. J. Syst. Softw. **86**(1), 100–107 (2013)
6. Coron, J.-S.: Resistance against differential power analysis for elliptic curve cryptosystems. In: Koç, Ç.K., Paar, C. (eds.) CHES 1999. LNCS, vol. 1717, pp. 292–302. Springer, Heidelberg (1999). doi:10.1007/3-540-48059-5_25
7. Doychev, G., Feld, D., Köpf, B., Mauborgne, L., Reineke, J.: Cacheaudit: a tool for the static analysis of cache side channels. In: Presented as Part of the 22nd USENIX Security Symposium (USENIX Security 13), pp. 431–446. USENIX, Washington, D.C. (2013)
8. Doychev, G., Köpf, B.: Rigorous analysis of software countermeasures against cache attacks (2016). https://arxiv.org/abs/1603.02187v2
9. Google Inc.: boringssl (2016). https://boringssl.googlesource.com/boringssl/
10. Gordon, D.M.: A survey of fast exponentiation methods. J. Algorithms **27**(1), 129–146 (1998)
11. Gutmann, P.: cryptlib (2016). https://www.cs.auckland.ac.nz/~pgut001/cryptlib/
12. INSIDE Secure Corporation: MatrixSSL (2016). http://www.matrixssl.org
13. Intel Corporation: Pin - A Dynamic Binary Instrumentation Tool, June 2012. https://software.intel.com/en-us/articles/pintool
14. Joye, M., Yen, S.-M.: The montgomery powering ladder. In: Kaliski, B.S., Koç, K., Paar, C. (eds.) CHES 2002. LNCS, vol. 2523, pp. 291–302. Springer, Heidelberg (2003). doi:10.1007/3-540-36400-5_22
15. Koç, Ç.K.: Analysis of sliding window techniques for exponentiation. Comput. Math. Appl. **30**, 17–24 (1995)
16. Knuth, D.: The Art of Computer Programming: Seminumerical Algorithms. Addison-Wesley Series in Computer Science and Information Processing. Addison-Wesley, Reading (1981)
17. Koch, W.: Libgcrypt (2016). https://www.gnu.org/software/libgcrypt/
18. Langley, A.: ctgrind - checking that functions are constant time with valgrind (2010). https://github.com/agl/ctgrind
19. Möller, N.: Nettle - a low-level cryptographic library (2016). https://www.lysator.liu.se/~nisse/nettle/
20. Molnar, D., Piotrowski, M., Schultz, D., Wagner, D.: The program counter security model: automatic detection and removal of control-flow side channel attacks. Cryptology ePrint Archive, Report 2005/368 (2005). http://eprint.iacr.org/2005/368
21. OpenBSD: LibreSSL (2016). http://www.libressl.org/

22. Percival, C.: Cache missing for fun and profit. In: Proceedings of BSDCan 2005 (2005)
23. Reparaz, O., Balasch, J., Verbauwhede, I.: Dude, is my code constant time? Cryptology ePrint Archive, Report 2016/1123 (2016). http://eprint.iacr.org/2016/1123
24. Rodrigues, B., Quintão Pereira, F.M., Aranha, D.F.: Sparse representation of implicit flows with applications to side-channel detection. In: Proceedings of the 25th International Conference on Compiler Construction, CC 2016, pp. 110–120. ACM, New York (2016)
25. Schneier, B.: Applied Cryptography (2nd Ed.): Protocols, Algorithms, and Source Code in C. Wiley, New York (1995)
26. The GNU project: The GNU Multiple Precision Arithmetic Library (2016). https://gmplib.org/
27. The OpenSSL Project: Changes between 0.9.7g and 0.9.7h, 11 October 2005. https://www.openssl.org/news/changelog.html
28. The OpenSSL Project: OpenSSL (2016). https://www.openssl.org/
29. wolfSSL: wolfSSL User Manual, March 2016. https://www.wolfssl.com/documentation/wolfSSL-Manual.pdf, v3.9.0
30. wolfSSL Inc.: wolfSSL Embedded SSL Library (2016). https://www.wolfssl.com
31. Yarom, Y., Falkner, K.: Flush+reload: a high resolution, low noise, l3 cache side-channel attack. In: Proceedings of the 23rd USENIX Security Symposium, San Diego, CA, USA, 20–22 August 2014, pp. 719–732 (2013)

An Analysis of the Learning Parity with Noise Assumption Against Fault Attacks

Francesco Berti[✉] and François-Xavier Standaert

ICTEAM/ELEN/Crypto Group, Université catholique de Louvain,
Louvain-la-neuve, Belgium
francesco.berti@uclouvain.be

Abstract. We provide a first security evaluation of LPN-based implementations against fault attacks. Our main result is to show that such implementations inherently have good features to resist these attacks. First, some prominent fault models (e.g. where an adversary flips bits in an implementation) are ineffective against LPN. Second, attacks taking advantage of more advanced fault models (e.g. where an adversary sets bits in an implementation) require significantly more samples than against standard symmetric cryptographic primitives such as block ciphers. Furthermore, the sampling complexity of these attacks strongly suffers from inaccurate fault insertion. Combined with the previous observation that the inner products computed in LPN implementations have an interesting algebraic structure for side-channel resistance via masking, these results therefore suggest LPN-based primitives as interesting candidates for physically secure implementations.

1 Introduction

Fault attacks exploit the possibility to force erroneous computations in cryptographic implementations [22]. In the context of symmetric cryptography, such attacks usually give rise to extremely powerful key recoveries. For example, a couple of random faults on the AES bytes are enough to recover its master key [28]. The Learning Parity with Noise (LPN) problem is an emerging cryptographic assumption that has been used to design various primitives over the last years [27]. Typical examples of its applications include identification protocols and MACs [8,10,15,20,21,23,24], but also PRGs, one-way functions [5], secret and public key encryption schemes [11,16]. However, despite their potential application for low-cost embedded devices, and to the best of our knowledge, the susceptibility of these primitives to fault attacks has not been studied yet.

In this paper, we propose a first investigation of the LPN assumption against fault attacks. In order to keep our conclusions general, we evaluate the resistance of two (serial and parallel) architectures for computing noisy inner products, that reasonably reflect the design principles of real-world implementations. We also study the impact of various types of faults against these architectures (i.e. bit flips vs. set bits, single vs. multiple, with varying accuracies).

© Springer International Publishing AG 2017
K. Lemke-Rust and M. Tunstall (Eds.): CARDIS 2016, LNCS 10146, pp. 245–264, 2017.
DOI: 10.1007/978-3-319-54669-8_15

Our main conclusion is that LPN-based primitives are surprisingly resistant against fault attacks by default. First, we can easily show that the most usual transient fault model (i.e. where we flip bits in an implementation) does not reveal more information than what would be obtained with standard (non physical) active attacks against LPN-based protocols. Second, even advanced fault models, such as when the adversary is able to set bits to a given value, require a substantial amount of fault to succeed. In the case of serial implementations, we show that attacks based on a maximum likelihood strategy can be mounted – yet succeed with significantly more samples than similar attacks against standard block ciphers such as the AES. Furthermore, these attacks strongly suffer from inaccurate faults. In the case of parallel implementations, the situation is even better (for the designer) as efficient attacks require multiple and accurate faults, and breaking these implementation essentially boils down to analyzing small LPN instances that require a large number of samples to be solved.

Since primitives based on LPN (and inner products) also have good properties for protection against side-channel attacks [1,12,13,26], our results therefore open the way towards more concrete investigations of their implementations, with low-cost security guarantees against both side-channel and fault attacks.

Admittedly, our general investigation of LPN implementations comes at the cost of less specialized conclusions regarding applicability. Yet, and for example, the proposed attacks can target the HB family of protocols [8,14,15,21,23].

2 Background

Let $(\mathbb{Z}_2, \oplus, \cdot)$ be the field of order 2 and consider the vector space $\mathbb{Z}_2^n$. Let $\mathbf{k} = (k_1, ..., k_n) \in \mathbb{Z}_2^n$ be a secret vector and $\mathbf{x} = (x_1, ..., x_n) \in \mathbb{Z}_2^n$ be a random vector. Let us denote by $\langle \mathbf{x} | \mathbf{k} \rangle$ the inner product of the vectors $\mathbf{x}$ and $\mathbf{k}$ in the vector space $\mathbb{Z}_2^n$, that is $\langle \mathbf{x} | \mathbf{k} \rangle = \bigoplus_{i=1}^{n} (x_i \cdot k_i)$. Let finally Ber_ϵ be the Bernoulli distribution with parameter ϵ (such that if $e \leftarrow \mathsf{Ber}_\epsilon$, then $\Pr[e = 1] = \epsilon$ and $\Pr[e = 0] = 1 - \epsilon$) We use the following definition of the LPN problem.

Definition 1 (LPN problem with parameter ϵ and dimension n). *Consider the distribution $\boldsymbol{D}_{k,\epsilon} := \{\boldsymbol{x} \leftarrow \mathbb{Z}_2^n, \nu \leftarrow \mathsf{Ber}(1, \epsilon) : (\boldsymbol{x}, y := \langle \boldsymbol{x} | \boldsymbol{k} \rangle \oplus \nu)\}$. Let $\mathcal{O}_{k,\epsilon}$ be an oracle outputting independent samples according to this distribution. The $\boldsymbol{LPN_\epsilon^n}$ problem is to find the secret vector $\boldsymbol{k}$ having obtained samples from the oracle. The LPN_ϵ^n problem is said to be (q, t, m, θ)-hard to solve if for any algorithm A, the following inequality holds:*

$$\Pr[\boldsymbol{k} \leftarrow \mathbb{Z}_2^n : A^{\mathcal{O}_{k,\epsilon}}(1^n) = \boldsymbol{k}] \leq \theta,$$

and A runs in time $< t$, memory $< m$ and makes $< q$ queries to $\mathcal{O}_{k,\epsilon}$.

We introduce the additional notation $\mathcal{Q} = \{(\mathbf{x}_j, y_j)\}_{1 \leq j \leq q}$ to denote a set of q outputs of the LPN oracle $\mathcal{O}_{\mathbf{k},\epsilon}$. In general, the LPN problem is believed to be hard for adversaries interacting only with such an oracle [6,19,25].

3   Evaluation Settings

Our goal is to analyze the hardness of the LPN problem against fault attacks [22]. In general, such physical attacks do not target the mathematical problems but their implementation. Therefore, this section describes the types of implementation and the types of faults that we consider for this purpose.

3.1   LPN Architectures

We consider serial and parallel architectures for the inner product computation that has to be performed by LPN implementations. An example of serial (resp. parallel) inner product computation is given in Fig. 1 (resp. Fig. 2). We use the notation $\mathcal{S}_{\mathbf{k},\epsilon}$ for serial implementations and the notation $\mathcal{P}_{\mathbf{k},\epsilon}$ for parallel ones. For simplicity, we will further denote the result of the AND and XOR intermediate results involved in these inner product computations by the notations A_i and B_j as represented in the figures. For an n-bit inner product computation, we have n ANDs and $n-1$ XORs in the serial architecture, and n ANDs and $\sum_{i=0}^{\log_2(n)-1} 2^i$ XORs in the parallel ones (the latter equals $n-1$ if n is a power of 2). For serial architectures, the depth of an intermediate XOR is its index, while for parallel ones, the depth of an intermediate XOR is $\lfloor \log_2(j) \rfloor$.

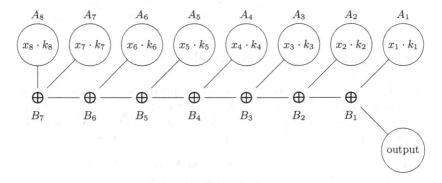

Fig. 1. Serial inner product architecture.

3.2   Fault Models

Based on the previous (generic) architectures, we will consider an adversary who does not only observe the outputs of the implementations $\mathcal{S}_{\mathbf{k},\epsilon}$ or $\mathcal{P}_{\mathbf{k},\epsilon}$ (for which the security would be identical as long as their result is XORed with a Bernoulli noise), but is also able to inject faults during their execution.

More precisely, we consider an adversary who is able to manipulate the intermediate results A_i's and B_j's. As generally considered in the literature on fault attacks, we will consider the following features for this adversary:

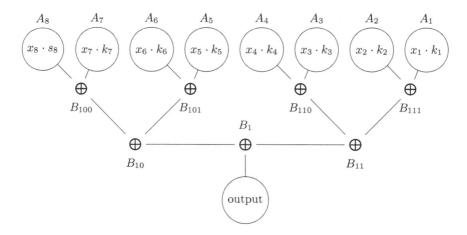

Fig. 2. Parallel inner product architecture.

1. *Fault model:* the adversary can either flip a bit or set it (to 0 or 1).
2. *Fault accuracy:* the adversary can either choose exactly the index of the inter-mediate ANDs and XORs he targets, or choose a set of indices so that the fault randomly happens on one of them (according to some distribution), which reflect the higher complexity of injecting accurate faults [3].
3. *Fault cardinality:* the adversary can inject a single fault or multiple faults.

4   Flipping Bits Is (mostly) Useless

We first observe that there are two possible options to flip bits in the inner product architectures of Figs. 1 and 2, namely targeting the ANDs inputs or targeting the XORs inputs and outputs. When targeting the ANDs inputs, one can affect either the public challenges $\mathbf{x}$'s or the key $\mathbf{k}$. In this respect:

1. *Flipping key bits does not modify the security of the LPN problem.* In stan-dard LPN every challenge $\mathbf{x}$ provides the adversary with a parity equation of the key bits. In this faulty version, one (or several) key bit(s) of this parity equation will simply be XORed with 1 (which is equally informative).
2. *Flipping challenge bits is equivalent to a man-in-the-middle attack* like the one on [14]. So while these attacks have to be considered at the protocol level (e.g. with [15]), they do not target the implementation of the inner product computations and we consider them out of the scope of this paper.

So we are essentially left with the case where we target the XORs inputs and outputs. In this context, we start with the observation that for our two architec-tures, $\mathcal{S}_{\mathbf{k},\epsilon}$ and $\mathcal{P}_{\mathbf{k},\epsilon}$, flipping a bit at any place of the computation is equivalent to performing $\oplus 1$ at the end of the computation of the inner product. This sim-ply results from the commutativity and associativity of the group operation $\oplus$.

Next, we have that an adversary exploiting this kind of faults can observe outputs of the form $\langle \mathbf{x} | \mathbf{k} \rangle \oplus \nu \oplus 1$ rather than $\langle \mathbf{x} | \mathbf{k} \rangle \oplus \nu$ in a standard LPN problem. In other words, the adversary can observe the distribution $\mathbf{D}_{\mathbf{k}, 1-\epsilon}$ rather than $\mathbf{D}_{\mathbf{k}, \epsilon}$. The complexity of solving the LPN problem is identical in both cases since one can trivially produce the samples of one distribution with the other.

So the important fault model where we flip bits is in fact quite irrelevant to attack LPN implementations, since it does not provide the adversary with better advantage than active (e.g. man-in-the-middle) attacks exploiting careful modifications of the challenges. In particular, flipping bits during the intermediate computations of serial or parallel inner product implementations is useless.

5 Setting Bits in Serial Implementations

We now analyze the security of the serial LPN implementation in case an adversary can take advantage of the (more informative) model where bits are set to zero. Essentially, such faults allow the adversary to simplify the LPN problem to small LPN instances (of size $n' < n$) and to exploit an extend-and-prune strategy similar to the one of [9]. Concretely, there are two possible situations that can occur. Either the resulting instances are so small that one can implement optimal attacks against LPN, where one just applies a maximum likelihood approach to recover key nibbles one by one. In this case, n' is small enough to be enumerated and the attack is in fact reminiscent of the template attacks used in the context of side-channel analysis [9]. Otherwise, the instances are such that n' is still too large to be exhaustively analyzed, in which case efficient algorithms such as [6,19,25] have to be exploited. We will see that the optimal strategy is easily applicable against serial implementations of LPN, while the more efficient ones will be required to evaluate parallel implementations in Sect. 6.

In this section, our goal is to analyze the security of serial LPN implementations against fault attacks in function of their main parameters. This naturally includes the LPN size parameter n and noise parameter ϵ. Additionally, we will consider the computational power of the adversary c (which corresponds to the number of key guesses he is able to make in a maximum likelihood attack), and the accuracy of the faults that we capture with a parameter Δ, which is the number of positions on which the fault can be inserted according to some distribution: $\Delta = 1$ means that the adversary can exactly select the position of the fault, $\Delta = 2$ means that the support of the distribution is 2, ... Based on these notations, we will consider an extend-and-prune strategy, where the adversary performs $\frac{n}{d}$ attacks against key nibbles of $d = \log_2(c)$ bits (for convenience, we assume c to be a power of 2). Following, we will first evaluate the success rate of an attack against a single key nibble and then its generalization to full keys. For simplicity, we will describe our attacks against single key nibbles using notations corresponding to the first key nibble. In case of accurate attacks (with $\Delta = 1$), this means that the fault is set on bit B_{d+1} of Fig. 1. In case of inaccurate attack, the fault will be set on positions ranging from $B_{d-\Delta+2}$ to B_{d+1}.

250 F. Berti and F.-X. Standaert

In practice, performing extend-and-prune attacks essentially requires to maximize the probability of each key nibble k^* after observing q queries of the form $(\mathbf{x}_j, y_j)$. For this purpose, we will start with the simple case of accurate fault attacks without computation and then investigate the more complex cases where the adversary exploits computation and the fault is not perfectly accurate. We will additionally combine different types of results. Namely, we will consider experimental attacks, that we will first explain based on exact formulas and then approximate using simple statistical tools, in order to gain intuition about how our main parameters influence the success rate of the attacks.

Remark 1. We next consider the fault distribution of inaccurate attacks to be uniform over Δ positions, which seems a natural first step to gain intuition about the impact of such inaccuracies. Indeed, the main goal in this paper is to put forward the interesting properties of LPN implementations against fault analysis based on standard models. Conceptually, there is nothing that prevents the following attacks to be applied to any type of distribution if they are given to the adversary. In case of concrete implementations, this would then require some kind of profiling, which we leave as an interesting scope for further research.

5.1 Accurate Fault Attacks Without Computation

In this simplest case, we perform extend-and-prune by dividing the key in blocks of a single bit, and repeat this process n times. We first show how to isolate and recover the first key bit k_1, then how to isolate and recover the jth key bit k_j, knowing the key bits $k_1, k_2, \ldots, k_{j-1}$. For this purpose, we set the output of the B_2 XOR to zero, and collect samples corresponding to plaintexts $\mathbf{x}$ with $x_1 = 1$. Setting this bit to zero implies that the output of the faulty computation is $y := x_1 \cdot k_1 \oplus \nu$, and using plaintexts $\mathbf{x}$ whose $x_1 = 1$ implies that $y = k_1 \oplus \nu$ (the other plaintexts do not reveal any information). Since both k_1 and $\nu \in \mathbb{Z}_2$, we obtain k_1 with probability $1 - \epsilon$ and $1 \oplus k_1$ with probability ϵ. Hence, we directly recover the key by performing a majority vote based on the collected samples, where votes for the wrong candidates can be simulated by a binomial random variable of parameters q (number of votes obtained) and ϵ (probability of obtaining that vote). We can compute the success rate of this process. Let $\Phi(s, q, \epsilon)$ be the cumulative function valued at sample s of the binomial distribution $B(q, \epsilon)$ and $\phi(s, q, \epsilon)$ be the corresponding probability mass function. The probability that the good candidate wins is the probability that the wrong candidate obtains less than half votes (and one half if the number of votes is tied), so that:

$$SR_1(q, \epsilon) = \Phi\left(\frac{q}{2}, q, \epsilon\right) - \frac{1}{2} \cdot \phi\left(\frac{q}{2}, q, \epsilon\right).$$

Figure 3 (1-bit nibble curves) illustrates that this theoretical success rate nicely matches the experimental one obtained based on 1000 independent experiments. By experiments, we mean simulated fault analyses, where the adversary performs template attacks with perfect models $\Pr[k^*|\mathbf{x}_i, y_i]$ obtained via theoretical prediction and confirmed by concrete profiling from $\mathbf{x}_i, y_i$ samples. Note that for

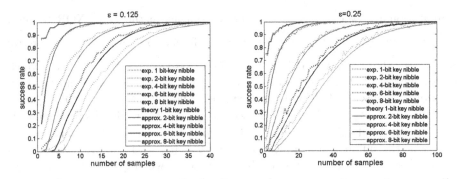

Fig. 3. Accurate fault attacks against a single key nibble.

such small nibbles, the success rate curve has a stepped (i.e. non continuous) shape which is due to the aforementioned possibility of tied votes.

Next, and knowing the first $j-1$ key bits, we can recover the jth one by setting the output of the B_{j+1} XOR to zero, and collecting plaintexts whose $x_j = 1$. As before, from the faulty computation we obtain $y := x_j \cdot k_j \oplus \left(\bigoplus_{i=1}^{j-1} x_i \cdot k_i \right) \oplus \nu$. Since we know the first $j-1$ key bits (and plaintext bits), we can easily subtract them, so that we are able to obtain $z := x_j \cdot k_j \oplus \nu$. Using only plaintexts whose $x_j = 1$ we obtain $z = k_j \oplus \nu$, i.e. the same situation as before, so we can recover the key bit k_j in the same way. We finally compute the success rate $SR_n(q, \epsilon)$ of the full key recovery process. For this purpose, we consider the simple strategy where we aim for a perfect pruning, i.e. we require single-nibble success rates such that no error will harm the full key recovery. In this case, the global success rate equals the probability of not doing errors at every step:

$$SR_n(q, \epsilon) = SR_1(q, \epsilon)^n.$$

If $N_s(n, \epsilon, \theta)$ is the minimum number of samples such that $SR_1(N_s(n, \epsilon, \theta), \epsilon) \geq \sqrt[n]{\theta}$, so that $SR_n(N_s(n, \epsilon, \theta), \epsilon) \geq \theta$, we obtain that we need $2 \cdot N_s(n, \epsilon, \theta) \cdot n$ samples to recover the full key with probability $\geq \theta$. The factor 2 is due to the fact that at each (j-th) step we discard the plaintexts whose $x_j = 0$.

Remark 2. A natural extension of the perfect pruning in this subsection would be to keep a list of the most likely keys for several key nibbles, e.g. thanks to enumeration [31]. The exploitation of computing power by considering larger key nibbles in the next subsection makes a first step in this direction.

5.2   Accurate Fault Attacks with Computation

We now show how to extend the previous attack by taking advantage of computational power. That is, instead of recovering the key bits one by one, we try to recover larger key nibbles one by one. For this purpose, and assuming a computational power of $c = 2^d$, we set the output of the B_{d+1} XOR to zero, thus obtaining $y := \left(\bigoplus_{i=1}^{d} x_i \cdot k_i\right) \oplus \nu$ from the faulty computation. As before we can observe that we have to discard the plaintexts $(x_1, ..., x_d) = (0, ..., 0)$, which appear with probability $\frac{1}{2^d}$, because they do not reveal any information. Furthermore, we observe that for a wrong subkey candidate $\mathbf{k}^*$, the probability that $y = (x_1, ..., x_d) \cdot (k_1^*, ..., k_d^*)$ is $\eta = (1 - \epsilon)\frac{2^{n-1}-1}{2^n-1} + \epsilon\frac{2^{n-1}}{2^n-1}$, while this probability is $1 - \epsilon$ for the good subkey candidate. Therefore, for each possible subkey $\mathbf{k}^*$ we can count the number of samples for which $y = (x_1, ..., x_d) \cdot (k_1^*, ..., k_d^*)$, which should be maximum for the good subkey candidate when a sufficient number of samples are observed. Unfortunately, although we can assume that number of right answers for a wrong key candidate is a binomial of parameters q (number of samples obtained) and η, whilst this second parameter is $1 - \epsilon$ for the good subkey, we cannot assume that these binomial random variables are independent, since they are produced with the same challenges $\mathbf{x}_i$'s. Yet, denoting them as $B_{\mathbf{k}^*}$ and under this independence assumption, we can approximate the success rate of an accurate fault attack against a d-bit nibble as:

$$SR_d(q, \epsilon, d) \simeq \prod_{\substack{\mathbf{k}^* \in \mathbb{Z}_2^d \\ \mathbf{k}^* \neq \mathbf{k}}} \Pr\left[B_{\mathbf{k}^*}(q, \eta) \lesssim B_{\mathbf{k}}(q, 1 - \epsilon)\right],$$

where we ignore the possibility of ties for simplicity. As illustrated in Fig. 3 for the larger nibbles, such a formula indeed provides a good approximation of the experimental success rates. Naturally, the positive impact of exploiting more computing power is not obvious in this figure, since it considers a single nibble recovery. In order to recover the other key nibbles, we then proceed as in the previous section and compute:

$$SR_n(q, \epsilon, d) = SR_d(q, \epsilon)^{\frac{n}{d}}, \tag{1}$$

since we have $\frac{n}{d}$ blocks of d bits to recover.[1] Again, if $N_s(\frac{n}{d}, \epsilon, \theta, d)$ is the minimum number of samples such that $SR_d(N_s(\frac{n}{d}, \epsilon, \theta), \epsilon) \geq \sqrt[n]{\theta^d}$, so that $SR_n(N_s(\frac{n}{d}, \epsilon, \theta), \epsilon)^{\frac{n}{d}} \geq \theta$, we obtain that we need $\frac{2^d}{2^d-1} \cdot N_s(\frac{n}{d}, \epsilon, \theta) \cdot \frac{n}{d}$ samples to recover the whole key with probability $\geq \theta$. The factor $\frac{2^d}{2^d-1}$ is due to the fact that at each step, we discard the plaintexts of which the bits corresponding to the target key nibble are all zeros (that occur with probability $\frac{1}{2^d}$).

Figure 4 illustrates the evolution of the success rate against a 1024-bit key, for $\epsilon = 0.125$ and $\epsilon = 0.25$ and computing powers ranging from 8-bit (which is instantaneously computed on a single desktop computed) to 32-bit. This time we clearly see the positive impact of exploiting computation from the data complexity point-of-view. We also observe the same "saturation effect" as when

---

[1] Intuitively, the independence assumption is reasonable since what we require is that for each key candidate $\mathbf{k}^*$ there exists enough plaintexts belonging to $\mathbb{Z}_2^d \setminus V(\langle \mathbf{x}|\mathbf{k} \oplus \mathbf{k}^*\rangle)$, with $V(\langle \mathbf{x}|\mathbf{k} \oplus \mathbf{k}^*\rangle)$ the hyperplane defined by the equation $\langle \mathbf{x}|\mathbf{k} \oplus \mathbf{k}^*\rangle = 0$.

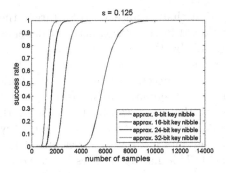
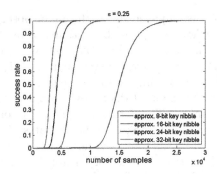

Fig. 4. Accurate fault attacks against a $n = 1024$-bit key.

exploiting enumeration in divide-and-conquer side-channel attacks [31], which typically suggests to limit the nibble size to 32 bits. Eventually, and interestingly, these results highlight that breaking a serial LPN implementation with accurate fault attacks requires a significantly larger number of faulty samples than for standard cryptographic primitives such as block ciphers [4,28].

5.3 Inaccurate Fault Attacks Without Computation

We next extend the previous analyses where the adversary cannot perfectly control the position of his faults. Again, we start with the simple case where we do not use any computation and want to recover the key bit by bit. In order to illustrate the intuitions behind inaccurate fault insertion, we start with an example where $\Delta = 2$ and we generalize it afterwards. Furthermore, and as previously, we only consider plaintexts $\mathbf{x}$ such that $x_1 = 1$.

Example with $\Delta = 2$. Let us suppose that the faulty computation gives $y := k_1 \oplus \nu$ with probability $\frac{1}{2}$ and $y := k_1 \oplus x_2 \cdot k_2 \oplus \nu$ with probability $\frac{1}{2}$. Denoting $W \simeq B(1, \frac{1}{2})$, we can write this outcome in a compact way as:

$$y := k_1 \oplus w \, (x_2 \cdot k_2) \oplus \nu.$$

Since we do not know the value of the bit k_2, we then have 2 possibilities:

- if $k_2 = 0$, $y = k_1 \oplus \nu$,
- if $k_2 = 1$, $y = k_1 \oplus w \cdot x_2 \oplus \nu$.

In the first case ($k_2 = 0$), we directly have $\Pr[y = k_1] = 1 - \epsilon = \frac{1}{2} + \frac{1-2\epsilon}{2}$. In the second case ($k_2 = 1$), $\Pr[y = k_1]$ becomes:

$$\Pr[w = 0, \nu = 0] + \Pr[w = 1, x_2 = 0, \nu = 0] + \Pr[w = 1, x_2 = 1, \nu = 1] = (*).$$

Since in LPN we obtain uniformly random samples, we have $\Pr[x_2 = 1] = \Pr[x_2 = 0] = \frac{1}{2}$. Further relying on the fact that the noise, the position of the fault and x_2 are independent, we obtain:

$$(*) = \frac{1}{2}(1 - \epsilon) + \frac{1}{2}\frac{1}{2}(1 - \epsilon) + \frac{1}{2}\frac{1}{2}(\epsilon) = \frac{1 - \epsilon}{2} + \frac{1}{4} = \frac{3 - 2\epsilon}{4} = \frac{1}{2} + \frac{1 - 2\epsilon}{4}.$$

This example leads to the main observation that despite we only target the first key bit k_1, the bias[2] that can be exploited in the attack actually depends on the other key bits that can be "covered" by the inaccurate faults (i.e. of which the index is lower than $\Delta + 1$), namely k_2 in the previous case. This leads to two important consequences. First, the success rate of inaccurate fault attacks against LPN is key-dependent. That is, there are (worst-case) keys that are more difficult to distinguish than others. Hence, we will next consider both average and worst-case success rates. Second, the fact that we target a single key bit while the faults actually cover several key bits inevitably makes our attack suboptimal, because of an imperfect model. This naturally gives incentive for considering attacks with computation as in the next section, since we can build perfect models again when $c > \Delta$. Interestingly, despite suboptimal the attacks without computation are functional, because the impact of the modeled key bit k_1 dominates over the impact of the other key bits in the bias expression.

Note that the success rate to recover the full key can be computed with the same formula as in the accurate case, by adapting the biases. Worst-case partial success rates have to be considered for perfect pruning (since in this case we want to recover each key nibble with probability one), while the average success rate could be exploited in the advanced strategies mentioned in Remark 2.

General case. Let Δ be the number of possible position of the fault. That is the fault can be in the output of the B_i XOR where $i = 2, ..., \Delta+1$. Let $r \leftarrow [2, ..., \Delta]$ be the actual position of a fault for one sample y. Let finally $P := [p_1, ..., p_\Delta]$ be the vector of the probabilities p_i that the fault is at the output of the B_{i+1} XOR (in our uniform errors case, $p_i = \frac{1}{\Delta}$). As previously, we have that if a fault occurs at the output of the B_2 XOR, we obtain $y = k_1 \oplus \nu$, whilst if it is at the output of the B_{r+1} XOR, we obtain $y = k_1 \oplus \left(\bigoplus_{i=2}^{r} x_i \cdot k_i \right) \oplus \nu$. For simplicity, we start by looking at the case where $k_2 = 1$, in which $\Pr\left[\bigoplus_{i=2}^{r} x_i \cdot k_i = 0 \right] = \frac{1}{2} = \Pr\left[\bigoplus_{i=2}^{r} x_i \cdot k_i = 1 \right]$ for all r's. Using the notation $W = B(1, 1-p_1)$, we can see an output of the faulty computation as $y := k_1 \oplus w \left(\bigoplus_{i=2}^{r} x_i \cdot k_i \right) \oplus \nu$ and compute:

$$
\Pr\left[y = k_1 \right] = \Pr\left[w = 0, \nu = 0 \right]
$$
$$
+ \Pr\left[w = 1, \left(\bigoplus_{i=2}^{r} x_i \cdot k_i \right) = 0, \nu = 0 \right]
$$
$$
+ \Pr\left[w = 1, \left(\bigoplus_{i=2}^{r} x_i \cdot k_i \right) = 1, \nu = 1 \right],
$$
$$
= p_1(1 - \epsilon) + (1 - p_1)\frac{1 - \epsilon}{2} + \frac{\epsilon}{2}(1 - p_1),
$$

---

[2] Defined as the distance from the uniform probability $\frac{1}{2}$.

$$= p_1(1 - \epsilon) + \frac{1 - p_1}{2} = \frac{1}{2} + \frac{p_1 - 2p_1\epsilon}{2},$$

$$= \frac{1}{2} + p_1\frac{1 - 2\epsilon}{2}. \tag{2}$$

From this equation, we clearly see that the inaccuracy of the fault decreases the bias by a factor $p_1 = \frac{1}{\Delta}$. Let us now look at the cases where $k_2 = 0$. Then, for any $\delta \in [2, \Delta]$ we have that if $(k_2, ..., k_\delta) = (0, ..., 0)$ and the fault is at the output of the B_{i+1} XOR with $i = 2, ..., \delta$, the output y equals to $k_1 \oplus \nu$ (i.e. is the same as if the fault is at the output of the B_2 XOR). So this case is captured by replacing p_1 in Eq. (2) by $\sum_{i=1}^{\delta} p_i$. Since this sum is larger than p_1, $\Pr[y = k_1]$ will be larger too and we will have a larger bias. More generally, it is easy to see that the increase of the bias depends only on the position of the first 1 in the key bits $(k_2, ..., k_\Delta)$. That is, the lowest bias is found for keys such that $k_2 = 1$, followed by keys such that $(k_2, k_3) = 01$ which have a slightly larger bias, ...

Based on the previous observations, we are finally able to compute $\Pr[y = k_1]$ for all possible keys. For this purpose, we define a vector $\mathbf{k}_{i,j} := (k_i, ..., k_j)$, such that we have 2 keys with $\Pr[y = k_1] = 1 - \epsilon$ (i.e. the 2 keys such that $\mathbf{k}_{2,\Delta} = \mathbf{0}$), 2 keys with $\Pr[y = k_1] = 1 - \epsilon - p_n\frac{1-2\epsilon}{2}$ (i.e. the 2 keys such that $\mathbf{k}_{2,\Delta-1} = \mathbf{0}$ and $k_\Delta = 1$), 4 keys with $\Pr[y = k_1] = 1 - \epsilon - (p_\Delta + p_{\Delta-1})\frac{1-2\epsilon}{2}$ (i.e. the 4 keys such that $\mathbf{k}_{2,\Delta-2} = \mathbf{0}$ and $k_{\Delta-1} = 1$, ...), until we have $2^{\Delta-1}$ keys with $\Pr[y = k_1] = 1 - \epsilon - \left(\sum_{i=2}^{\Delta} p_i\right)\frac{1-2\epsilon}{2} = \frac{1}{2} + p_1\frac{1-2\epsilon}{2}$. Hence, we can compute the average success rate in function of $SR_1(q, \epsilon)$ as defined in Sect. 5.2:

$$SR_1(q, \epsilon, P) := \frac{1}{2^\Delta}\left[2 \cdot SR_1(q, \epsilon) + \sum_{i=1}^{\Delta-1} 2^i \cdot SR_1\left(q, \epsilon + (\sum_{j=\Delta-i}^{\Delta} p_j)(1 - 2\epsilon)\right)\right].$$

We confirm that this prediction of the average success rate, and worst-case success rate $SR_1\left(q, \frac{1}{2} - \frac{p_1}{2}(1 - 2\epsilon)\right)$, matches experimental results in Fig. 5.

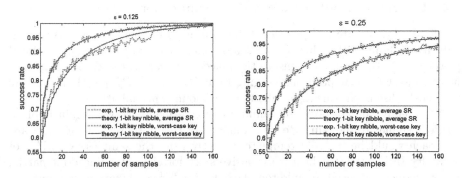

Fig. 5. Inaccurate fault attacks against a single key nibble with $\Delta = 4$.

Impact on the number of samples. We conclude this section by looking at the impact of a reduced bias due to inaccurate faults on the number of samples needed to perform successful attacks. For this purpose, we first recall that the success rate is the probability that the wrong key nibble (here bit) receives more votes than the good one. (to make this discussion simpler, we omit the case of ties). The number of votes for the wrong key nibble made with q samples is represented by a binomial random variable $X \sim B(q, \eta)$ of parameter $\eta := \frac{1}{2} - \frac{p_1 - 2p_1\epsilon}{2}$. We know that we have a confidence interval of level α for this random variable, that is $\left[\eta q - \frac{k_\alpha}{2}, \eta q + \frac{k_\alpha}{2} \right]$, and we want that all the values in this interval are lower than $\frac{q}{2}$. So we need that:

$$\eta q + \frac{k_\alpha}{2}\sigma(X) \lessgtr \frac{q}{2},$$

$$\frac{k_\alpha}{2}\sqrt{q(\eta)(1 - \eta)} \lessgtr q\left(\frac{1}{2} - \eta\right),$$

$$\frac{k_\alpha}{2}\frac{\sqrt{\eta - \eta^2}}{\frac{1}{2} - \eta} \lessgtr \sqrt{q}.$$

Defining $\tau := \frac{1}{2} - \eta$ we have $\eta - \eta^2 = \frac{1}{4} - \tau^2$ and the previous inequality becomes:

$$q^2 \gtrless \frac{k_\alpha^2}{4}\frac{\frac{1}{4} - \tau^2}{\tau^2} \gtrless \frac{k_\alpha^2}{4\tau^2}.$$

So we observe that if we multiply the bias τ by a factor $\frac{1}{\Delta}$ (as caused by Δ-inaccurate faults), we need to multiply the number of samples by a factor Δ^2.

Note that one possible way to mitigate the inaccuracy of the faults would be to filter the challenges so that in case there are Δ possible places for the fault, the adversary only keeps challenges such that the first Δ coordinates are $(1, 0, ..., 0)$. Yet, this filtering increases the data complexity exponentially (in 2^Δ) while the previous treatment of inaccuracies only does it quadratically.

5.4   Inaccurate Fault Attacks with Computation

We finally investigate the practically important case where the adversary can only insert fault with a limited accuracy, but where he has a computational power $c = 2^d$ that can compensate the inaccuracy parameter Δ, meaning that he can insert fault at positions ranging from $B_{d-\Delta+2}$ to B_{d+1} with $d > \Delta$. As previously discussed, this again allows us to mount optimal attacks.

Concretely, and in order to simplify our treatment, we will again apply a strategy similar to the template attack in [9]. For this purpose, a straightforward approach would be to build templates directly from the samples $(\mathbf{x}_i, y_i)_{i=1}^q$ of a "faulty LPN oracle", which is expensive since for characterizing d-bit partial inner products, we need to build templates for the 2^{2d} combinations of input and key. Luckily, it is actually possible to build such templates more efficiently. For this purpose, let again $P := (p_{d-\Delta+2}, \ldots, p_{d+1})$ be the vector of probabilities p_i

that the fault is at the output of the B_{i+1} XOR, and $p^i_{\mathbf{x},\mathbf{k}^*}$ be the probability that putting the fault at the output of the B_{i+1} XOR we obtain a 1. Clearly $p^i_{\mathbf{x},\mathbf{k}^*} = 1 - \epsilon$ if $\overset{i}{\underset{j=1}{\oplus}} x_j \cdot k^*_j = 1$ and ϵ if $\overset{i}{\underset{j=1}{\oplus}} x_j \cdot k^*_j = 0$. So by the law of total probability, we have $\Pr \left[y \overset{(f)}{=} 1 \right] = \overset{d}{\underset{i=d-\Delta+1}{\sum}} p_i \cdot p^i_{\mathbf{x},\mathbf{k}^*}$, where the (f) superscript is for faulty inner product outputs, which can be written in a compact way as:

$$\Pr \left[y \overset{(f)}{=} \langle \mathbf{x} | \mathbf{k}^* \rangle = 1 \right] = \sum_{i=d-\Delta+1}^{d} p_i \left((1 - \epsilon) \overset{i}{\underset{j=1}{\oplus}} x_j \cdot k^*_j + \epsilon (1 \oplus \overset{i}{\underset{j=1}{\oplus}} x_j \cdot k^*_j) \right).$$

Using the previous templates, we can now compute $\prod_{i=1}^{q} \Pr [y_i | \mathbf{k}^*, \mathbf{x}_i]$ for every candidate $\mathbf{k}^*$ and look for the one maximizing the likelihood of the noisy samples y_i. By defining $p_{\mathbf{x},\mathbf{k}^*} := \Pr \left[y \overset{(f)}{=} \langle \mathbf{x} | \mathbf{k}^* \rangle = 1 \right]$, we have $\Pr [y_i | \mathbf{k}^*, \mathbf{x}_i] = y_i \cdot p_{\mathbf{x}_i,\mathbf{k}^*} + (1 - y_i) \cdot (1 - p_{\mathbf{x}_i,\mathbf{k}^*})$. We can observe that $\Pr [0 | \mathbf{k}^*, \mathbf{x}_i] = \Pr [1 | \mathbf{k}^*, \mathbf{x}_i] = \frac{1}{2}$ iff $p_{\mathbf{x}_i,\mathbf{k}^*} = \frac{1}{2}$. Note that as in the previous section, there are keys that are easier/harder to attack depending on the value of their corresponding bias. Next, we can define the statistical distance between two key candidates as:

$$d(\mathbf{k}^*, \mathbf{k}^{**}) := \sum_{\mathbf{x} \in \mathbb{Z}_2^d \setminus \mathbf{0}} \left| \Pr \left[y \overset{(f)}{=} \langle \mathbf{x} | \mathbf{k}^* \rangle = 1 \right] - \Pr \left[y \overset{(f)}{=} \langle \mathbf{x} | \mathbf{k}^{**} \rangle = 1 \right] \right|, \quad (3)$$

and use it to compute the probability to distinguish the good key from an incorrect one. Here, we note that in theory, we should compute the probability to distinguish the correct key from all the incorrect ones. Yet, this would require characterizing the closeness of all the key candidates. For simplicity, we will compute an upper bound on the success rate, where we only compute the probability to distinguish the correct key from its nearest neighbour, i.e. the key candidate $\mathbf{k} \oplus \mathbf{01}$ for which we have flipped only the last bit of the correct key. As will be confirmed in our following experiments, this provides a good approximation of the actual success rate when the probability of success gets close to one. Note that for this key candidate, the probabilities in Eq. (3) are equal for $2^{d-1} - 1$ plaintexts (namely, those for which $\langle \mathbf{x} | \mathbf{01} \rangle = 0 = \langle \mathbf{x} | \mathbf{k}^{**} \oplus \mathbf{k}^* \rangle$), and their difference is $(1 - 2\epsilon) \sum_{i=d}^{n} p_i$ for the 2^{d-1} remaining samples.

In order to estimate the success rate, we now use to tools from [9], where the authors solved exactly this problem in the case of a template attack in which they try to distinguish two candidate subkeys $\mathbf{k}_1^*, \mathbf{k}_2^*$, using q leakage samples and assuming a Gaussian noise leading to an error probability:

$$\underset{err}{\Pr} := \frac{1}{2} erfc \left(\frac{\Theta}{2\sqrt{2}} \right),$$

with $\Theta^2 := (M_1 - M_2)^T \Sigma_q^{-1} (M_1 - M_2)$ and M_i is the vector containing the average value of q samples for the key $\mathbf{k}_i^*$ and Σ_q is the corresponding covariance matrix, modeling the noise distribution in these q samples. They additionally assume that the noise of every sample is iid for both candidate keys.

We simply apply this formula to the good subkey $\mathbf{k}$ and its nearest subkey $\mathbf{k}^*$ (i.e. $\mathbf{k} \oplus \mathbf{01}$), by taking the samples $y_1, ..., y_q$ and modeling them as a Bernoulli distribution $\mathrm{Ber}(p_{\mathbf{k},\mathbf{x}_i})$, with $i = 1, ..., q$. Denoting $M_1 := M_{\mathbf{k}}$ and $M_2 := M_{\mathbf{k}^*}$, we have $M_1 = (p_{\mathbf{k},\mathbf{x}_1}, ..., p_{\mathbf{k},\mathbf{x}_q})$ and $M_2 = (p_{\mathbf{k}^*,\mathbf{x}_1}, ..., p_{\mathbf{k}^*,\mathbf{x}_q})$. Therefore, on average, we find that $\frac{2^{n-1}-1}{2^n-1}q$ coordinates of these vectors are the same, and the others are $\pm p_{d+1}\frac{1-2\epsilon}{2}$. This means that for the vector $[M_1 - M_2]$ we have approximately $\frac{2^{n-1}-1}{2^n-1}q$ 0s and the remaining coordinates are $p_{d+1}\frac{1-2\epsilon}{2}$.

As for the covariance matrix, this is where key dependencies come into play. For simplicity, we only considered the worst-case (which is needed to compute the full key recovery success rate of our extend-and-prune strategy). Hence, we simply set it to a maximum $\Sigma = \mathbb{1} \cdot \frac{1}{4}$. As a result, we directly obtain the following bound of the success rate for worst-case keys and d-bit nibbles:

$$SR_d(q, \epsilon, P) \approx 1 - \frac{1}{2}erfc\left(\frac{\Theta}{2\sqrt{2}}\right),$$

with $\Theta = 2\sqrt{S(q)p_{d+1}\frac{1-2\epsilon}{2}}$ if we define $S(q) := \lfloor q\frac{2^{n-1}-1}{2^n-1}\rfloor$. As previously mentioned, and clear from Fig. 6, it starts from $\frac{1}{2}$ since we only distinguish two keys, and gets close to the actual success rate as the number of samples increases. We can then directly use Eq. (1) from Sect. 5.2 to obtain the bounds on the full key success rate of Fig. 7. Figure 8 in Appendix A additionally provides results for $\Delta = 8$ which confirms the simple intuition of inaccurate fault attacks without computation, that the data complexity of these attacks is proportional to Δ^2. In all cases, this data complexity is remarkably high.

Remark 3. The case of multiple faults is not very interesting in the context of serial implementation, since it is only the first bit set to zero (starting from the LSB) which matters in this case (as it cancels the effect of other faults).

Remark 4. The intermediate contexts, where the adversary exploits computation but his computational power $c = 2^d$ does not allow him to cover the full range of the possible faults (i.e. when $1 < d < \Delta$) could be analyzed with the same methodology as in this section, by simply adapting the distributions in hand. However, and as in the context of inaccurate fault attacks without computations discussed in Sect. 5.3, it would then lead to suboptimal attacks.

6   Setting Bits in Parallel Implementations

In this section, we complement the previous results with a discussion of the security of parallel LPN implementations against fault attacks. Interestingly, this discussion can be quite succint, since we can re-use most of the tools in the previous section. Essentially, the main difference between serial and parallel

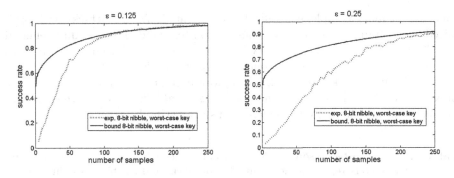

Fig. 6. Inaccurate fault attacks against a single key nibble with $\Delta = 4$.

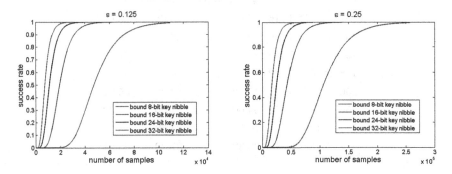

Fig. 7. Inaccurate fault attacks against a $n = 1024$-bit key with $\Delta = 4$.

implementations is that the latter ones can only be attacked efficiently in case adversaries can insert multiple and accurate faults. Hence, we will start our discussion with a description of these attacks. Then, we will argue why accuracy is in fact strictly needed in the case of parallel implementations, by looking at simple examples of (not too) inaccurate fault attacks with small Δ's.

Multiple and Accurate Faults. Say we consider a n-bit parallel LPN architecture of depth t (i.e. $n = 2^t$). Assuming that an adversary can insert m accurate faults, the best strategy is to cancel the left bit of the top node (i.e. B_{10} in Fig. 2), then cancel the left bit of the top node in the remaining right branch (i.e. B_{110} in Fig. 2), ..., so that one obtains samples of a reduced LPN problem of size $n' = 2^{t-m}$. If the fault cardinality is such that n' gets below 32 (which would correspond to a very powerful adversary), then the maximum likelihood attacks in the previous section directly apply. Otherwise, the (more realistic) adversary can only consider these smaller LPN instances and try to solve them with standard algorithms such as BKW [6], LF [25] or based on covering codes [19]. The complexities of some (efficient) attacks, borrowed from the recent work of Bogos et al. [7], can be found in Table 1 (where we report on classical values for the parameter ϵ, namely $\frac{1}{8}$ and $\frac{1}{4}$). Note that various other tradeoffs between data, time and memory complexity could be investigated. We list attacks with optimized time complexities since the main reason to abandon maximum likelihood attacks is that their time complexity becomes untractable for large n' values. In this respect, the only important conclusion of this table is that the overall complexity of fault attacks against LPN anyway becomes larger when leaving the maximum likelihood paradigm, and holds in general. This confirms the excellent properties of parallel LPN implementations against fault attacks.

Table 1. Complexitites to solve LPN with the LF1 algorithm $\log 2$ scale (a and b are technical parameters representing the number of blocks and the block size in LF1).

n'	ϵ	a	b	# of samples	Memory	Time
64	0.125	4	16	17.65	23.65	25.65
64	0.25	4	16	22.60	28.60	30.60
128	0.125	5	26	28.01	35.01	37.33
128	0.25	4	32	33.59	40.59	42.59
256	0.125	6	43	45.32	53.32	55.91
256	0.25	5	52	54.00	62.00	64.32
512	0.125	7	74	76.59	85.59	88.39
512	0.25	6	86	88.32	97.32	99.91

On the Need of Accuracy. Let us now consider a similar architecture and an adversary who can only insert a single (slightly) inaccurate fault with $\Delta = 2$. Then, the best strategy will be to hit either the left or the right bit of the top node (i.e. B_{10} or B_{11} in Fig. 2). Based on a reasoning similar to the one in Sect. 5.3 (recall the example with $\Delta = 2$), the adversary will then have to solve a $n' = 512$-bit LPN problem, with a probability $\frac{1}{2} + \frac{1-2\epsilon}{2} \cdot \frac{1}{2}$ (i.e. a halved bias) which is essentially as hard to solve as the original one. Furthermore, if the inaccuracy extends to more stages of the parallel LPN implementation, then any fault that occurs in an "already cancelled" branch of the implementation is lost. Hence, we have that accurate faults are in fact strictly necessary to carry out successful fault attacks against parallel LPN implementations.

7   Fault Attacks Against the Randomness

Before to conclude the paper, we finally note that all the attacks considered so far exploited non-permanent faults targeting inner product computations. Yet, in view of the probabilistic nature of the LPN assumption, a natural question to ask is whether directly targeting the randomness would not be more fruitful for the adversary. For example, and assuming that one can observe noisy samples of the form $y = \langle \mathbf{x} | \mathbf{k} \rangle \oplus \nu$, it is clear that a single permanent fault canceling ν allows breaking the LPN assumption with approximately n samples.

In this respect, we first mention that such permanent faults are generally harder to inject, and most of the literature on fault analysis focuses on non-permanent faults [17]. Hence, the good features of LPN implementations against fault attacks detailed in the previous sections are certainly a meaningful first step in the understanding of their physical security properties. Admittedly, permanent faults need to be prevented, and finding solutions to ensure this condition is an interesting scope for further research. Yet, we also note that this is a quite general issue and a requirement for the security of many cryptographic implementations relying on good randomness. For example, a single permanent fault on the randomness used in masked implementation directly breaks the uniformity property that is need for masking to deliver security guarantees [18].

Besides, the previous attack against the randomness generation can obviously be carried out with non-permanent faults, just by repeating them n times. Yet, here again, the accuracy of the fault insertion has to be high. Indeed, with perfect accuracy, the adversary will observe samples such that $\Pr[y = \langle \mathbf{x} | \mathbf{k} \rangle | \Delta = 1] = 1$. By contrast, as soon as the accuracy decreases, the samples become noisy again and their exploitation requires BKW-like algorithms to break LPN. In general, we have $\Pr[y = \langle \mathbf{x} | \mathbf{k} \rangle | \Delta] = \frac{\Delta+1}{2\Delta}$, meaning that already for $\Delta = 2$, we have $\epsilon = \frac{1}{4}$, therefore confirming the positive observations in the previous sections.

8   Conclusion and Open Problems

Our results show that fault attacks against LPN implementations (especially parallel ones) are significantly more challenging than similar attacks against standard symmetric cryptographic primitives such as block ciphers. Indeed they can only succeed if accurate fault insertion based on "set bit" models is possible, and even in this case, have quite high sampling requirements. For illustration, we analyzed some of the mainstream fault models. Yet, our evaluations are quite generic and could easily be extended to other fault models, leading to similar intuitions. For example, since it is mainly the position of the last erroneous bit that influences fault attacks against LPN, burst errors could be directly captured. This naturally suggests the further investigation of LPN implementations as an interesting research direction. Open problems include the study of advanced attack paths, e.g. going beyond the simple extend-and-prune strategy that we considered as a first step, or more challenging scenarii, e.g. if the faults and their positions follow an unknown (or imperfectly profiled) distribution. Real world experiments would naturally be interesting too, in order to evaluate the extent to which the conclusions of our generic analyses apply to actual devices. In this respect, it is worth mentioning that in concrete fault attacks, it may also happen that no fault occurs at all. Since in the context of LPN (where the challenges are always different) there is no direct way to verify whether a fault actually occurred, this could make the attack even harder (typically, increase the bias). In view of the algebraic structure of the inner products carried out by LPN implementations, combining them with error detection/correction tools appears as a natural goal as well (to further amplify the good properties of LPN with respect to fault attacks). Eventually, the extension of our work towards other learning problems such as LWE [30] or LWR [2] is certainly worth attention.

Acknowledgments. François-Xavier Standaert is a research associate of the Belgian Fund for Scientific Research (F.R.S.-FNRS). This work has been funded in parts by the ERC project 280141 and by the ARC project NANOSEC.

A   Additional figures

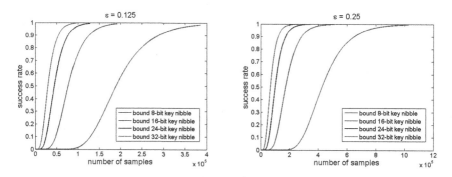

Fig. 8. Inaccurate fault attacks against a $n = 1024$-bit key with $\Delta = 8$.

References

1. Balasch, J., Faust, S., Gierlichs, B.: Inner product masking revisited. In: Oswald, E., Fischlin, M. (eds.) EUROCRYPT 2015. LNCS, vol. 9056, pp. 486–510. Springer, Heidelberg (2015). doi:10.1007/978-3-662-46800-5_19
2. Banerjee, A., Peikert, C., Rosen, A.: Pseudorandom functions and lattices. In: Pointcheval and Johansson [29], pp. 719–737 (2012)
3. Barenghi, A., Breveglieri, L., Koren, I., Naccache, D.: Fault injection attacks on cryptographic devices: theory, practice, and countermeasures. Proc. IEEE **100**(11), 3056–3076 (2012)
4. Biham, E., Shamir, A.: Differential fault analysis of secret key cryptosystems. In: Kaliski, B.S. (ed.) CRYPTO 1997. LNCS, vol. 1294, pp. 513–525. Springer, Heidelberg (1997). doi:10.1007/BFb0052259
5. Blum, A., Furst, M., Kearns, M., Lipton, R.J.: Cryptographic primitives based on hard learning problems. In: Stinson, D.R. (ed.) CRYPTO 1993. LNCS, vol. 773, pp. 278–291. Springer, Heidelberg (1994). doi:10.1007/3-540-48329-2_24
6. Blum, A., Kalai, A., Wasserman, H.: Noise-tolerant learning, the parity problem, and the statistical query model. In: Frances Yao, F., Luks, E.M. (eds.), Proceedings of the Thirty-Second Annual ACM Symposium on Theory of Computing, 21–23 May 2000, Portland, OR, USA, pp. 435–440. ACM (2000)

7. Bogos, S., Tramèr, F., Vaudenay, S.: On solving lPN using BKW and variants. IACR Cryptology ePrint Archive 2015:49 (2015)
8. Bringer, J., Chabanne, H., Dottax, E.: Hb^{++}: a lightweight authentication protocol secure against some attacks. In: Second International Workshop on Security, Privacy and Trust in Pervasive and Ubiquitous Computing (SecPerU 2006), 29 June 2006, Lyon, France, pp. 28–33 (2006)
9. Chari, S., Rao, J.R., Rohatgi, P.: Template attacks. In: Kaliski, B.S., Koç, K., Paar, C. (eds.) CHES 2002. LNCS, vol. 2523, pp. 13–28. Springer, Heidelberg (2003). doi:10.1007/3-540-36400-5_3
10. Dodis, Y., Kiltz, E., Pietrzak, K., Wichs, D.: Message authentication, revisited. In: Pointcheval and Johansson [29], pp. 355–374 (2012)
11. Duc, A., Vaudenay, S.: HELEN: a public-key cryptosystem based on the LPN and the decisional minimal distance problems. In: Youssef, A., Nitaj, A., Hassanien, A.E. (eds.) AFRICACRYPT 2013. LNCS, vol. 7918, pp. 107–126. Springer, Heidelberg (2013). doi:10.1007/978-3-642-38553-7_6
12. Dziembowski, S., Faust, S.: Leakage-resilient cryptography from the inner-product extractor. In: Lee, D.H., Wang, X. (eds.) ASIACRYPT 2011. LNCS, vol. 7073, pp. 702–721. Springer, Heidelberg (2011). doi:10.1007/978-3-642-25385-0_38
13. Gaspar, L., Leurent, G., Standaert, F.-X.: Hardware implementation and side-channel analysis of lapin. In: Benaloh, J. (ed.) CT-RSA 2014. LNCS, vol. 8366, pp. 206–226. Springer, Cham (2014). doi:10.1007/978-3-319-04852-9_11
14. Gilbert, H., Robshaw, M., Sibert, H.: Active attack against HB+: a provably secure lightweight authentication protocol. Electron. Lett. **41**(21), 1169–1170 (2005)
15. Gilbert, H., Robshaw, M.J.B., Seurin, Y.: Hb$^{\#}$: increasing the security and efficiency of Hb*. In: Smart, N. (ed.) EUROCRYPT 2008. LNCS, vol. 4965, pp. 361–378. Springer, Heidelberg (2008). doi:10.1007/978-3-540-78967-3_21
16. Gilbert, H., Robshaw, M.J.B., Seurin, Y.: How to encrypt with the LPN problem. In: Aceto, L., Damgård, I., Goldberg, L.A., Halldórsson, M.M., Ingólfsdóttir, A., Walukiewicz, I. (eds.) ICALP 2008. LNCS, vol. 5126, pp. 679–690. Springer, Heidelberg (2008). doi:10.1007/978-3-540-70583-3_55
17. Giraud, C., Thiebeauld, H.: A survey on fault attacks. In: Quisquater, J.-J., Paradinas, P., Deswarte, Y., El Kalam, A.A. (eds.) Smart Card Research and Advanced Applications VI. IFIP, vol. 153, pp. 159–176. Springer, Heidelberg (2008). doi:10.1007/1-4020-8147-2_11
18. Grosso, V., Standaert, F.-X., Faust, S.: Masking vs. multiparty computation: how large is the gap for aes? J. Cryptographic Eng. **4**(1), 47–57 (2014)
19. Guo, Q., Johansson, T., Löndahl, C.: Solving LPN using covering codes. In: Sarkar, P., Iwata, T. (eds.) ASIACRYPT 2014. LNCS, vol. 8873, pp. 1–20. Springer, Heidelberg (2014). doi:10.1007/978-3-662-45611-8_1
20. Heyse, S., Kiltz, E., Lyubashevsky, V., Paar, C., Pietrzak, K.: Lapin: an efficient authentication protocol based on ring-LPN. In: Canteaut, A. (ed.) FSE 2012. LNCS, vol. 7549, pp. 346–365. Springer, Heidelberg (2012). doi:10.1007/978-3-642-34047-5_20
21. Hopper, N.J., Blum, M.: Secure human identification protocols. In: Boyd, C. (ed.) ASIACRYPT 2001. LNCS, vol. 2248, pp. 52–66. Springer, Heidelberg (2001). doi:10.1007/3-540-45682-1_4
22. Joye, M., Tunstall, M. (eds.): Fault Analysis in Cryptography. Information Security and Cryptography. Springer, Heidelberg (2012)
23. Juels, A., Weis, S.A.: Authenticating pervasive devices with human protocols. In: Shoup, V. (ed.) CRYPTO 2005. LNCS, vol. 3621, pp. 293–308. Springer, Heidelberg (2005). doi:10.1007/11535218_18

24. Kiltz, E., Pietrzak, K., Cash, D., Jain, A., Venturi, D.: Efficient authentication from hard learning problems. In: Paterson, K.G. (ed.) EUROCRYPT 2011. LNCS, vol. 6632, pp. 7–26. Springer, Heidelberg (2011). doi:10.1007/978-3-642-20465-4_3
25. Levieil, É., Fouque, P.-A.: An improved LPN algorithm. In: Prisco, R., Yung, M. (eds.) SCN 2006. LNCS, vol. 4116, pp. 348–359. Springer, Heidelberg (2006). doi:10.1007/11832072_24
26. Medwed, M., Standaert, F.-X.: Extractors against side-channel attacks: weak or strong? J. Cryptographic. Engineering 1(3), 231–241 (2011)
27. Pietrzak, K.: Cryptography from learning parity with noise. In: Bieliková, M., Friedrich, G., Gottlob, G., Katzenbeisser, S., Turán, G. (eds.) SOFSEM 2012. LNCS, vol. 7147, pp. 99–114. Springer, Heidelberg (2012). doi:10.1007/978-3-642-27660-6_9
28. Piret, G., Quisquater, J.-J.: A differential fault attack technique against SPN structures, with application to the AES and KHAZAD. In: Walter, C.D., Koç, Ç.K., Paar, C. (eds.) CHES 2003. LNCS, vol. 2779, pp. 77–88. Springer, Heidelberg (2003). doi:10.1007/978-3-540-45238-6_7
29. Pointcheval, D., Johansson, T. (eds.): EUROCRYPT 2012. LNCS, vol. 7237. Springer, Heidelberg (2012)
30. Regev, O.: On lattices, learning with errors, random linear codes, and cryptography. In: Gabow, H.N., Fagin, R. (eds.) Proceedings of the 37th Annual ACM Symposium on Theory of Computing, 22–24 May 2005, Baltimore, MD, USA, pp. 84–93. ACM (2005)
31. Veyrat-Charvillon, N., Gérard, B., Renauld, M., Standaert, F.-X.: An optimal key enumeration algorithm and its application to side-channel attacks. In: Knudsen, L.R., Wu, H. (eds.) SAC 2012. LNCS, vol. 7707, pp. 390–406. Springer, Heidelberg (2013). doi:10.1007/978-3-642-35999-6_25

Author Index

Printed in the United States
By Bookmasters